Behavioral Corporate Finance

Concepts and Cases for Teaching Behavioral Finance

The McGraw-Hill/Irwin Series in Finance, Insurance and Real Estate

Stephen A. Ross
Franco Modigliani Professor of Finance and Economics
Sloan School of Management
Massachusetts Institute of Technology
Consulting Editor

FINANCIAL MANAGEMENT

Block, Hirt, and Danielsen
Foundations of Financial Management
Sixteenth Edition

Brealey, Myers, and Allen
Principles of Corporate Finance
Twelfth Edition

Brealey, Myers, and Marcus
Fundamentals of Corporate Finance
Ninth Edition

Brooks
FinGame Online 5.0

Bruner
Case Studies in Finance: Managing for Corporate Value Creation
Eighth Edition

DeMello
Cases in Finance
Third Edition

Grinblatt (editor)
Stephen A. Ross, Mentor: Influence through Generations

Grinblatt and Titman
Financial Markets and Corporate Strategy
Second Edition

Higgins
Analysis for Financial Management
Eleventh Edition

Ross, Westerfield, and Jaffe
Corporate Finance
Eleventh Edition

Ross, Westerfield, Jaffe, and Jordan
Corporate Finance: Core Principles and Applications
Fifth Edition

Ross, Westerfield, and Jordan
Essentials of Corporate Finance
Ninth Edition

Ross, Westerfield, and Jordan
Fundamentals of Corporate Finance
Eleventh Edition

Shefrin
Behavioral Corporate Finance: Decisions that Create Value
Second Edition

INVESTMENTS

Bodie, Kane, and Marcus
Essentials of Investments
Tenth Edition

Bodie, Kane, and Marcus
Investments
Tenth Edition

Hirt and Block
Fundamentals of Investment Management
Tenth Edition

Jordan, Miller, and Dolvin
Fundamentals of Investments: Valuation and Management
Eighth Edition

FINANCIAL INSTITUTIONS AND MARKETS

Rose and Hudgins
Bank Management and Financial Services
Niinth Edition

Rose and Marquis
Financial Institutions and Markets
Eleventh Edition

Saunders and Cornett
Financial Institutions Management: A Risk Management Approach
Ninth Edition

Saunders and Cornett
Financial Markets and Institutions: Approach
Sixth Edition

INTERNATIONAL FINANCE

Eun and Resnick
International Financial Management
Eighth Edition

REAL ESTATE

Brueggeman and Fisher
Real Estate Finance and Investments
Fifteenth Edition

Ling and Archer
Real Estate Principles: A Value Approach
Fifth Edition

FINANCIAL PLANNING AND INSURANCE

Allen, Melone, Rosenbloom, and Mahoney
Pension Planning: Pension, Profit-Sharing, and Other Deferred Compensation Plans
Eleventh Edition

Altfest
Personal Financial Planning
Second Edition

Harrington and Niehaus
Risk Management and Insurance
Second Edition

Kapoor, Dlabay, Hughes, and Hart
Focus on Personal Finance: An Active Approach to Help You Achieve Financial Literacy
Fifth Edition

Kapoor, Dlabay, Hughes, and Hart
Personal Finance
Eleventh Edition

Walker and Walker
Personal Finance: Building Your Future
Second Edition

Behavioral Corporate Finance

Concepts and Cases for Teaching Behavioral Finance

Second Edition

Hersh Shefrin

Department of Finance
Santa Clara University

Mc Graw Hill Education

BEHAVIORAL CORPORATE FINANCE: CONCEPTS AND CASES FOR TEACHING BEHAVIORAL FINANCE, SECOND EDITION

Published by McGraw-Hill Education, 2 Penn Plaza, New York, NY 10121.

This book is printed on acid-free paper.

1 2 3 4 5 6 7 8 9 QTN 21 20 19 18 17

ISBN 978-1-259-27720-7
MHID 1-259-27720-8

Chief Product Officer, SVP Products & Markets: *G. Scott Virkler*
Vice President, General Manager, Products & Markets: *Marty Lange*
Managing Director: *James Heine*
Brand Manager: *Chuck Synovec*
Product Developer: *Noelle Bathurst*
Marketing Development Manager: *Julie Wolfe*
Director, Content Design & Delivery: *Linda Avenarius*
Program Manager: *Mark Christianson*
Content Project Managers: *Melissa M. Leick & Karen Jozefowicz*
Buyer: *Laura Fuller*
Design: *Studio Montage, Inc.*
Content Licensing Specialists: *Beth Thole*
Cover Image: *Shutterstock/SFIO CRACHO*
Compositor: *MPS Limited*
Printer: *Quad/Graphics*

All credits appearing on page or at the end of the book are considered to be an extension of the copyright page.

Library of Congress Cataloging-in-Publication Data

CIP to come

mheducation.com/highered

To my wife Arna
for her unfailing support
and gracious forbearance
during the many hours I spent developing
the manuscripts for both editions;

and to my students for their invaluable
feedback from working through the ideas
in this book.

About the Author

Hersh Shefrin *Santa Clara University*

Hersh Shefrin, who holds the Mario L. Belotti Chair in the Department of Finance at the Leavey School of Business, is one of the pioneers of behavioral finance. He has published widely in the area and writes for both academics and practitioners. Professor Shefrin regularly teaches behavioral finance courses and often speaks on the subject to financial executives, portfolio managers, security analysts, risk managers, and financial planners both in the U.S. and abroad.

In 1999, his book, *Beyond Greed and Fear: Understanding Behavioral Finance and the Psychology of Investing,* was published by Harvard Business School Press. This is the first comprehensive treatment of behavioral finance written specifically for practitioners. In 2002, Oxford University Press, who assumed publication of the book, released an edition with a revised preface to reflect recent events and developments.

In 2001, Professor Shefrin edited a three-volume collection, entitled *Behavioral Finance,* published by Edward Elgar. In addition to seminal papers in this rapidly developing field, these volumes contain some of the pioneering works in psychology, upon which behavioral finance is based.

In 2005, his book, *A Behavioral Approach to Asset Pricing,* was published by Elsevier. This is the first book to develop behavioral pricing kernel theory, thereby providing a unified, comprehensive behavioral approach to the main elements of asset pricing theory: stochastic discount factor, mean-variance portfolios, beta, option pricing, and the term structure of interest rates. A second edition of this book was published in 2008.

In 2008, after the publication of the first edition of this book, Professor Shefrin published a related book titled *Ending the Management Illusion,* which described how behavioral corporate finance could be taught using a simulation game. The gaming approach places students in a decision environment in which both their intellects and emotions are engaged. Students work together in groups, making decisions to run a simulated company, in a setting that provides them with an opportunity to identify their own psychological tendencies, the tendencies of others, and to develop processes and group cultures that mitigate their vulnerability to behavioral pitfalls.

In 2010, Professor Shefrin published a monograph titled *Behavioralizing* Finance. The monograph discusses both the strengths and weaknesses to the behavioral approach, and suggests some directions for strengthening the weaknesses.

In 2016, Professor Shefrin published a book titled *Behavioral Risk Management*. As the title suggests, the book describes the applicability of behavioral concepts to risk management, suggesting that risk managers augment their quantitative skill sets to include psychological elements. Risk management is a very broad area, as most corporate finance textbooks make clear, and applies to corporate finance.

Professor Shefrin's scholarly articles have appeared in the *Journal of Finance,* the *Journal of Financial Economics,* the *Review of Financial Studies,* the *Journal of Financial and Quantitative Analysis, Financial Management,* the *Financial Analysts Journal,* the *Journal of Portfolio Management,* and the *Journal of Economic Behavior & Organization.*

Professor Shefrin completed his PhD at the London School of Economics in the economics of uncertainty; he earned a Master of Mathematics from the University of Waterloo and a BS (Honours) in economics and mathematics from the University of Manitoba. He also holds an honorary doctorate from the University of Oulu, Finland.

Brief Contents

Table of Contents

Chapter 4
Capital Budgeting 85

Chapter 5
Inefficient Markets and Corporate Decisions 110

Chapter 6
Perceptions about Risk and Return 131

Chapter 7
Capital Structure 149

Chapter 10
Mergers and Acquisitions 227

Chapter 11
Financial Management and Group Process 257

Preface to the Second Edition

GOALS AND STRUCTURE

The second edition of *Behavioral Corporate Finance* comes a decade after the publication of the first edition, which was the first textbook dedicated to providing instructors with a comprehensive pedagogical approach for teaching students how behavioral concepts apply to corporate finance. This second edition contains a great deal of new material, as the academic literature in behavioral corporate finance a decade ago was nascent. Notably, in the last 10 years this literature has mushroomed, and so the second edition has much upon which to draw.

Feedback from adopters of the first edition provides testimony to the fact that the examples and cases in the first edition are unique in bringing behavioral corporate finance alive. This is especially true of the minicases that conclude each chapter of the first edition. The second edition contains a completely new set of minicases. However, almost all of the minicases used in the first edition are still available in the Additional Resources (available online) that accompany each chapter.

The goals and structure of the second edition are the same as in the first edition. The primary goal is to identify the key psychological obstacles to value maximizing behavior, along with steps that managers can take to mitigate the effects of these obstacles. In this respect, instructors should view this book as a complement to traditional texts in corporate finance, not as a substitute. Notably, neither students nor instructors require a background in psychology to understand the key psychological concepts. All the key concepts can be grasped intuitively, and are easily related to financial decisions.

The second edition can be viewed as something of an out-of-sample test. Most of the examples and cases identified psychological phenomena in specific companies. The second edition provides an opportunity to trace the implications of those phenomena over the subsequent decade. Readers can judge for themselves whether the rest of those stories were random outcomes, or instead natural outcomes of the underlying psychological phenomena being present. The same remark applies to the book *Ending the Management Illusion*, which is a companion treatment to the first edition and analyzes a completely different set of companies. Readers can judge for themselves whether, after the publication of the book, the companies identified as being psychologically smart went on to become successful and whether those that were identified as being psychologically challenged went on to exhibit poor performance, if not outright failure.

Based upon advice from reviewers, the second edition features two new chapters, and some rearrangement of chapter order from the first edition. The first new chapter, Chapter 1, introduces the psychological foundations in depth. As a result, instructors no longer need to rely on online Additional Resources for this material.

The second new chapter is Chapter 13, on investments. This chapter extends the discussion from the application of behavioral concepts to corporate finance alone to their application to investments. As a result, the book can be used to teach dedicated courses in behavioral finance, not just corporate finance. To this end, instructors can use the book to teach behavioral finance in much the same order that they teach traditional finance: corporate finance first, followed by investments. At the same time, the book has a modular structure, and therefore can be used as a secondary text in regular investment courses as well as regular corporate finance courses. In this regard, Chapter 1, which provides the behavioral foundations, Chapter 3 on valuation, and Chapter 5 on market efficiency apply to investments as well to corporate finance.

As was mentioned in the Preface to the first edition, many traditional finance textbooks, in both corporate finance and investments, have added behavioral chapters. These additions serve as testimonials to the importance of behavioral ideas for finance. At the same time, there is a limit to how much can be accomplished within the confines of a single chapter, especially when it comes to integrating behavioral concepts into the treatment of traditional topics. Coverage of behavioral issues in traditional texts through a single-chapter approach has tended to be at best surface level, providing students with a behavioral flavor but not with the in-depth skills required to understand, identify, and deal with behavioral phenomena.

Teaching behavioral corporate finance is much more effective when the primary focus is a specific topic such as capital budgeting or capital structure, and the discussion focuses on the psychological dimension of the topic in question. In contrast, placing primary focus on psychological phenomena rather than specific corporate finance topics shifts attention away from integration. A similar remark applies to investments. For example, lumping technical analysis and behavioral finance into a single chapter, as some authors do, is not only misleading but also takes focus away from the very significant behavioral dimension in almost all other aspects of investment. This book provides instructors in mainstream finance courses with a resource that will allow them to identify the behavioral dimension in each topic they teach, and offer their students an integrated approach that combines traditional and behavioral perspectives.

ORGANIZATIONAL DESIGN

This book identifies the key behavioral concepts associated with every major topic in corporate finance: capital budgeting, capital structure, valuation, dividend policy, corporate governance, and mergers and acquisitions. However, the book provides only a brief summary of the traditional approach to each topic, whose purpose is to provide context. Instructors are assumed to teach the traditional approach from the traditional textbook of their choice. Instructors who use this book as a behavioral supplement in a traditional finance course can cover topics in the traditional manner, and then follow up the discussion by introducing the behavioral dimension. Instructors who use this book to teach a behavioral finance course can build on prior finance courses, and briefly summarize the traditional approach before introducing the behavioral approach to each topic. Questions and minicases appearing at the end of the chapters are designed to help students recognize the strength, magnitude, and persistence of behavioral phenomena in financial decision making.

Chapter 11 broadens the discussion of Chapter 9 from the first edition and makes the point that financial management means more than corporate finance. Rather, financial management entails the integration of corporate finance and management, meaning the incorporation of the psychological dimension into corporate financial decision making. Failures in financial management, especially risk management, lie at the heart of the global financial crisis. Examples from the financial crisis illustrate the main ideas in the chapter.

With a few exceptions, each chapter is devoted to a traditional topic. The exceptions are Chapters 1, 2, 11, and 13. Chapters 1 and 2 introduce the key psychological concepts used throughout the book. Chapter 1 provides a detailed presentation of 10 important psychological concepts, with the emphasis on psychology, not finance. Chapter 2 is devoted to explaining how these concepts apply to finance, and it is a prerequisite for every subsequent chapter. Every other chapter explains how concepts developed in Chapters 1 and 2 apply to traditional topics in corporate finance and to investments. Notably, Chapter 2 has been written to be self-contained, and so those wishing to proceed directly to the application of the the 10 key psychological concepts can do so without working first through Chapter 1.

For example, Chapter 1 introduces students to the concept of excessive optimism, and Chapter 2 describes how it impacted the decisions of the CEO of a specific firm. Chapter 3 then describes how excessive optimism affects valuation. Chapter 4 describes how excessive optimism affects capital budgeting. Chapter 7 describes how excessive optimism affects capital structure. The main issue is not to be repetitive about the fact that corporate managers tend to be excessively optimistic. The main issue is to explain how excessive optimism impacts the different decisions that managers are called upon to make.

Chapter 11 is entitled Financial Management and Group Process, and does not have an obvious counterpart in traditional textbooks on corporate finance. This chapter makes the point that financial management involves more than just corporate finance, but instead entails the integration of corporate finance and management.

Chapters follow a set format. Behavioral objectives for learning introduce each chapter. Most chapters have a section that provides a brief overview of the traditional approach to the topic at hand. The remainder of the chapter then focuses on developing the behavioral concepts and applications.

In order to help students focus on the underlying psychological issues, "Concept Preview Questions" are used. These are intended to help students reflect on how their own minds approach information and decision tasks. Thematic boxes, labeled "Behavioral Pitfalls" provide brief illustrations of business situations that feature the psychological phenomena being discussed. Hints for mitigating bias and error are provided in thematic boxes labeled "Corporate Nudges," or in the case of Chapter 13 "Investor Nudges."

Chapter summaries review the main points of the chapter in relation to the learning objectives. Chapter questions provide focused exercises to help students learn the key points in the chapter. Every chapter concludes with a minicase, allowing students the opportunity to develop the skills of recognizing psychological phenomena within the context of real world events.

The behavioral objectives, concept preview questions, thematic boxes and chapter summaries contain the major points in the book. Illustrative examples, anecdotes and cases serve as the most effective way of communicating general findings and ideas. Most students relate easily to stories. However, the stories are only intended to communicate the main points. The general evidence is based on the academic studies described in the book.

As was mentioned above, Chapters 1 and 2 are prerequisites to all the remaining chapters. However, all remaining chapters essentially stand alone, so that instructors have the flexibility to choose whichever chapters they deem appropriate, and in whatever order they find most useful.

INTENDED MARKET: CORPORATE FINANCE COURSES

I have written *Behavioral Corporate Finance* for use in any course devoted to teaching either corporate finance or behavioral finance. For traditional courses in corporate finance, I see the book being used as a supplement to any traditional textbook that serves as the primary course text. This pairing of a traditional primary corporate finance text and *Behavioral Corporate Finance* provides a powerful way to augment the teaching of traditional skills with an understanding of the psychological factors that influence the application of these skills in practice. In this respect, *Behavioral Corporate Finance* contains many real-world examples and case studies, designed to bring the behavioral concepts to life. Similar remarks apply to courses in Investment, which can draw on Chapter 13.

Behavioral pitfalls represent one of the most important obstacles to the successful implementation of the skills taught in traditional corporate finance courses. When it comes to improving the financial decision process, understanding these pitfalls is absolutely essential. Therefore, a crucial challenge is to teach students nudging techniques for avoiding psychological pitfalls identified in the behavioral decision literature, as well as how to deal with others that do fall into the associated traps.

INSTRUCTOR RESOURCES

All of the instructor resources for this text are available on the book web site at **www.mhhe.com/shefrin2e.** We put them in one place for easier access and convenience.

- The ***Instructor's Manual*** includes a chapter overview, learning objectives, key terms, and presentation of the material which organizes the material around the PowerPoint Presentation. Solutions to the end of chapter questions and minicases are also provided.
- ***PowerPoint Presentation Slides*** contain key points and summaries to help instructors give lectures on the main ideas in the chapter.
- ***Test Bank,*** prepared by David Distad of the University of California, Berkeley, contains a variety of true/false questions, multiple choice, and essay questions. Complete answers are provided for all test questions and problems.
- ***Additional Minicases and Case Analysis Questions*** for selected chapters are referenced in the text and available online.

For those interested in using *Behavioral Corporate Finance* as a text in a course dedicated to behavioral finance, additional teaching resources are also provided on the book web site. These resources expand the material presented in most chapters and have been referenced in the text. In addition, separate chapters dealing with real options and investments are also available on the web.

Acknowledgments

In the course of writing this book I benefited from discussions with managers, academics, consultants, and students. I learned a great deal from my fellow members of the Santa Clara Valley chapter of Financial Executives International. I especially thank those who gave guest lectures to my classes about how they practice corporate finance in their firms. Their insights were invaluable. My biggest debt is to the students I taught in Santa Clara University's executive MBA program, and to my wife Arna. My executive MBA students all had at least 10 years of management experience. By teaching them both traditional and behavioral corporate finance, I learned how to structure the approach in the book. Among the individuals to whom I would like to express appreciation are: Martha Amram, Herzel Ashkenazi, Blair Baker, Eric Benhamou, Brigida Bergkamp, Ray Bingham, Bill Black, Tony Blagrove, David Bostwick, Alon Brav, Judy Bruner, Marshall Burak, Larry Carter, Kris Chellam, Jeff Clarke, Tom Cupples, Greg Davies, George Davis, Patricia Dechow, Robert Dunham, Jeremy DeGroot, Rajiv Dutta, Denise Esguerra-Aguilar, Rami Fernandez, Jennifer Fromm, Diane Gale, Ken Goldman, John Graham, Artie Green, Robyn Greenwood, Sal Gutierrez, Campbell Harvey, Dirk Hackbarth, John Heywood, David Hirshleifer, Mike Hope, Kuno Huisman, Mark Keil, Marc Kramer, Mira Ma, Fred Kurland, Bruce Lange, Eddie Le, Sonia Li, Tim Loughran, Ulrike Malmendier, Greg Matz, Webb McKinney, Laura McLeod, Manoj Mittal, Chris Paisley, Bill Palmer, Phuong Quach, John Payne, William Pitney, Alex Potts, Betsy Raphael, George Reyes, Eduardo Repetto, Brian Reynolds, Jay Ritter, Chris Robell, Mark Rubash, Christine .Russell, Stephen Schaefer, Claire Silverman, Gurkirpal Singh, Bryce Skaff, Paul Slovic, Scott Smart, Song Ma, Meir Statman, Tom Stein, Don Taylor, Ed Teach, Frans Tempelaar, Alex Triantis, Paul Tufano, George Vera, Robert Wayman, Ben Walker, KipWitter, Arnold Wood, Jeffrey Wurgler, and David Young.

I am indebted to the following people for their insightful reviews of the proposal and various drafts of *Behavioral Corporate Finance* and their suggestions in the preparation of the 1st and 2nd editions.

Paul Adams,
University of Cincinnati
Malcolm Baker,
Harvard Business School
Candy Bianco,
Bentley College
Kirt Butler,
Michigan State University
Joseph Chen,
University of Southern California
Werner DeBondt,
DePaul University
David Distad,
University of California, Berkeley
Robert Duvic,
University of Texas at Austin
Christophe Faugere,
State University of New York, Albany
Joseph J. French
University of Northern Colorado
University of Maryland
Gordon Hanka
Vanderbilt University

Hugh Hunter,
San Diego State University
Nancy Jay,
Mercer University
D. Scott Lee,
Texas A&M University
David Lins,
University of Illinois, Urbana-Champaign
Tim Manuel,
University of Montana
Joe Messina,
San Francisco State University
Shabnam Mousavi
Johns Hopkins University
Roni Michaely,
Cornell University
Terrance Odean,
University of California, Berkeley
Dilip Patro,
Rutgers University
Raghavendra Rau,
Cambridge University
Thomas Rietz,
University of Iowa
Robert Ritchey,
Texas Tech University
Scott Smart,
Indiana University
Richard Taffler,
Warwick University, UK
Bijesh Tolia,
Chicago State University
P.V. Viswanath,
Pace University
John Wald,
Rutgers University
Arthur Wilson
George Washington University

In connection with this second edition, I want to thank Charles Synovec, Executive Brand Manager; Noelle Bathurst, Senior Product Developer; and Tara Slagle, Senior Content Project Manager. In connection with the first edition, I want to acknowledge the direction and coaching by Chuck Synovec, Noelle Bathurst, Julie Wolfe, Melissa Leick, Laura Fuller, Tobi Philips, Vivek Khandelwal, Debra Boxill, and Karen Jozefowicz, on the development, design, editing, and the production of this book.

Finally, I would like to acknowledge financial support for the first edition provided by the Dean Witter Foundation and the Leavey School of Business at Santa Clara University. Lastly, my wife Arna contributed many behavioral examples from her own work experience. She was especially gracious about my having devoted untold hours developing the manuscript and then producing this second edition.

Hersh Shefrin
Santa Clara University

Chapter **One**

Behavioral Foundations

The main objective of this chapter is for students to demonstrate that they can describe 10 specific psychological phenomena that impact the judgments and choices that normal people make about decision tasks that feature risk. These phenomena are divided into two groups: heuristics and biases, and framing effects.

After completing this chapter students will be able to:

1. Identify key biases that typically arise when people make judgments about risk.
2. Explain why reliance on heuristics, while unavoidable, leaves people vulnerable to making biased judgments.
3. Recognize that framing effects lead people's attitudes toward taking risk to be highly dependent on the circumstances in which they find themselves.

1.1 TRADITIONAL CORPORATE FINANCIAL DECISIONS AND PSYCHOLOGICAL TASKS

A wealth of psychological research over the last 50 years provides important insights into how normal people make judgments and choices about risky alternatives. Over the same period, research conducted by financial academics provides important insights into how financial executives should consider making judgments and decisions about corporate risk, and to some extent what executives do in practice. This book will help you to connect these two research streams, and in the course of doing so it will provide you with insights about the degree to which psychological pitfalls create imperfections in corporate decision making and reductions in corporate value. The book will also provide guidance about how to create value by mitigating vulnerability to these pitfalls.

To help fix ideas, consider a small example. Imagine a firm is contemplating a new one-year project which requires it to spend \$3.2 million at the end of this year, in the anticipation of receiving a return at the end of the following year. The project is cyclical, as the financial executives at the firm believe that the actual value of the future cash flow from the project will strongly depend on the state of the economy during the next year. The project also features high risk, as cash flow will be especially high if the economy is strong but especially low if the economy is weak. Typically, for projects of comparable risk, the firm seeks an expected return of 35 percent.

Suppose that the economy was stagnant last year, and that economists' current outlook for next year is that there is a very high chance that growth will continue to be stagnant. Suppose too that most economists agree that there is a low chance of moderate growth and a very low chance of a boom. The consensus view is that a recession is not likely, but if one materializes it is half as likely to be severe as mild.

The financial executives typically rely on these forecasts to form their own judgments, which they combine with other information such as recent stock market performance. In this regard, the stock market increased by 25 percent during the last twelve months, the stock of the average firm in their industry increased by 18 percent, and the stock of their own firm increased by 12 percent.

In assessing their proposed project, the executives estimate that its cash flows will be \$46.9 million in the event of a boom, \$31.9 million if the economy exhibits moderate growth, \$1.9 million if the economy is stagnant, –\$8 million in the case of a mild recession, and –\$13 in the case of a severe recession.

Put yourself in the position of a financial executive who has the responsibility of deciding whether to adopt this project. Suppose that you place a lot of trust in the cash flow estimates, as well as in the economists' general assessment. Would you feel that you have enough information to make an informed decision about whether to adopt the project?

The standard textbook approach to project selection revolves around discounted expected cash flows. In theory, the computation of expected cash flows would require quantitative probabilities for the alternative states of the economy, not simply the qualitative descriptors mentioned above. Therefore, financial executives who sought to base their decision on the kind of reasoning found in traditional corporate finance textbooks would need to convert the economists' qualitative descriptors, along with other information such as stock market performance, into numerical probabilities. Imagine that they do so, and assign a probability of 6 percent to a boom, 1 percent to moderate growth, 90 percent to a stagnant economy, 1 percent to a mild recession, and 2 percent to a severe recession. Exhibit 1-1 summarizes the information in this example.

Based on the executives' probability judgments, the expected cash flow from the project would be \$4.5 million, whose present value at 35 percent turns out to be

EXHIBIT 1-1 **Forecasted Cash Flows for a Hypothetical Project, with Associated Gains and Losses, Conditional on the Future State of the Economy Along with Economists' Qualitative Probabilistic Assessments and Managers' Quantitative Probabilistic Assessments**

Future State of Economy	Economists' Probability Assessments	Managers' Probability Assessments	Cash Flow	Cash Flow (Gain/Loss)
Severe recession	Highly unlikely	2%	–\$13.1	–\$16.3
Mild recession	Not likely	1%	–\$8.1	–\$11.3
Stagnant economy	Very high chance	90%	\$1.9	–\$1.3
Low-to-moderate growth	Low chance	1%	\$31.9	\$28.7
Boom	Very low chance	6%	\$46.9	\$43.7

$3.4 million. Notably, $3.4 million exceeds the $3.2 million required capital investment, which according to traditional textbook analysis suggests that the financial executives should adopt the project.

There are two important psychological points to note in the example. The first point pertains to the fact that the financial executives were not given quantitative probabilities, but instead had to make their own subjective judgments about what numbers to use, based on a mix of qualitative and quantitative information available to them. Notice from Exhibit 1-1 that executives assign a probability of 6 percent to a boom, which is much higher than the 1 percent they assign to low-to-moderate growth. Given that economists characterized low-to-moderate growth as being more likely than a boom, financial executives' probability assignment might reflect judgmental biases or a psychological tendency to overweight probabilities of extreme events. A similar remark applies to the probabilities that executives assign to a recession.

The second point concerns the gains and losses associated with the project, where the gain is expressed as "payback" defined as cash flow minus initial investment. See the rightmost column in Exhibit 1-1. Notice that the probability of the project incurring a loss is 93 percent, with gains being generated if the economy grows. Psychologically, being super sensitive to losses might lead the executives to reject the project, despite its positive net present value.

The two points just mentioned relate to the primary focus of this chapter, whose purpose is to introduce ten specific psychological phenomena that underlie the behavioral approach to corporate finance. To be sure, there are other psychological phenomena discussed in the book, besides the ones introduced in this chapter. However, the ten phenomena that form the heart of this chapter provide the foundational material for everything else in the book.

Notably, these ten phenomena impact investors just as they impact the managers of a firm. Investors also form judgments about firms' future cash flows, especially when they face choices about trading the securities of those firms. An important issue that arises in the behavioral approach is that both managers and investors often need to consider the psychological phenomena impacting other people, as well as themselves, when making their own judgments and decisions.

Dual Systems

heuristic
A rule of thumb used to arrive at a judgment or make a decision.

frame
Synonymous for description.

System 1
The fast, automatic, and intuitive processes associated with thinking.

In this chapter you will learn about biases associated with **heuristics,** or rules of thumb, upon which people rely in order to arrive at their judgments and make decisions, as well as how people's choices are influenced by the manner in which they **frame** their decision tasks with respect to gains and losses. Accordingly, the remainder of this chapter is organized into four main sections, the first three of which are respectively devoted to biases, heuristics, and framing effects; these sections introduce and describe 10 specific psychological phenomena. The fourth section discusses psychological and neurological frameworks to explain the factors underlying people's judgments and decisions about risk, as well as ways to improve both of these tasks.

Many aspects of the 10 phenomena take place below the level of consciousness. In this regard, psychologists suggest that we can think of our brains as having two systems, an intuitive system they call **System 1,** which is fast, and a more deliberative

System 2
The slow, deliberate, conscious processes associated with thinking.

system they call **System 2,** which is slow. Although both systems engage in calculation, we are consciously more aware of the calculations when they are done by System 2, such as computing the present value of a stream of cash flows. The calculations performed by System 1 are more automatic, such as when making a turn while driving a car or running to catch a ball.

The operations that System 1 makes are quite impressive, given the absence of conscious calculation. At the same time, human intuition is imperfect, which is why we are prone to make errors in judgment and choices that are imprudent. It is easy to suggest that the remedy is to rely on System 2 for judgment and decision making. However, System 2 requires much more effort than System 1, and we typically lack the mental resources and capabilities necessary for System 2 perfection.

The term "dual systems" is shorthand for the System 1/System 2 conceptual framework. An important reason to study behavioral corporate finance is to investigate how dual systems influence judgments and decisions that are made in a corporate financial environment. In this regard, much of what is taught in traditional corporate finance textbooks pertains to processes that System 2 carries out. Behavioral corporate finance adds explicit consideration of System 1 issues to the mix, with the intent to help managers make better decisions.

The next three sections discuss the results of experiments that psychologists have used to uncover the 10 psychological phenomena that form the heart of this chapter. In order to appreciate the discussion that follows, it is vitally important to complete the behavioral questionnaire, which is available in Additional Resources to Chapter 1. This questionnaire can be downloaded from the book web site at **www.mhhe.com/shefrin2e.** After completing the behavioral questionnaire, please continue your reading of this chapter, which provides a detailed discussion of each of the 10 phenomena.

Each of the next three sections is divided into subsections, with each subsection introducing one of the ten foundational psychological phenomena. The subsections feature a three-pronged 3-D structure, namely: description, diagnostic question, and discussion. A subsection begins with a brief description of a psychological phenomenon. This is followed by an example of a diagnostic question that psychologists have used to identify the phenomenon in question. The ensuing discussion indicates how people generally respond to the question, and what the response pattern means for the phenomenon being discussed.

1.2 BIASES

Bias
A predisposition toward making a specific type of error.

A **bias** is a predisposition towards making a specific type of error.

Excessive Optimism

Description

Psychologists have concluded that people are *excessively optimistic,* by which they mean unrealistically optimistic. More precisely, people tend to overestimate how frequently they will experience favorable outcomes and underestimate how frequently they will experience unfavorable outcomes.

Diagnostic Question

Consider the following four specific events that might happen to you during your lifetime and answer the question that appears thereafter.

1. Being fired from a job
2. Your work recognized with award
3. Living past 80
4. Having your car stolen

Compared to other people of the same gender as you in this class, what do you think are the chances that each of these events will happen to you? The choices range from much less than average, through average, to much more than average. Enter a column of numbers from 1 to 4 on a blank page, and record your answers next to each event number. For example, consider event 1, being fired from a job. If you think that being fired from a job is as likely to happen to you as to anyone else, record a 7 beside event 1.

1. 100% less (no chance)
2. 80% less
3. 60% less
4. 40% less
5. 20% less
6. 10% less
7. Average
8. 10% more
9. 20% more
10. 40% more
11. 60% more
12. 80% more
13. 100% more
14. 3 times average
15. 5 times average

Discussion

In the preceding diagnostic question, people can rate how likely they are to experience particular events relative to other people who are similar to them. A rating of 7 means that a person feels that an event is as likely to happen to them as to anyone else in similar circumstances.[1] Some of the events are favorable, and some are unfavorable. The unfavorable events are being fired from a job and having your car stolen. The favorable events are your work recognized with an award, and living past 80.

The four events under discussion are part of a general study involving 42 life events, of which 18 are favorable and 24 are unfavorable. The 42 events are described in the Additional Resources to Chapter 1, which is available online at the book web site. The questionnaire you answered as part of this chapter comprised an 18-question subset of the set of 42. If everyone held objectively correct beliefs, then the average response across the class for all events should be 7. Typically the average rating for the unfavorable events is below 7, while the average rating for the favorable events is above 7.[2] This means that people believe that unfavorable events are less likely to happen to them than to other people, but favorable events are more likely to happen to them than to other people. While this may be true for some people, it cannot be true for everyone. The general conclusion is that people tend to be excessively optimistic.[3]

excessive optimism
People overestimate how frequently they will experience favorable outcomes and underestimate how frequently they will experience unfavorable outcomes.

The original study on **excessive optimism** was conducted in the 1970s and used undergraduate students at an American university as subjects. The general results have been replicated many times and are robust, applying both to undergraduate students and to working professionals of all ages, both in the United States and internationally. In respect to the four life events discussed here, typical average class responses for the question about being fired lie in the range 3.8 to 5.2. This range corresponds to judgments that are between 44 percent and 18 percent less than the average, respectively.[4] Typical ranges for the other three questions are 7.5 to 9.1 for your work being recognized with an award, 7.1 to 7.9 for living past 80, and 5.1 to 6.3 for having your car stolen. For these ranges, every unit deviation from 7.0 corresponds to 10 percent in probability.

Psychologists have identified a separate concept of optimism, called "dispositional optimism," which is about having a positive general outlook on life. Dispositional optimism can be measured on a scale of 0 to 100, with scores above 50 corresponding to optimism and scores below 50 corresponding to pessimism.

Dispositional optimism and excessive optimism are positively related, but weakly so. For undergraduate finance majors, a 10-point increase in dispositional optimism on average increases the probability attached to favorable events by approximately 3 percent, and decreases the probability attached to unfavorable events by approximately 2 percent. However, the correlation between dispositional optimism and excessive optimism is low. Moreover, for an international group of investment professionals, the correlation is effectively zero, suggesting the need for caution when basing statements about excessive optimism on measures of dispositional optimism.[5]

The diagnostic question for optimism that involves living past the age of 80 is of special interest. In practice, assessments of length of life can be used to proxy for optimism. The use of this proxy has led to the conclusion that excessively optimistic people are more likely to believe that future economic conditions will improve. They are also more entrepreneurial and work more hours than people who are less optimistic.[6]

Overconfidence

overconfidence
People know less than they think they know and view themselves as better than they actually are.

Psychologists have found that people are generally overconfident when it comes to their knowledge and ability to complete difficult tasks. **Overconfidence** is a bias that pertains to how well people understand the limits of their knowledge, their own abilities, or both.

Description

People who are *overconfident* about their level of knowledge think they know more than they actually know. People who are overconfident about their abilities think they are better than they actually are. This overconfidence does not necessarily mean that these people are ignorant or incompetent. It just means that in their own eyes they are smarter and better than is actually the case.

Psychologists test for overconfidence about knowledge by asking knowledge-based questions such as the following.[7]

Diagnostic Question

Based on your own knowledge, and without using any additional sources, what is your best guess about the length, in miles, of the Amazon River? This is a difficult question for most people to answer, and it is unrealistic to assume that they will provide an accurate response. For this reason, suppose that we also ask for a confidence interval, meaning a low guess and a high guess, with the width of the interval reflecting a person's degree of confidence in his or her response. For example, we might ask people to structure their confidence intervals so that they feel 90 percent confident that their low and high guesses would bracket the answer they would find by conducting an Internet search about the length of the Amazon. If you have not yet done so for the Amazon River question, try it now by providing your best guess, a low guess, and a high guess, structured to define a 90 percent confidence interval.

A confidence interval for a single question is somewhat informative. More informative is to ask people to provide best guesses and confidence intervals for a series of difficult questions, say 10, so that we can point out that a person who is well calibrated would expect that for nine of the ten questions, the "true" numbers provided by an Internet search would lie within the confidence intervals.

Discussion

An Internet search for the length of the Amazon River yields an answer of 4,000 miles. If 4,000 lies between your low guess and your high guess, give yourself a hit. Otherwise, give yourself a miss. The answers to the 10 difficult questions in the behavioral questionnaire can be found in endnote 7 at the end of this material. People who are well-calibrated should expect to score nine hits for the 10 questions.[8]

When people set their confidence intervals too narrowly, their hit rates can be expected to be less than nine. Such people are overconfident about their knowledge. When they set their confidence intervals too widely, their hit rates can be expected to be 10. Such people are typically underconfident about their knowledge.

How well do people do on these questions? Typically, the most frequent number of hits, and the average number of hits, is about 4, with the mean being approximately 4.5. For a typical class, the standard deviation is approximately 2.5: the response associated with being well calibrated lies two standard deviations above the most frequent number of hits. That is, when it comes to difficult questions, people are typically very overconfident about their knowledge. They do not realize how little they know.

In respect to the overconfidence questions, what is the percentage of people responding who are well-calibrated? The answer turns out to be about 3.5 percent. Virtually everyone else is overconfident. Nevertheless, occasionally someone will achieve a hit rate of 100 percent and appear to be underconfident. But this is a relatively rare occurrence.[9]

In order to test for overconfidence in respect to ability, psychologists often pose the following question to people.

Diagnostic Question

Relative to all the people in the class, how would you rate yourself as a driver? (1) Above average? (2) Average? or (3) Below average? Here average is defined as the median.

Discussion

By definition, the median lies exactly in the middle, with the population equally divided on either side. The point of the last question is that very few people rate themselves below average. Instead, almost everyone rates themselves as either above average or average. This notion of overconfidence is sometimes called the **better than average effect.**

better than average effect
People tend to rate themselves above average rather than below average.

In a typical class, 45 to 55 percent might rate themselves as above average and 30 to 45 percent might rate themselves as average. The proportion of those rating themselves as below average are fewer in number, typically 10 percent or less. Notably, for undergraduates, the responses for above average tend to be at the high end of the range. Some people fault the wording in the question for not specifying a criterion on which to judge driving ability, suggesting that they chose criteria on which they indeed judge themselves to be above average. In a sense, this proves the point: people prefer to regard themselves as above average, if possible. Virtually nobody likes being below average.

Confirmation Bias

People who overlook information that disconfirms positions which they are evaluating or views which they hold in favor of information that confirms those positions or views are said to exhibit **confirmation bias.**[10]

confirmation bias
People attach too much importance to information that supports positions which they are evaluating or views which they hold relative to information that runs counter to those positions or views.

Description

People often spend too much time searching for reasons to support why a position they are evaluating or a view they hold are correct and too little time searching for reasons that might lead them to conclude that the position or their views are incorrect.

Confirmation bias pertains to the manner in which people either seek information or make use of the information at their disposal. Psychologists have concluded that many people are vulnerable to confirmation bias. This conclusion is based on the study of hypothesis evaluation tasks such as the following.

Diagnostic Question

Imagine that you are presented with four cards placed flat on a table in front of you. There is a letter appearing on one side of the card and a number on the other side of the card. You see the following on the four cards: a, b, 2, and 3.

a	b	2	3

Suppose you are asked to test the following hypothesis about these four cards: "Any card having a vowel on one side has an even number on the other side." Imagine that you are asked to select those cards, and only those cards, that will determine whether the hypothesis is true. That is, please select the minimum number of cards that will enable you to determine whether or not the hypothesis is true. Of the four cards, which would you turn over to verify the hypothesis?

Discussion

In this card task, most people turn over the card with the *a*, and some turn over the card with the *2* as well. The proportion turning over just the *a* and the *2* tends to vary between 30 and 70 percent. Typically less than a third choose to turn over just the *a* and the *3*. Yet, turning over only the *a* and *3* turns out to be the correct answer. This is because the efficient way of testing the validity of the hypothesis is to follow the "innocent until proven guilty" maxim and turn over only the cards that might falsify the hypothesis.

Consider in turn the falsification potential of each card. Suppose we turn over the card featuring the *a*. We will find either an even number or an odd number. If we find an even number, we have evidence supporting the hypothesis. However, if we find an odd number, we know that the hypothesis is false. Next, suppose we turn over the card with the *b*. This card provides us with no evidence to judge the validity of the hypothesis, since the hypothesis says nothing about cards featuring consonants. Now consider the card with a *2* on it. If we turn it over, we might find a vowel. This would be consistent with the hypothesis. Alternatively, we might find a consonant. That would be irrelevant to the hypothesis. Hence, this card offers no potential for falsification. Last, suppose that we turn over the card with the *3* on it. If we find a vowel, we know that the hypothesis is false. A consonant provides no information to support or falsify the hypothesis. Thus, the only two cards that offer the potential for falsification are the *a* and the *3*. However, most people choose *a* and *2*, or *a* alone. Notice that while *a* allows for both confirmation and falsification, *2* allows for confirmation only.[11]

Illusion of Control

When a person makes a decision, the outcome typically depends on a combination of luck and skill. Psychologists have concluded people have an exaggerated view of how much control they exert over outcomes. The associated bias is known as the **illusion of control.**

illusion of control
People overestimate the extent to which they can control events.

Description

The more control a person has over the outcome, the less the influence of chance and the more the influence of skill.

Diagnostic Question[12]

Imagine that you agree to participate in a baseball pool. The pool works as follows. Lying in front of you are two identical piles of baseball cards, with each pile containing 227 cards. The face of each card displays the picture of a different baseball player. The organizer of the baseball pool asks you to look through the pile, select one card, and show it to her. After you have done so, the organizer looks through the second (duplicate) pile, finds the twin of the card you selected, and deposits the twin into a brown cardboard carton. In order to participate, you pay $1 to the pool organizer. Because you were the first participant approached, when the pool organizer approaches the next participant, she will do so with two identical pools containing 226 cards, not 227 cards. After all the cards have been sold, the organizer then plans to draw exactly one card from the brown cardboard carton. The owner of the winning card will receive a $50 prize.

Suppose that all the cards have been sold, but the drawing has yet to take place. The pool organizer approaches you to say that someone who really wanted to participate cannot, because all the cards have been sold. She asks you how much you would be willing to accept in exchange for the card you drew. What is the minimum amount you would ask for to give up your card?

Discussion

When the study using the preceding question was first run, only half the participants were allowed to choose their own cards from the pile of 227 cards. Each person who was not allowed to choose a card was instead handed a card by the pool organizer. Apart from that change, everything else was the same for the two groups of participants, including the valuation question at the end.

Is it important that people be able to choose their own cards instead of being handed their cards? Does it affect their valuations? Is a pool participant more likely to win the $50 just because he or she selected the card instead of being handed the card? Of course not; the winner of the pool is determined entirely by a chance drawing. The odds of winning $50 from a single card in this pool are 1 in 227. The expected payoff is $0.22. And participants have been asked to pay $1 per card no matter who selects the card.

In the actual study, among participants who selected their own cards, the typical response was $8.67. In the alternative version, where the organizer selected the card, the typical response was $1.96.

What accounts for the difference? Psychologists have concluded that the illusion of control leads people to place a higher value on their cards when they select the cards than when the organizer selects their cards. That is, people seem to act as if they can control the odds of winning the pool by selecting the card themselves rather than letting somebody else do it. However the odds are the same, no matter who selects the card. Being able to control the odds is an illusion.

A subsidiary finding concerns overvaluation. First, people agree to pay $1 for a risky expected payoff amounting to $0.22. Second, they place a minimum value on the card well in excess of $1, let alone $0.22. Once they own that card, it increases dramatically in value.

For the previous diagnostic questions, the typical results when administered to a given class of students tend to conform to the original experimental findings almost all of the time. However, the same statement does not apply to the baseball pool question, where it is not unusual for the group choosing their own cards to provide a valuation that is lower than the group that was handed their cards. In addition, there can be considerable variation in valuations, some of which are much less than those reported in the original experiment. That this is the case suggests the need for more caution when applying the concept of illusion of control.

1.3 HEURISTICS

Representativeness

In asking about the extent to which an object or idea fits a stereotype, people are asking how representative that object or idea is for the class to which it belongs. Psychologists refer to the underlying principle as **representativeness.**

representativeness
People make judgments based on stereotypic thinking, asking how representative an object or idea is for the class to which it belongs.

conjunction fallacy
People misjudge the probability that several events occur simultaneously relative to the probabilities of those events occurring separately.

Description

People often make judgments and predictions by relying on heuristics that make use of analogues and stereotypes. Psychologists have concluded that people place too much reliance on representativeness and suggest that representativeness-based thinking can result in systematic errors. One such error is known as the **conjunction fallacy** and was studied through the use of the following question.[13]

Diagnostic Question

Imagine that you hear about a 31-year-old woman named Linda from people who know her quite well. They tell you that she is single, outspoken, and very bright. When she was a student, she was deeply concerned with issues of social justice. Linda's friends neglect to tell you about her current interests and career. The question about Linda in the behavioral questionnaire provided you with several alternatives, which included the following:

1. Linda is a feminist, active in the women's movement.
2. Linda is a psychiatric social worker.
3. Linda is a bank teller.
4. Linda is a bank teller and is active in the women's movement.

The diagnostic question asks you to rank these possibilities about Linda from top to bottom by assigning 1 to what you regard as the most likely possibility.

Discussion

In answering this question, people often put activity in the women's movement and psychiatric social worker at the top of their lists. The situation that people judge to be least likely is bank teller.

How do people arrive at these assessments? Psychologists suggest that they consider each situation as a category and ask how representative Linda is of the category. Since the description of Linda is highly representative of their impression of someone active in the women's movement, they judge that Linda is highly likely to be in the women's movement. Similarly, since Linda does not seem to fit the stereotype of a bank teller, they judge that Linda is unlikely to be a bank teller.

Because heuristics are shortcuts, they may also lead their users astray. For example, consider two of the choices for Linda, item 3 (Linda is a bank teller) and item 4 (Linda is a bank teller and is active in the women's movement). As Exhibit 1-2 demonstrates, feminist bank tellers are members of the category of bank

EXHIBIT 1-2
Venn Diagram for Three Choices in Linda Problem

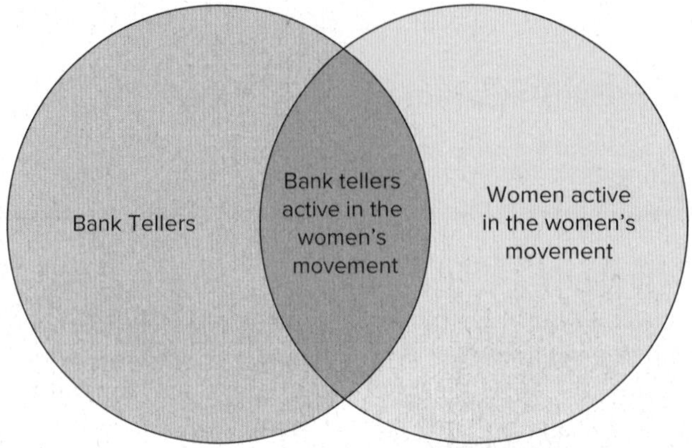

tellers. Therefore, it cannot be more probable for Linda to be a feminist bank teller than just a bank teller. This would violate one of the laws of probability. Yet, most people respond to the Linda question by assigning a higher likelihood to item 4 (feminist bank teller) than they do to item 3 (bank teller).[14] It is typical for between 67 and 80 percent of a class to provide responses exhibiting the conjunction fallacy for this question.

The event that Linda is both a bank teller and is active in the women's movement is an example of the conjunction of two events. In this respect, the typical response to the Linda question constitutes a *conjunction fallacy*.

Availability

Psychologists have concluded that people tend to attach more weight to information that is more readily available than to information that is less readily available. They call the propensity to overrely on information that is readily available, especially from memory, the **availability** heuristic.

availability
People overweight information that is readily available and intuitive relative to information that is less salient and more abstract, thereby biasing judgments.

Description

People typically rely on their own experiences and memories when forming judgments of risk. In other words, salience matters. This conclusion is based on studies that pose questions such as the following.

Diagnostic Question

Consider the danger of death or injury stemming from four sources, all involving water:

1. Shark attacks
2. Hurricanes
3. Rip currents
4. Floods

Which item in this list involves the most danger to people?

Discussion

Most people think about the risks associated with the above four sources by trying to recall events associated with each, and basing their judgments of relative frequency on the ease with which such events come to mind. Memories record both personal experiences and information obtained through the media.

In August 2005, Hurricane Katrina struck the gulf states, and damaged the levee system that protected New Orleans. The resulting flood destroyed the city and was the main media story day after day. The resulting death toll from Katrina was more than 1,500. Before Katrina, the death toll from hurricanes and floods had been much lower. In 2004, four successive hurricanes struck Florida, in what was viewed as a highly unusual event. The resulting death toll from all four storms was about 100, quite a high number at the time.

The media reports attacks by sharks on swimmers and surfers, often with a level of drama that rivals the reporting of many floods and hurricanes. Stories about rip currents receive occasional coverage in the media, usually when someone has drowned as a result.

Before Hurricane Katrina, most people ranked shark attacks or floods as posing the most danger. Few people chose rip currents. Yet, according to the U.S. Lifesaving Association, riptides pose the most danger. Using data reported for the years 1994–2014, the United States Lifesaving Association reported that rip currents are the primary cause of distress leading to rescue by lifeguards at surf beaches, comprising more than 80 percent of incidents. The Association reports that between 2010 and 2014, there were on average approximately 72,700 rescues per year, and 111 deaths from drowning. The National Oceanic and Atmospheric Administration (NOAA) reports that between 2004 and 2014, the average number of deaths per year from floods was 75 and from hurricanes it was 108. Although the percentage of people ranking rip currents is somewhat variable from class to class, they are typically rated first about 50 percent less often than the top rated item, be it hurricanes or floods.

Anchoring and Adjustment

A number that people have in their minds can serve to anchor their judgments just as a dropped anchor keeps a boat from drifting too far. Psychologists have concluded that people are susceptible to a bias known as **anchoring and adjustment.**

anchoring and adjustment
People form an estimate by beginning with an initial number and adjusting to reflect new information or circumstances. However, they tend to make insufficient adjustments relative to that number, thereby leading to anchoring bias.

Description

When forming judgments, people have a tendency to become anchored on numbers in their heads and do not make sufficient adjustments relative to the anchor. The following two-part question has been used to study anchoring.

Diagnostic Question

Record the last three digits of your home phone number. Now add 400 to the last three digits of your home phone number. Call the sum X.

1. Without looking up the answer anywhere, do you think that Attila the Hun was defeated in Europe at the Battle of the Catalaunian Plains before or after the year X?
2. Without looking up the answer anywhere, provide your best guess about the actual year that Attila the Hun was defeated at the Battle of the Catalaunian Plains.

Discussion

Most people do not know their history well enough to remember that Attila the Hun was defeated at the Battle of the Catalaunian Plains in 451 CE. Because most people do not know the date, they have to estimate it based on whatever recollections they have. Mean predictions are highly variable across different classes, typically lying between 415 and 1100. Mean responses for Europeans tend to be much closer to 451 than non-Europeans.

Consider the first of the two parts of the preceding question. The first question is intended to provide a context for the way they think about the second question. The issue here is whether people arrive at their prediction of the year of Attila's defeat by beginning with X and adjusting up or down. Specifically, do they anchor on X but not adjust sufficiently?

There is no rational reason to expect that people's predictions should in any way be correlated with the last three digits of their phone numbers. Yet in practice, people's responses are so correlated, with the sign of the correlation being positive. At the same time, correlations are often statistically insignificant unless class sizes are very large, well over a hundred.

Affect Heuristic

Description

affect
An emotional feeling.

When psychologists use the word **affect,** they are referring to the specific quality of goodness or badness. This quality is typically experienced as a feeling state, possibly consciously but not always, with goodness being experienced positively and badness being experienced negatively. People's affective responses occur rapidly and automatically, and relate to what is called their "affect pool." This pool consists of a "library" of positive and negative mental markers that people associate, either consciously or unconsciously, with the images stored in their memories. When people engage in the mental shortcut of basing their decisions on the contents of their affect pools instead of weighing the pros and cons of various alternatives, or retrieving relevant information from their memories, they are said to rely on the **affect heuristic.** In this regard, psychologists note that retrieving relevant information from memory and then processing this information relies on other heuristics such as availability and representativeness. In contrast, the affective heuristic is more of a "quick and dirty" shortcut.

affect heuristic
Basing decisions primarily on intuition, instinct, and gut feeling.

Diagnostic Question

Imagine that you have an opportunity to win $10 by randomly drawing a white bean from one of two jars, denoted Jar 1 and Jar 2. Jar 1 contains 10 beans, of which one is white and the rest are black. Jar 2 contains 100 beans, of which seven are white and the rest are black. You can choose the jar from which the drawing will take place. Which jar would you choose, Jar 1 or Jar 2?

Discussion

Jar 2 contains more white beans than Jar 1. This fact turns out to be important in the way people make choices in this decision task.

When psychologists conducted an experiment based on the above diagnostic question, in which real jars with real beans were used, they found that a majority of subjects selected Jar 2 over Jar 1, even though Jar 1 featured a higher probability of winning the $10. Moreover, many people stated that although they recognized that the probability of winning was higher with Jar 1, they found themselves emotionally drawn to choose Jar 2. In essence, people underweighted the denominator when implicitly computing the odds of winning depending on which jar they selected. Psychologists named the phenomenon "ratio bias" and concluded that the visual stimulus of seeing a higher absolute number of beans in Jar 2 than Jar 1 was the driving factor. Jar 2 generated a higher level of positive affect than Jar 1.

The role of affect in choice can be illustrated by another experiment. In this experiment, experienced forensic psychologists and psychiatrists were asked to recommend whether to release a mental patient, Mr. Jones, who might be violent within six months of being discharged from the hospital. Notably, the subjects based their recommendations on information provided by other clinical experts. When the information in question was described as "20 out of every 100 patients similar to Mr. Jones are estimated to commit an act of violence," they were twice as likely to recommend against discharge than when the information was described as "patients similar to Mr. Jones are estimated to have a 20 percent chance of committing an act of violence." The psychologists concluded that the first description generated much more negative affect than the second.[15]

Interacting Phenomena

Description

Psychologists have discovered that one behavioral phenomenon can affect another. In this respect, consider the extent to which excessive optimism is related to the following four issues:

1. The perceived controllability of the event.
2. The desirability of the event.
3. The perceived probability of the event, reflecting previous personal experience—effectively the degree to which the person is familiar with the event.
4. The degree to which people view themselves as representative of the type of persons to whom the event occurs.

Diagnostic Question

The question pertaining to excessive optimism involves a series of possible life events. Please assess each of these events on the specified criteria.

A. For each of the life events, assign a controllability category number. The list of choices includes:

   1. There is nothing one can do that will change the likelihood that the event will take place.
   2. There are things one can do to have a moderate effect on the chances that the event will occur.
   3. The event is completely controllable.

B. For each of the life events, assign a desirability number on a scale of 1 to 9 where 1 means extremely undesirable, 5 is neutral, and 9 means extremely desirable.
C. For each of the life events, assign a category number for familiarity, where the categories range from "The event has not happened to anyone I know," and "The event has happened to me more than once."
D. For each of the life events, assign a category number for mental imaging, where the categories are

1. No particular person with a high chance comes to mind.
2. When I think about the event, a clear picture comes to mind of a particular type of person to whom it is likely to happen.

Discussion

The general findings about excessive optimism is that its magnitude is related to other psychological variables. In this regard, one of the most important issues for corporate finance involves the connection between control and excessive optimism. The more that people report they are in control of a situation, the greater their optimism about how the situation will turn out.

Wishful thinking also affects optimism. People are more optimistic about events that are desirable than events that are undesirable.

Availability through personal experience also affects optimism. The more familiar people feel with a situation, the greater their optimism about how the situation will turn out. People are more optimistic about events that have happened to them than about events that have not happened to anyone that they know.

Representativeness also affects optimism. When people have a clear picture of the type of person to whom the event is likely to happen, and see themselves as resembling that person, they are inclined to be especially optimistic. This phenomenon is accentuated, the more likely people view the event as being.

1.4 FRAMING EFFECTS

framing effect
A person's decisions are influenced by the manner in which the setting for the decision is described.

Framing effects pertain to the manner in which people's choices are influenced by the descriptions of the decision tasks they face. This section uses a series of questions to discuss two types of framing effects.

Loss Aversion

Description

People feel a loss more intensely than a gain of the same magnitude.

Diagnostic Question

Imagine a 50–50 risk involving a coin toss where you lose $500 if the coin toss comes up tails, but win a different amount if the coin toss comes up heads. What is the lowest amount you would have to win in this risky alternative in order to accept the risk?

Discussion

loss aversion
Psychologically, people experience a loss more acutely than a gain of the same magnitude.

Psychological studies find that people's responses to this question suggest that they experience a loss roughly 2.5 times as intensely as a gain of the same magnitude. This phenomenon is called **loss aversion.** In this regard, the way a person answers the preceding diagnostic question provides an indication of how loss averse he or she is. For example, we can say that a person whose response to the question is $1,250 has a coefficient of loss aversion of 2.5, since $1,250 is 2.5 times larger than the $500 he or she might lose in the event a tail comes up. Notably, loss aversion leads people to be conservative about taking risk

The psychological concept of framing is synonymous with "description," as in the phrase "framing of a decision task." Suppose you were told that you would be paid $500 to participate in an experiment in which you would have the opportunity to take a 50–50 risk where you might lose $500 or win an unspecified amount. The experimenter will place the amount you might gain on a piece of paper face down in front of you, and will then ask you the diagnostic question above. Once you have provided your answer, the experimenter will turn over the piece of paper, and if your answer is less than or equal to the amount of the gain shown, you will face the risk. Otherwise, the experiment will terminate at that point, and you will collect your participation fee. If you do face the risk, then at the end of the experiment, you will receive the sum of the participation fee and the outcome of the risk.

Will you answer the diagnostic question differently when it is part of an experiment with a $500 participation fee than not? When there is a participation fee, will you ignore it when answering the question because you receive it regardless of how you answer the diagnostic question? Or will you instead think about the diagnostic question in net winning terms, seeing yourself as either winning $0 or winning some amount plus $500?

People who ignore the $500 participation fee when answering the diagnostic question continue to frame the outcome associated with a tail as a $500 loss and for most, losses loom larger than gains. Those who instead frame the outcome associated with a tail as a $0 gain do not perceive themselves as facing a potential loss, and so loss aversion is not operative for them in this particular situation.

In the diagnostic question, loss aversion leads people to ask for a higher gain in order to take a risk in which they might lose money. Those who frame the choice as being only in the domain of gains would be inclined to ask for a zero gain in the event of a head than in the original version of the diagnostic question, netting either zero or $500.

fourfold pattern
When probabilities of nonzero extreme outcomes are moderate, people are risk averse in the domain of gains, and risk seeking in the domain of losses. When probabilities of extreme nonzero outcomes are small, people are risk seeking in the domain of gains, and risk averse in the domain of losses.

The Fourfold Risk Pattern

In contrast to loss aversion, which applies to risks involving a mixture of possible gains and losses, the **fourfold pattern** applies to risks whose possible outcomes are either only gains or only losses. Below you will find an explanation of the fourfold pattern through four examples. Together the four examples illustrate how people's willingness to take risk can depend on the circumstances in which they find themselves, rather than being the same in all circumstances.

Description: Pattern One

For risks in which the probabilities attached to nonzero gains are not too small, people are inclined to be risk-averse.

Diagnostic Question

Suppose that you face a choice between two risks. Which of the two would you choose?

A. 90% chance of winning $2,000.
   10% chance of zero.

B. 45% chance of winning $4,000.
   55% chance of zero.

Discussion

The probabilities attached to nonzero outcomes in both A and B are moderate, not small. Moreover, both risks in the above decision task feature an expected gain of $1,800. However, B is riskier than A. Most people choose A over B when facing this choice, which is consistent with risk-averse behavior.

Description: Pattern Two

For risks in which the probabilities attached to nonzero gains are quite small, people are inclined to be risk-seeking.

Diagnostic Question

Suppose that you face a choice between two risks. Which of the two would you choose?

C. $2,000 with probability .002.
   0 with probability .998.

D. $4,000 with probability .001.
   0 with probability .999.

Discussion

The probabilities attached to nonzero outcomes in both C and D are small. Moreover, both risks in the above decision task feature an expected gain of $4. However, D is riskier than C. Most people choose D over C when facing this choice, which is consistent with risk-seeking behavior.

Description: Pattern Three

For risks in which the probabilities attached to nonzero losses are not too small, people are inclined to be risk-seeking.

Diagnostic Question

Suppose that you face a choice between two risks. Which of the two would you choose?

E. 90% chance of losing \$2,000.
   10% chance of losing \$0.

F. 45% chance of losing \$4,000.
   55% chance of losing \$0.

Discussion

The probabilities attached to nonzero losses in both E and F are moderate, not small. Moreover, both risks in the above decision task feature an expected loss of \$1,800. However, F is riskier than E. Most people choose F over E when facing this choice, which is consistent with risk-seeking behavior.

Description: Pattern Four

For risks in which the probabilities attached to nonzero losses are quite small, people are inclined to be risk-averse.

Diagnostic Question

Suppose that you face a choice between two risks. Which of the two would you choose?

G. Lose \$2,000 with probability .002.
   Lose 0 with probability .998.

H. Lose \$4,000 with probability .001.
   Lose \$0 with probability .999.

Discussion

The probabilities attached to nonzero losses in both G and H are small. Moreover, both risks in the above decision task feature an expected loss of \$4. However, H is riskier than G. Most people choose G over H when facing this choice, which is consistent with risk-averse behavior.

Exhibit 1-3 summarizes the fourfold pattern.

Framing Pitfalls

In a behavioral context, a "decision frame" is synonymous with the description of a decision task. For example, consider the following decision task:

Suppose that you face the following pair of concurrent decisions, with the outcome of your first decision being determined tomorrow afternoon and the outcome

EXHIBIT 1-3 **Fourfold Pattern Associated with Decision Tasks in Which the Risks Involve Either Gains Only or Losses Only**

	Gains	Losses
Probabilities moderate	Risk averse	Risk seeking
Probabilities small	Risk seeking	Risk averse

of your second decision being determined tomorrow evening. Examine both decisions, and then make your choices, keeping in mind that the outcomes are one-shot deals.

First decision: Choose between

I. A sure gain of $2,400.

J. A 25 percent chance to gain $10,000 and a 75 percent chance to gain nothing.

Second decision: Choose between

K. A sure loss of $7,500.

L. A 75 percent chance to lose $10,000 and a 25 percent chance to lose nothing.

The frame used to describe this decision task presents the choice as consisting of two concurrent decisions, one in the domain of gains and the second in the domain of losses. When people are presented with the task framed in this way, they tend to choose the combination "I and L." In the context of the fourfold pattern, it is easy to understand why. When considering the first part of the task, they perceive themselves to be choosing in the domain of gains, with the probability of a nonzero gain not being small, and as a result tend to exhibit risk-averse behavior. When considering the second part of the task, they perceive themselves to be choosing in the domain of losses, with the probability of a nonzero loss not being small, and as a result tend to exhibit risk-seeking behavior.

Notice that the combination of separate decisions in the concurrent decision task involves mixed gains and losses. In this regard, the combination I and L effectively adds $2,400 to the outcome of L. Therefore, I and L is a risk featuring a 25 percent probability of incurring a $2,400 gain and a 75 percent probability of incurring a $7,600 loss. However, because of the way the decision task is framed, most people do not think about it this way. As a result, the fourfold pattern effectively drives their choices, with loss aversion playing no role despite the presence of mixed gains and losses.

There is a deeper framing issue here as well. The combination J and K is a better choice than I and L. The combination J and K offers a 25 percent probability of a $2,500 gain and a 75 percent probability of a $7,500 loss. Notice that J and K offers the same probabilities as I and L, but $100 more regardless of whether the outcome is a gain or a loss: $2,500 versus $2,400 and −$7,500 versus −$7,600. Nevertheless, because of framing, I and L emerges the most popular choice combination and few people choose J and K. Exhibit 1-4 summarizes the structure of all four combinations.

The choice of L over K in the concurrent choice problem reflects more than the tendency to be risk-seeking in the domain of losses. It also reflects a feature known as "aversion to a sure loss." In this case, choosing K represents accepting the sure loss, and choosing L represents the **aversion to a sure loss.** People who are averse to a sure loss are actually willing to take actuarially unfair risks, hoping to beat the odds, in order to avoid sure losses.

aversion to a sure loss
People choose to accept an actuarially unfair risk in an attempt to avoid a sure loss.

Aversion to a sure loss is an issue that arises at several points in this book. Although both "loss aversion" and "aversion to a sure loss" seem like similar terms,

EXHIBIT 1-4 Alternative Frame for the Concurrent Choice Problem

	Probability	Outcome		Probability	Outcome
I	100%	2,400	I and K	100%	–$5,100
J	75%	0	I and L	25%	$2,400
	25%	10,000		75%	–$7,600
K	100%	–7,500	J and K	75%	–$7,500
				25%	$2,500
L	25%	0	J and L	18.75%	$0
	75%	–10,000		56.25%	–$10,000
				6.25%	$10,000
				18.75%	$0

keep in mind that they are different concepts. Aversion to a sure loss entails the *willingness to accept* risk in order to avert a sure loss. Loss aversion entails the *reluctance to accept* risk when both gains and losses are possible, because psychologically losses loom larger than gains.

Prospect Theory

prospect theory
A general psychological approach that describes the way people make choices among risky alternatives.

Prospect theory is a formal framework that presents a set of organizing principles to explain the framing issues described above. The theory was developed by psychologists Daniel Kahneman and Amos Tversky, for which Kahneman was awarded an Economics Nobel Prize in 2002.[16] In making the award, the Nobel committee explicitly cited prospect theory, thereby suggesting that they would have conferred the award on Tversky, had he not died several years before.

According to prospect theory, people act as if their incentives are to make choices as though using a criterion similar to expected cash flow. You can think of constructing the formula for this criterion by beginning with the formula for expected cash flow and then substituting alternatives for cash flows and probabilities. In the substitution, the alternative to cash flow is the mental sensation an individual experiences from anticipating the gain or loss associated with that cash flow. Replace each probability with the mental sensation associated with anticipating that probability, along with the relative ranking of its associated cash flow. For the sake of reference, call the resulting formula "prospect theory expected value."

psychophysics
The diminishing marginal impact associated with successive increases in stimuli.

A single psychological principle called **psychophysics** defines the character of these mental sensations. According to psychophysics, mental sensations increase with the magnitude of both cash flows and probabilities, but less than proportionally.

The psychophysics principle provides prospect theory with the power to explain the fourfold pattern that includes aversion to a sure loss. In this regard, the mental sensations associated with anticipating a sequence of successive gains increase, but at a decreasing rate. A similar statement applies to successive losses. Likewise, the mental sensations from anticipating successive increases in the probability of an extreme event increases with the likelihood with which the event occurs, but at a decreasing rate. The latter statement holds up to a point, in that the mental sensations from anticipating successive decreases in the probability of a highly likely event decreases with the probability of the event, but again at a decreasing rate.

Prospect theory explains loss aversion by treating the mental sensations associated with the anticipation of losses to be larger than the corresponding sensations associated with the anticipation of gains. According to prospect theory, an individual frames choices in terms of gains and losses relative to a **reference point.** Cash flows above the reference point are framed as gains while cash flows below the reference point are framed as losses. As the earlier discussion emphasized, there can be ambiguity attached to how people set reference points, and how they frame the consequences of the decisions they make. Notably, people can frame their decisions narrowly or broadly, which in turn can impact the decisions they make. A good example is the earlier discussion about alternatives I, J, K, and L. People who engage in **narrow framing** and treat risks in isolation are prone to choose I and L, whereas those who frame risks more broadly are inclined to choose the superior combination of J and K.

reference point
Benchmark used to measure gains and losses.

narrow framing
Treating a risk in isolation.

Prospect theory expanded our understanding of how attitude to risk depends on circumstances. Before prospect theory, there was a tendency to treat risk attitude as univariate, and to measure it using a question such as the following: Imagine that you face a choice about whether to stay in your current job, which involves no risk to your wealth, or to take a new job, which features a risk. The risk is that with a probability of 50 percent, your future wealth will either double or be cut by x percent. Think about what the value of x would have to be so that you would be indifferent between the two options. Notably the variable $1/x - 1$ can be used to measure a concept called the "coefficient of relative risk aversion." The higher the value of x, the more tolerance a person shows to bearing risk.

For a more formal discussion of prospect theory, see Additional Resources to Chapter 1, which is available online.

Aspiration Points

There are natural reference points, such as zero for earnings per share. Reference points can also be aspirational, such as the 52-week high for a stock price. SP/A theory is a psychologically based theory of choice emphasizing that while gains and losses can be defined relative to one reference point, an individual might also aspire to achieve a different reference point, which is usually higher. This aspiration point separates success from failure, as opposed to gain from loss.[17]

Like prospect theory, SP/A theory has a psychophysics structure for its treatment of probabilities. However, unlike prospect theory, **SP/A theory** interprets the mental associations in terms of emotions, most notably fear and hope. Fear leads to the overweighting of rare unfavorable events, while hope leads to the overweighting of rare favorable events. According to SP/A theory, people act as if their incentives are to make choices by balancing the perceived probability of being successful against "behavioral" expected value, of which prospect theory expected value is an example.

SP/A theory
A psychological theory of risk taking focused on security to address fear, potential to address hope, and the need for success in respect to aspiration.

March-Shapira framework
A model with two reference (focal) points, one low (survival) and one high (aspiration), with only one point operative at any one time, and risk appetite increasing with the absolute distance between the current situation and the reference point.

One way of adapting these ideas from individual choice to firm choice is to consider firms as having two potential reference points, called focal points, one for survival and the other for aspiration. At any one time, only the first focal point will be operative, depending on the extent to which a firm experiences financial distress along with the personality traits of its executives and board members. According to the theory, known as the **March-Shapira framework**, a distressed firm takes low risk but increases that risk as the level of distress declines.[18] For a non-distressed firm, the theory postulates that when a firm is operating below aspiration, and therefore experiencing a shortfall, it takes on relatively high risk. However, as the shortfall shrinks the amount of risk declines. When the shortfall turns into a surplus, risk falls discontinuously at the juncture, but then increases with the magnitude of the surplus.

1.5 MITIGATING PITFALLS

Biases such as excessive optimism and overconfidence illustrate faulty judgments. The framing effect associated with the concurrent choice problem (involving choices I, J, K, and L) illustrates faulty decision making. Faulty judgments and faulty decisions are part of the normal human experience. Because by nature people are imperfect, expect mistakes. At the same time, there is an expression about not letting the perfect be the enemy of the good, which in this case means not letting the impossibility of perfection stand in the way of seeking ways to mitigate mistakes.

debiasing
A process for mitigating bias.

nudge
A form of weak intervention for helping people to avoid psychological pitfalls and make better choices.

The most common behavioral terms for mitigating mistakes are "nudges," "**debiasing,**" and "cognitive repairs." These vary from small-scale interventions called **nudges,**[19] to large-scale interventions such as shifts in organizational culture. Although discussion of large-scale interventions is mostly confined to Chapter 10, throughout this book readers will find tips about corporate nudges. These tips are set out as thematic boxes bearing the title "Corporate Nudges," and structured to identify the error or bias, briefly explain why it happens, describe how it happens, and offer a nudge for doing something about it.

The purposeful design of decision frames to facilitate effective decision making is called "choice architecture." Good choice architects understand that there are numerous challenges in getting people to change their behavior.

The rest of this section describes some of the general issues of which good choice architects need to be cognizant. Many people get set in their ways and resist change, a tendency known as "status quo bias." Many profess through their System 2 that they wish to change, but find that they lack self-control in that their System 1 is resistant to going along. Many are excessively optimistic, but because not all are so for the same reason, choice architects might need to take a nuanced approach. For some, the main reason for excessive optimism is emotional in that some people simply feel hopeful. For others the main reasons have more to do with specific factors such as people perceiving themselves as in control, engaging in wishful thinking, being familiar with the decision task, or perceiving themselves as representative of successful people. Knowing the source of the excessive optimism can sometimes help choice architects devise ways to provide feedback to decision makers in order to help them be aware of their biases.

Choice architects understand the challenges that arise because people sometimes make poor decisions as a result of their attention being drawn to factors of secondary importance rather than factors of primary importance. The factors that attract and keep our attention relate to brain chemistry—for example, the specific brain region known as the posterior cingulate cortex. In this regard, people for whom these regions exhibit higher density are better at maintaining focus. Therefore, choice architects need to understand that interventions that work for some will not work for all.

Brain structure is particularly germane when it comes to risk taking, a critical aspect of corporate finance. Neuroscientists have identified heightened activity in the brain region known as the nucleus accumbens, which is involved in positive emotional states such as feelings of "excitement," as increasing the salience of potential gains and with it subsequent risk taking. Analogously, they have identified heightened activity in the brain region known as the anterior insula, which is associated with negative emotional states such as feelings of "anxiety," as increasing the salience of potential losses and subsequent risk avoidance.[20]

testosterone
A steroid hormone associated with risk taking, aggression, and sexuality.

cortisol
A steroid hormone generated during prolonged periods of stress.

Levels of steroid hormones such as **testosterone** and **cortisol** also impact risk taking. Prior success tends to induce increases in testosterone and decreases in cortisol, both of which are associated with higher risk taking.[21] Elevated testosterone is associated with success and feeling like a winner, physically manifested in high power poses such as raised arms.[22] The neurotransmitter dopamine is a critical ingredient in the neuro-reward system. In this regard, good choice architects will appreciate that strings of successes that lead to heightened levels of testosterone and dopamine often result in extreme overconfidence.

prefrontal cortex
The front part of the human brain associated with higher-order thinking and executive function.

Perhaps the best known psychology experiment in self-control is the "marshmallow test" investigating how children are successfully able to face temptation and delay gratification in order to obtain two marshmallows instead of one.[23] Brain chemistry also plays a role in self-control. In this case, specific regions of the part of the brain associated with executive function, known as the **prefrontal cortex,** play critical roles, one being the ventromedial prefrontal cortex (vmPFC) and the other being the dorsolateral prefrontal cortex (DLpfc), so named for where they are located in the brain. Activity within the vmPFC is associated with pleasure, such as the belief one is drinking expensive wine. When most people face a decision between giving in to temptation and delaying gratification, their vmPFC regions will become active. Researchers have found that those able to resist the temptation will have activated and engaged DLpfc regions as well, whereas those unable to resist the temptation will not.[24]

Food choices are often good ways to explain interventions. Suppose that according to Systems 2, a person entering a lunch cafeteria professes that she would be better off choosing fruit for dessert instead of a pastry. Choice architects have learned that by structuring the choice so that the fruit is attractively displayed early on, and the pastry placed further along, more people will choose fruit over pastry. The attractive fruit display activates their reward systems and they make the choices without needing to confront the stronger temptation of having to choose between fruit and pastry with both options in front of them.

In some cases, choice architects will find it better to leave well enough alone, despite the pitfalls and imperfections. For example, take the Linda problem discussed in Section 1.3, and the fact that most people form judgments in this problem by relying on representativeness. Rather than relying on their subjective impressions about the alternatives to be ranked in the Linda problem, people could instead do research to identify the relative frequencies associated with these choices and then apply **Bayes' rule** to arrive at a ranking. Bayes' rule stipulates that for two events D and F, the conditional probability of F given D, P(F|D), can be computed as P(F) × P(D|F)/P(D). Most people find it extremely difficult to carry out this procedure. If representativeness-based thinking leads them to do a decent job of rank ordering most of the possibilities, then despite succumbing to the conjunction fallacy, they might be better off relying on the heuristic rather than poorly executing a Bayesian procedure. For them, less information might be better than more.

Bayes rule
The relationship linking the probabilities of two events F and D expressed as P(F|D) = P(F) × P(D|F) /P(D), where P(F) is called the prior and P(F|D) is called the posterior.

To recap, choice architects can offer decision-making improvements by keeping in mind a set of factors. These factors relate to psychological incentive issues including the elements that activate neurological systems and attention, awareness of how people respond to different frames, an appreciation of defaults, provisions for giving decision makers feedback, expecting mistakes instead of perfection, and promoting frames for dealing with complex choices that take psychological phenomena into account.

Summary

Traditional corporate finance textbooks focus more on what corporate managers should do rather than what they actually do. The behavioral approach seeks to investigate what they actually do, why they do it, and to offer suggestions for how they might do a better job when it is possible.

This chapter introduces 10 psychological phenomena that are hardwired. Psychologists suggest that we can think of our brains as having two systems: an intuitive system they call System 1, which is fast, and a more deliberative system they call System 2, which is slow. System 1 activities tend to be automatic, and its calculations feel effortless, as when we are driving a car or running to catch a ball. System 2 activities feel more like work, as in the preparation of cash flow forecasts for the purpose of undertaking discounted cash flow analysis.

Like everyone else, managers make professional decisions using the processes of both System 1 and System 2. Some decisions are very sophisticated, and require significant System 2 activity. Much of professional education is aimed at enhancing System 2 skills. As impressive as people can be, few—if any—are perfect. Each of us, to some degree, is vulnerable to some or all of the 10 phenomena at the heart of this chapter.

The 10 phenomena comprise three categories: biases, heuristics, and framing effects. Biases and heuristics mostly pertain to imperfect judgments. Framing effects pertain to choices among alternatives, and some framing effects are associated with imperfect decisions. In this regard, one of the major lessons to be learned from studying framing effects is that people's psychological attitude toward risk taking is often circumstantial.

In a sense, the route to better decisions is to develop a greater reliance on System 2 for judgment and decision making. However, keep in mind that System 2 requires much more effort than System 1, and people typically lack the mental resources and perhaps the capabilities necessary for System 2 perfection. Moreover, managers might compute net present value, but if net present value and their intuition point in different directions, managers might be more prone to follow their intuition.

Figuring out how to make better decisions typically requires working within the system, meaning the joint interaction of System 1 and System 2. Working within the system requires knowledge of choice architecture. In some circumstances, people can make better decisions by reframing their decision tasks. Remember the adage: the way to solve an important problem is to ask the right question. Sometimes others will be able to recommend architectural changes that nudge "us" into better decisions. Other times, "we" might be able to ask themselves questions that promote self-nudging.

Additional Behavioral Readings

Barberis, N. C., "Thirty Years of Prospect Theory in Economics: A Review and Assessment," *Journal of Economic Perspectives* 27, no. 1 (Winter 2013), pp. 173–196.

Gilovich, T., D. Griffin, and D. Kahneman, *Heuristics and Biases: The Psychology of Intuitive Judgment* (Cambridge, UK: Cambridge University Press, 2002).

Kahneman, D. and A. Tversky "Prospect Theory: An Analysis of Decision Making under Risk," *Econometrica* 5, no. 2 (1979), pp. 263–291.

Kahneman, D., *Thinking, Fast and Slow* (New York: Farrar, Straus, and Giroux, 2011).

Key Terms

affect, *14*
affect heuristic, *14*
anchoring and adjustment, *13*
availability, *12*
aversion to a sure loss, *20*
Bayes rule, *25*
better than average effect, *8*
bias, *4*
confirmation bias, *8*
conjunction fallacy, *11*
cortisol, *24*
debiasing, *23*
excessive optimism, *6*
fourfold pattern, *17*
frame, *3*
framing effect, *16*
heuristic, *3*
illusion of control, *9*
loss aversion, *17*
March-Shapira framework, *23*
narrow framing, *22*
nudge, *23*
overconfidence, *6*
prefrontal cortex, *24*
prospect theory, *21*
psychophysics, *21*
reference point, *22*
representativeness, *11*
SP/A theory, *22*
System 1, *3*
System 2, *4*
testosterone, *24*

Explore the Web

www.nobelprize.org/mediaplayer/?id=531
Nobel prize lecture by Daniel Kahneman, 2002.

www.psych-it.com.au/Psychlopedia/article.asp?id=238
Discussing optimism bias.

www.psychologytoday.com/blog/the-art-thinking-clearly/201306/the-overconfidence-effect
Discussing overconfidence bias.

www.npr.org/2016/06/24/483112809/www.npr.org/programs/ted-radio-hour/483080945/nudge
Explaining the concept of nudge.

Chapter Questions

1. Imagine a decision task in which you are to choose between two alternatives that involve blindly drawing a single chip from one of two urns, labeled A and B respectively. Both urns contain colored balls. The proportion of the different colors is described below. Also described below are the payoffs from drawing a ball of a specific color from each of the two urns. Your task is to decide from which urn you would draw a ball, urn A or urn B?

	Urn A		Urn B	
	Probability	**Outcome**	**Probability**	**Outcome**
Yellow	2%	–$15	2%	–$15
Blue	1%	–$15	1%	–$10
Green	1%	$30	1%	$45
Red	6%	$45	6%	$45
White	90%	$0	90%	$0

2. Imagine yourself at a conference center, where there are two groups meeting in adjoining rooms, one a group of lawyers and the other a group of engineers. In fact, the room with lawyers contains 30 lawyers and the room with engineers contains 70 engineers. Someone named Jack is attending a meeting in one of these two rooms. Here is what we are told about Jack: he is a 45-year-old man who is married and has four children. He is generally conservative, careful, and ambitious. He shows no interest in political and social issues and spends most of his free time on his many hobbies, which include home carpentry, sailing, and mathematical puzzles. What probability would you assign to Jack being an engineer?
3. Suppose that you are offered the opportunity to accept a risk involving the toss of a fair coin, in which you will win $450 if heads comes up and lose $450 if tails comes up.
   a. Would you accept this opportunity or reject it?
   b. If the stake size was changed to $225 from $450, would you accept the opportunity or reject it?
4. Consider a trivia test consisting of 10 questions for you to answer from memory alone. In addition to giving your best guess, consider a range: a low guess and a high guess so that you feel 90 percent confident that the right answer will lie between your low guess and your high guess. Try not to make the range between your low guess and high guess too narrow. Otherwise, you will appear overconfident. At the same time, try not to make

the range between your low guess and high guess too wide. This will make you appear underconfident. If you are well-calibrated, you should expect that only one out of the 10 correct answers you provide does not lie between your low guess and your high guess.

After each question, write down three numbers, your best guess, low guess, and high guess.[25]

a. What is the average weight of an adult blue whale, in pounds?

b. In what year did Leonardo da Vinci paint the *Mona Lisa*?

c. How many independent countries were there at the end of the year 2000?

d. What is the air distance, in miles, from Paris, France to Sydney, Australia?

e. How many bones are in the human body?

f. How many combatants were killed in World War I?

g. How many books were in the U.S. Library of Congress at the end of the year 2000?

h. In miles, how long is the Danube River?

i. In miles per hour, how fast does the Earth spin at the equator?

j. How many transistors are in Intel's Pentium III processor?

5. Imagine 100 book bags, each of which contains 1,000 poker chips. Forty-five bags contain 700 black chips and 300 red chips. The other 55 bags contain 300 black chips and 700 red chips. You cannot see inside any of the bags. One of the bags is selected at random by means of a coin toss.

   Consider the following three questions about the book bag.

   a. What probability would you assign to the event that the selected bag contains predominantly black chips?

   b. Now imagine that 12 chips are drawn, with replacement, from the selected bag. These 12 draws produce 8 blacks and 4 reds. Would you use the new information about the drawing of chips to revise your probability that the selected bag contains predominantly black chips? If so, what new probability would you assign?

   c. In addition to giving your best probability estimate in question b, consider a range: a low estimate and a high estimate so that you feel 90 percent confident that the right answer will lie between your low estimate and your high estimate. Try not to make the range between your low estimate and high estimate too narrow. Otherwise, you will appear overconfident. At the same time, try not to make the range between your low estimate and high estimate too wide. This will make you appear underconfident. If you are well-calibrated, you should expect the true probability to lie outside the range between your low estimate and your high estimate one time in ten.

6. Suppose that a university is attempting to predict the grade point average (GPA) of some graduating students based upon their high school GPA levels. GPA scores lie between 0 and 4. Below are some data for undergraduates at a university located in California. Historically, the mean high school GPA of students who entered as freshmen and graduated was 3.44 (standard deviation was 0.36). The mean college GPA of those same students was 3.08 (standard deviation 0.40). This question asks you to predict the college GPA scores of three graduating students, based solely on their high school GPA scores. The three high school GPA scores are 2.2, 3.0, and

3.8. Write down your predictions for each of the three students, along with a brief explanation of your thought process.

7. An episode of the BBC program *Horizons* featured the following experiment. A researcher in a park with a lot of pedestrians invited passersby to examine an unopened bottle of wine, which the researcher stated he had just purchased at a nearby wine shop, and estimate the price the researcher had paid. Before participants actually came up with their estimates, the researcher asked them to pull a ping pong ball from a bag, keeping their eyes closed. The researcher indicated that each ball in the bag had a number between 1 and 100 written on it. However, this was not true, as all the ping pong balls had the same number.

   The experiment was conducted twice, on two different days, with two different groups of participants. The first group of people drew a ping pong ball with the number 10, while the second group drew a ping pong ball with the number 65. After seeing the number on the ball, the researcher asked each participant for his or her estimate of the wine's price. The first group estimated the cost to be between \$10 and \$30, while the second group guessed much higher, between \$40 and \$100. Discuss what psychological phenomenon might explain this behavior pattern.

8. In connection with chapter question 2, answer the following questions.

   a. What probability would you assign to Jack being an engineer if the question instead stated that the room with lawyers has 70 lawyers and the room with engineers contains 30 engineers?

   b. In your opinion, what proportion of engineers match Jack's description?

   c. In your opinion, what proportion of lawyers match Jack's description?

   d. Did you ask these questions of yourself when answering question 2, yes or no?

9. Imagine a decision task in which you are to choose between two alternatives that involve blindly drawing a single chip from one of two urns, labeled A and B respectively. Both urns contain colored balls. The proportion of the different colors is described below. Also described below are the payoffs from drawing a ball of a specific color from each of the two urns. Your task is to decide from which urn you would draw a ball, urn A or urn B.

	Urn A		**Urn B**	
	Probability	**Outcome**	**Probability**	**Outcome**
Yellow	3%	–\$15	2%	–\$15
Green	1%	\$30	1%	–\$10
Red	6%	\$45	7%	\$45
White	90%	\$0	90%	\$0

10. Excel has a function, BINOM.DIST, for the binomial probability distribution. This function computes the probability of drawing x successes in n independent trials when the probability of drawing a success is p. Do you see a role for the binomial distribution in finance? Do any of the problems in the problem set for this chapter strike you as directly relating to the binomial distribution, and if so which one or ones? In answering this question, do not change any of your previous answers.

Additional Resources and Materials for Chapter 1 Are Available at www.mhhe.com/shefrin2e

Minicase

Panama Canal

In one of the world's greatest engineering feats, the United States built the Panama Canal. The project took 10 years and was completed in August 1914. The United States operated the waterway for the remainder of the twentieth century, but a treaty between the United States and Panama resulted in the Panama Canal Authority (ACP) assuming command of the waterway. This they did at the end of 1999.

Over the course of the twentieth century, the volume of world shipping grew greatly, and with it the volume of traffic through the Panama Canal. Notably, ship sizes also grew, to the point where the largest container ships were too big to traverse the waterway. Partly out of fear that its canal would become obsolete, the ACP made the decision to build new locks that would handle the larger container ships. In 2007 they put out a request for proposal (RFP), soliciting bids for the project.

The lowest bid came from a consortium called Grupo Unidos por el Canal that was led by the Spanish firm Sacyr Vallehermoso. The consortium's members included firms from Panama, Belgium, and Italy. Their bid, $3.1 billion, was approximately $1 billion lower than the next lowest bid. Notably, the other bidders included Bechtel, one of the most experienced engineering and construction firms in the world.

In accepting the consortium's bid in July 2009, the ACP set a goal of completing the project in time for the 100-year anniversary of the original canal. However, the consortium missed the August 2014 deadline, and the first container ship passed through the new locks in June 2016.

The *New York Times* documented a series of problems between 2009 and 2016.[26] The problems involved leaks in concrete, insufficient water to support large ships in the canal, a shift from stable locomotives for guiding ships to less stable tugboats, insufficient margin for error from a new lock design that was too narrow, the identification of earthquake faults beneath the canal, and a cost overrun whereby $3.1 billion rose to $5.25 billion. Below is a capsule summary of the main points in coverage by the *Times*.

The locks are made from concrete and reinforcing steel bars, and the consortium chose low-quality ingredients for the concrete. According to a 2010 confidential analysis from the firm Hill International, which was commissioned by the consortium's insurer, the consortium's budget for concrete was 71 percent smaller than that of the next lowest bidder. Moreover, the raw material for concrete, known as aggregate, was excavated from the Pacific side of the canal, and generally regarded as being of questionable quality for making concrete. It was for that reason that Bechtel, in preparing its bid, had planned to import aggregate. During the testing phase in 2015, cracks emerged in the concrete lining the lock walls, and water rushed through the cracks, requiring the insertion of additional steel reinforcing bars. The *Times* quoted one concrete expert who monitored the situation for his criticism of the project having used the wrong mix of concrete ingredients as well as substandard pouring practices. Although characterizing the project's approach to fixing problems as trial-and-error, the ACP described itself as "confident" about the concrete lasting for a century.

The Panama Canal features two sets of locks, one on the Pacific side and one on the Atlantic side, with a 50-mile-long artificial lake between the two sets. This lake has to be deep enough to support large ships as they go from one side of the canal to the other. The lake also supplies most of Panama's drinking water. From the time the ACP took control of the canal, they recognized that an expansion project would require more water and planned for a series of dams that would address the issue. However, building new dams would have displaced many low-income Panamanians, and political protests led to the idea being shelved. Despite warnings in 2008 from both the Inter-American Development Bank and the World Bank about a shortfall of fresh water, the project leaders decided that they could address the problem by conserving water in large water-saving basins. While a clever solution, in 2016 drought conditions caused the level of the lake to decline, and as a result the ACP issued an advisory that large ships would have to lighten their loads considerably.

The original Canal uses locomotives to guide ships into and out of the locks. Although these have been very effective over time, especially in bad weather, the ACP decided to replace the locomotives with tugboats. The decision was made based on a lock system in Belgium (Berendrecht), which uses tugboats to guide large ships. While versatile, the tugboats are less stable than the locomotives, and not as capable of providing stability to large ships during turbulent weather. Moreover, they are more stable going backward than forward, yet will have to go forward much of the time. According to union representatives in Panama, the ACP did not include canal workers in the planning process, and in addition ignored important differences between Panama's canal and the one in Berendrecht.

In 2003 a feasibility study requested by the ACP concluded that the new locks should be at least 328 feet longer and 40 feet wider than the ships going through. Because the largest container ships are approximately 1,200 feet long and 160 feet wide, the new locks would have to be about 1,528 feet long and 200 feet wide. However, they are instead 1,400 feet long and 180 feet wide. Tugboats are approximately 100 feet long. That leaves very little margin for error for the tug boats to move alongside the ships, especially on windy days.

In November 2007 reports by one geologist working for the ACP and another working for the U.S. Embassy in Panama indicated that Panama faced a much higher earthquake risk than was previously believed. The then Panamanian president responded by saying that the geologists had insulted his republic.

In June 2016, the first large ship went through the new locks.[27] At the time, the executive vice-president of engineering and administration at the ACP stated that the *New York Times* coverage was out of date and addressed only challenges that had occurred during the construction phase but were resolved.

Case Analysis Questions

1. Of the 10 psychological phenomena introduced in Chapter 1, identify which ones apply to the minicase, and give reasons to support your answer.
2. The *Times* article notes that three days after the ACP awarded a $158 million contract to the Spanish firm that manufactures the tugboats, the son of the canal administrator joined the law firm representing the tugboat manufacturer. Discuss whether such a relationship presents any potential conflicts of interest.
3. The U.S. Army Corps of Engineers maintains locks and dams on U.S. waterways, and engages consultants to analyze the kinds of issues described in the minicase. One of these consultants points out that even if it is below standard, concrete might last a hundred years because it continues to gain compressive strength and generally the concrete is not heavily loaded.[28] He also notes that the problem with locks and dams on such canals is not so much the concrete, but the steel gates that open and close once or twice an hour over the course of decades. The associated changes from tension to compression tend to create long-term problems, an issue which surfaced at the locks in Sault Ste. Marie, Michigan and posed a major threat to the U.S. economy.[29] In this respect, lock gates can become serious maintenance problems, and can take several months to repair or replace. In mentioning lock gates, the *Times* article points out that the gates in the original canal weigh several hundred tons and are finely balanced, but mentions little more than this. Discuss whether, by saying only what it did about the locks and nothing more, the Times article reflects any of the psychological phenomena described in Chapter 1.

Chapter Two

Introduction to Behavioral Analysis

The main objective of this chapter is for students to learn to structure questions as the first step in applying the 10 foundational psychological phenomena to behavioral corporate issues. Because these phenomena pertain to common human traits, they affect both managers and investors. Certainly, managers need to understand how these phenomena impact their own judgments and decisions; however, they also need to understand the decisions of other managers as well as the investing public whose trading activities establish market prices.

After completing this chapter students will be able to structure questions as they engage in behavioral analysis to:

1. Identify the key biases that lead managers to make faulty financial judgments about risky alternatives.
2. Explain why reliance on heuristics and susceptibility to framing effects render managers vulnerable to making faulty decisions that reduce firm value.
3. Recognize that investors are susceptible to the same biases as managers and that mispricing stemming from investor errors can cause managers to make faulty decisions that reduce firm value.

2.1 TRADITIONAL TREATMENT OF CORPORATE FINANCIAL DECISIONS

Firms raise funds by borrowing on lines of credit, issuing commercial paper, selling corporate bonds, issuing new equity, and generating operating cash flows. Firms use funds when they undertake projects, acquire fixed assets, build inventory, pay dividends, engage in mergers and acquisitions, and deal with legal and regulatory issues.

The traditional value-maximizing approach is based on discounted cash flow (DCF) analysis. Virtually all the decisions just mentioned involve risk. Because the cash flows are uncertain, expected or mean values are used to assess value. Risk enters into the analysis through the discount rate that is applied to the expected cash flows. According to DCF analysis, projects should be undertaken if the present value of the expected future cash flows exceeds the initial investment required. In the same vein, funding decisions should be made in order to maximize the value of the firm, based on DCF analysis. For example, the use of debt provides a tax shield, which managers should balance or trade off against potential bankruptcy costs.

In theory, managers serve the interests of investors, the owners of the firm. In practice, the interests of managers and investors might not be perfectly aligned. Conflicts of interest are known as agency conflicts, in that investors are principals whose interests are being served by managers acting as their agents. In general, agency conflicts may prevent the firm's managers from making decisions that result in full value maximization. In these situations, the attendant costs are known as agency costs.

For organizational purposes, imagine that managers seek to maximize an objective function measuring performance. This objective function is a sum of terms such as the present value of the firm's after-tax cash flows from operations and investment, the value associated with its financing strategy, and net benefits associated with managerial interests such as compensation and perquisites. The summation of all three components is often called *adjusted present value* (APV). Notably, in the traditional setting, markets are efficient so that managers and investors agree on how valuation reflects available information.

Managers' decision environment is simplest when these components are independent of each other, so that decisions about operations, financing, and compensation feature no interactions. When this is the case, we can consider decisions about capital budgeting and capital structure separately, with decisions about investment made to maximize net present value (NPV), and decisions about capital structure made to trade off the benefits of tax shields against the costs associated with financial distress. However, in practice, there will be interactions. For example, financing costs might be too high to justify a project whose net present value is otherwise positive, or interest payments associated with high debt levels might be used to provide managerial discipline in an attempt to counteract the potential for agency conflicts. Information asymmetries between managers and investors can also complicate matters, as investors seek to make inferences about what managers know based on their actions.

2.2 BEHAVIORAL TREATMENT OF CORPORATE FINANCIAL DECISIONS

The traditional material taught in corporate finance courses offers powerful techniques that in theory help managers to make value-maximizing decisions for their firms. Yet, in practice, psychological pitfalls hamper managers in applying these techniques correctly. The purpose of this text is to make students aware of potential psychological pitfalls as they arise in the various decision tasks that financial managers confront, and to offer advice on how to mitigate the impact of these pitfalls.

The behavioral pitfalls discussed in this text are not unique to managers, but are prevalent across the general population, impacting investors as well as managers.

Many of these pitfalls were identified by psychologists Daniel Kahneman and the late Amos Tversky. Their work was recognized with a Nobel Prize in Economics, awarded to Kahneman in 2002, jointly with economist Vernon Smith, who pioneered the use of experimental techniques to study markets.

Although executives are prone to experiencing the same psychological phenomena as the general population, the evidence indicates that for some phenomena they do so with greater intensity. In particular, chief executives exhibit more dispositional optimism and less risk aversion than the general population, features which are accentuated among CEOs who are taller and younger than their counterparts, and who are also male. CEOs also exhibit greater dispositional optimism than their CFOs, which is a trait that many CFOs have noticed.[1]

Because psychologically induced mistakes can be, and often are, very expensive, studying behavioral corporate finance is vital. Exhibit 2-1 provides a thumbnail sketch of the main points in the chapter. The chapter discusses how the 10 foundational psychological phenomena introduced in Chapter 1 lead managers to make faulty decisions, thereby reducing the values of their firms.

Like agency conflicts, behavioral phenomena also cause managers to take actions that are detrimental to the interests of shareholders. However, behavioral costs are the result of managers' mistakes, not the result of managers having different interests

EXHIBIT 2-1 **How Psychology Affects Financial Decisions**

Psychological Phenomenon	Example of Faulty Financial Decision	Resulting Outcome for Firm
1. Biases		
Excessive optimism	Delay cost cutting during a business recession	Lower profits
Overconfidence	Make inferior acquisitions when cash-rich	Reduce firm value because risk underestimated
Confirmation bias	Ignore information that is counter to current viewpoint	Lower profits from delayed reaction to changing environment
Illusion of control	Overestimate own degree of control	Incur higher costs than necessary
2. Heuristics		
Representativeness	Choose wrong projects based on biased forecasts	Reduce firm value because net present value (NPV) not maximized
Availability	Choose wrong projects based on biased forecasts	Reduce firm value because of misjudged priorities and risks
Anchoring	Become fixated on a number and adjust insufficiently	Reduce firm value because of biased growth forecasts
Affect	Rely on instincts instead of formal valuation analysis	Reduce firm value because negative NPV projects adopted
3. Framing effects		
Loss aversion	Losses loom larger than gains of the same size	Foregone tax shield benefits because of aversion to debt
Fourfold pattern	Throw good money after bad in losing projects	Reduce firm value because of a negative NPV decision

from investors. The distinction is important in that the two sources of cost typically require very different remedies. Remedies for agency conflicts tend to emphasize the manipulation of incentives. Remedies for behavioral pitfalls tend to emphasize training and process.

For organizational purposes, imagine that in a behavioral environment, managers seek to maximize a performance objective, just as they do in a traditional setting. However, unlike the traditional setting, psychological pitfalls might prevent managers from achieving perfect maximization—for example because of behaviors described in Exhibit 2-1.

Moreover, because psychological pitfalls can also impact the judgments of investors, managers might judge value differently from the markets even when all information is common. When psychological pitfalls distort market prices, we say that prices reflect **sentiment**. When managers perceive sentiment in the market, they might view themselves as having opportunities to engage in behaviors that reflect catering and market timing. **Catering** entails actions that exploit sentiment in order to increase a firm's stock price. **Market timing** entails actions that take advantage of mispriced securities, such as issuing new equity when stocks are overvalued.

Sentiment
Distortion in market prices caused by psychological phenomena

Catering
Actions that exploit sentiment to increase the market price of securities.

Market timing
Actions that take advantage of securities being mispriced at different points in time.

Just as we speak of traditional APV, we can speak of behavioral APV. Behavioral APV incorporates the impacts of psychological phenomena that affect managers directly, as well as the effects that stem from catering and market timing.

The remainder of the chapter provides two examples that serve as vehicles in helping students learn to apply psychological concepts when analyzing corporate financial issues. The first example pertains to Sun Microsystems, known mostly for manufacturing hardware such as servers, and to a lesser extent software such as the programming language Java, which transmits web pages over the Internet. The second example pertains to Merck, known for developing and selling a wide a variety of pharmaceutical products.

In working through the examples, a major objective is to structure questions that generate discussion around the issues described in Exhibit 2-1. The example involving Sun Microsystems is used to focus on biases and heuristics, while the example involving Merck is used to focus on framing effects.

2.3 ANALYZING BIASES

The discussion about Sun Microsystems in the nearby Behavioral Pitfalls box is based on an article that appeared in *Businessweek*. For the sake of exposition, the discussion below takes the characterizations described in the article as accurate, and then proceeds to analyze them.

As you read the discussion about Sun in the Behavioral Pitfalls box, try to identify two sets of concepts, first the psychological attributes of Sun's chief executive officer (CEO) Scott McNealy, and second the decisions made by Sun's managers. The manner in which psychological attributes impact managers' decisions about investment and financing lies at the core of behavioral corporate finance. Although most of the examples in this chapter involve decisions made by the CEO, the

Behavioral Pitfalls: Scott McNealy and Sun Microsystems

The cover story in the July 26, 2004, issue of *Businessweek* is about Scott McNealy, the chief executive officer of high-technology firm Sun Microsystems. Sun is known as a leading manufacturer of servers and for having invented the Internet software programming language Java. The *Businessweek* article uses the following adjectives to describe Scott McNealy: optimistic, smart, acerbic, cocky, and combative. These are all psychological traits that influenced McNealy's business decisions.

McNealy was one of Sun Microsystem's founders, became its CEO in 1984, and had a history of being willing to take major risks in order to avoid disaster. During the 1980s, against the advice of his executives, he decided to substitute Sun's own microprocessors for those manufactured by Motorola. That decision turned out well for Sun.

During the 1990s, Sun's competitors produced servers that used Microsoft's Windows operating systems. McNealy instead chose to invest in servers that ran Sun's own software Solaris. That decision also turned out well, as Solaris came to be highly praised for its speed, reliability, and security. Sun's sales, profits, and cash holdings soared, and it dramatically increased its spending on a great many research and development projects. During the technology stock market bubble in the late 1990s, which peaked in March 2000, Sun's price-to-earnings ratio (P/E) soared to 119.

Sun's fortunes changed with the onset of an economic recession in 2001. Wall Street analysts called for Sun to cut costs. However, McNealy was optimistic that the recession would be short-lived. In 2001, during a conference call with analysts, he said about business cycles: "We don't have rolling waves. We seem to have real edges." Instead of cutting costs during the recession, Sun invested heavily in new projects. In justifying that decision, McNealy stated: "The Internet is still wildly underhyped, underutilized, and underimplemented. I think we're looking at the largest equipment business in the history of anything. The growth opportunities are stunning."

Cisco Systems is the leading producer of router products used on the Internet. On March 8, 2001, Cisco announced that because the economic downturn looked like it would last much longer than expected, it was going to lay off 18 percent of its workforce. Some of Sun's executives wanted to follow suit. One stated: "When times are hard, you've got to shoot activities that aren't making money." Chief Operating Officer Ed Zander proposed major cuts. However, McNealy refused to do so, and Zander subsequently resigned.

In an effort to cut costs, Sun's customers sought low-end servers. McNealy initially dismissed their concerns. Later, Sun spent $2 billion to acquire Cobalt, a manufacturer of low-cost servers. However, after the acquisition, Sun chose to limit Cobalt's budget, and McNealy later admitted that the acquisition was a mistake.

The economic downturn was much longer than McNealy had forecast. In the next three years, Sun lost a third of its market share, its sales fell by 48 percent, and its stock price fell from $64 in 2000 to about $4 in 2004. Its net income turned negative in 2002, with a loss of $587 million. Losses in 2003 and 2004 totalled $3.4 billion and $388 million respectively, the result of both reduced demand for its computers from major corporate customers and greater competition from IBM, Hewlett-Packard (HP), and Dell.

Source: J. Kerstetter and P. Burrows, "Sun: A CEO's Last Stand," *Businessweek*, July 26, 2004, Bloomberg.

psychological traits described affect managers at all levels of the firm. Indeed, they affect most people, be they managers or not.

Recall from Chapter 1 that a bias is a predisposition toward error. This section discusses whether four specific biases were manifest within Sun's processes, with the four biases being excessive optimism, overconfidence, confirmation bias, and the illusion of control.

Excessive Optimism

When people exhibit excessive optimism, they overestimate how frequently they will experience favorable outcomes and underestimate how frequently they will experience unfavorable outcomes.

Delayed Cost Cutting and Value Loss

There is evidence suggesting that when press coverage describes an executive as "optimistic," that the executive being discussed is excessively optimistic. In this regard, the *Businessweek* magazine article specifically included *"optimistic"* among the list of attributes to describe Sun's CEO Scott McNealy. Therefore, a natural question to ask is whether excessive optimism affected McNealy's decisions as a manager. For example, is there evidence that excessive optimism led him to delay cost-cutting measures, which resulted in steep losses for Sun? Notably, the general evidence suggests that people who report that economic conditions will improve are twice as optimistic as those who report that economic conditions will either stay the same or get worse.[2]

Was McNealy excessively optimistic when he predicted that the recession of 2001 would be brief, albeit with extreme changes (sharp edges)? The National Bureau of Economic Research (NBER) is officially responsible for determining when economic recessions begin and end in the United States. According to the NBER, the U.S. economy entered a recession in March 2001, and the recession lasted until November 2001, a period of nine months that was neither brief nor atypical.

The slowdown was longer for firms engaging in business investment. Sun Microsystems' customers are other firms. When those firms purchase Sun's servers, they are engaging in business investment. During the 2001 recession, investment fell for six consecutive quarters, twice as long as the period real gross domestic product (GDP) fell.

Scott McNealy's prediction that the recession of 2001 would be brief was excessively optimistic. Was his prediction necessarily biased? In other words, might Scott McNealy's prediction about the recession of 2001 have been reasonable, even though it was wrong after the fact?

Between World War II and 2000, the average length of a U.S. recession was 11.6 months. During those recessions, real gross domestic investment tended to fall for 12 months. The recession before 2001 occurred in 1990–1991 and featured two consecutive quarters of negative growth in real GDP. During the recession of 1990–1991, real gross domestic investment fell for 12 months.

What are we to conclude? There is nothing in the historical record to suggest that recessions would be brief affairs. The more reasonable conclusion might be that Scott McNealy's prediction was biased in the direction of optimism and that his optimism led him to delay cost cutting, thereby destroying value at his firm.

Sentiment: Excessively Optimistic Sun Stockholders

During the stock market bubble between January 1997 and June 2000, irrational exuberance drove up the prices of both the S&P 500 and Sun's stock. Exhibit 2-2 displays the market value of Sun's equity between 1986 and 2003. An investor who held the S&P 500 during this period would have seen his or her investment almost double. An investor who held Sun stock during this period would have seen his or her stock increase by more than fourteen fold. No firm the size of Sun has historically merited a price-to-earnings ratio (P/E) over 100. In March 2000, at the height of the bubble, Sun's P/E reached 119, reflecting the sentiment of the time.[3]

It seems plausible that the spectacular rise in Sun's stock price encouraged some of the excessive optimism experienced by Sun's managers. In this text, considerable

EXHIBIT 2-2
Sun Microsystems' Market Capitalization 1986–2003

Source: Center for Research in Security Prices.

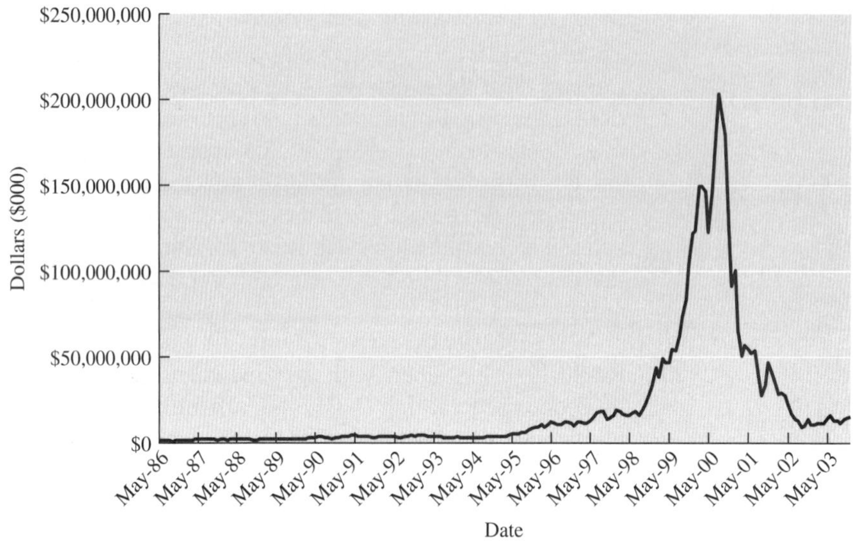

space is devoted to explaining why blindly trusting market prices can lead even the best-intentioned managers to make faulty decisions about investment policy, financing, and acquisitions.

Overconfidence

In general, overconfidence relates to difficult tasks and abilities. Overconfidence is a bias that pertains to how well people understand their own abilities and the limits of their knowledge. People who are overconfident about their abilities think they are better than they actually are. People who are overconfident about their level of knowledge think they know more than they actually know. This overconfidence does not necessarily mean that these people are ignorant or incompetent. It just means that in their own eyes they are smarter and better than is actually the case.

Overconfidence about Ability

Among the attributes used in the *Businessweek* article to describe Scott McNealy are *cocky* and *smart.* The appearance of these adjectives naturally leads to the question of whether Scott McNealy is overconfident, as cockiness is a symptom of overconfidence. Overconfident people can certainly be smart, just not quite as smart as they think they are. Moreover, people can learn to be overconfident, as a result of past successes.[4] McNealy had achieved major successes in the past, particularly in his decision to support Sun's own software over Microsoft's software.

Overconfident managers tend to make poor decisions about both investments and mergers and acquisitions, especially if their firms are cash-rich. Sun's increased spending on research and development in 2000 and its acquisition of Cobalt are cases in point. Both resulted in dramatic reductions in Sun's market value. In March 2004, analysts issued very negative reports about Sun. McNealy responded by pointing out that the firm was hardly likely to become distressed, given that it held more than $5 billion in cash.

EXHIBIT 2-3
GDP Growth Rates During U.S. Recessions (Inflation Adjusted)

Source: Federal Reserve Bank of St. Louis, Economic Data (FRED), **research.stlouisfed .org/fred2 /categories/22.**

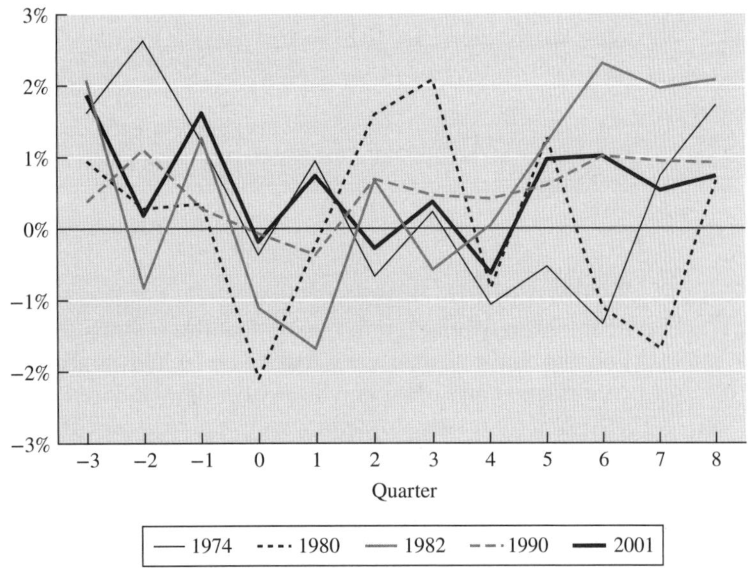

Overconfidence about Knowledge

Was Scott McNealy overconfident about his knowledge of U.S. business cycles? He was certainly confident that the 2001 recession would be sharp-edged, by which he meant that it would feature a sharp downturn followed by a sharp upturn. Was it?

Exhibit 2-3 contrasts the manner in which GDP growth behaved in the quarters just before, during, and after a recession for all recessions between 1974 and 2001. Quarter 0 marks the onset of recession. The heavy line in the exhibit depicts the recession of 2001. You can decide for yourself whether the recession in 2001 was markedly brief or sharp-edged, relative to its predecessors.

CONCEPT PREVIEW
Question 2.1

Five cards are placed in front of you as shown. All cards are either green-backed or red-backed. Cards 1 and 5 are face down, and the other three are face up.

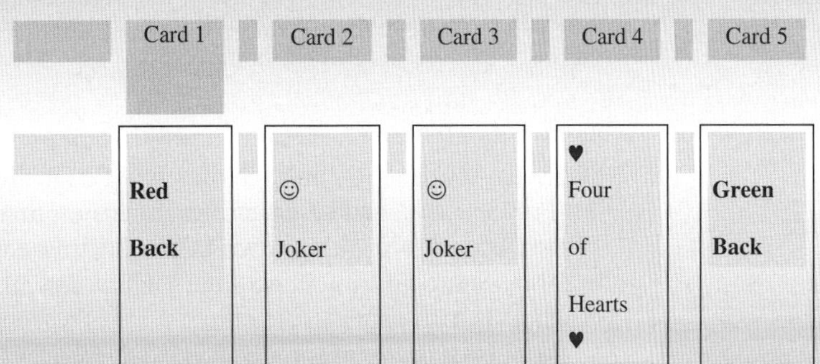

Suppose you are asked to test the following hypothesis about these five cards: "Each card that has a green back on one side has a joker on the other side." In particular, select those cards and only those cards that will determine whether the statement is true. That is, select the *minimum number of cards* that will enable you to determine whether or not the statement is true. Of the five cards, which would you turn over?

Confirmation Bias

People who overlook information that disconfirms their views in favor of information that confirms their views are said to exhibit confirmation bias. People exhibiting confirmation bias often only hear what they want to hear. They spend too much time searching for reasons to support why their views are right and too little time searching for reasons that might lead them to conclude that their views are wrong.

In Concept preview question 2.1, asking for cards displaying jokers to be turned over reflects confirmation bias. The principle is the same as in the diagnostic question for confirmation bias in Chapter 1. Only the green backed card and the four of hearts can provide evidence that disconfirms the hypothesis.

Turning a Blind Eye

Is there anything in the *Businessweek* magazine article to suggest that Scott McNealy exhibited confirmation bias? The article mentions that in late 2000, executives at Sun learned that the revenues of industry leader Cisco Systems were declining dramatically and began to suggest that a cost-cutting program be put in place at Sun. In March 2001, Cisco Systems laid off 18 percent of its workforce. However, this information did not confirm McNealy's view about recessions being short. Despite the recommendations of his upper-level executives, McNealy refused to approve any cost cutting at Sun.

Illusion of Control

When a person makes a decision, the outcome typically depends on a combination of luck and skill. Those who have an exaggerated view of how much control they exert over outcomes exhibit the illusion of control. As was discussed in Chapter 1, psychological studies have found that an increase in perceived control leads to an increase in excessive optimism.

Not Made Here

Did Scott McNealy exhibit the illusion of control? Although not mentioned earlier, the *Businessweek* article describes a decision that Sun's managers had to make in 1997: whether to use their own microchips for Sun servers or to use Intel's chips. In 1997, Sun could purchase Intel's chips for 30 percent less than what it cost to produce its own comparable chips.

Despite the desire of some Sun executives to buy Intel chips instead of making their own, Scott McNealy felt that Sun's chip design group exerted enough control to close the gap. In a short meeting, McNealy ordered that Sun would not feature "Intel Inside." Seven years later, Intel chips were twice as fast as those produced by Sun. In retrospect, McNealy describes his decision to not use Intel chips as one of his biggest regrets.

2.4 ANALYZING HEURISTICS

A heuristic is a rule of thumb. This section discusses representativeness, availability, anchoring and adjustment, and affect.

Representativeness

People often make judgments and predictions by relying on heuristics that make use of analogues and stereotypes. Psychologists refer to the underlying principle as representativeness. In asking about the extent to which an object or idea fits a stereotype, people are asking how representative that object or idea is for the class to which it belongs. In general, people place too much reliance on representativeness, and representativeness-based thinking can result in bias.

The Internet Represents the Overall Economy

Relatively speaking, Internet firms have a short history. During this history, the growth rate in sales of the typical or representative Internet firm featured extreme movements. Scott McNealy is quoted as having said in early 2001: "The Internet is still wildly underhyped, underutilized, and underimplemented. I think we're looking at the largest equipment business in the history of anything. The growth opportunities are stunning."

The *Businessweek* article reported that Scott McNealy believed that the Internet had fundamentally changed the U.S. economy and that the Internet was critical to a great many firms. Is there reason to believe that Scott McNealy relied on representativeness? Representativeness-based reasoning might have led him to conclude that because of the growing importance of the Internet in the economy, and because Internet firms experience brief sharp swings in business conditions, the U.S. economy as a whole would experience brief sharp swings rather than rolling waves.

Availability

People exhibit the availability heuristic when they rely on information that is more readily available than information that is less readily available.

Out of Sight, Out of Mind

Sun played a principal role in a large law suit against rival firm Microsoft that received national attention. The dispute had extended out several years and had become quite personal between Scott McNealy and Microsoft's founder Bill Gates. As such, it was in the forefront of McNealy's mind and highly salient. Did the dispute lead him to exhibit availability bias?

Sun's upper-level executives communicated their concerns that the Microsoft suit had distracted McNealy from focusing on the needs expressed by Sun's customers.

Customers themselves echoed this concern. They had been asking for low-end servers in order to cut costs during the downturn. With Microsoft on his mind, McNealy paid little attention to customers' requests. In April 2004, Sun and Microsoft announced that Sun had dropped its suit, in exchange for a cash settlement and technology agreement. In July 2004, Sun was offering low-end servers and McNealy was claiming that Sun was more focused than any of its competitors.

Anchoring and Adjustment

People often develop quick estimates by beginning with an initial number with which they are familiar and then adjusting that number to reflect new information or circumstances. Just as a dropped anchor keeps a boat from drifting too far, the initial numbers with which managers begin can serve to anchor their judgments. The heuristic has come to be called anchoring and adjustment. The attendant bias is known as anchoring bias. When forming judgments, people have a tendency to become anchored on numbers in their heads and do not make sufficient adjustments relative to the anchor.

Anchored to Growth

Were Sun's managers anchored on their past growth rates? During its most successful period, the turn of the century, Sun's earnings growth rate reached 50 percent per quarter, faster than competitors Microsoft, Intel, and Dell. That rate was not sustainable on a permanent basis. In forming forecasts going forward, the question is how to adjust relative to the 50 percent. If Sun's executives became anchored on the 50 percent, then even if they adjusted their forecasts of future growth downwards, they would be psychologically disposed to adjust insufficiently. That is the nature of anchoring bias. In this case, anchoring would have contributed to excessively optimistic forecasts of growth.

Affect Heuristic

Most people base their decisions on what feels right to them emotionally. Psychologists use the technical term affect to mean emotional feeling, and they use the term affect heuristic to describe behavior that places heavy reliance on intuition or "gut feeling." As with other heuristics, the affect heuristic involves mental shortcuts that can predispose managers to bias.

Acquisitions That Feel Right but Destroy Value

Michael Lehman joined Sun's board of directors in 2002. Before that he was Sun's chief financial officer (CFO). In 2000, Lehman described Sun's decision process for making acquisitions. He stated: "Now, in determining the price we are willing to pay for such acquisitions, we are not nearly as formal as the corporate finance textbooks suggest we perhaps ought to be. Our approach to acquisition pricing is more intuitive."[5]

Remember that intuition is based on affect. In contrast, the formal textbook approach to corporate decision making is based on the net present value (NPV) of the acquisition being positive, or at worst zero. When the NPV of an acquisition is greater or equal to zero, the fair value of that acquisition is at least as high as the number of dollars invested making the acquisition.

Lehman explained that the managers at Sun did not say to themselves: "For every dollar we invest, we're going to get at least an NPV of one dollar in return." (Lehman likely misspoke here, having used NPV when he meant PV.) He went on to say that instead of relying on DCF, the managers at Sun asked how an "acquisition will enhance our overall capabilities, and how that enhancement will contribute to our overall market value."

Intuition is important, make no mistake about it. Experience is valuable, and firms pay for experienced managers. Indeed, the emotions that managers feel are a manifestation of their minds making associations with the memories of past experiences. However, experience is not a substitute for careful analysis. Acquisitions that feel right might well feature negative NPV. Think back to Sun's experience with Cobalt.

2.5 VALUE DESTRUCTION AND SUN'S ENDGAME

Businessweek's July 2004 cover story on Sun Microsystems described how the security analysts who followed Sun reacted when the firm failed to reduce its costs after the recession of 2001. Their comments, along with media coverage such as the *Businessweek* article, constituted clear warnings that Sun needed to change its business strategy.

Subsequently, Sun's losses continued to mount, with net income still negative in 2005 at –\$107 million. In February 2006, Michael Lehman rejoined the firm as CFO, and analysts expressed the hope that he would institute cost-cutting measures. Two months later, the firm reported a fiscal third-quarter loss of \$217 million, which included \$87 million in costs associated with two acquisitions and \$57 million in costs from stock-based compensation. Shortly thereafter, Scott McNealy resigned as CEO and was replaced by Sun's chief operating officer Jonathan Schwartz. Notably, McNealy remained as chairman and also stayed on as an employee of the firm.

In taking over as CEO, Schwartz announced that he wanted to hold the line on costs and focus aggressively on growth opportunities rather than reduce headcount. Nevertheless, in June 2006 Sun announced that over the subsequent six months it would lay off 4,000 to 5,000 employees, comprising 11 to 13 percent of its work force. Schwartz then began to reshape Sun's strategy by shifting its focus from hardware to software, while maintaining control of all the major aspects of its technology, both hardware and software.

Exhibit 2-4 displays the trajectory of Sun's sales and net income for the period 1995 through 2009. In 2007 and 2008, Sun's net income turned positive at \$473 million and \$403 million, respectively. However, by June 2009 its net income was again negative, at –\$2.23 billion, and Sun announced that it planned to reduce the number of its employees by 6,000, from 33,000. A month earlier, in May 2009, Sun agreed to be acquired by software firm Oracle for \$7.4 billion. Oracle had a history of making major reductions in headcount at firms it acquired, and analysts

EXHIBIT 2-4
Sun Microsystems Sales and Net Income, 1995–2009

Source: Compustat.

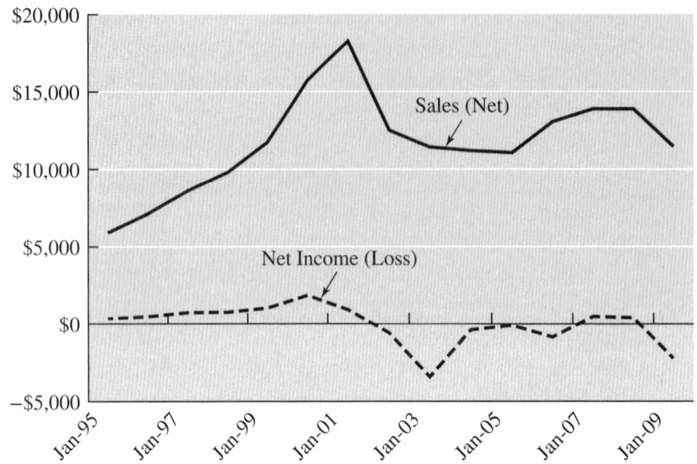

predicted that it would do so at Sun. Most of Sun's executives, including McNealy and Schwartz, resigned after the acquisition became final.

A year after Oracle acquired Sun, *Fortune* magazine interviewed Scott McNealy, asking him what had gone wrong at Sun during his overall tenure as well as the firm's final years as an independent company.[6] McNealy joked that his interviewer didn't have enough video storage to record all his mistakes. He then made two specific points about what he might have done differently.

First, McNealy stated that during the technology bubble, Sun's stock price was about 10 times its revenue, which for a hardware company was unsustainable, he suggested. Although he pointed out that Sun had monetized the valuation very well, he said that perhaps he might have tried to talk the analysts into not running up Sun's stock to the extent that they did.

Second, McNealy noted that he might have hired a chief operating officer during his tenure as CEO, rather than undertaking the responsibility himself at a time in his life when he had four children with whom he also wanted to spend his time. He noted that he did spend time with his children and that he was thrilled with how things had turned out for him personally.

There are several issues that McNealy might have mentioned in his interview, but did not. A discussion of these issues appears in the Additional Resources to Chapter 2.

2.6 ANALYZING FRAMING EFFECTS

To discuss how framing effects might impact corporate financial decision making, consider the history of Merck, a firm quite different from Sun, which is discussed in the nearby Behavioral Pitfalls box. Merck is one of the best-known pharmaceutical firms in the world.

Behavioral Pitfalls: Judy Lewent and Merck

Judy Lewent joined Merck in 1980, and became its CFO 10 years later. In doing so she became the first woman in the United States to serve as CFO of a major corporation. And Merck was undeniably a major corporation. During the 1980s and 1990s, it was recognized as America's Most Admired Company in *Fortune* magazine's annual survey, winning that honor seven times, more frequently than any other firm.

In 1972, Lewent completed her Master of Science in business at the Sloan School, Massachusetts Institute of Technology (MIT), studying under some of the major academics in finance: Fischer Black, Myron Scholes, and Stewart Myers. Before joining Merck, she worked as an analyst at several financial institutions and in 1976 moved to pharmaceutical firm Pfizer.

In 1994 Lewent was one of the most respected CFOs in the United States. That year the *Harvard Business Review* published an interview with her, which they entitled "Scientific Management at Merck: An Interview with CFO Judy Lewent." However, in 2004, *CFO* magazine ran an article entitled "What Will Judy Do?" asking whether she would be able to keep her job. What happened?

The short answer to the last question is that in September 2004 Merck recalled its blockbuster drug Vioxx, a drug that had contributed 8.7 percent of the firm's global revenues that year. The long answer is more complicated and requires a short history of the firm.

According to *Fortune* magazine's annual reputation survey, Merck was one of America's most admired companies. In fact, for the seven straight years between 1986 and 1992, Merck ranked as America's most admired company. Merck gained its exalted status by producing a series of blockbuster drugs, such as Vasotec for the treatment of blood pressure, Prinivil for cardiac medication, Pepcid and Prilosec for ulcers, and Mevacor to lower cholesterol.

The year 1999 was auspicious for Merck. That year the five drugs mentioned earned Merck $4.38 billion in U.S. sales and royalties, at a time when its total net sales were $32.7 billion. At the same time, there were dark financial clouds on the horizon. Pharmaceutical products typically receive patent protection for a period of 17 years. By the end of 2001, all five of the major drugs mentioned were due to go off patent.

The pharmaceutical industry is also regulated. In the United States, the Food and Drug Administration (FDA) must approve all new drugs as being safe and effective. To establish safety and efficacy, pharmaceutical firms collect data for submission to the FDA, using clinical trials to test new drugs in small samples involving both animals and people.

In May 1999, the FDA approved Vioxx to treat pain. However, it asked Merck to conduct a new large postapproval trial in order to extend its study of the side effect profile of Vioxx in respect to stomach ulcers. The issue was important, in that existing painkillers that were already on the market, such as aspirin and naproxen (for example, Aleve), caused stomach irritation. Merck's earlier studies showed that Vioxx did not irritate people's stomachs.

Because aspirin reduces blood clotting, it reduces the incidence of heart attacks and strokes. Vioxx does not, a fact of which Merck's scientists and executives were well aware.

Surprisingly, Merck's postapproval study appeared to show that Vioxx actually caused heart attacks and strokes. However, the firm's executives resisted that interpretation and invested heavily in promoting the drug. Then, in September 2004 a new separate Merck study of colon polyps also found that Vioxx caused heart attacks and strokes.[7] Merck's managers belatedly recalled the drug and prepared for the lawsuits to come. Between September 27 and November 5, its stock price fell from $44.46 to $26.21.

Sources: A. Mathews and B. Martinez, "E-Mails Suggest Early Vioxx Worries—As Evidence of Heart Risk Rose, Merck Officials Played Hardball; One Internal Message: 'Dodge!'" *The Wall Street Journal,* November 2, 2004; "Scientific Management at Merck: An Interview with CFO Judy Lewent," *Harvard Business Review,* Jan–Feb, 1994; Kate O'Sullivan, "What Will Judy Do?" *CFO Magazine,* December 3, 2004.

CONCEPT PREVIEW
Question 2.2

Only one in 10,000 chemicals that are investigated for their drug potential actually turns out to be successful in the sense of becoming a prescription drug. Moreover, completing the process often takes at least a decade. Suppose that a pharmaceutical firm explores 1,000 chemicals, and that the success probability for one chemical is independent of the others. What do you think the probability is that the firm will successfully produce at least two prescription drugs?

The "one in 10,000 probability" in Concept Preview Question 2.2 is a statistic Judy Lewent frequently mentioned. Applying the binomial probability distribution to this question produces an answer of 9.5 percent. As was mentioned in the Behavioral Pitfalls box about Judy Lewent, one thing that set her apart from other CFOs was her application of scientific methodology to make judgments of, and decisions about, risk. In this regard, she developed Monte Carlo simulation models to assess Merck's long-term risks, and used real option techniques to manage those risks. Although these techniques are described in corporate finance textbooks, they are not well used in practice. Lewent's model became the basis of Merck's research planning framework, seeking to capture all its risks and long-term development timetables to show how they play out over a 20-year time horizon.

In theory, decisions about capital structure—the mix of debt and equity on a firm's balance sheet—reflect judgments about risk. In respect to capital structure, Lewent stated the following in 2012: "This is certainly true in the research pharmaceutical industry, which carries by definition significant risk. And when the risks become real and not just theoretical, that's when the value of a prudent capital structure becomes evident. A capital structure that enables the company to continue to pay dividends and fund R&D can mean the difference between weathering the storm or sinking into oblivion."[8] In regard to dividends, in 2006 she stated: "In the fourth quarter of 2004, we had a call with analysts. I won't say the most important, but one of the most important questions asked was, 'Is the dividend secure?' And I could [answer with] an unequivocal 'yes.'"[9]

With the preceding comments as a backdrop, consider two framing issues at Merck, one relating to its decisions about capital structure and the other relating to its decisions about Vioxx. Given Lewent's remarks, it is clear that she perceives these issues as being interconnected.

Loss Aversion

Loss aversion leads people to behave in risk-averse fashion when facing alternatives that feature the possibility of both gain and loss.

Traditional textbooks in corporate finance teach that debt can be used to shield investors from corporate taxes. Yet many firms appear to take on less debt than textbook theory suggests, thereby leaving tax shield dollars on the table.[10]

Consider Merck's debt policy. Has Merck been averse to debt? Exhibit 2-5 displays the time paths of three variables between 1983 and 2014: Merck's leverage measured as total assets to common equity, its times interest earned, its total liabilities to total assets, and its return on common equity. All of these variables are based on book value, not market values.

Exhibit 2-5 shows that Merck's total debt has typically been below 50 percent of its assets during the time period displayed. Financial textbooks suggest that decisions about debt be made using market values rather than debt values. Consider the period before 2004 when Merck withdrew Vioxx from the market. During this time, the market value of Merck's equity averaged six times the book value of its equity during the period. Therefore, in market terms Merck's debt was a much lower fraction of its assets than shown in Exhibit 2-5.

In the traditional trade-off theory approach to debt policy, managers balance the benefits of additional tax shields against the costs of possible future financial distress

EXHIBIT 2-5
Merck's Capital Structure and ROE 1983–2014

Source: Compustat.

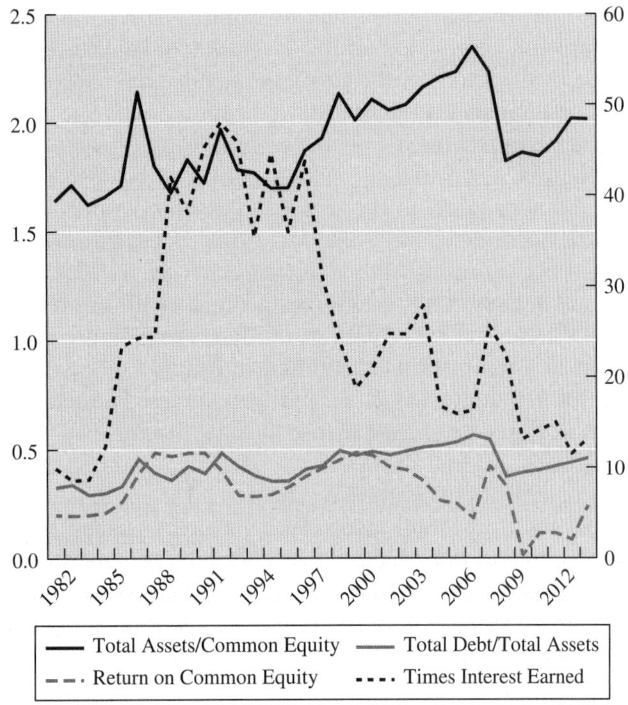

stemming from excessive debt. Firms having large amounts of tangible assets that can be sold to service debt, if need be, have lower expected distress costs than firms whose assets are mostly intangible. Of course, Merck would have significant intangible assets stemming from research and development. Those assets largely reside in the brains of its scientists and managers. As a result, Merck's executives would have to be concerned that the firm's scientists and managers might react to financial distress by leaving the firm, taking with them a large portion of the firm's intangible assets. A concern about losing intangible assets might reasonably lead the firm to shy away from taking on too much debt.

Such a concern is not hypothetical. After Merck withdrew Vioxx from the market, the price of its stock fell by more than a third over the next two months. That drop made Merck a strong takeover candidate, and its directors began to worry about talented managers leaving the firm. In response, Merck filed a new compensation plan for top executives with the Securities and Exchange Commission. The new plan featured one-time severance payments of up to triple executives' salary and bonus, along with other perquisites like health benefits, should Merck be acquired and the executives lose their jobs.

This change in compensation suggests that there are alternatives to addressing brain drain besides the assumption of lower debt. Moreover, it is important to ask whether in the late 1980s and throughout the 1990s the risk of distress was reasonable or instead was overblown. Between 1988 and 2001, Merck had a high tax bill, held a large amount in cash, and had several blockbuster drugs. Its high cash holdings

(10 to 20 percent of sales) and blockbuster drugs with many years remaining of patent protection provided for low risk as far as bankruptcy was concerned.

Several editions of the corporate finance textbook co authored by Judy Lewent's corporate finance professor Stewart Myers, along with Richard Brealey and Franklin Allen, analyze Merck's decision about capital structure. The tenth edition focuses on the year 2008, when Merck's market-to-book ratio (for equity) was about 3.6. The authors examine the impact of a $1 billion dollar recapitalization in which Merck borrows $1 billion and uses the proceeds to repurchase shares. They argue that doing so raises Merck's intrinsic value by $350 million, and conclude: "It's hard to believe that Merck's financial managers are simply missing the boat."[11]

By taking on more debt in the late 1980s and early 1990s, Merck could have reduced a tax bill that amounted to roughly 60 percent of its cash holdings. As Exhibit 2-5 shows, Merck generally maintained its leverage between 1982 and 1997, even as its return on equity rose and stabilized.

Brealey, Myers, and Allen examine two possible explanations for Merck's conservative debt policy, the first involving the combination of corporate and personal taxes, and the second involving bankruptcy costs. They find that the inclusion of personal taxes does reduce the advantage to debt somewhat, but does not eliminate it. As for bankruptcy, they state the following about Merck: "It could borrow enough to save tens of millions of dollars without raising a whisker of concern about possible financial distress . . . Merck illustrates an odd fact about real-life capital structures. The most profitable companies borrow the least."[12]

This last statement naturally leads to the following question: Is the underlying issue psychological and related to reference points and loss aversion? To answer this question, suppose that the operative reference point for a firm is aspirational in the sense of the March-Shapira model described in Chapter 1, with the firm perceiving its current position as a success, relative to its aspiration. In this case, loss aversion becomes central and tends to induce a low-risk/low leverage strategy. However, if the operative reference point for a firm is aspirational, but the firm views achieving aspiration as challenging, then risk seeking in the domain of losses rather than loss aversion becomes central, in which case the firm would choose a high-risk/high leverage strategy.

It is also possible that Lewent's models showed the risks of financial distress to be considerably higher than those outside the firm perceived them to be. Even if that were the case, that would not explain the general pattern that the most profitable companies borrow the least, whereas a reference point-based argument would.

Aversion to a Sure Loss

Recall from Chapter 1 that aversion to a sure loss can lead people to choose a risky alternative instead of accepting a sure loss, even when the odds are against them. In doing so, they choose risk hoping to beat the odds, in an effort to break even.

In 1999, the executives at Merck were watching the clock tick down, as five of their most successful products were due to go off patent in 2000 and 2001. One possible scenario was that the firm would be unable to find new products to replace the lost profits from the ones going off patent. Merck continued to be one of America's most admired companies throughout the 1990s, a state of affairs to which its executives had become accustomed. It is plausible to suggest that if the firm's profits declined, these executives would have difficulty adjusting psychologically from their days of past glory. As a result, they might have used past profitability as an aspirational reference point and framed the lower forecasted profit situation as a loss relative to that reference point.

After the FDA approved Vioxx in May 1999, Merck's executives were hoping that its sales would help them to avoid entering the domain of psychological losses, meaning lower profits. However, the results from its postapproval clinical study, code named VIGOR (for Vioxx Gastrointestinal Outcomes Research), indicating that Vioxx might actually cause heart attacks and strokes, presented the executives with a dilemma involving two alternatives.

The first alternative, called second line therapy, was to promote Vioxx for a small market, namely people who needed pain relief, whose sensitive stomachs did not tolerate drugs like aspirin and naproxen, and who were not prone to heart problems. This alternative was akin to accepting a sure loss (meaning, lower profits). The second alternative, called first line therapy, was to try and beat the odds, hoping that the negative findings from VIGOR would not carry over to the general population. The second alternative involved promoting Vioxx as a general painkiller for the whole market, downplaying the cardiac side effect profile, and hoping for blockbuster sales.

People who view themselves in the domain of losses are much more prone to accept risks than people who view themselves in the domain of gains. Because of the looming patent expiration on its older drugs, Merck executives felt the pressure to make Vioxx a major success. They chose the risky alternative.

Researchers at Stanford University, Harvard University, and the Cleveland Clinic wrote scientific articles that raised concerns about Vioxx's safety. Merck challenged these concerns and continued to promote Vioxx as safe. In February 2001, the FDA issued a letter to Merck's CEO at the time, Ray Gilmartin, chastising the firm for deceptive promotional practices. In August 2004, a researcher from the FDA's drug-safety office presented data that showed that higher doses of Vioxx correlated with a tripled risk of a heart attack or sudden cardiac death. Merck responded by issuing a press release reiterating its confidence in the safety and efficacy of its drug.

Between 2000 and 2004, twenty-eight million people took Vioxx. After Merck finally withdrew Vioxx from the market, the British medical journal *The Lancet* wrote that the firm should have made that decision several years earlier. In December 2004, the best estimates were that the lawsuits against Merck would total $18 billion.

In February 2005, by a vote of 17 to 15, members of an FDA advisory panel recommended that Vioxx was safe enough to be sold in the United States, as long as its package label carried strict warnings about the risk of heart attacks and strokes. The vote led Merck to inform the FDA that it was considering requesting permission to reintroduce Vioxx. However, in the end it chose not to do so.

Lawsuits and Aftermath

In August 2005, a Texas jury rendered its verdict on the first of the Vioxx trials, finding Merck liable for the death of 59-year-old marathon runner Robert Ernst who had taken the drug. The jury award of $253 million jolted Merck executives, and Merck's market capitalization fell by 7.7 percent after the announcement of the jury's verdict.

Jury members indicated that they were particularly troubled that Merck executives had knowledge of Vioxx's negative side-effect profile before they placed the drug on the market, but took actions to conceal that knowledge from the public. Although Texas law requires the amount of the actual award to be much less than $253 million, and Merck planned to appeal the verdict, the outcome of the trial set an important precedent for the remaining Vioxx suits, which numbered 4,200 at the time. On August 22, 2005, *The Wall Street Journal* reported that after the verdict was announced, analysts' estimate of the value of Merck's legal liability increased to $30 billion, raising questions about Merck's long-term ability to survive.

Some analysts estimated Merck's legal liability to be even more, at $50 billion. However, in the end, Merck's chief counsel Kenneth Frazier was able to craft a strategy that proved far less expensive for the firm. That strategy centered on framing, the ability of Merck's lawyers to be able to frame the scientific issues for juries in ways jury members found intuitive. Notably, Merck won a series of important Vioxx cases, and in 2007 reached a $4.85 billion settlement with most of the remaining plaintiffs. Two years after having withdrawn Vioxx, Merck's stock price rebounded to $46, and the firm was beating analysts' consensus earnings estimates.

In 2005 CEO and chairman Gilmartin retired from Merck, and was replaced by long-time Merck employee Richard Clark, who had been CEO of Merck's Medco Health Solutions. As can be seen from the ROE trajectory in Exhibit 2-4, Merck's profitability limped along thereafter. In 2013, its total returns lagged behind almost all of its competitors over one-five-, and ten-year horizons. In 2006 and 2007 Merck launched five new drugs that drove its earnings for the next several years. However, after 2007 it did not launch a drug for which annual sales were more than $1 billion.

Moreover, Merck encountered another image-tarnishing problem when it was criticized, along with its partner Schering-Plough, of having avoided analyzing the results of a trial of the cholesterol drug Vytorin. Eventually, the results of clinical trials showed that Vytorin was no more effective than an inexpensive generic. The number of prescriptions of Vytorin fell from 22 million in 2007 to fewer than 4.6 million in 2012. In addition, Merck paid $688 million to settle a lawsuit with shareholders who alleged that the firm had intentionally withheld unfavorable clinical trial data.

In January 2011, Kenneth Frazier replaced Clark as CEO. In 2012, Merck experienced more bad news with one of its heart drugs and another for treating osteoporosis. Frazier hired a new head of research and development to reshape the firm's focus.

In the aftermath of the Vioxx incident, Brealey, Myers, and Allen did not change their perspective on Merck's capital structure. They acknowledged that the firm had set aside $5 billion for legal costs and settlements, but pointed out that the firm's credit rating was not damaged, its cash flow remained sufficient to fund its investments (including research and development), and it had maintained its regular dividend.

Lewent resigned from Merck in 2007. Although she had been a strong candidate to be the firm's next CEO, replacing Gilmartin, the board instead chose Clark. Moreover, Clark installed an executive named Peter Loescher as global marketing chief and designated him, not Lewent, as his number two executive.

In 2011, Lewent was inducted into the Hall of Fame of Financial Executives International (FEI), the professional association of financial managers. For her reflections on being inducted, see her comments in Additional Resources for Chapter 2.

2.7 DEBIASING AND NUDGES

The psychological phenomena described in this chapter are systematic and persistent. Although they vary in incidence and degree from person to person, by and large the average responses are similar across different groups of people. What can be done to reduce these errors and biases? How can people debias?

Debiasing turns out to be an enormous challenge. Psychologists have repeatedly demonstrated that recognizing our errors and biases does not lead us to change our behavior automatically. The psychology that underlies errors and biases is remarkably resistant to change.[13] That is not to say that people cannot learn to avoid mistakes. People can learn. However, people learn slowly, and the task of debiasing requires great effort.

Debiasing is more difficult in some situations than in others. Situations where people receive quick, clear feedback about the results of their actions are more conducive to debiasing efforts than situations where the feedback is slow, and outcomes are influenced by many factors. Unfortunately, many of the tasks in corporate finance feature long lags between the time decisions are made and the time the outcomes occur, as well as sources of risk that can obscure the underlying biases.

Throughout this textbook, you will encounter tips and suggestions for mitigating bias. These tips and suggestions appear in boxes labeled Corporate Nudges. As you read these tips, remember to keep your expectations modest. Debiasing is a process that rarely produces quick results. The tips and suggestions produce progress, but rarely miracles. In respect to corporate finance, managers make errors both individually and in groups. Mitigating bias at both levels requires

Corporate Nudges

Errors or biases: Accepting an actuarially unfair risk.
Why does it happen? Aversion to a sure loss, aspirational risk seeking.
How does it happen? When faced with the prospect of a sure loss, people try to beat the odds.
What can be done about it? First, view decision tasks broadly, rather than narrowly, remembering that over the course of a lifetime, risks are faced repeatedly. Because of the law of averages, accepting an actuarially unfair risk as a policy is likely to produce inferior results over the long term. Second, reframe by resetting reference points in order to accept losses and treat sunk costs as sunk. Try using stock phrases such as "that's water under the bridge" and "don't cry over spilled milk" as helpful reminders.

the use of explicit procedures and the exercise of discipline. Debiasing requires major effort.

The Corporate Nudges box at the bottom of page 51 contains an example of debiasing that builds on the earlier discussion about aversion to a sure loss. The example provides some advice on steps that managers can take to mitigate their vulnerability to faulty decisions that reduce value.

Finally, a cautionary note: Absolute perfection is rarely attainable, and sometimes it is best to leave well enough alone. Indeed, moderate degrees of dispositional optimism and overconfidence can be good things. Economists report that moderate optimists display financial habits that tend to be prudent. However, it is possible to have too much of a good thing: extreme optimists display behaviors that are generally unwise.[14] Certainly, some measure of excessive optimism and overconfidence is essential for leadership. However, leaders for whom these biases are extreme place their organizations at risk in respect to value destruction, if not survival.

Summary

Heuristics, biases, and framing effects impede managers from making the best use of the traditional tools of corporate finance, causing them to make faulty decisions that destroy value. This chapter illustrates types of questions to ask when applying psychological concepts to analyze behavioral issues in corporate finance.

The main biases discussed in the chapter are excessive optimism, overconfidence, confirmation bias, and the illusion of control. Managers are inclined to choose negative net-present-value projects because they are excessively optimistic about the future prospects of their firms, overconfident about the risks they face, discount information that does not support their views, and exaggerate the extent of control they wield over final outcomes.

The main heuristics discussed relate to representativeness, availability, anchoring and adjustment, and affect. Managers are prone to make faulty decisions about uses of funds because they place too much reliance on stereotypic thinking when forming judgments, attach too much emphasis to information that is readily available, become overly fixated on specific numbers in their analyses, and place too much reliance on intuition.

The main topics discussed in the section on framing effects are loss aversion and the four-fold risk pattern, especially aspiration-based risk behavior and aversion to a sure loss. Managers' attitudes toward risk typically vary with the circumstances in which they find themselves. Circumstances can vary according to the firm's position relative to its aspirations and financial position. Notably, managers are inclined to make faulty decisions about investment policy and financing because they are unduly sensitive about potential future losses and find it difficult to accept losses that have already occurred.

Managers need to be aware that psychological phenomena also cause investor errors that can result in the mispricing of the securities issued by their firms. Mispricing raises issues about catering behavior and market timing. At the same time, managers need to be concerned with their own vunerability to bias. Avoiding bias, or debiasing, is a major challenge that generally requires a sophisticated, disciplined approach.

Additional Behavioral Readings

Baker, M. and J. Wurgler, "Behavioral Corporate Finance: A Current Survey." Handbook of the Economics of Finance. Vol. 2. Edited by G. M. Constantinides, M. Harris, and R. M. Stulz. Handbooks in Economics. New York, NY: Elsevier, 2012.

Bernstein, P., *Against the Gods: The Remarkable Story of Risk.* New York: John Wiley and Sons, 1996.

Belsky, G. and T. Gilovich, *Why Smart People Make Big Money Mistakes and How to Correct Them: Lessons from the New Science of Behavioral Economics.* New York: Simon & Schuster, 2000.

Key Terms

Catering, *35* Market timing, *35* Sentiment, *35*

Explore the Web

http://www.forbes.com/2009/04/06/sun-microsystems-enterprise-technology-enterprise-tech-sun.html
This web site contains an analysis of Sun Microsystems's business strategy by Andy Greenberg and Brian Caulfield, "Sun's Six Biggest Mistakes," April 7, 2009.

http://money.cnn.com/video/technology/2011/02/28/ctd_mcnealy_sun_oracle.fortune/
This web site contains an interview by *Fortune* magazine editor Adam Lashinsky with Scott McNealy.

http://www.cancer.net.nz/Vioxx_warning_letter_misleading_marketing.html
This web site contains the warning letter that the FDA sent to Merck in 2001.

http://mitsloanexperts.mit.edu/mit-sloan-alumna-judy-lewent-on-the-future-of-finance/
This web site contains remarks made by Judy Lewent, in "MIT Sloan Alumna Judy Lewent on the Future of Finance," January 9, 2012.

http://knowledge.wharton.upenn.edu/article/mercks-judy-lewent-once-again-talking-about-the-future/
This web site contains the article "Merck's Judy Lewent: Once Again, 'Talking About the Future,'" November 1, 2006.

http://www.world-nuclear.org/info/safety-and-security/safety-of-plants/fukushima-accident/
This web site contains an analysis by the World Nuclear Association, "Fukushima Accident," updated October 2015.

Chapter Questions

1. Does the chapter present any information that would lead you to conclude that managers at Sun Microsystems were averse to a sure loss? Discuss.
2. During its most profitable years in the late 1990s, Sun did not carry any debt. In 1999, Sun paid $138.6 million in taxes. Compare the situation at Sun with the situation at Merck in respect to their debt policies.
3. Discuss Scott McNealy's comments about sentiment in his interview with *Fortune* magazine. In your answer, describe any valuation metric Scott McNealy mentions. Do McNealy's comments suggest that Sun engaged either in catering behavior or market timing during the technology bubble?
4. Discuss the comment Scott McNealy made in his interview about not having hired a chief operating officer.
5. You can find Sun's statement of cash flows on the book web site. Do these statements suggest that Sun engaged in market timing during the technology bubble?

www.mhhe.com/shefrin2e

6. Did Merck's managers exhibit confirmation bias in their assessment of Vioxx? Discuss this question.
7. At the beginning of 2001, Merck's CFO Judy Lewent predicted that Vioxx sales for the year would be between $3 and $3.5 billion. In June she qualified her prediction to say that although Vioxx sales would be closer to the lower end of the prediction range, four of their top five drugs would achieve the upper end of their prediction ranges. One month later, she stated that Merck's research pipeline was as productive as at any other time in the firm's history. However, in August the *Journal of the American Medical Association* published a study linking Vioxx to an increased risk of heart attack and stroke. Immediately thereafter, sales of Vioxx began to slow. In 2001 Vioxx sales were $2.3 billion. In 2002 Vioxx sales were $2.5 billion. In light of the graph of return on equity displayed in Exhibit 2-5, discuss whether the events just described reflect any behavioral biases.
8. Merck's VIGOR study used 8,000 subjects. Notably, Merck chose to include only subjects whose risk of experiencing a heart attack was low. Half the subjects in the study received Vioxx, and the other half received naproxen. Of those receiving Vioxx, 20 had heart attacks. Of those receiving naproxen, four had heart attacks. Many medical researchers believe that naproxen does not reduce the incidence of heart attacks. Suppose that this is the case. From the vantage point of 1999, discuss whether the study outcome was just a fluke, with Vioxx actually being no riskier than naproxen when it comes to heart attacks.
9. On November 2, 2004, *The Wall Street Journal* published an article describing the manner in which Merck's executives made decisions about Vioxx. *The Wall Street Journal* article pointed out that the November 2000 issue of *The New England Journal of Medicine* included an article describing the results of the VIGOR study. *The New England Journal of Medicine* article stated that Vioxx did not significantly increase the incidence of heart attacks among patients who did not appear to be at high risk of having a heart attack. Notably, Merck had excluded subjects whose risk of experiencing a heart attack was anything but low. In retrospect, the executive editor of *The New England Journal,* Gregory Curfman, told *The Wall Street Journal* that his journal did not have all the details that were available to the FDA. He stated that his journal concentrated its efforts on ensuring that the text of the article accurately represented the data presented in the article. The authors of the article were academics who received consulting contracts or research grants from Merck and employees of Merck. Can you detect any behavioral issues and agency conflict issues (meaning general conflicts of interest) in the preceding discussion?
10. Compare two positions about Merck's handling of Vioxx. The first position is that Merck should have warned patients about the enhanced risk of heart attack or stroke (after prolonged use of the drug) with prominent language on drug packaging and ads. Eric Topol, director of San Diego's Scripps Translational Science Institute, called Merck's deficient labeling "a serious, prolonged problem about being honest about the risks." The thrust of this position is that had Merck done so, Vioxx might still be on the market. The second position is articulated by a legal complaint filed in 2015 against Merck by the Kuwait Investment Authority, Aegon Investment Management BV and Transamerica Funds. These investors had withdrawn from the settlement Merck had negotiated some years earlier. The complaint alleges that Merck was aware of the risks posed by Vioxx relating to strokes and heart attacks before it won FDA approval in 1999 and could have withdrawn its new drug application. However, the firm instead placed the drug on the market in order to compete against competitor Pfizer's drug Celebrex.

Additional Resources and Materials for Chapter 2 Are Available at www.mhhe.com/shefrin 2e

Minicase

Nuclear Meltdown at Fukushima Daiichi

On March 11, 2011, an earthquake of magnitude 9 on the Richter scale occurred off the northeast coast of Japan. This was the largest ever recorded in the country, and it generated a powerful tsunami that caused major damage in Japan. Tsunami waves reached 128 feet (39 meters) and penetrated inland for as much as 6 miles (10 kilometers).

According to the country's National Police Agency, the number of deaths exceeded 15,000 with at least 2,500 people unaccounted for. The Japanese government estimated total damages from the disaster to be in the vicinity of $300 billion.[15] This event had ongoing long-term consequences. Japan shut down all of its nuclear reactors until 2015, switching to more expensive alternatives such as oil.[16]

Included in the damage was the destruction of the Fukushima Daiichi power plant, which experienced the meltdown of some of its nuclear fuel rods. Earthquakes and tsunamis are well recognized risks in Japan, and the 2011 combination of earthquake and tsunami was a case of very bad luck. According to the World Nuclear Association, the reactors proved to have been robust seismically, but vulnerable to the ensuing tsunami.[17] In response to the earthquake, Fukushima Daiichi's operating reactors shut down automatically, as planned, with backup generators being used to supply power in order to keep the reactor cores from overheating. However, when the tsunami arrived an hour after the earthquake struck, it swamped the backup generators and the emergency core cooling systems subsequently failed.

Consider how risks associated with earthquakes and tsunamis were assessed, both in the planning stage for building the Fukushima Daiichi plant and in the subsequent period when it was in operation. In this regard, the plant was commissioned in 1971 and operated by the Tokyo Electric Power Company (TEPCO), was built by General Electric, and was regulated by Japan's Nuclear and Industrial Safety Agency (NISA).

During the time that the Fukushima Daiichi plant was built, the standard was to plan for a major seismic event that was expected to occur only once in 10,000 years. The International Atomic Energy Agency (IAEA) stipulates that best practice for assessing the risks of earthquakes and tsunamis should include the feasible collection of data on prehistoric and historic earthquakes and tsunamis in the region of a nuclear power plant.

Originally, TEPCO and NISA agreed on a plant design in which the seawater intake buildings were located 12 feet (4 meters) above sea level and the main plant buildings were located at the top of a slope that was 30 feet (10 meters) above sea level. The basis for these decisions was an earthquake that occurred in 1960 off the coast of Chile, which generated a tsunami having a height of 10 feet (3.1 meters).

Japan experiences approximately 1,500 earthquakes every year, with minor tremors occurring on a near-daily basis and major destructive seismic events well documented. More than 20 quakes occurred in the twentieth century of magnitude 6.3 or greater. Notably, about the same number occurred between the years 2000 and 2015. In 1936, 1978, and 2005, three major earthquakes occurred near Miyagi off the east coast of the Japanese island of Honshū, all with magnitudes between 7.2 and 7.5. The 2005 quake caused casualties, building collapses, and power outages; it also triggered a tsunami warning and shook buildings 200 miles away in Tokyo.

Tsumamis occur much less frequently than earthquakes, as they are only associated with some major earthquakes that occur under the ocean. A compilation of historical tsunamis in and around Japan includes 12 events that have occurred since 1498, for which the maximum amplitude exceeded 30 feet (10 meters), with six having exceeded 60 feet (20 meters). In the previous century eight tsunamis have been recorded in the region around Japan with maximum amplitudes exceeding 30 feet (10 meters), generated by earthquakes of magnitude 7.7 to 8.4 on the Richter scale, and occurring on average once every 12 years. Two earthquakes of magnitude 7.7 generated tsunamis with heights of 45 feet (15 meters) and over 90 feet (30 meters) respectively, one in 1983 and the other in 1993. Subsequent academic research discovered sedimentary layers suggesting that massive tsunamis occur once every thousand years or so, with the most recent episode having occurred in the year 869, as a result of an earthquake measuring 8.3 on the Richter scale.

Fukushima Daiichi's existence coincided with meltdowns at two nuclear power plants, one at Three Mile Island in 1979 and the other at Chernobyl, Ukraine in 1986. Unlike Fukushima Daiichi, neither Three Mile Island nor Chernobyl was located on a sea coast and using seawater for cooling. However, a plant in France located at Blayais did so, and experienced an incident that was relevant to the Fukushima Daiichi plant.[18] The plant at Blayais was protected from storm surges, by dikes. In 1999 an eight-foot-high (2.5 meter) storm surge overflowed the plant's dikes and flooded a pumping station. In order to prevent a reactor meltdown, the pumping system needs to carry heat from the reactor rods to a heat "sink," in this case the nearby estuary. A breakdown in the pumping system can prove dangerous. The decision makers at Blayais decided that it was prudent to shut down all reactors at the site. Thereafter, an investigation conducted by French authorities found not only that the dikes were too low, but also that the rooms which contained emergency equipment were not sufficiently protected from flooding.

These nuclear incidents prompted the institution of stricter safety standards across the globe. The U.S. Nuclear Regulatory Commission specifies that reactor designs meet a 1-in-10,000-year core damage frequency. The threshold requirement for U.S. utilities is 1 in 100,000 years. In 2015, the best of operating plants in operation were at 1 in 1 million. Future plants will likely be built to a standard of approximately 1 in 10 million.

A report published by the Carnegie Endowment analyzed the judgments and decisions in connection with the Fukushima Daiichi meltdown.[19] The report makes a series of points that are summarized below.

In January 2011, the Headquarters for Earthquake Research Promotion, which is funded by the Japanese government, repeated its judgment that there is a 99 percent probability that a magnitude 7.5 earthquake would strike the region within 30 years. Given that the magnitude of the actual earthquake was 9, the report characterizes the outcome as "a sobering warning against overconfidence in hazard prediction."

In 2002, the Japan Society of Civil Engineers developed a methodology to determine "runup," meaning how a tsunami would behave when it reached the sloped area on which the nuclear power plants rested. That methodology prompted TEPCO to increase the design-basis tsunami at Fukushima Daiichi to 18 feet from 10 feet (5.7 meters from 3.1 meters). However, the Carnegie report faults TEPCO's analysis for underestimating the height of the runup that would occur when the tsunami reached the sloped area.

Within Japan there is great confidence in the reliability of the country's power supply. The report describes the comments of a Japanese executive who characterized the prevalent implicit assumption that any loss in electrical power from the grid would be restored within 30 minutes. As it happened, the power plant at Fukushima Daiichi had six external power lines to Japan's grid, and all were destroyed by the earthquake. The emergency diesel generators did begin operating, for the most part successfully, until the tsunami struck.

In 2008, TEPCO performed computer modeling that suggested that the tsunami hazard to the Fukushima Daiichi plant had been severely underestimated. The associated simulations were based on the earthquake that occurred in the year 869. At the time, TEPCO indicated that it did not consider the simulation to be reliable, and therefore planned to investigate the issue further with the Japan Society of Civil Engineers. However, it never did so. Moreover, TEPCO waited three years before informing NISA of its results, which it did on March 7, 2011, four days before the disaster.

The Carnegie report summarizes judgments about TEPCO's decisions made by executives and safety experts who had many years of experience in nuclear power programs outside of Japan and at the IAEA, as well as knowledge of Japan's nuclear power program. These experts suggest that TEPCO did not put into practice lessons learned from the body of international knowledge that accumulated during the four-decade operating lifetime of the Fukushima Daiichi plant. The report faults TEPCO for not having installed emergency power equipment and cooling pumps in dedicated, bunkered, watertight buildings or compartments; not having moved emergency diesel generators and other emergency power sources to higher ground on the plant site; not having established watertight connections between emergency power supplies and the plant; and not having built dikes and seawalls to protect against a severe tsunami.

The Carnegie report emphasizes the value of taking such actions, pointing to the fact that one Japanese utility, Japan Atomic Power Company (JAPC), was in the process of carrying out such improvements. The tsunami struck one of its plants located approximately 100 miles south of Fukushima. JAPC had taken steps to make its pump rooms watertight and to build a seawall to protect against flooding in two pits that housed the pump rooms. In areas where pipes had been made watertight, they functioned as planned, preventing a bad situation from becoming worse.

Although the Carnegie report offers no conclusive prioritization of the various factors that contributed to shortcomings in TEPCO's risk assessment, it does offer comments and suggestions. The first comment pertains to the asymmetry between perceptions about earthquakes and perceptions about tsunamis. In this regard, the culture in Japan is highly informed about dangers associated with seismic activity. As a result the country has firm and robust technical requirements for its nuclear power plants, and indeed all of its civil engineering structures. In contrast, the country has been slower to recognize the potential danger posed by tsunamis and other external events.

The second comment is that both Japanese executives and regulators noted the presence of a general Japanese cultural bias against openly discussing worst-case scenarios. Prior to the Fukushima Daiichi meltdown, there was little interest in public discussion or media coverage about tsunami safety.

The third comment is that most Japanese regulations do not require probabilistic safety assessments, such as "1 in 10,000" or "1 in a million," in order to demonstrate that plants are protected against the threat of severe external events. And while some Japanese decision makers have examined the concept, probabilistic assessments have played no role in actual decision making.

The fourth comment pertains to characterization. The Carnegie report communicates the views of some Japanese experts who stated that the accident at Fukushima Daiichi serves to illustrate "supreme overconfidence by decision makers that Japan's nuclear power program would never suffer a severe accident." The report notes that the discussion about blackouts in the 1990 safety guide only described power interruptions of 30 minutes or less. The report provides another example to illustrate "excessive confidence," namely that Japanese plant owners chose to expose their firms to unlimited liability in the event of an accident in order to communicate to local populations the confidence they had in the safety of their power plants.

The accident resulted in an enormous cleanup challenge. When TEPCO built the plant, they cut away a hillside to shorten the distance from the plant to the ocean, which increased the threat from incursions of groundwater into plant facilities. Because cracks developed in the basement floors of reactor buildings after the accident, groundwater began seeping into damaged reactor buildings and creating all kinds of problems. The water became radioactive and has had to be collected into large containers on site, to limit ocean contamination. Moreover, the accumulated water has prevented TEPCO crews from cleaning up reactor fuel. In 2016, TEPCO began to freeze a large area of ground in order to create an artificial permafrost ice wall that would serve as a barrier. The wall was built by the Japanese central government at a cost of $320 million, and was intended to provide protection for at least five years so that cleanup crews could address the myriad of complex cleanup issues. Some suggested that the ice wall solution was much more expensive, not completely effective, and offered very few advantages over conventional solutions such as walls built from concrete or steel. In this regard, a researcher from an independent radiation-monitoring group characterized the ice wall strategy as "a Hail Mary play."[20]

Case Analysis Questions

1. Identify the psychological phenomena in the minicase. Prioritize the phenomena from most important to least important. Begin your answer by defining the phenomena, and then describing their role in the minicase. As part of your answer, discuss the implications of avoiding probabilistic safety assessments when planning the design of a nuclear reactor such as Fukushima Daiichi.
2. As of July 2015, 30 countries worldwide are operating 438 nuclear reactors for electricity generation and 67 new nuclear plants are under construction in 15 countries. Nuclear power plants provided 10.9 percent of the world's electricity production in 2012. In 2014, 13 countries relied on nuclear energy to supply at least one-quarter of their total electricity. As of 2015, there have been three major reactor accidents in the history of civil nuclear power—Three Mile Island, Chernobyl, and Fukushima Daiichi. One was contained without harm to anyone, the next involved an intense fire without provision for containment, and the third severely tested the containment, allowing some release of radioactivity. These are the only major accidents to have occurred in over 15,000 cumulative reactor-years of commercial nuclear power operation in 33 countries.

   Given a standard of 1 in 10,000 years, use the binomial distribution to compute the probability that there will be three or more "core meltdowns" in 15,000 cumulative reactor-years.[21] How does your answer change when the standard is 1 in 10 million?

Chapter Three

Valuation

The main objective of this chapter is for students to demonstrate that they can identify how heuristics and framing affect the way managers and analysts value firms.

After completing this chapter students will be able to:

1. Explain why some financial executives and analysts rely on valuation heuristics instead of textbook techniques that emphasize intrinsic value.
2. Describe the main heuristics that financial executives and analysts use to compute value.
3. Identify the biases that arise in connection with the use of valuation heuristics.
4. Identify the biases that arise in connection with the use of traditional textbook techniques that emphasize intrinsic value.

3.1 TRADITIONAL APPROACH TO VALUATION

The two most prominent approaches to valuation are *intrinsic valuation* and *valuation by comparables*. The former is based on discounted cash flow (DCF) analysis, while the latter is mostly based on ratios such as price-to-earnings and price-to-sales.

The most general DCF approach to the intrinsic valuation of a firm involves its future free cash flows. The annual free cash flow to a firm is the cash the firm generates in a year that is available to be paid to its investors. Free cash flow (*FCF*) is generated from a firm's operating activities, net of investments in fixed assets and changes in working capital. The standard textbook formula for free cash flow is *EBIT(1 − tax rate) + depreciation − investment − change in working capital*. The intrinsic value V_F of a firm is the present value of its expected free cash flow stream, discounted at its cost of capital k_W, plus the value of its current cash. It is common to divide the free cash flow into two horizons, respectively called the intermediate horizon and the terminal horizon. During the terminal horizon, which begins in period $T + 1$, free cash flow is expected to grow at a constant rate g, with present value PV_T being given by the formula $FCF_{T+1}/(k_W - g)$. A fuller discussion of free cash flows can be found in the Additional Resources to Chapter 3, which is posted on the book web site.

The intrinsic value of a firm's equity, V_E, can be obtained in several ways. The first is by subtracting the intrinsic value of the firm's debt from its intrinsic value V_F.

The second is by using the dividend discount method (DDM), which involves computing the present value of the firm's expected dividend stream, discounted at the required return on equity k_E.

A third way to compute V_E is through the formula $E_1/k_E + PVGO$, where E_1 denotes expected earnings next period and *PVGO* represents the firm's present value of growth opportunities.[1] A firm has positive growth opportunities when the expected return on its future projects exceeds the required return on those projects. Effectively, *PVGO* is the net present value of a firm's current and future projects.

A fourth way to compute V_E is through the formula $BE + PV(expected\ EVA\ stream)$. Here *BE* is a firm's current book value of equity and *EVA* stands for economic value added. Economic value added for the firm is the difference between net operating profit after tax (NOPAT, effectively earnings before interest and tax minus tax), and a charge to capital defined as the product of the cost of capital and book value of assets.

Notably, the PVGO approach provides a formula for a firm's intrinsic forward P/E ratio V/E_1, namely $[k_E \times (1 - PVGO/V_E)]^{-1}$. This formula implies that intrinsic P/E is decreasing in the firm's required return on equity k_E and increasing in the proportion of its intrinsic value that stems from its growth opportunities. Similarly, the economic value added approach provides a formula for a firm's intrinsic market-to-book ratio V_E/BE, namely $[1 + PV(EVA\ stream)/BE]$. This formula implies that when a firm expects that in the future it will earn exactly its cost of capital, then its intrinsic market-to-book ratio will be unity.

valuation by comparables
Valuation based on comparison of a specific firm's characteristics with the characteristics of comparable firms

Valuation by comparables focuses on the relationship between the market value of a firm's equity, and the characteristics of that firm relative to similar firms to see if the relationships are comparable. For example, in valuing a specific firm's stock, financial analysts might use the valuation formula $P = P/E \times E$, where P/E is their judgment of the appropriate value of forward-looking P_0/E_1 and E_1 is their estimate of the firm's earnings over the next year. What estimate of P/E to use in the analysis, and how much confidence to have in this estimate, might depend on how the firm's "trailing P/E" (written as P_0/E_0 and defined as current price divided by current earnings), compares to the trailing P/E ratios of similar firms.

In addition, analysts tend to repeat the analysis for other ratios such as price-to-sales, price-to-book (also known as market-to-book), price-to-cash flow, and PEG defined as P/E divided by the estimated growth rate of a firm. Doing so provides a range of possible values for a firm's stock, leading each analyst to make a judgment call about where in the associated range to place his or her final valuation estimate.

3.2 TARGET PRICE HEURISTICS

The formulas underlying present value analysis have been rigorously derived as part of a well-established theory. Nevertheless, in practice, equity valuation strongly reflects the use of heuristics and therefore vulnerability to biases. In this regard, valuation by comparables is a heuristic technique: it is based on formulas that are true by definition (tautologies), relies on judgments of similarity that depend on how representative a firm is in the class of its comparables, and reconciles possibly diverse valuation estimates associated with different ratios by using instinct (gut feel or affect). Recall the discussion about representativeness and the affect heuristic in Chapters 1 and 2.

Both analysts and financial executives rely on a combination of discounted cash flow (DCF) and valuation by comparables.[2] This chapter focuses on the heuristic nature of valuation methodologies and on the biases associated with their implementation in practice. In this respect, much of the chapter focuses on security analysts' estimates of future values known as "price targets."

The general evidence indicates that analysts are prone to a series of specific biases when setting price targets. They overweigh past sales growth and underweigh the level of past earnings. They tend to overvalue firms that report losses, particularly when those losses are extreme. They tend to undervalue firms that have large cash flows more than firms that have large accruals, and they are prone to misvalue firms with high profit margins.[3] The next part of the discussion specifies the equations used in three particular price target heuristics associated with valuation by comparables.

P/E Heuristic

Valuation based on the P/E ratio involves the product of two terms: a P/E ratio and an earnings estimate. The P/E ratio is a forward P/E, having the form P_0/E_1, where P_0 denotes current price and E_1 denotes the forecast of earnings per share for the next year. Security analysts rely on the **P/E heuristic** more than any other technique.[4]

P/E heuristic
An approach to valuation based on multiplying a P/E ratio and an earnings forecast.

The valuation identity is given by $P_0 = P_0/E_1 \times E_1$. In order to forecast the price P_1 a year hence, apply the relationship $P_1 = P_1/E_2 \times E_2$. Here the challenge is to arrive at sensible forecasts of the P/E ratio that will apply a year hence and earnings per share two years hence.

PEG Heuristic

A firm's PEG ratio is defined as its P/E ratio divided by its expected earnings growth rate per year (actually 100 × expected earnings growth rate). The premise underlying the use of PEG-based valuation is that the stocks of high-growth firms merit higher P/E ratios than the stocks of low-growth firms. To compute the value of a firm's stock based on its PEG ratio, multiply the following three terms: its PEG ratio, an estimate of future earnings per share, and an estimate of expected earnings growth.

PEG heuristic
An approach to valuation based on multiplying a PEG ratio, an earnings forecast, and a forecast of the growth rate.

The valuation identity is given by $P_0 = \text{PEG} \times E_1 \times G$, where G is 100 × growth rate. As with the P/E heuristic, the **PEG heuristic** can be used to forecast price P_1 a year hence. Doing so requires forecasts of the PEG ratio that will apply a year hence, earnings per share two years hence, and the growth rate that will apply over the forecast period.

Price-to-Sales Heuristic

price-to-sales heuristic
An approach to valuation based on multiplying a price-to-sales ratio and a sales forecast.

The **price-to-sales heuristic** has the same structure as the P/E heuristic, except that future sales are substituted for future earnings. The valuation identity is given by $P_0 = P_0/S_1 \times S_1$, where S stands for sales.

3.3 A CFO'S RELIANCE ON VALUATION HEURISTICS

In order to make the ideas about valuation heuristics and biases concrete, this chapter uses the case of the major online auction firm eBay as a vehicle for discussion. eBay's users use its site to buy and sell items such as antiques, art, jewelry, books, collectibles, and automotive parts.

The initial public offering (IPO) for eBay took place in September 1998. In 2002 eBay acquired the Internet payment provider PayPal in a $1.4 billion stock deal, thereby providing its users with a safe and reliable way to make their online purchases. By the end of 2002 eBay was one of the most successful Internet companies in the world. A $100 investment in eBay stock at the time of its IPO would have grown to more than $640 by May 2003. In contrast, the return to both the S&P 500 and the Nasdaq Composite index during the same period was close to zero, if not negative.

On May 20, 2003, eBay's stock closed at $97.75, having risen by more than 44 percent from the beginning of the year. That increase gave eBay a market valuation higher than the market valuations of both General Motors and McDonald's. On that day the consensus analyst estimate of its earnings per share (EPS) for the coming four quarters was $1.56. That produced a forward P/E for eBay of 62.7.[5]

CONCEPT PREVIEW
Question 3.1

After Internet stock prices had generally soared in May 2003, the *San Jose Mercury News* asked whether the rapid increase was due to solid fundamentals or 1999-style bandwagon investing. Investors were asking the same question. If you were a financial executive at eBay, what combination of traditional and heuristic valuation techniques would you use to answer this question?

Consider next how the financial executives at eBay actually approached valuation at the time. See the Behavior Pitfalls box "Attaching a Value to eBay."[6,7]

Both eBay's chief financial officer and vice president for corporate finance were highly educated and experienced. Despite all the emphasis in corporate finance textbooks on discounted cash flow analysis, many financial executives rely on heuristics instead of the fundamental valuation techniques taught in textbooks. Heuristics are simpler to use: P/E, PEG, and price-to-sales require very few variables and involve simple formulas. As such they have intuitive appeal, the basis for the affect heuristic. The discussion in the nearby box vividly illustrates this point. The DCF-based analyses taught in textbooks require far more detail than the heuristic techniques, involve more complex formulas, and are far less intuitive.

3.4 HOW ANALYSTS VALUE FIRMS: AN ILLUSTRATIVE EXAMPLE

Analyst Mary Meeker

The Behavioral Pitfalls box on page 62 illustrates how the financial executives at eBay approached the value of their firm. Essentially, they relied on the PEG heuristic

Behavioral Pitfalls: Attaching a Value to eBay

On April 1, 2003, Rajiv Dutta, eBay's chief financial officer (CFO) addressed a chapter meeting of Financial Executives International (FEI). During his presentation he discussed the manner in which eBay's executives respond to investors who suggest that the firm's stock is overvalued. He indicated that eBay's executives take skeptical investors through the following PEG-based analysis.

In March 2003, eBay's P/E ratio was 79, which some investors took to imply that its stock price was too high. However, Dutta suggested that a valuation based on P/E alone failed to factor in earnings growth. In this respect, he suggested comparing the stock of eBay to the stock of the large retail firm Wal-Mart, and using the PEG ratio as the valuation metric. According to *Fortune* magazine, Wal-Mart was the most admired company in America during 2003.

On May 20, 2003, eBay's forward-looking P/E ratio was 66.7, while Wal-Mart's P/E ratio was 22.7. On a P/E basis, eBay appeared to be over twice as expensive as Wal-Mart. However, Dutta pointed out that analysts were expecting eBay to grow by 42.5 percent, while they were only expecting Wal-Mart to grow by 14 percent. As a result, eBay's PEG was 1.56, which was actually lower than Wal-Mart's PEG of 1.62. By the PEG metric, eBay was actually cheaper than Wal-Mart, a point that eBay's CFO emphasized.

In May 2003 Mark Rubash, eBay's vice president for corporate finance and investor relations, explicitly stated that the firm's managers did not track return on equity and were uncertain about the value of their firm's cost of capital. Based on conversations with investors and perhaps analysts, they believed their cost of capital to be in the range of 11 to 12 percent. However, they claimed not to compute their cost of capital, say, by using a textbook framework such as the capital asset pricing model (CAPM), or by factoring their historical return on equity into their valuation analysis. Given the high and accelerating growth rates they were witnessing during 2003, eBay's executives stated, frankly, that they had very little idea about the intrinsic value of their firm's stock.

To assess the above discussion in hindsight, a brief chronology of eBay for the period 2004 through 2014 appears later in the chapter, with further detail provided in the Additional Resources to Chapter 3.

to assess whether or not their stock price seemed to be fairly priced. However, they did little analysis beyond that.

What about security analysts? One of their main tasks is to assess value. Do they rely on DCF? Do they use heuristics, and if so which ones? In the Spring of 2003, 24 analysts followed eBay. Among these, the most well known was Mary Meeker from the firm Morgan Stanley. She led a team of analysts, hereafter called the Morgan Stanley team, which conducted an analysis of eBay using a series of valuation techniques, each of which gave a different price target (also known as a target price) for eBay. Her April 2003 report offers a rich set of insights into how analysts apply these various techniques. Before describing the details, refer to the Behavioral Pitfalls box "Wal-Marting of the Web" for some background information on Mary Meeker.

The Morgan Stanley Team's Mid-2004 Price Target for eBay

At the time the Morgan Stanley team released their April 2003 report, eBay's price was $89.22. The team's task was to develop a price target for eBay over the subsequent 12 months. In undertaking this task, they used all three valuation heuristics described earlier, as well as a discounted cash flow (DCF) computation.

Exhibit 3-1 provides a summary of the components of the Morgan Stanley team's price target analysis. For each of the first three heuristics, the team computed a low, high, and intermediate guess, which they called downside, upside, and base

Behavioral Pitfalls: Wal-Marting of the Web

During the late 1990s Mary Meeker was a security analyst at Morgan Stanley and was one of the highest-paid analysts on Wall Street, having earned approximately $15 million in 1999 and $23 million in 2000. At the time, she placed very high valuations on some Internet firms, and as a result came to be called Queen of the Internet.

In 1998, *Time Magazine* interviewed Mary Meeker, asking her to justify the high valuations of Internet companies that prevailed at the time. She began by stating that the development of the commercial Internet was "the biggest new technology cycle ever."

Continuing, she pointed out that just as the traditional retailer Wal-Mart came to dominate the retail sector, web-based counterparts would emerge and dominate Internet commerce. Mary Meeker described the phenomenon as the "Wal-Marting of the Web."

Wal-Mart had built its business by beating its competition in regard to convenience, product selection, and low prices. She argued that the Internet provided the opportunity for other firms to follow Wal-Mart, but on the web.

In 2000, after a period of excessive optimism, if not irrational exuberance, the prices of many Internet stocks fell dramatically. This event has been described as the bursting of the dot-com bubble. In May 2002 *Fortune* magazine placed Mary Meeker's picture on their cover and asked if investors could ever trust Wall Street again.

In the wake of the collapse in stock prices, regulators from New York State's attorney general's office and the U.S. Securities and Exchange Commission launched a major investigation. Among those investigated was Mary Meeker. In 2003, the attorney general's office and the SEC criticized her valuations as excessive, but they did not bring charges against her.

On February 23, 2004, *The Wall Street Journal* ran a feature titled "Ah, the 1990s" updating the fates of key Wall Street personalities from the 1990s stock market bubble. Regarding Mary Meeker, the article notes that she was recently named Morgan Stanley's coleader of tech-sector research. In August 2004, Meeker told *Newsweek* and *CBS.MarketWatch.Com* that she was not going to be hiding out any more. The press duly noted that her stock picks were outperforming the market. In 2010, Meeker left Morgan Stanley and moved to California to join the venture capital firm Kleiner Perkins Caufield & Byers (KPCB) as a partner. In the ensuing years she came to be recognized as one of the world's leading experts on digital technology.

Sources: M. Meeker and M. Murray Buechner, "Q&A: Morgan's Mary Meeker: Look for the Net's 'Top Dogs'," *Time,* April 1, 1998; E. S. Browning, "Ah, the 1990," *The Wall Street Journal,* February 23, 2004; F. Barnako, "Mary Meeker Is Still a Believer," *CBS.MarketWatch .com,* August 23, 2004; C. Gasparino and S. Craig, "Meeker Won't Face Securities-Fraud Charges," *The Wall Street Journal,* April 3, 2003; C. Gasparino, "Climbing Back Up; Ready to Reign Again, Wall Street's Fallen 'Queen of the Net' Tells *Newsweek:* 'I'm not hiding out anymore,'" *Newsweek,* August 30, 2004.

respectively. They then averaged these together with their DCF valuation to arrive at a price target of $106 per share.[8]

Exhibit 3-2 describes the assumptions and computations that underlie the average target values displayed in Exhibit 3-1. In Exhibit 3-2, an E after a year (for example, 2004E) designates that the numbers are estimates, not actual values. In all cases price targets were computed for year-end 2004 and then discounted back to mid-2004. To arrive at their price target for December 2004, the team used a P/E value of 40 for 2005, the midpoint of 47 and 33 shown in the table. For sales, they used the gross global sales activity on all eBay web sites, called gross merchandise sales (GMS).

As can be seen in Exhibit 3-1, the Morgan Stanley team used a DCF approach, applied to eBay's free cash flows. This computation is the only one of the four that purports to derive the price target in terms of intrinsic or fundamental value.

A firm generates positive free cash flows when its after-tax cash flows from operations are positive and it does not spend all those after-tax flows acquiring

EXHIBIT 3-1
Summary of Components in Mary Meeker's Price Target Analysis of eBay

Source: Mary Meeker and Brian Pitz, "CQ1 Results: Tales of a Growth Machine," Morgan Stanley Analyst Report on eBay, April 23, 2003.

Technique	Downside	Upside	Base
P/E	$74	$111	$ 84
PEG	45	91	68
Price-to-sales	97	210	154
Discounted cash flow			117
Average			$104
Upside adjusted average			$106

EXHIBIT 3-2 Valuation Methodologies in the Morgan Stanley Team's Price Target Analysis of eBay

Source: Mary Meeker and Brian Pitz, "CQ1 Results: Tales of a Growth Machine," Morgan Stanley Analyst Report on eBay, April 23, 2003.

	Year			
	2002	2003E	2004E	2005E
EPS at 32% growth	$0.86	$1.14	$1.50	$1.98
EPS at 38% growth	$0.86	$1.19	$1.64	$2.26
GMS/share at 38% growth	$39.53	$54.55	$75.27	$103.88
P/E	103	63	47	33

Method	P/E Ratio	PEG Ratio	Price-to-Sales Ratio	EPS	Growth	GMS Sales per Share	Price Target Dec 2004	Price Target (Discounted)
P/E	40			$2.26			$90	$84
PEG		1.5		1.50	32		72	68
Price-to-sales			1.5	2.26		$103.88	156	154

working capital and new fixed assets. In this respect, working capital is to be understood to mean "operational working capital," namely the change in net working capital for items only associated with cash flow from operations but not cash flows from financing or cash and marketable securities. Therefore, annual free cash flow comprises cash flow generated by the firm within the year that is available to be paid to the firm's investors. This available cash flow consists of cash flow actually paid to investors together with the increase in the firm's cash and marketable securities. In this respect, the firm's investors are its debtholders and shareholders, so that cash paid to investors consists of interest, repayment of principal net of new debt, dividends, and share repurchases net of new stock issues.

Exhibit 3-3 displays the DCF valuation table from the Morgan Stanley team's April 2003 report. The heart of their DCF analysis consists of the forecasts for eBay's revenues and its earnings before interest, taxes, depreciation, and amortization (EBITDA).

The free cash flows for eBay are displayed in Exhibit 3-3. The present value of the firm's expected free cash flows, plus the value of its current cash and marketable securities, comprise the value of the entire firm.

EXHIBIT 3-3 Free Cash Flow Computation in Mary Meeker's Price Target Analysis of eBay

Note: Values given are in $ thousands.

Source: Mary Meeker and Brian Pitz, "CQ1 Results: Tales of a Growth Machine," Morgan Stanley Analyst Report on eBay, April 23, 2003.

	2000	2001	2002	2003E	2004E	2005E	2006E	2007E	2008E	2009E	2010E	2011E on
Revenue	431,424	748,821	1,214,100	2,050,492	2,829,679	3,763,473	4,907,751	6,287,602	7,857,002	9,582,843	11,400,983	
EBITDA	84,072	229,438	444,614	723,735	1,005,276	1,401,682	1,853,230	2,426,297	3,110,990	3,985,085	4,982,032	
Taxes	—	—	—	—	—	140,168	370,646	849,204	1,088,846	1,394,780	1,743,711	
Change in working capital	47,582	41,091	(39,232)	26,792	(6,849)	58,695	(9,709)	52,096	(7,375)	53,278	(4,105)	
Capital expenditures	49,753	57,420	138,670	188,908	190,000	190,000	190,000	190,000	190,000	190,000	190,000	
Free cash flow	(13,263)	130,927	345,176	508,035	822,125	1,012,819	1,302,292	1,334,997	1,839,519	2,347,027	3,052,426	65,321,907

Price Target—Dec 31, 2003

Present value eBay free cash flows	$36,478,759
Less debt	$79,592
Plus cash	$2,280,857
eBay's full value	$38,680,023
Shares outstanding ('000)	330,259
Discount rate	12%
Future growth rate	7%
DCF per share value	$117

Note that we use a Hurdle Rate rather than the Weighted Average Cost of Capital (WACC) as the discount rate for our DCF analysis. We believe that a Hurdle Rate is more appropriate because it more accurately reflects what we view as company-specific risks. We calculate the Cost of Equity at 9.5 percent based on a risk-free rate of 3.9 percent taken from the 10-year U.S. Government Bond Yield as of 10/31/02; a risk premium of 4.0 percent from Morgan Stanley Economics Research estimates of expected equity risk premium; and beta of 1.38 from Bloomberg relative to the S&P 500 as of 10/31/02. Note that eBay's debt is immaterial.

In their April 2003 report, the Morgan Stanley team forecast free cash flows through the end of 2010. They used a terminal value to capture the free cash flows that would occur after 2010 and discounted these at a rate of 12 percent.[9] In Exhibit 3-3, they obtained their $65.3 billion terminal value in 2011 by assuming that free cash flows would grow at the rate of 7 percent from 2011 on, and then valued the future expected free cash flow stream beginning in 2011 using the constant-growth-rate perpetuity formula. Specifically, they forecast that free cash flows in 2011 would be $3,266,096 = 1.07 × $3,052,426. They then applied the perpetuity formula:

$$PV = \frac{\$3{,}266{,}096}{0.12 - 0.07} = \$65{,}321{,}907$$

The Morgan Stanley team computed the present value of the free cash flow stream by summing the discounted free cash flow values for every year between 2004E and the terminal year. As shown in Exhibit 3-3, that sum came to $36.5 billion. Then they added eBay's $2.3 billion cash holdings to arrive at the value of the firm as a whole and subtracted the value of eBay's $79 million in debt to arrive at the value of eBay's equity. The net result was $38 billion, which the team called eBay's "full value." Dividing full value by eBay's shares outstanding (from Exhibit 3-3) resulted in a target value of about $117 per share at year-end 2003.[10] In using this amount, they did not take the future value of the $117 to mid-2004.

3.5 VALUATION HEURISTICS AND BIASES: IN FORESIGHT

This section uses the Morgan Stanley eBay report and eBay CFO Rajiv Dutta's valuation perspective about valuing the company as vehicles to discuss identifying valuation heuristics and biases. Keep in mind that the discussion is intended to be illustrative, and it is important to avoid overgeneralizing on the basis of a single example. The drawing of broad conclusions needs to be based on fairly large samples: because of luck, good judgments in foresight can look bad in hindsight, and vice versa.

For this reason, this section focuses on two approaches, one foresight-focused and the other hindsight-focused. The foresight-focused approach seeks to identify biases based on information available at the time the judgments were made, and ignoring what we now know in hindsight. The hindsight-focused approach examines those judgments in light of how actual events played out. Both approaches provide different insights, and offer different lessons about how to improve the process of valuation.

Optimism Bias: In Foresight

The Behavioral Pitfalls box "Attaching a Value to eBay" describes how in 2003 eBay's financial executives thought about the value of their firm. They were uncertain as to how to conduct an evaluation, engaged in no discounted cash flow analysis, and viewed the market price as justifiable on the basis of PEG. In contrast, Mary Meeker and her analyst team at Morgan Stanley had a methodology for valuing eBay featuring discounted cash flow analysis along with a series of price target heuristics, one of which involved PEG. This section discusses the presence of bias in the valuation judgments described in the previous section. In this regard, the focus on eBay simply provides a vehicle for making the discussion concrete. The general ideas apply widely. Notably, the Morgan Stanley analysts' focus on DCF, P/E, PEG, and P/S is common in the analyst community.

Recall the discussion of optimism bias from Chapter 1. On April 23, 2003, *The Wall Street Journal* published an article suggesting that the analysts following eBay were excessively optimistic about eBay's future revenue stream. The article pointed out that the Morgan Stanley team's forecast for the period ending in 2010 was the most optimistic. Nick Wingfield, the author of *The Wall Street Journal* article, laid out several possible scenarios that might support the optimistic revenue forecasts, and concluded that 30 percent revenue growth forecasts for eBay were unduly optimistic. Notably, this judgment applies to the assumptions stated in Exhibits 3-2 and 3-3.

EXHIBIT 3-4
Year Over Year Growth Rates in Morgan Stanley 2003 Report on eBay, for Revenue, EBITDA, and Free Cash Flow

Source of data: Morgan Stanley Report on eBay, April 2003.

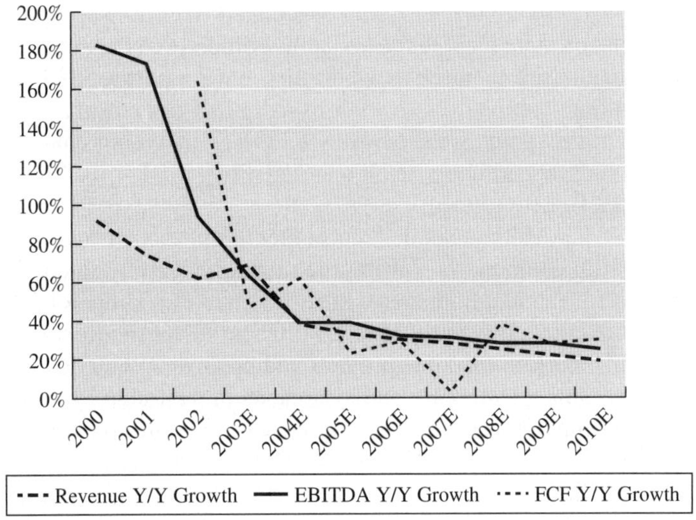

In the Morgan Stanley report, the 30 percent assumption pertains to P/E, PEG, and P/S. However, the free cash flow analysis also involves longer-term forecasts. Exhibit 3-4 illustrates the growth rates of three critical inputs, namely revenues, EBITDA, and free cash flows. Over the forecast period from year-end 2003 through 2010, revenue growth declines from 38 percent to 19 percent, EBITDA growth declines from 39 percent to 25 percent, and free cash flow growth declines from 62 percent to 30 percent.

Plausibly, the short-term 30 percent forecasts might have been optimistic, when made. In this regard, a reasonable question to pose might be whether the very rapid growth rates for revenue and EBITDA in the period 2000 through 2002 served as anchors for the forecasts in 2003 through 2010?

More importantly, from an intrinsic valuation point of view, the short-term growth rates are much less important than the growth rate associated with terminal value. The free cash flows from 2004 through 2010 only comprise 19 percent of the \$36.5 billion value that Morgan Stanley analysts assigned to all of eBay's future free cash flows. Terminal value comprised the lion's share, namely 81 percent.

Looking back at Exhibit 3-3, we can see that free cash flows were expected to grow at 7 percent during the terminal horizon beginning in 2011. That is, the Morgan Stanley analysts forecasted that beginning in 2011, eBay's free cash flows would grow at 7 percent forever. According to World Bank Statistics,[11] GDP growth in 2003 was approximately 4 percent and the GDP deflator was about 2 percent. The two together total 6 percent, which is a full percentage point less than the 7 percent forecast for eBay. The difference is small for a single year, but compounding out to eternity is another matter. If eBay were to grow 1 percent faster than the U.S. economy, it would eventually become the U.S. economy.

There are deeper issues associated with the question of whether the forecast inputs feature bias. Think about the competitive dynamic in which currently successful firms find themselves when they have a competitive advantage. Successful firms attract competitors seeking to reduce, if not eliminate, that competitive advantage. On this point, in 2014 eBay CEO Devin Wenig characterized eBay's competitive landscape as being "a more competitive market," adding: "We are not going to have the field to [ourselves]."[12]

The Morgan Stanley report mentions Amazon and Google as being two of eBay's main competitors. During the time a firm enjoys a competitive advantage, its projects feature a higher rate of return than the competitive rate of return. Notably it is the competitive rate of return that serves as the discount rate associated with positive net present value projects and positive PVGO. However, competitive advantage is usually temporary and disappears in the long run along with positive PVGO. The terminal horizon is the long term. Therefore, only in very unusual circumstances would we expect positive PVGO during the terminal horizon.

Unless they are magicians, firms have to invest enough, both in fixed assets and working capital, in order to grow. Take another look at Exhibit 3-3 to see what the Morgan Stanley group was forecasting in respect to eBay's capital expenditures (CapEx). Notice that during the period 2004 through 2010, CapEx is flat at $190 million every year, even as eBay's forecasted growth is soaring, as displayed in Exhibit 3-4. This suggests that the forecasted CapEx is too low to support the forecasted growth.

There is a particular condition that must hold if PVGO is to be zero in the terminal horizon. As is discussed in the Additional Resources for this chapter, the condition stipulates that the fraction of after-tax EBIT that is allocated to the sum of CapEx (net of replacing depreciated assets) and the change in net working capital must equal the ratio g/k, where g is the growth rate and k is the discount rate. Since Morgan Stanley assumed that g would be 7 percent and k would be 12 percent, g/k is 58.3 percent. Is there any hint that eBay is planning to invest 58.3 percent of its after-tax EBIT on net CapEx and working capital?

The sum of net CapEx and working capital is just the difference between after-tax EBIT and free cash flow. We can use this fact to compute the time series of the ratio "net CapEx and working capital to after-tax EBIT" for the period 2004 through 2010. The ratio averages 7.8 percent during the period, and declines from 10.1 percent in 2004 to 3.1 percent in 2010. It reaches a maximum of 13 percent in 2005, which is still a far cry from 58.3 percent.

There are at least three conclusions that one might draw at this point. The first is that eBay's intellectual capital and brand is so powerful and persistent that the firm will be able to maintain a competitive advantage in the terminal period with minimal investment. Given the competitive dynamic in high technology, this possibility is unrealistic. The second is that eBay's investment levels, if continued into the terminal horizon, are far too low to support a growth rate of 7 percent. If we stick with 7 percent, then the level of free cash flows during the terminal horizon will have to be much lower than the Morgan Stanley team assumes. Third, if we stick with the level of investment, then eBay's growth rate during the terminal horizon will have to be much lower than 7 percent.

Either lower free cash flows or a lower growth rate, or both, will result in a lower DCF valuation for eBay. The result is bias, namely excessive optimism, resulting from biased inputs used in the DCF analysis. The specific form of optimism pertains to the implicit assumption that there are positive growth opportunities during the terminal horizon, a feature called **"growth opportunities bias."**

growth opportunities bias
Unwarranted assumption of positive growth opportunities during the terminal horizon.

What would eBay's price per share be if we maintain its investment policy into the terminal horizon, but require that PVGO be zero after 2010? To answer that question, consider a growth rate g that would be consistent with zero PVGO. To find such a growth rate, suppose that the fraction of eBay's after-tax EBIT going to net CapEx and working capital during the terminal horizon is the average value during the period 2006–2010. That average turns out to be 6.3%, which given the equation $g/k = 6.3\%$. With k assumed to be 12%, g must be 0.76%. If we redo the computation in Exhibit 3-3 with this value of g, we obtain a price per share of $65.

Biases Associated with P/E, PEG, and PVGO: In Foresight

CONCEPT PREVIEW
Question 3.2

In traditional textbook valuation analysis, what variables determine whether the stock of a firm has a low intrinsic P/E ratio or a high P/E ratio?

Textbook theory stipulates that intrinsic P/E is a function of two variables, required return and the fraction of a firm's value that derives from growth opportunities PVGO. When a firm has zero growth opportunities, meaning its PVGO is equal to zero, then its intrinsic forward P/E is $1/k_E$, where k_E is the required return on equity. However, as PVGO becomes positive, P/E rises above $1/k_E$. As PVGO approaches P_0, P_0/E_1 rises to infinity.

Notably, in April 2003, the Morgan Stanley team titled their report on eBay "Tales of a Growth Machine" in order to emphasize growth as the justification for their price target of $106, with its associated P/E being in the vicinity of 50. Notably, that value of P/E is indirect, obtained by taking the future value of the price target at year-end 2004 divided by forecasted EPS for 2005 given 38 percent growth.

Other analysts covering eBay used even higher values than the Morgan Stanley team for P/E. For example, a Prudential report on eBay, dated May 12, 2003, used a P/E ratio of 75.[13] The Prudential analysts assessed the value of eBay stock at $108, not that different from Morgan Stanley's $106. However, their valuations involved an EPS forecast of $1.43 for fiscal year 2003 and an EPS estimate of $2.15 for 2004, implying a growth rate of 50 percent, much higher than the corresponding forecasts of the Morgan Stanley team.

As a general matter, analysts rely heavily on the P/E heuristic to arrive at price targets, but their reports rarely, if ever, use techniques that emphasize growth opportunities (in the sense of PVGO), despite the prominence of growth opportunity-based formulas in finance textbooks. This is not to say that analysts ignore growth; they most certainly do not. However, they are inclined to focus on growth in EPS rather than growth in future NPV that forms the basis for PVGO.

Are analysts, and for that matter CFOs, inclined to form judgments of P/E in which they implicitly view high earnings growth as representative of high PVGO? In other words, do analysts and CFOs succumb to representativeness bias when forming judgments about P/E? To be sure, reliance on a PEG-based valuation heuristic is consistent with the answer being yes. In this respect, think back to Rajiv Dutta's argument in the Behavioral Pitfalls box "Attaching a Value to eBay," as well as the Morgan Stanley team's use of a PEG heuristic in arriving at a price target.

The PEG heuristic specifically states that P/E is proportional to earnings growth. Notably, legendary money manager Peter Lynch, in his book *One Up on Wall Street,* explicitly stated that for companies whose stocks are fairly valued, P/E will equal the growth rate. In contrast, standard investment textbooks warn about using PEG, indicating that it is a Wall Street rule of thumb that has shortcomings. A major shortcoming is that the value of PEG for the S&P 500 has fluctuated widely over time, in the range 1 to 1.5. In addition, keep in mind that in theory, a firm with zero PVGO will have a P/E ratio equal to $1/k_E$ no matter what its growth rate. Indeed, its growth rate will be determined by the dividend payout ratio and return on equity, with a higher payout lowering g but not P/E. There are many zero PVGO firms—most children cannot be above average—and therefore their PEG ratios are not pegged to a specific number like 1.5.

In contrast to the PEG perspective in which P/E is proportional to growth rate g, textbook theory tells us something quite different about intrinsic P/E, required return, and PVGO. Recall that the Morgan Stanley team's discussion of eBay used a rate of 12 percent to discount eBay's future cash flows, thereby treating 12 percent as eBay's required return k_E. The intrinsic forward P/E ratio of a firm with zero growth opportunities and a required return of 12 percent is 8.33 (1/0.12). At the same time, the Morgan Stanley team used a P/E ratio of 40 in their P/E valuation heuristic. If this P/E were intrinsic, then a value of 40 would imply that eBay had significant PVGO. Textbook finance theory stipulates that in order for a firm to have positive PVGO, its expected return on equity (ROE) must exceed its required return. In contrast, firms for which expected ROE equals k_E have zero growth opportunities.

Consider how, between the time eBay went public in 1998 and the time the Morgan Stanley team issued its April 2003 report, the firm's actual ROE compared to its required return. Between 1998 and 2002, eBay's ROE rose from 5 percent to a maximum of 10 percent, with an average ROE of 6.1 percent for the period.

Even though its annual growth rate of its EBITDA exceeded 90 percent every year from 2000 through 2002, its ROE never rose to the required return of 12 percent used in the Morgan Stanley report—although this does not mean that looking forward in mid-2003, eBay necessarily had zero growth opportunities and that a P/E ratio of 40 for 2005 was unjustified. However, the history of ROE up to that point does not support the intrinsic value of P/E being 40. Therefore, any justification for intrinsic P/E being that high would require identifying the magnitude of growth opportunities explicitly and in a systematic fashion.

Biases Related to the 1/*n* Heuristic: In Foresight

Consider the methodology used in Exhibit 3-1, whereby the four price target components were equally weighted. Despite the enormous dispersion in values associated with P/E, PEG, price-to-sales, and DCF, the Morgan Stanley team simply averaged the numbers, which, in their words, "combine to an average fair value of about $106."

1/*n* heuristic
A decision rule based on using the simple average of a series of variables.

The **1/*n* heuristic** is a rule of thumb that assigns the same weight to each technique component, as if they are all equally valid. In particular, textbook-favored DCF receives the same weight as the PEG heuristic, which has no basis in textbook theory. Some psychologists call the 1/*n* heuristic "tallying" and suggest that it is reasonable to use it in complex environments when the level of understanding is poor.

Valuation is certainly complex, and perhaps the wide range of valuation estimates associated with the Morgan Stanley team's four techniques suggests that they have a poor understanding of the drivers of eBay's stock market value. In this regard, the P/E ratio associated with the Morgan Stanley team's DCF-based estimate of $117 was 56, suggesting strong growth opportunities. Given that eBay's stock was trading at $89.22 a share when the report was released, a price target of $117 corresponds to an expected return of 31 percent. As 31 percent exceeds the required return of 12 percent, the implication is that eBay's stock is intrinsically undervalued.

That being said, Exhibit 3-1 tells us that the Morgan Stanley team's valuations directly based on P/E and PEG imply that eBay's stock was overvalued. The key assumption underlying the overvaluation was not the team's forecast for earnings growth, but its assumption about P/E, which the report predicted would decline from 63 to 33 between 2003 and 2005.

In applying the 1/*n* heuristic, the Morgan Stanley team assigned equal weight to the two overvaluation components and the two undervaluation components in Exhibit 3-1. At the same time, the tone of the Morgan Stanley 2003 report did not reflect the weighting and was very upbeat, calling many of eBay's elements "outstanding." The report noted that the number of "what's good" items they analyzed vastly outnumbered the number of "what's bad" items, and the analyst team's recommendation for eBay stock was "overweight." Moreover, the report indicated that all the positive trends gave the team "more confidence" in the firm's long term outlook, leading them to have much more comfort creating long-term forecasts.

A general issue associated with the *1/n* heuristic is that the judgments it generates are highly dependent on the composition of the choice menu. For example, when applied to portfolio selection in retirement plans, the *1/n* heuristic leads investors to overweigh equities when their choice menu features more equity funds than bond funds, and to underweigh equities when the reverse holds.

The Morgan Stanley team's reliance on the *1/n* heuristic implies that they assign a weight of 25 percent to eBay's stock being driven by intrinsic value. The other 75 percent reflect mispricing, with techniques based on P/E and PEG suggesting that eBay's stock was overvalued, and price-to-sales suggesting it was undervalued. Notably, if the Morgan Stanley team were to drop one of the techniques, such as the one based on PEG, the *1/n* heuristic would imply that the weight attached to intrinsic value would increase to 33 percent from 25 percent. In this regard, the Morgan Stanley team later dropped its use of the PEG-based technique—but that is getting ahead of ourselves.

Biases Using the CAPM Heuristic: In Foresight

As was noted in Exhibit 3-3, the Morgan Stanley team used the CAPM to come up with a discount rate of 12 percent for its forecasted free cash flow stream. Notably, they arrived at the 12 percent rate by using a CAPM expected return of 9.5 percent, to which they added 2.5 percent reflecting "company-specific risks." Of course, traditional textbooks argue that in a CAPM world, investors will not be compensated with higher expected returns for bearing non-market risk.

In practice, the estimates for the risk premium are wide and varied. The average textbook estimate of the market risk premium has been 6.5 percent. However, the range of values for the market risk premium across different finance textbooks has been wide—0 to 10 percent. And it has varied over time. In 2003, the range was 5 to 8 percent.

Survey evidence from 2011 for the United States shows that analysts have the lowest estimates for the market risk premium, at 5 percent, followed by financial executives at 5.6 percent and academics at 5.7 percent. However, there is more agreement among analysts about the value of the market risk premium than among the other two groups. The Morgan Stanley estimate of 4 percent fits the general pattern for analysts, as it lay below the range of academic estimates for 2003.

Estimates for beta are wide and varied.[14] Historical betas, computed over fixed windows of time such as 60 months, exhibit considerable variation over time for the same stock. The Morgan Stanley team drew their estimate of beta, 1.38, from Bloomberg. A month later, Reuters reported that eBay's beta was 1.09. A straight CAPM regression of eBay's risk premium against that of the S&P 500 for the prior 24 months yields an estimated beta of 1.9. An estimate based on 60 months yields an estimated beta of 2.8, but the early portion of the sample occurred close to eBay's IPO.

3.6 VALUATION HEURISTICS AND BIASES: IN HINDSIGHT

To evaluate the Morgan Stanley team's 2003 forecasts in hindsight, consider eBay's cumulative returns for the period May 2003 through December 2014. These are displayed in Exhibit 3-5, along with the cumulative returns for the S&P 500. A detailed chronology of eBay's history for this period is provided in the Additional Resources for this chapter.

Exhibit 3-5 shows that a $1 investment in eBay at the end of April 2003 would have produced $2.41, while a $1 investment in the S&P 500 would have produced $2.25. These values correspond to an annualized geometric return of 7.9 percent for eBay and 7.2 percent for the S&P 500. Not surprisingly, eBay's stock return volatility was much higher than that of the S&P 500.

Consider the price target for mid-2004, which the Morgan Stanley price target established in April 2003. How did that turn out? In August 2003, eBay split its

EXHIBIT 3-5
Cumulative Returns to eBay and S&P 500 Between April 2003 and December 2014

Source: Center for Research in Security Prices.

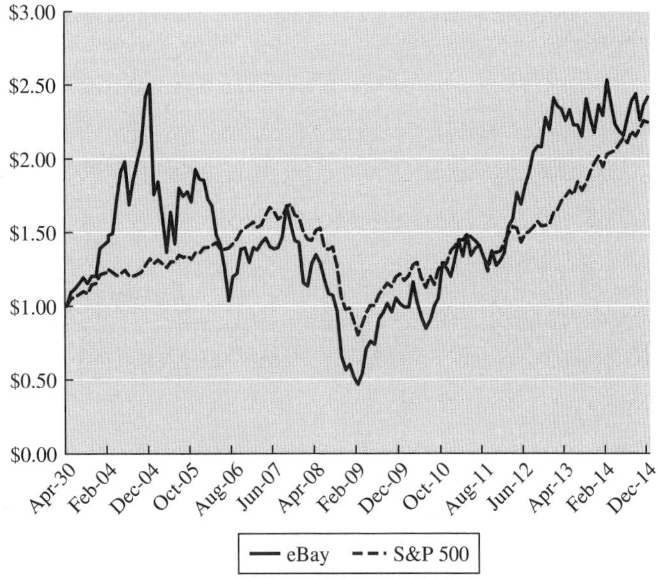

stock 2-for-1. At the end of June 2004, eBay's stock price reached $180 (on a pre-split basis), well above the Morgan Stanley team's price target of $106. Therefore, in hindsight, some might have felt justified in concluding that if anything the Morgan Stanley team was too pessimistic, not optimistic about eBay's prospects.[15]

Turning to overconfidence, notice that Exhibit 3-1 displays the Morgan Stanley team's low to high ranges for three of the four valuation components, which effectively serve as confidence intervals. Averaging the low and high values yields a range from $72 to $137. Given that $180 lies well above the high end of the range, it seems reasonable to conclude that the Morgan Stanley team was overconfident in establishing its price target.

As Exhibit 3-5 shows, eBay's stock return was very high during the early period. At year-end 2004 the firm's stock price closed (pre-split) at $232, with analysts' consensus P/E for eBay at 70, well above 47, which was the value for P/E that the Morgan Stanley team had forecast in their April 2003 report.

At the same time, consider not just price targets for 2004 that were established in 2003, but the long-term forecasts that provided the inputs for these price targets. In this regard, examine Exhibit 3-5 to see what happened from 2005 onward. Analysts' optimistic recommendations about eBay changed on January 20, 2005, when the firm announced that it had missed analysts' consensus earnings forecast by a penny a share. At the time, eBay CEO Meg Whitman indicated that future earnings would be lower because of higher advertising costs and reinvestment. In response to the announcement, eBay's stock price fell by 20 percent to $81 per share.

Investors were largely disappointed with the performance of eBay's stock until 2009, reflecting managerial decisions that had not turned out well. Thereafter, a change in management and strategy led to better performance for the firm and its stock, as can be seen in Exhibit 3-5 for the period late 2009 through December 2014.

EXHIBIT 3-6 Comparison of Morgan Stanley Forecasts from April 2003 to Actual Values for Period 2003 Through 2010

Source of data: Top panel is from Morgan Stanley Report on eBay, April 2003. Bottom panel is from Compustat, accessed through WRDS.

Forecast ($ Thousands)	2003E	2004E	2005E	2006E	2007E	2008E	2009E	2010E
Revenue	2,050,492	2,829,679	3,763,473	4,907,751	6,287,602	7,857,002	9,582,843	11,400,983
EBITDA	723,735	1,005,276	1,401,682	1,853,230	2,426,297	3,110,990	3,985,085	4,982,032
Taxes	—	—	140,168	370,646	849,204	1,088,846	1,394,780	1,743,711
Change in Working Capital	26,792	(6,849)	58,695	(9,709)	52,096	(7,375)	53,278	(4,105)
Capital Expenditures	188,908	190,000	190,000	190,000	190,000	190,000	190,000	190,000
Free Cash Flow	508,035	822,125	1,012,819	1,302,292	1,334,997	1,839,519	2,347,027	3,052,426
Actual ($ Thousands)	2003	2004	2005	2006	2007	2008	2009	2010
Revenue	2,165,096	3,271,309	4,552,401	5,969,741	7,672,329	8,541,261	8,727,362	9,156,274
EBITDA	818,209	1,312,932	1,819,872	1,967,508	2,605,825	2,844,615	2,649,098	2,837,473
Taxes	3,237	8,234	3,478	5,916	10,474	7,759	6,050	54
Change in Working Capital	29,432	190,588	4,242	(204,674)	172,318	147,623	(220,575)	899,102
Capital Expenditures	365,384	292,838	338,281	515,448	453,967	565,890	567,094	723,912
Free Cash Flow	420,156	821,272	1,473,871	1,650,818	1,969,066	2,123,343	2,296,529	1,214,405

With this history as a backdrop, how did the Morgan Stanley team's long-term forecast turn out in respect to sales, EBITDA, CapEx, working capital, and free cash flow? Exhibit 3-6 displays the comparison. We can see that the Morgan Stanley team was reasonably accurate in their forecasts for revenue and EBITDA up through the end of 2008 when the global financial crisis occurred. They were less accurate in their forecasts of taxes, working capital, and capital expenditures. Nevertheless, their forecasts of eBay's free cash flows were, if anything, too low through the end of 2009. Only in 2010 did eBay's actual free cash flow fall short of the Morgan Stanley team's forecast.

Given the difficulty of forecasting the future of a firm like eBay, the degree to which the Morgan Stanley team's forecasts for the intermediate horizon came close to the actual values is noteworthy. As for 2010 when free cash flow was well below its forecasted value, that might have been a lagged effect from the financial crisis, as revenues and EBITDA were both significantly lower than forecast.

Turning next to the terminal period, remember that more than 80 percent of the value in the 2003 Morgan Stanley price target of eBay came from terminal value, and terminal value is heavily dependent on the forecast of free cash flow in 2010. Therefore, if the 2003 DCF computation was intended to provide an estimate of eBay's intrinsic value at the time, the magnitudes of free cash flow in 2011 and the growth rate of those cash flows from 2011 onward are both crucial.

Exhibit 3-7 contrasts forecasted and actual free cash flows for the period 2002 through 2014. Here 2002, which corresponds to the actual value, is displayed as a starting value for both series. There are three important points to note from

EXHIBIT 3-7
Comparison of Morgan Stanley Team's Forecast of Free Cash Flows with Actual Free Cash Flows, 2003–2014, $million

Source of data: Morgan Stanley Report on eBay, April 2003, and Compustat accessed through WRDS.

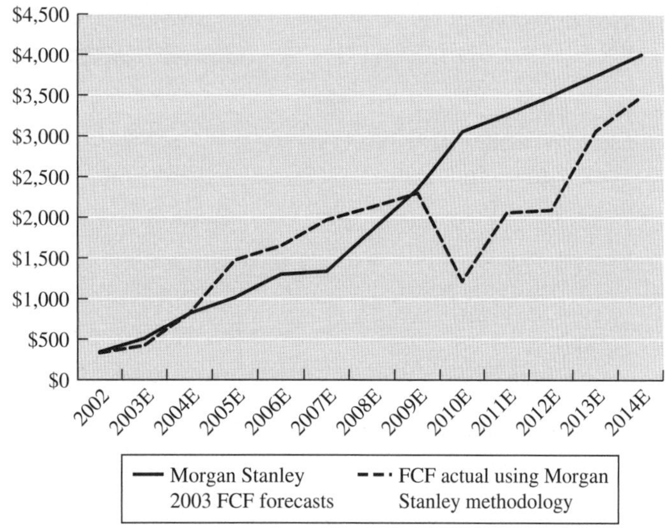

Exhibit 3-7 for the period beginning in 2011. First, actual FCF lay below forecasted FCF. Second, the growth rate of FCF after 2010 is highly variable, but does appear to be consistent with the forecasted growth rate after 2011. It just began at a lower level.

Third, by 2010 the Morgan Stanley team, with some but not all of the original members, had changed parts of its approach. For one thing, it dropped the use of the PEG heuristic. For another, it modified its views on the long-term growth rate of free cash flows, and lowered its forecast from 7 percent to 4.5 percent, with the terminal horizon beginning in 2020. This modification is highly significant, and raises the following question: In 2003, did the Morgan Stanley team exhibit bias by choosing a terminal horizon that began too early and featured too high a long-term growth rate, not so much for the period around 2011, but for the period further into the future that would begin later, such as in 2020? Coming back to the discussion of CAPM, a CAPM regression for the period May 2003 through December 2014 produces an estimate of beta that is 1.5, with an estimated alpha that is effectively zero. In hindsight, the Morgan Stanley team's 1.38 estimate of beta was a little low, but within range of the subsequent actual value of 1.5 for the period. The team's estimate of 4 percent for the market risk premium was much lower than its historical value and its value for the intermediate horizon. The annualized geometric return for the S&P 500 was 7.2 percent, its annualized arithmetic return was 8.2 percent, and its annualized arithmetic risk premium was 6.8 percent.

3.7 BIASES ASSOCIATED WITH FREE CASH FLOW FORMULA

The Morgan Stanley team used the textbook formula for free cash flow in its DCF analysis. It is important to understand the basis for this formula, and how it relates to the value of a firm and the value of its equity.

Corporate Nudges

Errors or biases: Misvaluing stocks.
Why does it happen? Managers and analysts rely on crude heuristics to measure fundamental value, use biased forecasts of future cash flows, and misframe free cash flows.
How does it happen? Managers and analysts find heuristics based on P/E, PEG, and price-to-sales to be simpler and more intuitive than DCF. Moreover, managers and analysts are prone to using cash flows that reflect biases stemming from excessive optimism and misframing.
What can be done about it? Managers and analysts can:

- Apply a variety of valuation techniques that are firmly grounded in textbook theory, in addition to crude ratio-based heuristics, and weight them sensibly.
- Ensure that terminal value based on free cash flow features zero PVGO, and if not, have a reasonable explanation for why not.
- Develop confidence intervals for valuation judgments that can be calibrated over time.
- Avoid the dogmatic use of heuristics that tie P/E to earnings growth.
- Prepare free cash flow forecasts based on cash flow from operations, cash flow from investment, and interest paid.

The textbook formula for the free cash flow FCF of a firm is:

$$\text{FCF} = \text{EBIT}(1 - \text{tax rate}) + \text{Depreciation} - \text{CapEx} - \text{Change in Working Capital}$$

An alternative formula for free cash flow is based on items appearing in the Statement of Cash Flows. The alternative formula is to add cash flow from operations and interest paid, and then to subtract cash flow from investment (where a positive entry for investment is interpreted as a cash outflow).

Technically, the most important issue relating to the two formulas for computing free cash flow is that CapEx is only one component of cash flow from investment. Conceptually, the most important issue is that the textbook formula might feature bias and not yield the amount of cash per year a firm generates that is available to be paid to its investors. Cash flow available to be paid to investors is the sum of cash flow actually paid and cash flow added to cash and marketable securities. A discussion in the Additional Resources to Chapter 3 uses eBay's financial statements to illustrate that between 2002 and 2014 the present value of cash flow available to be paid to the firm's investors was roughly one-third of the value associated with the free cash flows computed using the textbook formula. In retrospect, investors who relied on the textbook formula for free cash flow to estimate the amount of cash eBay generated that was available to be paid to them should have felt duped.

3.8 AGENCY CONFLICTS

It is important to keep in mind that analysts face conflicts of interest. Analysts are not necessarily objective evaluators, but instead are agents of financial organizations that seek to do business with the firms being covered. These organizations earn fees from firms' raising external capital, and earn commissions from the trading of their securities. In respect to Morgan Stanley, that point is prominently noted in a text box on the first page of the Morgan Stanley team's report.

The managers of firms prefer favorable coverage from analysts to unfavorable coverage. Therefore, analysts whose firms seek to do business with the companies that analysts cover have an incentive to generate favorable reports. This agency conflict may induce analysts to be excessively optimistic about their forecasts of earnings and cash flows. The agency conflict might also induce analysts to view valuation heuristics as alternative instruments that can provide numbers they want to deliver. In other words, excessive optimism and the reliance on heuristics may have an agency conflict component as well as a behavioral component.

The general evidence is that agency issues explain some but not all of the biases in analysts' price targets. An important indication of the impact of agency considerations is that the forecasted returns implied by analysts' price targets are unjustifiably higher for firms that raise external financing than those that do not. Price target-based forecasted returns are also positively related to trading volume, controlling for firm size—and yet, realized returns and volume are uncorrelated.

Summary

The main takeaway from this chapter is that heuristics and biases play a major role in valuation. The financial world is an imperfect place. This is not to say that financial textbooks fail to offer rigorous techniques for doing valuation. Textbooks do provide structured valuation processes, some of which are quite sophisticated. Nevertheless, in practice, a lot of valuation is heuristically driven. This chapter has concentrated on the case of a single firm, eBay, to illustrate the point. To be sure, it is important to refrain from overgeneralizing from a single case, and the chapter minicase provides an opportunity to investigate valuation issues for another firm and the judgments of other analysts.

Optimism, overconfidence, representativeness, and anchoring are psychological phenomena that arose several times in the discussion about eBay, and were manifest in questions such as the following: Did the Morgan Stanley team's assumed growth rate for terminal value reflect excessive optimism? Was the fact that the actual stock price lay outside their forecast range imply that they were overconfident? Do analysts generally view earnings growth as representative of growth opportunities in the sense of PVGO? Do analysts' free cash flow forecasts for the terminal period implicitly assume positive growth opportunities? In arriving at a discount rate, do analysts anchor on estimates based on the CAPM? Do CFOs rely on a PEG heuristic because they regard earnings growth as the basis for P/E? Do analysts, financial executives, and investors misframe free cash flows because they employ the textbook definition of free cash flow when that definition is overly simplistic? Although it is difficult to be definitive, good arguments can be made that the answer to each of these questions is yes.

Several factors contribute to the reliance on valuation heuristics instead of the fundamental valuation techniques taught in textbooks. Heuristics are simpler to use: P/E, PEG, and price-to-sales require very few variables and involve simple formulas compared to the DCF-based analyses taught in textbooks.

Moreover, analysts face agency conflicts. They need to manage relations with the managers of the firms they cover. Hence, they might choose valuation heuristics strategically, in order to arrive at numbers that will please managers.

Additional Behavioral Readings

Martin, J. and J. W. Petty, *Value Based Management.* Boston: Harvard Business School Press, 2000.

Montier, J., *Behavioural Finance.* West Sussex, UK: Wiley, 2002.

Rappaport, A. and M. Mauboussin, *Expectations Investing.* Boston: Harvard Business School Press, 2002.

Wingfield, N., "Stock of eBay Acts Like . . . eBay, But How Can Shares Stay Lofty? The Bullish Projections Assume Gigantic Rise in Online Shopping," *The Wall Street Journal,* April 23, 2003.

"eBay at Bear, Stearns & Co. Inc. 16th Annual Technology Conference – Final," *FD (FAIR DISCLOSURE) WIRE,* June 8, 2005.

"eBay Inc at Citi Global Technology Conference – Final," *CQ FD Disclosure,* September 4, 2014.

Bhatia, S., "The History of eBay," *The Telegraph Online,* November 17, 2015.

Key Terms

1/*n* heuristic, *71*
growth opportunities bias, *69*
P/E heuristic, *60*
PEG heuristic, *60*
price-to-sales heuristic, *60*
valuation by comparables, *59*

Explore the Web

www.ebay.com
The web site for eBay contains financial information about the firm, as well as serving as a gateway to the firm's transaction services.

www.morganstanley.com
The web site for Morgan Stanley has an interesting section where institutional investors can view sample reports.

www.aetna.com
The web site for Aetna has several sections of interest, especially Who We Are and Investors.

Chapter Questions

1. In its April 2003 report, the Morgan Stanley team computed EBITDA as "Adjusted Operating Income plus Depreciation Addback." The adjustment in question is to "Reported Operating Income." The report explained the adjustment as follows: "eBay includes unusual items such as amortization of stock compensation in operating expenses and then adjusts these with 'add back charges.' Adjusted operating income removes these items from operating expenses and treats them directly as 'below-the-line' unusual items." That is, the adjustment moves line items from their position as components of reported operating income further down in the income statement. As a result, the value of EBITDA used in the report is higher than it would have been had reported operating income been used instead. Discuss the relevance of the approach taken in the report.
2. In the spring of 2003, analysts at Prudential established a target price for eBay, justifying the P/E values in their analysis by appeal to PEG. Their report stated that their assumptions of a P/E of 75 to multiply 2003 earnings, and a P/E of 50 to multiply 2004 earnings

   > . . . equates to P/E/G ratios of 1.5 and 1.0, respectively, which we believe are reasonable, compared with those of other growth companies. We note that the S&P 500 currently trades at approximately 16.5 times forward-year earnings, equating to a P/E/G ratio of 1.3.

   Discuss the reasoning of the Prudential analysts.
3. In 2005, eBay CFO Rajiv Dutta stated that eBay's investments were reflected in the firm's income statement rather than its balance sheet. Discuss the extent to which Dutta's perspective, in foresight, was reflected in the Morgan Stanley team's April 2003 report. Then discuss whether both Dutta's perspective and the Morgan Stanley team's forecasts of CapEx were accurate in hindsight.
4. The column "Ahead of the Tape" that appeared in the February 13, 2004, issue of *The Wall Street Journal* states that prudent investors prefer to value firms using free cash flow instead of EBITDA. The article explains that the typical definition of free cash flow is cash flow from operations minus capital expenditure, not EBITDA minus capital expenditure. Discuss these comments.
5. Analyst Safa Rashtchy developed his 2010 forecast for eBay's revenue by assuming that its annual growth would be about a 30 percent compounded annual growth rate between 2002 and 2010. In the previous year, eBay's revenue had grown at the rate of 62 percent, and the firm forecast that its revenue would increase by 58 percent in 2003. Which, if any, of the behavioral elements described in Chapter 1 might have affected Rashtchy's long-term forecast?
6. Consider the following excerpt from a Prudential report on Wal-Mart, dated May 13, 2003.[16] The report states:

   > We are maintaining our Hold rating on Wal-Mart as we believe the stock's current valuation of 28 times our 2003 EPS estimate of $2.01 adequately reflects the company's 13% 5-year EPS growth rate . . . Wal-Mart is currently trading at 28.2 times our 2003 EPS estimate of $2.01, a 57% premium to S&P 500. This is not far from the retailer's five-year average high premium of 59%. The stock is also close to its 52-week high of $59.30, achieved in May 2002. It is difficult for us to envision investors paying an even larger premium, particularly for 13% projected growth. We believe the stock will continue to hover around a 55% premium to the market multiple or 27.9 times. Using this valuation and our 2003 EPS estimate of $2.01 yields a 12-month price target of $56, up from $55.

   Discuss the merits of the valuation technique mentioned in this excerpt, with reference to the contents of the chapter.
7. Consider the assumptions in Exhibit 3-2 that underlie the valuations associated with P/E, PEG, and price-to-sales. Analyze the degree to which these assumptions are mutually

consistent, and correspondingly whether the heuristic equations were properly applied. In addition, discuss what to make of the wide dispersion in the three associated valuations.

8. In respect to the Morgan Stanley 2003 report on eBay, eBay's annualized geometric return between May 2003 and December 2014 was 7.9 percent, its annualized arithmetic return was 14.2 percent, and its annualized arithmetic risk premium was 12.7 percent. In light of this information, how would you judge the Morgan Stanley team's assumption of a 12 percent discount rate?
9. On April 23, 2003, *The Wall Street Journal* published an article suggesting that the analysts following eBay were excessively optimistic about eBay's future revenue stream. The article pointed out that the second most optimistic analyst was Safa Rashtchy, the author of the U.S. Bancorp Piper Jaffray report. The author of the article, Nick Wingfield, interviewed Safa Rashtchy and asked him to consider whether his 30 percent revenue growth forecasts for eBay were unduly optimistic. Wingfield reported that Rashtchy reacted by reconsidering his assumption that eBay could grow at a 30 percent compounded rate between 2002 and 2010.[17] On January 20, 2005, eBay announced that it had missed analysts' consensus earnings forecast by a penny a share. In response to the announcement, eBay's stock price fell by 20 percent to $81 per share. Thereupon, Rashtchy downgraded his recommendation on eBay from "outperform" to "market perform," stating that the stock had been priced for perfection. He also lowered his earnings estimate for 2005 by 5.3 percent, but maintained his price target of $101 per share. Discuss Rashtchy's judgments about eBay.
10. In the section of the book web site for this chapter, you will find an Excel file containing counterparts to the free cash flow table in Exhibit 3-3, but for forecasts and valuations made in 2010 and 2013. Use the analysis described in the chapter to investigate whether the terminal growth rates assumed in these tables is consistent with PVGO being zero. For this purpose, assume that over time, eBay maintains a constant ratio of depreciation to CapEx, and that this ratio is 52 percent.[18] For this purpose, assume that over time, eBay maintains a constant 52 percent ratio of depreciation to CapEx.
11. For the period 2010 through 2014, the Morgan Stanley team's 2010 report on eBay forecasted that free cash flow would on average grow by 5.7 percent. Free cash flow actually grew by an average growth rate of 16.7 percent during this period. Discuss the nature of this forecast error from a behavioral perspective.
12. In 2010, the Morgan Stanley analysts covering eBay had stopped using PEG to value eBay, relying on P/E, P/S, and discounted values of free cash flows. In 2013, they dropped P/E and P/S, and only used discounted free cash flows. In 2015, they based their price targets primarily on P/E, and claimed to rely on discounted values of free cash flows as "support" and a "sanity check." How would you interpret these changes over time in valuation methodology?
13. The Morgan Stanley report on eBay, dated July 23, 2015, established a one-year forward price target of $29 per share.[19] At the time of the report, eBay's stock price was $28.45, which the report noted implied a target price appreciation of 2 percent. The discounted free cash flow analysis in the report contained three cases, a base case involving a target price per share of $34, a bull case involving a price of $38 per share (and implicit target return of 34 percent), and a bear case involving a price per share of $24 (and implicit target return of −16 percent). The report used $24 to $38 as its interval forecast range and $29 as its point forecast. A spreadsheet for the base case is provided at the book web site, and shows that the report discounted eBay's free cash flows at8 percent, described as its WACC, and used a terminal growth rate of 1 percent. Check to see if the free cash flow computations were done correctly. Then discuss the methodology the Morgan Stanley team used to arrive at their forecasts.

Additional Resources and Materials for Chapter 3 Are Available at www.mhhe.com/shefrin2e

Minicase

Aetna

Based in Hartford, Connecticut, Aetna is a large diversified health care benefits firm. It serves approximately 44 million people, making it the third-largest American managed care organization (MCO) by membership. Its members are diverse, being composed of employer groups, health plans, health care providers, governmental units, government-sponsored plans, labor groups, individuals, and expatriates. Aetna is a global company. Its global health care benefits support approximately half a million members residing in almost every country. The firm offers a wide range of health care insurance products that include medical, dental, pharmacy, group life, and disability plans, as well as Medicaid health care management services.

In May 2013, Aetna completed the acquisition of the MCO Coventry Health Care Inc. in a cash and stock deal worth $5.7 billion. It did so to strengthen its presence in government-financed health care. By doing so, Aetna added approximately 3.7 million medical members and 1.5 million Medicare Part D members. At the time, the firm's guidance was for full-year operating earnings estimate to fall in the range of $5.70 to $5.85 a share.

At the end of July 2013, Aetna announced that its second-quarter earnings had risen by 17 percent, reflecting its growth in membership and revenue. Total medical membership had grown to 22 million as of June 30, from 18.3 million in the previous quarter. As a result, the firm increased its full-year operating earnings estimate to a range of $5.80 to $5.90 per share. At the beginning of 2013, the firm forecast that adjusted earnings would be at least $5.40 per share, but had already raised the forecast three times.

The weak economic conditions that followed the global financial crisis and great recession had led consumers to reduce their health care expenditures, which in turn restrained costs in Aetna's commercial insurance business, as well as competitors such as UnitedHealth Group and WellPoint. For the quarter, the amount of premiums Aetna used to pay patient medical costs, known as its *total medical benefit ratio,* was 82.5 percent, compared to 82.4 percent a year earlier and 81.9 percent during the previous quarter. At the same time, there was awareness that an improving U.S. economy would induce consumers to resume their previous patterns of health-care usage.

Aetna's CEO Mark Bertolini indicated that he was cautiously optimistic about prospects for 2014, when new health care exchanges were expected to begin operating, as required by the Patient Protection and Affordable Health Care Act, so-called Obamacare. In a July conference call with analysts, Bertolini expressed his optimism when he described being "increasingly confident that we will grow both operating earnings and operating EPS in 2014." Bertolini's caution stemmed from concerns about exchange readiness and rates, which would affect the profitability of participating in the exchanges, many of which were run by the states. In this regard, Bertolini said to analysts: "I will tell you we remain very cautious if not more cautious." Aetna's CFO Shawn Guertin explained what that caution meant for the number of states where Aetna might participate in 2014 when the exchanges would first begin operating. He stated that the financial projections were "working to push the number downward, and not up."[20]

For its second quarter the consensus analyst earnings forecast from Thomson Reuters was for earnings per share (EPS) of $1.41 on revenue of $11.99 billion. Actual revenue turned out to be $11.54 billion, an increase of 31 percent, but Aetna reported EPS of $1.49 a share, corresponding to earnings of $536 million, up from $457.6 million or $1.32 a year earlier. Operating earnings increased to $1.52 a share from $1.31 the previous year, which led the firm to change its guidance for full-year operating earnings, as was mentioned above.

From the beginning of 2013 until the end of July, Aetna's stock increased by 38 percent, and it closed at $64.17 on July 31. Even before its second quarter earnings announcement, analysts had begun revising their price targets upward. Earlier in July, a Jefferies analyst raised his price target from $74 to $77. Immediately after the announcement, Citigroup increased its price target from $68 to $72, noting that "Aetna should have the fastest earnings growth among the large-cap plans in 2014/2015, and yet it trades at the lowest multiple in the group."[21] During the first week of August Cantor Fitzgerald increased its price target from $60 to $65 a share. In mid-September, Bank of America/Merrill Lynch stated that Aetna's current valuation overly discounted the risks associated with health care reform and exchanges, and increased its price target from $68 to $79.

The consensus analyst forecast for Aetna's third-quarter EPS was $1.52 per share on approximately $12.87 billion in revenue. On October 28, Aetna announced that its third-quarter earnings had increased by 4 percent to $518.6 million, or $1.38 per share on revenue of $13.04 billion. The firm noted that excluding items such as integration costs, its adjusted EPS was $1.50 per share. In respect to the negative earnings surprise, the lead Citigroup analyst covering Aetna commented that even in its previous conference call, the firm had talked down third-quarter earnings.

In its announcement, Aetna explained that poor performance from two products and federal budget cuts that year had hurt its Medicare business (Medicare Advantage, MA). Health care costs, which were its largest expense, had increased 57 percent in the quarter. The firm reiterated that its 2013 adjusted earnings would range between $5.80 and $5.90 per share. The market response to Aetna's third-quarter earnings announcement was a decline in its stock price by 1.9 percent to $60.63, but the stock's October close a few days later was at $62.70.

The reports of analysts covering Aetna, whose stock ticker is AET, were varied in their price targets and associated methodologies. Below are four examples.

Jefferies: In its report dated October 29, when Aetna's stock was trading at $61.78, Jefferies stated the following, noting that it was maintaining its price target of $77 from July:

> We continue to believe AET can modestly grow earnings next year and increase EPS 15%+ in 2015. 3Q results were uneventful, but the company guided to a 2014 EPS floor that implies modest growth and improves visibility. AET's 12/12 Investor Day will bring more 2014 clarity. We reiterate our Buy rating on AET, which is the cheapest MCO stock (9.8x/8.4x 2014-15E EPS) . . .
>
> Valuation/Risks: Our $77 PT reflects a P/E multiple of 12.4x our 2014E EPS. AET trades at 9.8x our 2014E EPS, which is below the broader peer average of 10.7x and its historical 11.1x. Risks: 1) spike in cost trend, 2) Coventry integration, 3) Exchanges, 4) 2014 MA headwinds . . .
>
> The price targets are based on several methodologies which may include, but are not restricted to, analyses of market risk, growth rate, revenue stream, discounted cash flow (DCF), EBITDA, EPS, cash flow (CF), free cash flow (FCF), EV/EBITDA, P/E, PE/growth, P/CF, P/FCF, premium (discount)/average group EV/EBITDA, premium (discount)/average group P/E, sum of the parts, net asset value, dividend returns, and return on equity (ROE) over the next 12 months.

Cantor Fitzgerald: In its report dated October 29, when Aetna's stock was trading at $61.78, Cantor Fitzgerald stated the following:

> We are maintaining our 2013–14 earnings estimates, $65 price target and HOLD rating. Although, strictly speaking, 3Q:13 was a slight miss, it was mostly in line, and the company expects 2014 EPS to be at least flat with this year's guidance of $5.80–$5.90. The company's Medicare book, half of which is group (experienced rated), is reporting higher loss ratios, and management is cautious about the 2014 outlook for the individual MA business, but Aetna is less exposed than other national carriers and says that its exchange business (focused on catastrophic and bronze plans) will not materially increase its individual book, which accounts for 3% of revenue.
>
> We arrive at our $65 price target for AET by comparing its current valuation on 2014 estimated earnings with that of other large commercial plans and the stock's own trading history. Our target price equates to 10.8x our 2014 EPS estimate of $6.00. At its current valuation of 10.3x our 2014 EPS estimate, AET trades roughly at parity with the group, consistent with its traditional in-line valuation, despite the potentially transformative changes in senior management in recent years and the 5/7/13 acquisition of Coventry Healthcare.

Leerink Swann: In its report dated November 19, when Aetna's stock was trading at $65.08, Leerink Swann stated the following:

> We use an absolute and relative P/E multiple-based approach to valuation on the average of our 2014 and 2015 EPS estimates. We combine the P/E-based approach with a DCF model that points to the intrinsic value of the company . . .
>
> Valuation has pulled back to 10x P/E with 2014E earnings upside the most important catalyst. Our 12–18 month Price Target of $72 contemplates a P/E of 10.5x the average of 2014 + 2015 estimated EPS views . . . (See Exhibit 3-8.)

ValuEngine: In its report dated November 19, when Aetna's stock was trading at $64.75, ValuEngine had a one-year price target of $67.28 for Aetna, and stated the following:

> **FAIR MARKET VALUATION PRICE:** Based on available data as of Nov. 19, 2013, we believe that AET should be trading at $49.68. This makes AET 30.32% overvalued. Fair Value indicates what we believe the stock should be trading at today if the stock market were perfectly efficient and everything traded at its true worth. For AET, we base this on actual earnings per share (EPS) for the previous four quarters

EXHIBIT 3-8 **Leerink Swann Free Cash Flow Table for Aetna**

Dec Yr	1Q	2Q	3Q	4Q	FYRev	1Q	2Q	3Q	4Q	FY	EPS	P/E
2012A	$8,864.00	$8,827.00	$8.899.00	$8.955.00	$35,545.00		$1.34	$1.31	$1.55	$0.94	$5.13	12.7x
2013E	$9,507.0A	$11,537.0A	$12,994. 0A	$13,694. 00	$47,754.00		$1.50A	$1.52A	$1.50A	$1.36	$5.87	11.1x
2014E	—	—	—	—	$56,118.00		—	—	—	—	$6.32	10.3x
2015E	—	—	—	—	$59,672.00		—	—	—	—	$7.03	9.3x

AET DCF Valuation

Source: Company Reports, Leerink Swann Research Estimates.

	2009	2010	2011	2012	2013E	2014E	2015E	2016E	2017E	2018E	2019E	Terminal Value	Terminal Year
Operating Revenues	$33,643	$32,962	$32,681	$34,628	$46,851	$55,099	$58,493	$62,402	$66,463	$70,516	$74,580		$78,309
% Growth	9.6%	–2.0%	–0.9%	6.0%	35.3%	17.6%	6.2%	6.7%	6.5%	6.1%	5.8%		5.0%
EBIT	$1,079	$1,572	$2,373	$2,045	$2,732	$2,937	$2,886	$2,847	$2,793	$2,663	$2,491		$1,958
% Margin	3.2%	4.8%	7.3%	5.9%	5.8%	5.3%	4.9%	4.6%	4.2%	3.8%	3.3%		2.5%
Investment Income	$1,036	$1,056	$931	$917	$882	$1,021	$1,291	$1,440	$1,611	$1,841	$2,097		$2,202
Operating Income	$2,115	$2,629	$3,304	$2,963	$3,614	$3,958	$4,177	$4,287	$4,404	$4,504	$4,588		$4,159
% Margin	6.30%	8.00%	10.10%	8.60%	7.70%	7.20%	7.10%	6.90%	6.60%	6.40%	6.20%		5.30%
Taxes	–767	–953	–1,198	–1,074	–1,311	–1,435	–1,515	–1,555	–1,597	–1,633	–1,664		–1,508
NOPAT	$1,348	$1,675	$2,106	$1,888	$2,303	$2,523	$2,662	$2,732	$2,807	$2,871	$2,924		$2,651
(+) D&A				$450	$703	$826	$877	$936	$997	$1,058	$1,119	$1,17	
(–) CapEx				–338	–609	–735	–799	–874	–953	–1,034	–1,119	–1,175	
(–) Chg. in Working Cap.				292	1,834	1,237	509	586	609	608	610	559	
Free Cash Flow				$2,292	$4,231	$3,852	$3,249	$3,381	$3,460	$3,502	$3,534	$42,804	$3,210
Reform Haircut				0%	0%	0%	0%	0%	0%	0%	0%	0%	0%
Adjusted Free Cash Flow				$2,292	$4,231	$3,852	$3,249	$3,381	$3,460	$3,502	$3,534	$42,804	$3,210
Misc. Operating Metrics													
D&A					1.3%	1.5%	1.5%	1.5%	1.5%	1.5%	1.5%	1.5%	1.5%
CapEx					1.0%	1.3%	1.3%	1.4%	1.4%	1.4%	1.5%	1.5%	1.5%
ΔWC/ΔRevs.					–15.0%	–15.0%	–15.0%	–15.0%	–15.0%	–15.0%	–15.0%	–15.0%	–15.0%
Years Out				0	0.3	1.3	2.3	3.3	4.3	5.3	6.3	7.3	
Discount Factor @ 9.0%				1	0.979	0.898	0.824	0.756	0.693	0.636	0.584	0.535	
PV of Cash Flows				$2,292	$4,141	$3,458	$2,676	$2,555	$2,399	$2,228	$2,062	$22,916	
PV of Forecast Period FCFs	$23,950												
PV of Terminal Value	$22,916												
Enterprise Value	$46,866												
Equity Value per Share Calculation													
Enterprise Value	$46,866												
(–) Debt	($8,350)												
(+) Cash	$990												
Equity Value	$39,507												
Diluted Shares	368												
Value Per Share	$107.44												

Source: Company Reports, Leerink Swann Research Estimates.

of $5.60, forecasted EPS for the next four quarters of $6.16, and correlations to the 30-year Treasury bond yield of 3.50% . . . ..

FORECASTED TARGET PRICES: The predictive variables used in ValuEngine's forecast target price models include both proprietary and well-established forecasting variables derived from credible financial research studies and publications. Our forecasting models capture, among other things, several important tendencies that stock price consistently exhibit: Short-term price reversals, Intermediate-term momentum continuation, and Long-term price reversals. We use a distinct forecasting model for each time horizon and for every industry. We then apply the most advanced statistical/econometric techniques to ensure that our stock return forecasts are as reliable as possible . . .

We present a valuation based on one of three market ratios: PEG (price to trailing 4 quarter earnings ratio, divided by the consensus analyst forecasted next year EPS growth), P/E (price to forward 4 quarter earnings ratio), and P/S ratio (price to trailing 4 quarter sales). Among the three, PEG is the most informative as it reflects both the price/earnings ratio and expected future EPS growth, while P/E is better than P/S. For each given stock, we apply the PEG to give a fair value assessment if both its trailing 4 quarter EPS and forecasted EPS growth rate are positive. If its forecasted EPS growth is negative but its forward 4 quarter EPS is positive, we apply the P/E to give a fair value for the stock as of today. Otherwise, we resort to the P/S to assess its fair value.

To establish a valuation standard, we use both (i) the average historical market ratio of the stock over the past 10 years (or however long there is data available for the stock), and (ii) the average market ratio today of five comparable stocks in the same sector and from companies of similar size. These two alternative perspectives should give you a good idea about where this stock's valuation stands today.

1. Valuation Based on AET's Past PEG: Over the past 10 years, AET's average PEG is 2.84. AET earned $5.60 per share in its recent 4 quarters. The analyst consensus estimate is $6.16 for its 4 quarter forward EPS. AET's current price sales ratio is 0.55. The following assessment is based on multiplying the historical PEG with recent 4 quarter EPS and the forecasted EPS growth rate over the next 4 quarters for AET.

Fair Value	
Historical Average PEG	2.84
PEG-Based Fair Value	$159.75

2. Valuation Based on Comparables' PEG: AET's comparables are CNC, HNT, HUM, WCG and WLP. The current PEG average of these comparables is 1.66. AET earned $5.60 per share in its recent 4 quarters. The analyst consensus estimate is $6.16 for its 4-quarter-forward EPS. AET's current price sales ratio is 0.55. The following assessment is based on multiplying comparable stocks' average PEG today with AET's recent 4 quarter EPS and the forecasted EPS growth rate over the next 4 quarters.

Comparables' PEG	
Comparables	Current PEG
CNC	0.69
HNT	n/a
HUM	n/a
WCG	2.64
WLP	n/a

Fair Value	
Comparable Stocks Ag PEG	1.66
Comparable PEG-Based Fair Value	$93.72

An Excel file containing historical financial statements for Aetna is available on the book web site, **www.mhhe.com/shefrin2e.**

Case Analysis Questions

1. What insights from the discussion of the Morgan Stanley 2003 report on eBay apply to the 2013 report on Aetna by Jefferies?
2. What insights from the discussion of the Morgan Stanley 2003 report on eBay apply to the 2013 report on Aetna by Cantor Fitzgerald?
3. What insights from the discussion of the Morgan Stanley 2003 report on eBay apply to the 2013 report on Aetna by Leerink Swann?
4. What insights from the discussion of the Morgan Stanley 2003 report on eBay apply to the 2013 report on Aetna by ValuEngine?
5. How would you use behavioral concepts to explain generally why different analysts arrive at different price targets?

Chapter Four

Capital Budgeting

The main objective of this chapter is for students to demonstrate that they can identify the manner in which heuristics, biases and framing effects adversely impact managers' forecasts of project cash flows and their decisions about project adoption and termination.

After completing this chapter students will be able to:

1. Explain why excessive optimism and overconfidence lead managers to adopt negative net-present-value projects because of cost overruns, revenue shortfalls, and late completion times.
2. Explain why the combination of aversion to a sure loss, regret, and confirmation bias leads managers to continue failing projects when they should terminate those projects.
3. Explain why managers who avoid discounted cash flow analysis and instead rely exclusively on the affect heuristic are prone to select low-value projects over high-value projects.
4. Distinguish between the remedies appropriate to agency conflicts and the remedies appropriate to behavioral biases.

4.1 TRADITIONAL TREATMENT OF CAPITAL BUDGETING

The traditional approach to capital budgeting emphasizes different criteria for assessing project cash flows, including the manner in which project risk is incorporated into the analysis. The most important criterion that academics recommend for deciding whether or not to adopt a project is net present value (NPV). In theory, NPV measures the incremental fundamental value the project would create for the firm's investors, were it to be adopted.

The starting point for obtaining the project discount rate is typically the firm's cost of capital, the expected return that investors require in order to hold the firm's long-term debt and equity. In theory, the cost of capital is estimated as a weighted average of its constituent components, where the weights are market values. In practice, managers confront a series of challenges in deriving appropriate discount rates. These challenges involve having to rely on asset pricing models to estimate the cost of equity and having to adjust the cost of capital to reflect differential project risk, taxes, and transaction costs.

A close cousin of NPV is the concept of internal rate of return (IRR). Any discount rate that leads a project's cash flows to have an NPV of zero is said to be an IRR for the project. Some managers may use IRR in deciding whether or not to adopt a project. A typical decision rule is to accept a project if it has an IRR that is at least as high as the required return k. Notably, a project may have more than one IRR. This can happen when there is more than one change in sign in the project's expected cash flow stream.

Some firms use a payback rule to evaluate project proposals. The payback period is defined as the length of time it takes for the sum of future cash flows to cover the initial investment. Traditional textbooks are often critical of the payback rule, as it is not value-based.

4.2 THE PLANNING FALLACY

CONCEPT PREVIEW
Question 4.1

Consider four different types of tasks you undertook in the past, for which you had deadlines.

1. Everyday tasks around the home
2. Holiday shopping
3. Completing income tax returns
4. School assignments

On average, how accurate are you in predicting when you will complete the tasks described above, relative to your plans?

1. Much earlier than predicted
2. Earlier than predicted
3. As predicted
4. Later than predicted
5. Much later than predicted

Now consider a different question about these tasks. The next time you plan to do each of these tasks, how do you predict the outcomes will turn out?

1. Much earlier than predicted
2. Earlier than predicted
3. As predicted
4. Later than predicted
5. Much later than predicted

the planning fallacy
Establishing excessively optimistic and overconfident plans that fail to take into account past excessive optimism and overconfidence.

Even though there is a fair amount of dispersion in the way that people answer these questions, people tend to be more optimistic about being earlier on completing the next project than they were on past projects. This phenomenon, of failing to learn the lessons of the past about planning times, is called "**the planning fallacy**." The planning fallacy is remarkably resilient.

The heart of the planning fallacy is that people do not take their own past tardiness sufficiently into account when making predictions about how long it will take them to complete future tasks. For the most part, it seems that people act as if they ignore the past. Instead they formulate their plans as though they will complete these tasks as predicted rather than, as in the past, later than predicted. Moreover, on average they end up completing those tasks later than predicted, just as they had in the past.

In the business world, a great many projects come in over budget, miss their deadlines, and fail to deliver on all promised features. Although most managers are aware of these general tendencies, they fail to adjust for these tendencies in preparing forecasts for future projects. The planning fallacy is alive and thriving in the business world.

Planning typically involves laying out a set of steps to complete a task. Basically, people who succumb to the planning fallacy do not appreciate the vast number of ways in which the future might unfold. Instead, they get fixated on an imagined specific scenario or story, which is natural as people often think in narrative terms.

Moreover, the planning story in people's minds usually has a happy ending: and therein lies the rub. The typical planner establishes as his or her planned scenario an optimistic scenario in which very little or nothing goes wrong. In other words, the typical planner does not give enough attention to the manner in which his or her plans might fail.

Psychologists who study the planning fallacy suggest that its key driver is people paying excessive attention to narratives, and overweighing occurrence of steps associated with planned scenarios. After all, the steps associated with planned scenarios should terminate in success. Naturally, having a planned scenario terminate successfully is quite reasonable. Some might call this having "vision." The difficulty is that the steps in the successful plan are highly salient, whereas the competing failure scenarios are less salient.

Biased inputs typically produce faulty decisions. The planning fallacy combines different psychological biases: excessive optimism, overconfidence, and confirmation bias play critical roles. In addition, aspiration-based risk seeking and aversion to a sure loss can also be involved. In order to illustrate how the planning fallacy plays out in practice, consider an example involving the development of two airliners, Airbus's 380 and Boeing's 787.

The Planning Fallacy in Aircraft Manufacturing

In the late 1990s, Boeing and Airbus dominated airline manufacturing, with Boeing being the larger firm. In December 2000, Airbus adopted a project for a new large aircraft, the Airbus A380. The executives at Airbus promised to begin delivering the Airbus 380 in early 2006, about five years after the launch of the project.

In 2003, Boeing executives decided to develop a large aircraft of their own, the 787, which they later called the Dreamliner. A surge of advance orders made the 787 the fastest-selling new jet in history.

In 2006, the date for delivering the A380 to customers was fast approaching, and the A380 was not ready to be delivered. Something had gone wrong with the wiring in the plane's electrical system. In June 2006 Airbus announced a postponement to its delivery schedule, saying that of the 25 aircraft it originally promised customers by 2007 it would only deliver nine.

As for Boeing, delays in the development of the 787 became endemic, and the project went billions over budget. When Boeing unveiled a model of the Dreamliner on July 8, 2007, its CEO told the crowd that the plane would fly within two months; however, it was more than two years before the plane's first test flight in December 2009. Although Boeing's plans had initially called for it to deliver the first 787 to All Nippon Airways in February 2011, delivery took place in September and began carrying customers in October. In the United States, United Airlines began flying the Dreamliner in November 2012. However, starting in January 2013 the 787 experienced a series of technical issues, one of which was a battery problem that led the Federal Aviation Administration to ground all 787s in the United States until the problem was resolved.

The experiences of Boeing and Airbus serve as typical examples of the planning fallacy. In these kinds of cases, the devil is usually in the details, and additional details are provided in Additional Resources for Chapter 4.

4.3 EXCESSIVE OPTIMISM AND OVERCONFIDENCE IN CAPITAL BUDGETING

Excessive optimism leads managers to develop upwardly biased forecasts of project cash flows. This section reviews evidence, and provides additional examples that pertain to the pervasive nature of excessive optimism in both the public and private sector capital budgeting.[1]

Excessive Optimism in Public-Sector Projects

Cost overruns in the military certainly have a long history. A study published in 1966 found the following ratios of actual costs to forecasted costs for the following series of items: missiles (4.9), bombers (3.0), fighter planes (1.7), and cargo tankers (1.2).[2]

One need not look far for civilian examples of excessive optimism. Boston's central artery/tunnel project, called the "Big Dig," is known to be the most expensive highway project in the United States. The Big Dig was approved in 1985 for $2.6 billion, but as the project neared completion in 2005, the final cost turned out to be closer to $15 billion. After the tunnel went into operation, leaking water required the closure of the tunnel system every night for repairs. The leaks caused at least one fatal accident, stemming from a large ceiling tile which fell onto an automobile, killing the driver.

The Denver airport opened in 1995 a year behind schedule. The major delay was caused by problems with the automated baggage-handling system and cost the city of Denver approximately $1 million per day. For transportation infrastructure projects, actual costs have, on average, been 28 percent higher than estimated costs, and costs have been underestimated on 9 out of every 10 projects.[3]

Moreover, cost underestimation does not appear to have decreased over the past 70 years.

Excessive optimism also afflicts revenue forecasts. Actual passenger traffic on European rail projects has been, on average, 39 percent less than had been forecast.

Excessive Optimism in Private-Sector Projects

Many studies document overruns in the private sector, in terms of both costs and time to completion. Only 42 percent of large systems projects, lasting at least a year, come in on budget. And only 37 percent come in on schedule.[4] For example, the ratio of actual costs to forecasted costs, for research and development in new chemical entities by one particular pharmaceutical firm, was 2.25. In the case of a second such firm, the corresponding figure was 3.66 for projects requiring large or medium[5] technological advances.[6] Studies of the mining industry suggest that the net present value of the average mining project has been negative.[7] Of course, there are also exceptions to the general rule of cost overruns.[8]

When it comes to sales forecasts, the evidence is mixed. Some studies found that sales forecasts for new products tend to be systematically optimistic.[9] Yet at least one study in the pharmaceutical industry found that on average, actual sales exceeded forecasted sales.[10]

A dramatic example of excessively optimistic revenue forecasts involves the Channel Tunnel (the Anglo-French tunnel). In the opening year of the Channel Tunnel, traffic was one-fifth of what planners had forecast.[11] Between 1987 and June 2005 shares of Eurotunnel, the firm that operates the Channel Tunnel, lost more than 95 percent of their value. In 2007, the firm restructured €5 billion of debt by swapping it for equity. As a result, the equity held by the firm's 750,000 original shareholders lost most of its value. Subsequently, the firm's cash flows improved. It paid its first dividend in 2009, 14 years late. In 2014, it was successfully paying down its €3.7 billion debt. Revenues were growing. Still, the tunnel system was operating at half capacity when it had been forecast to operate at full capacity. *The Financial Times* quoted Douglas McNeill, investment director and analyst at Charles Stanley, for his remarks about "the dangers of over-optimism" in respect to infrastructure projects."[12]

Software projects may not be especially capital intensive, but because of their intangible character they may be especially vulnerable to excessively optimistic forecasts. Indeed in 1988 the publication *Computing* contained an article whose title asked: "Why do so many projects still miss deadlines and bust budgets?"[13] The first sentence of the article provided the answer, citing excessive optimism as the culprit.

In respect to software and information technology failures, the excessive optimism described in 1988 persists. Consider three dimensions on which software projects are typically evaluated: (1) budget, (2) schedule, and (3) functions and performance.

A study by the Standish Group,[14] which has been ongoing since 1993, documents performance on these three dimensions. For the year 2000, and based on all projects in the study survey, budget cost overruns ran at 1.45; completion time overruns were 1.63; and of the originally specified features and functions, 67 percent were available on the released project. These findings were actually an improvement over prior years.[15] The general findings reported by the Standish Group are similar in nature to the findings reported earlier. However, critiques pointing to the influence of agency issues in respect to the Standish findings suggest the need for some caution.[16]

In any event, the Standish group assigns projects to three categories: succeeded, challenged, and failures. Success is defined as projects that delivered results on time, within budget, and with all required features and functions. Projects are defined as challenged if they were delivered late, went over budget, and/or were delivered with less than the requested features and functions. Complete failures are defined in the event of cancellation prior to delivery or project deliverables that were never used post completion. Exhibit 4-1 displays the trajectory of this breakdown over time.

Projects differ in important ways. Standish reports that low- and medium-risk projects appear to be excessively pessimistic, not optimistic. However, the opposite holds true in respect to high-risk projects. For high-risk projects actually experiencing difficulty on two of the three evaluation criteria previously mentioned (budget, schedule, and functions and performance), the most probable status report received by executives is that the project is performing well on all three criteria.[17] Project performance also differs by size and complexity. Exhibit 4-2 displays findings for project size for the period 2011 through 2015. The impact of complexity is similar to size.[18]

For the largest and most highly publicized software failures between 1988 and 1998, a study focusing on these failures identified the top two causes of these failures.[19] The top cause is "project objectives not fully specified," and this is closely followed by "bad planning and estimating." In respect to the latter, the study stated that the

EXHIBIT 4-1
Software Project Performance Over Time: Standish Group Findings

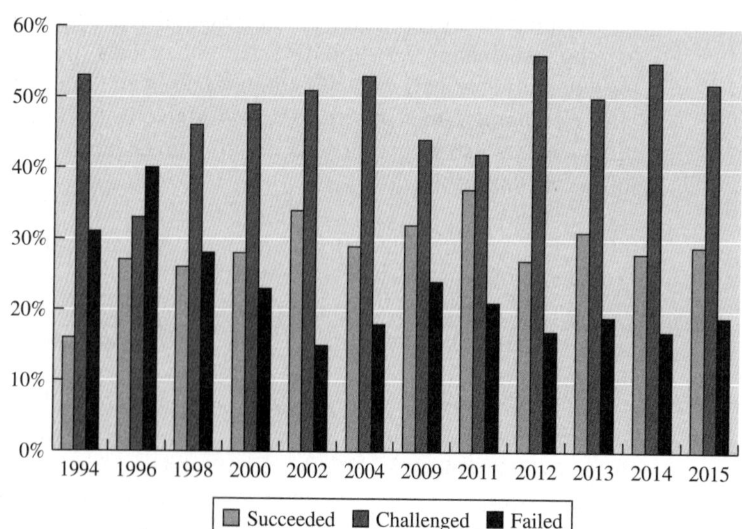

EXHIBIT 4-2
Project Performance By Size: Percentages Across Project Size Sum to 100%

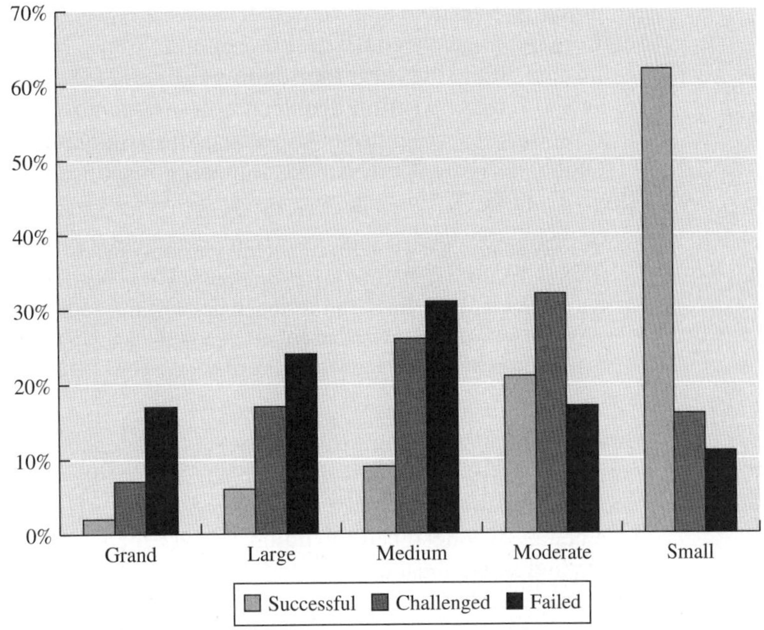

most common problem in building software systems is underestimating costs. Fifty-five percent of the failures documented in the study involved no risk management. Although survey respondents indicated that 38 percent did make use of risk management, half claimed that they did not use the risk findings once the project was under way. All of the features mentioned above were evident in 2013 and 2014 at the highly problematic launch of the web sites for the health care exchanges associated with the Patient Protection and Affordable Health Care Act, so-called ObamaCare. The government had hired private contractors to build the system of web sites.

In financial institutions, loans correspond to projects, as they are commitments of capital in exchange for expected future cash flows. There is evidence that when loan officers are able to exercise discretion, they tend to approve more loan applications on days that are sunnier, suggesting that they are more optimistic on sunnier days than overcast days. Notably, loans approved on sunny days experience significantly higher defaults than loans approved on overcast days.[20]

Agency Conflict Determinants of Excessive Optimism

To be sure, psychologically induced bias provides only part of the explanation for excessively optimistic project forecasts. The private interests of managers, such as the desire to engage in empire building, also serve as contributing factors. These private-interest issues give rise to agency conflicts. Agency conflicts are as pertinent to public-sector projects as to private-sector projects. In the traditional textbook approach, compensation policy is viewed as the key to dealing with optimistic forecasts that are agency-based. However, psychologically induced optimism might not be as amenable to compensation-based remedies. Some of the examples that appear later in the chapter illustrate this point.

Some people hold the view that excessively optimistic project forecasts stem entirely from agency conflicts. For example, Bent Flyvbjerg, Mette Skamris Holm, and Soren Buhl study transportation projects in Europe. At one stage they appear to have taken the position that agency conflicts, not psychological factors, explain forecast bias, referring to the prevalence of these biases as "lying."

Others disagree. Consider the following response by Paul Morrell, a partner at Davis Langdon & Everest.

> It really annoys me when Flyvbjerg talks about lying. To tell a lie, you have to know the truth and subvert it. It's not as if people are working out the true cost of a project and then lying about it. I'm sure deceit is sometimes a factor—construction represents a sizeable chunk of human endeavour, so nobody, least of all a social scientist, should be surprised to find that it demonstrates every kind of human behaviour, from honest effort to outright villainy.

In a similar vein, John McCready, head of regeneration at the accounting firm Ernst & Young, stated: "I worked on the Channel Tunnel, and the forecasts were not cooked deliberately to make them too optimistic. The engineers designed the tunnels before they designed the trains, so later there were a lot of design changes for health and safety reasons."

Managers who use incentives alone to deal with excessively optimistic cash flow forecasts, because they believe that optimism stems from agency conflicts alone, are likely to experience unpleasant surprises.

Flyvbjerg's later work added clarity to his perception of the role that agency issues play in capital budgeting, relative to excessive optimism. His position is that lying behavior (also known as strategic misrepresentation) is likely to be the dominant driver of cost and time overruns when pressure from organizational politics is high. In contrast, excessive optimism is likely to be the dominant driver of cost and time overruns when pressure from organizational politics is low.

Overconfidence

Overconfidence leads managers to be surprised more frequently than they had anticipated. In respect to capital budgeting, overconfidence leads managers to underestimate project risk. As an example of overconfident managers being surprised, consider the nearby Behavioral Pitfalls box describing the chronology of the global communications firm Iridium.

At the same time, overconfidence can have positive as well as negative effects. When it comes to innovative industries, overconfident managers generally invest more than non-overconfident managers, receive more patents and patent citations, and have more successful research and development projects.[21] Not surprisingly, the stocks of their firms display greater volatility.

Psychological Determinants of Excessive Optimism and Overconfidence

Excessive optimism and overconfidence are critical aspects of the planning fallacy. Evidence from survey data provides an indication of the degree to which optimism

Behavioral Pitfalls: Iridium

In 1987, some of the engineers at the electronics firm Motorola conceived of the idea of using a global satellite system to build a worldwide telephone network, thereby enabling customers to place and receive calls from anywhere in the world. The engineers proposed the project in a presentation to top executives at Motorola: Robert Galvin (the CEO), John Mitchell, and William Weisz.

The initial presentation took about two hours. The proposed global satellite mobile telephone project was very ambitious, requiring a capital investment of several billion dollars.

What was Motorola's CEO Robert Galvin's reaction? Did he find the proposal attractive? Did he ask for a DCF-based analysis in order to assess the net present value of the proposed project?

In Robert Galvin's own words, "with no further review, the three of us approved the project on that first sitting." They asked for no cash flow forecasts. Therefore, no discounting. No NPV. No IRR. Not even a payback analysis.

The project led to the creation of a new firm, to be called Iridium, with Motorola as its principal investor. Iridium was neither a small-scale project, nor a short-term project. It required an investment of $5 billion over 11 years, before generating revenues, making it one of the largest private-sector projects in the world.

During the 11-year investment period, Iridium's engineers achieved several technical successes. In November 1998, Iridium began to offer phone service to customers in remote locations. Yet, to the chagrin of its investors, the project proved to be a commercial failure. Within a year, Iridium had filed for bankruptcy protection and was sold to private investors for $25 million.

The failure stemmed from a series of faulty judgments and decisions that Motorola had made. The firm's executives underestimated the risk associated with the number of customers. Iridium's target market consisted of business executives who engage in frequent international travel. Its potential customer base comprised about eight million people. Despite 1½ million inquiries from potential customers, its subscriber base turned out to be a mere 20,000. Why the low number? The answer involves a series of *four* surprises.

1. *Indoors/outdoors.* Engineers discovered that their phones worked outdoors, but not indoors. This technical difficulty was totally unanticipated.
2. *Cellular competition.* In 1987, cell phones were expensive and used by only a few technically oriented individuals. A decade later, when Iridium took its service to market, cellular phones had become widespread in the general population. Interviewed in 2003, Robert Galvin stated: "I did not anticipate that by the time the Iridium product would finally be able to present itself to the world that the cellular telephone business would be so pervasive."[22]
3. *Size.* Iridium's telephone could not be made to be as small as a cellular phone. Cellular phones could fit in the palm of a user's hand. Iridium's phone was as large as a hand and required a long antenna. Users of cell phones viewed Iridium's phone as inconvenient.
4. *Cost.* Iridium's phones sold for over $3,000 each. At the time, the price of a cellular phone was about $100. Moreover, Iridium charged high rates for airtime, between $4 and $10 per minute.

Source: H. Wolinsky, "Iridium Failure Brought Motorola Back Down to Earth," *Chicago Sun-Times,* September 25, 2003.

and overconfidence impact CEOs and CFOs in the United States relative to others.[23] Consider what this evidence tells us.

For the general population, the standard range for dispositional optimism is 59.7 to 63.1, where the scale goes from 0 to 100, and 50 connotes neutral, scores lying above 50 connote optimism, and scores lying below 50 connote pessimism. By way of comparison, a sample of approximately 300 undergraduate finance majors, sampled over five years, featured a dispositional optimism score of 60.8.

CEOs are much more optimistic than the general population. Their mean score for dispositional optimism is 84.8. In a way this is not surprising. There is a good argument to be made that in selecting CEOs from pools of managers, corporate boards tend to emphasize traits such as optimism and confidence that are helpful in respect to the promotion process.[24] In this regard, CEOs are considerably more optimistic than CFOs, whose mean dispositional optimism score is 74.5. While having lower scores than that of CEOs, CFOs also display considerably more dispositional optimism than the general population.

Although dispositional optimism pertains to having a rosy outlook on life, it is conceptually different from excessive optimism, which pertains to biased probabilities. The discussion in Chapter 1 noted that the correlation between these two aspects of optimism is not high, and cautions against drawing strong conclusions about excessive optimism based on evidence about dispositional optimism.[25] Inferences about excessive optimism for CFOs can be inferred from studies involving market predictions made by CFOs. In this regard, on average CFOs' estimate of the market risk premium is approximately two percent *below* the 5.5 percent figure associated with estimates made by academics. This evidence, which is discussed in greater detail in Chapter 6, does not suggest excessive optimism on the part of CFOs.

In regard to overconfidence, the evidence is strong that CFOs are overconfident about their knowledge of market movements. As with responses to the trivia quiz question that was discussed in Chapter 1, CFOs' forecasts of market returns feature 80 percent confidence intervals that are roughly five times too narrow.

Across CFOs, there is considerable variation in respect to excessive optimism and overconfidence, with these differences impacting corporate investment. The evidence indicates that corporate investment is positively related to both optimism and overconfidence.[26] In this respect, corporate investment is defined as annual net investments scaled by lagged total assets. Measures of optimism and overconfidence are derived from predictions of 10-year market-wide stock returns, and subjective 80 percent confidence intervals associated with these predictions. Relative to base level investment, a one standard deviation change in optimism is associated with a 10 percent change in investment activity, while a one standard deviation change in overconfidence is associated with a 7 percent change in activity.

The discussion in Chapter 1 pointed out that several elements drive excessive optimism, namely perceived control, desirability, representativeness, and familiarity. The nature of these elements suggests that CFOs are more likely to be optimistic about tasks that are under their control and familiar to them than future market returns. Perceived control has also been identified as a key factor driving overconfidence.

The psychological evidence indicates that increased perceived control is associated with lower perceived risk. This relationship turns out to be particularly strong among white males. White males who perceive risks as lower than others tend to trust experts and engineers more than others, especially when it comes to making the proper decisions about managing the risks from technology. In respect to Iridium, recall from the contents of the Behavioral Pitfall box on page 93 that Motorola's executives adopted the satellite project on the basis of one two-hour meeting with a group of engineers and insufficient analysis of the attendant risks.[27]

Another contributor to managerial overconfidence is inadequate planning and risk management. When it comes to risk, out of sight is typically out of mind. Therefore people become more confident when they themselves have to generate a list of risks as compared to the list being generated for them. This is an example of availability bias. The general point is that failure to engage in adequate risk planning leads to overconfidence.

Evidence of availability bias comes from a 2003 survey of risk managers and financial executives, jointly conducted by the Financial Executives Research Foundation, the insurance organization FM Global, and The National Association of Corporate Treasurers.[28] The study found that risk managers and financial executives do not share the same view about the hazards that affect the earnings of their firms. Risk managers are more familiar with insurable risks, such as property-related hazards, whereas financial executives are more familiar with hazards associated with improper management.

In the study, risk managers viewed the top risk as being due to fire and explosion, whereas financial executives viewed the top risk as being related to improper management and employee practices. Risk managers favored property-related hazards over other hazards, with the corresponding weights being 70-30. In contrast, financial executives gave 50-50 (equal weights) to property-related hazards and other hazards. Somewhat relatedly, survey evidence indicates that risk managers exhibit less dispositional optimism than CFOs, 71.4 versus 74.5.

4.4 PROJECT ADOPTION CRITERIA

Discounted cash flow (DCF) techniques form the basis of traditional capital budgeting analysis. The discussion about the planning fallacy makes clear that even if firms rely on DCF, the analysis is only as good as the quality of its inputs. Moreover, the discussion in Chapter 1 pointed out that people's natural way of making decisions about risk does not always conform to DCF. This section reviews the major survey evidence about the capital budgeting techniques that financial managers use in practice.

What do financial managers generally say about the criteria that they use to guide their capital budgeting decisions?[29] To answer this question, consider evidence based on a survey conducted by a group at Duke University of chief financial officers (CFOs) who belong to the organization Financial Executives International (FEI).[30] The survey evidence[31] tells us that although corporate practice has been moving in the direction of textbook theory, the overall picture is mixed.[32]

The FEI survey asked financial managers how frequently their firms use a host of techniques when deciding which projects or acquisitions to pursue. The top two choices identified by survey respondents were IRR and NPV. Specifically, 75 percent of CFOs reported that their firms use IRR and 75 percent reported the use of NPV.[33] On a scale of 0 to 4, where 4 is very important, the mean responses associated with both IRR and NPV were about 3.1.

Interestingly, 57 percent of CFOs reported using the payback rule. Academics are quite critical of the use of the payback rule for at least two reasons. First, the payback rule does not involve discounting and therefore ignores the time value of money.[34] Second, the payback rule attaches zero weight to cash flows that arrive after the payback period. Some argue that the use of the payback rule is rational for firms that are severely capital constrained.

The FEI survey found that the payback rule is used by older, longer-tenure CEOs without MBA degrees. However, the survey also failed to find a relationship between the use of the payback rule and degree of leverage, credit rating, or dividend policy. In consequence, the survey authors conclude that the use of the payback rule stems from a lack of managerial sophistication.

The Importance of Intuition

As previously mentioned, financial executives report that they use NPV and IRR with equal frequency. However, in corporate executive surveys that have been conducted since 1977, IRR or some variant of return has been cited much more frequently than NPV. Notably, these surveys were essentially conducted in large firms.

Consider some examples. For years Sun Microsystems, the manufacturer of servers described in Chapter 2, based its capital budgeting decisions on a measure the company called RONABIT (return on net assets before interest and tax). Applied Materials, one of the largest manufacturers of semiconductor manufacturing equipment, bases its capital budgeting decisions on a return measure the company calls ROOPA (return on operating assets). Xilinx, one of the major manufacturers of programmable chips, bases its decisions on ROIC (return on invested capital).

Why was the payback rule the predominant capital budgeting criterion for so long, and why do return measures seem to have an edge over NPV, the criterion emphasized in traditional textbooks on corporate finance?

Comparing NPV, IRR, and the payback rule, the payback rule is the most intuitive of the three measures and NPV is the least intuitive. The basic idea underlying the payback rule is very straightforward: how long a period it takes for the cumulative project cash flows to cover the initial investment. Return measures such as IRR, RONABIT, ROOPA, and ROIC come next. Most people interpret IRR as the rate of return from investing in the project. This may or may not be correct, but most people generally have reasonable intuition about what rate of return means, as in interest earned on bank deposits.

The concept of NPV is much less intuitive. Managers rarely think of NPV as the incremental wealth that a project generates for investors. They instead think about NPV in terms of its defining formula, which is abstract and unintuitive for most. Indeed many managers think of a zero NPV project as mediocre, as if it was just breaking even profitwise, rather than earning a competitive return.

Comfort is important. As was mentioned, 25 percent of the participants in the FEI survey reported using neither NPV nor IRR. People are more comfortable relying on criteria that they find intuitive than on criteria they find harder to understand.

A follow-up survey conducted by the Duke group examined the role of intuition, also known as "gut feel," in the way managers allocate capital across divisions.[35]

They found that approximately half of survey respondents rate "gut feel" as important or very important. While significant, gut feel ranks lower than other criteria such as the "NPV ranking of a project" which almost 80 percent of respondents rated as important. Also ranked higher than gut feel were, in order: the reputation of the divisional manager in terms of delivering on previous projects, the confidence of the divisional manager in the project, the timing of projects' cash flows, protecting market share, and the return on previous projects earned by the division proposing the project.

The Affect Heuristic

Chapter 1 introduced the concept of the affect heuristic. Managers who rely on the affect heuristic base their decisions not only on financial analysis, but also on whether the decision they propose making feels right emotionally. That is a major reason why many firms continue to rely on payback, even when they compute IRR and NPV. Indeed, some managers rely exclusively on the affect heuristic, even for major projects.

Choice, Value, and the Affect Heuristic

The Iridium example, described in the Behavioral Pitfalls box displayed earlier, illustrates the perils of relying on intuitive judgment when making capital budgeting decisions. People's intuition about choice and value are not always the same.

CONCEPT PREVIEW
Question 4.2

Imagine a bingo cage containing 36 balls, numbered from 1 to 36. Consider two risky alternatives whose outcomes depend on the number on a single ball drawn from the bingo cage.

A. If the number drawn is 29 or less, you win $20; otherwise you win $0.
B. If the number drawn is 30 or more, you win $90; otherwise you win $0.

1. What is the maximum amount you would be willing to pay for the opportunity to face alternative A?
2. What is the maximum amount you would be willing to pay for the opportunity to face alternative B?
3. If you could only choose one of these alternatives, which one would you choose, A or B?

Decisions about capital budgeting involve choices about uncertain cash flows. In Concept Preview Question 4.2, you are asked to consider two alternatives where the amount you might win or lose is an uncertain cash flow. Psychological studies have used this question to investigate how people make decisions and assign values when the outcomes are risky. The major conclusion from these studies is that people rely heavily on the affect heuristic, and that doing so leads them to attach a lower value to the alternative they choose than the alternative they reject.

In Concept Preview Question 4.2, alternative B offers a higher expected payoff ($17.50) than does alternative A ($16.10). Many people, typically 40 percent, assign

willingness to pay
How much a person or group is willing to pay to acquire something.

preference reversal
Choosing low-value alternatives over high-value alternatives.

a higher **willingness to pay** (WTP) to the riskier alternative B than the safer alternative A. Notably, many respondents typically assign a lower valuation to the alternative they choose than the alternative they reject. Psychologists suggest that this phenomenon, called **preference reversal,** occurs because people use a different mental process to make a choice than they do to assess value (WTP). Specifically, when choosing between alternatives A and B, the chance of winning generates more of an emotional (affective) response than the amount won. However, when assessing value, the reverse is true: amount won generates more of an affective response than the chance of winning.[36]

One interesting study redid Concept Preview Question 4.2 and changed the $0 outcome in alternative B to a loss of 50 cents. Although counterintuitive, that change made alternative B a more attractive choice than alternative A, thereby reducing the degree of the preference reversal. The study concluded that the 50 cent loss served as a more striking contrast for the $90 win than did $0, thereby increasing the affective response attached to the $90.

What is the takeaway? Decisions about project adoption and termination involve risk. Managers who do not base these decisions on NPV, but instead rely on subjective judgment, are prone to preference reversal, meaning they are prone to selecting projects with lower values in place of projects with higher values.

outside view
Taking a perspective on a project by comparing the characteristics of a specific project with a large population of projects which are similar in nature.

inside view
Taking a perspective on a project by focusing on the details specific to that particular project.

reference class forecasting
Past, similar projects that are small enough in number to compare to the given project, but large enough to enable meaningful statistical analysis.

Corporate Nudges

Errors or biases: Excessive optimism, overconfidence, preference reversal

Why does it happen? Reliance on the affect heuristic, perceived control, familiarity, representativeness, anchoring, desirability.

How does it happen? Perceived control predisposes managers to be both excessively optimistic and overconfident. Familiarity, representativeness, wishful thinking, and anchoring bias, in combination with the substitution of intuition for financial analysis, accentuate this predisposition.

What can be done about it? The core advice for dealing with the planning fallacy is to adopt what is known as the **outside view,** to be distinguished from the **inside view,** which is more common. In this regard, the inside view focuses on project specifics, while the outside view emphasizes general success rates. **Reference class forecasting,** which invokes the outside view, involves three steps:[37]

1. For a given project, identify a relevant reference class of past, similar projects that are small enough to be compared meaningfully to the given project, but large enough to enable meaningful statistical analysis.
2. Obtain historical data that is rich enough to develop probability distributions for the relevant class.
3. Establish unbiased cash flow projections for the given project by benchmarking it against the reference class probability distribution.

4.5 RELUCTANCE TO TERMINATE LOSING PROJECTS

Once projects are adopted, managers face subsequent decisions about whether to continue these projects or terminate them. What makes the follow-on decision especially important is the presence of excessive optimism. If excessive optimism is systematically at work in capital budgeting, then managers will undertake more negative net-present-value projects than they anticipate. As a result, they will have to face the question of whether to abandon failing projects more frequently than they anticipated.

Interestingly, although survey evidence shows that 97 percent of firms use cost-of-capital techniques to evaluate new projects, the same survey shows that only 73 percent do so when deciding whether or not to abandon existing projects.[38] However, the issue here is not whether firms use cost-of-capital techniques when deciding whether or not to abandon projects. The issue is whether firms make negative net-present-value decisions by delaying the decision to abandon failing projects.

Aversion to a Sure Loss

As in the discussion about project adoption, avoiding DCF and NPV analysis means that capital budgeting decisions involve subjective judgment. And subjective judgment leads managers to be vulnerable to behavioral biases. In the case of project termination decisions, the most important bias is aversion to a sure loss.

CONCEPT PREVIEW
Question 4.3

1. Suppose that you faced a situation where you had to choose between a sure loss of $7,400, and a risky alternative that featured a 75 percent chance to lose $10,000 and a 25 percent chance to lose nothing. Would you choose to accept the sure loss of $7,400 or choose the risky alternative?
2. Suppose that you had an opportunity to choose a risky alternative where there was a 25 percent chance you could win $7,400, but a 75 percent chance you would lose $2,600. Would you be willing to accept the risk?

As discussed in Chapter 2, breaking even is a key issue. In the first part of Concept Preview Question 4.3, part 1, both the risk-free alternative and the risky alternative are framed in the domain of losses. Most people are averse to accepting a sure loss and therefore choose the risky alternative in this situation.

However, suppose that the person who faces the choice described in Concept Preview Question 4.3, part 1, could come to terms with that loss. Coming to terms with the loss, psychologically, means that he or she treats the $7,400 as an irrelevant **sunk cost**. Having done so, he or she then frames the question as between choosing a risk-free $0, or facing a 25 percent probability of a $7,400 gain and a 75 probability of a $2,600 loss.

sunk cost
An expenditure made in the past that is irrevocable.

Notice that this choice is exactly what Concept Preview Question 4.3, part 2, offers and that almost everyone rejects the risky alternative. Loss aversion typically leads people to choose a risk-free $0 over an expected loss of

\$100 (= 0.25 × 7,400 − 0.75 × 2,600). However, aversion to a sure loss leads them to choose an expected loss of \$7,500 (= 0.75 × 10,000 + 0.25 × 0) over a sure loss of \$7,400.

What are we to conclude? People who accept losses reset their reference point so that they no longer perceive the status quo to be in the domain of losses. As a result, loss aversion typically induces them to reject the actuarially unfair alternative, whereas aversion to a sure loss leads them to choose the actuarially unfair alternative.

The framing issues associated with decisions involving sunk costs are complex. Imagine that the decision task in part 2 of Concept Preview Question 4.3 is presented to someone who has incurred a recent prior loss of \$7,400. The combination of the prior loss and the risks associated with the decision task involves choices that are now numerically identical to the decision task described in part 1 of Concept Preview Question 4.3. However, when the decision task is framed according to part 1, the majority of respondents accept the risk, whereas when the decision task is framed according to part 2, explicitly mentioning the prior loss, the majority of respondents reject the risk. This feature is part of a phenomenon known as **quasi-hedonic editing,** which emphasizes the importance of prior losses and gains.

quasi-hedonic editing
After a recent prior gain, people are more willing to take risks that will not jeopardize the recent gain, whereas after a recent prior loss, they become less willing to take a subsequent risk that would accentuate the recent loss.

Consider survey evidence about how CEOs and CFOs respond to a prior loss. The survey instrument asked respondents the following question:

> Last year your company invested \$5 million in a project that was expected to generate cash flows of \$10 million after one year. A year has passed and the project yielded nothing. Now you have the opportunity to invest an additional sum in this same project. There is a 20 percent chance that the project will generate a \$10 million cash flow in a year's time and nothing thereafter. There is an 80 percent chance that the new investment will generate nothing at all. How much would you be willing to invest today?

Notice that the expected future cash flow from continued investment is \$2 million. Therefore, a modest investment would generate positive NPV. Of course, any investment amount exceeding \$2 million would produce a negative NPV, assuming a positive discount rate.

The survey evidence indicates that CEOs display quasi-hedonic editing more strongly than CFOs. Whereas 76 percent of CEOs refuse to invest anything more in the project, 59 percent of CFOs make the same decision. At the same time, there is considerable heterogeneity across respondents. For CEOs willing to invest some positive amount in continuing the project, the mean investment amount for CEOs was \$4.4 million and for CFOs it was \$2.5 million. In this regard, for both CEOs and CFOs, the two highest investment amount quintiles of respondents willing to invest positive amounts were associated with negative NPV. Notably, members of these groups feature high dispositional optimism, with the figure being especially high for the top quintile (92.6 for CEOs and 88.2 for CFOs).

The standard measure of risk aversion discussed in Chapter 1 also provides insight about the responses of CEOs and CFOs to the above question. CFOs with the lowest risk aversion are willing to invest considerably more than those with higher

Behavioral Pitfalls: Sony

In 1946, Masaru Ibuka and Akio Morita founded Sony. In 1961, Sony began to develop a color television receiver based on the Chromatron picture tube. Ibuka led a two-year effort to develop a commercial prototype and process technology. By September 1964, Ibuka's team had succeeded in developing a prototype. However, they had not developed a commercially viable manufacturing process.

Ibuka committed Sony to mass-produce color television sets before his engineers had developed a cost-effective mass-production process. A chronicler of the events indicated that Ibuka alone was confident. He had the product announced and displayed in Sony's showroom. Consumer reaction was enthusiastic.

Sony invested in a new facility to house the production assembly. Ibuka announced that the color television would be Sony's top priority. He placed 150 people on its assembly line.

To Ibuka's chagrin, the production process yielded only two or three usable picture tubes per thousand produced. The retail price of Sony's color television set was $550, but the cost of production was more than double that amount. There was a sharp difference of opinion within the Sony leadership about the appropriate course of action. Morita wanted to terminate the project. However, Ibuka refused.

Sony continued to produce and sell Chromatron sets, eventually selling 13,000 sets, each one at a loss. In November 1966, Sony's financial managers announced that Sony was close to ruin. Only then did Ibuka agree to terminate the project.

Source: J. Nathan, *Sony: The Private Life.* Boston: Houghton Mifflin Company, 1999.

risk aversion, $1.16 million versus $0.78. For CEOs, the same general pattern holds, but is weaker than for CFOs.

For firms whose prior annual stock market return has been negative, the more negative the return, the larger the subsequent volatility. For firms whose prior annual stock market return has been positive, the more positive the return, the larger the subsequent volatility. This behavior pattern is consistent with aversion to a sure loss, and more broadly with the March-Shapira framework described in Chapter 1.[39]

Escalation of Commitment

escalation of commitment
The tendency to throw good money after bad.

There is research documenting that managers often put more money into a failure for which they feel responsible than into a success.[40] This phenomenon is known as the **escalation of commitment.** Apparently, decision makers who feel responsible for a failure are inclined to be more retrospectively oriented than those who were not responsible for a failure. Retrospective means that they search for evidence to confirm that their prior decision was a reasonable course of action.

Visibility

visibility
How salient a project or activity is to others.

One very important finding is that the size of the sunk cost does not alter the tendency of managers to be retrospective or to escalate the level of expenditure. However, the **visibility** of the decision that resulted in failure does impact both. In this respect, think about a manager like Masaru Ibuka. See the nearby Behavioral Pitfalls box. He was seen as a champion for a project that was prone to being viewed as a highly visible failure. Someone in this position is likely to be especially retrospective.

Regret

regret
An emotion occurring when people imagine having taken a different decision than the one they actually took, one that would have turned out favorably rather than unfavorably.

After an unfavorable outcome that stems from a past decision, many people experience the emotion of **regret**. This emotion occurs when people imagine having taken a different decision than the one they actually took, one that would have turned out favorably rather than unfavorably. In order to avoid experiencing regret, many managers will put off terminating losing projects, so as not to have to admit to having made a mistake.

Feelings of regret for short-term decisions often occur when it is easy to imagine having followed a different course of action than the one actually taken. A prime example of this type of situation involves deviating from a conventional way of doing things. For this reason, people who are regret-averse tend to favor the status quo, a behavior pattern referred to as **status quo bias**.

status quo bias
inertia, reluctance to make changes from default positions.

Neuroscientific studies find evidence of regret being experienced in particular regions of the brain (such as the orbitofrontal cortex and the ventral striatum). Particularly striking is a finding that specific neural regret signals are generated within the ventral striatum. Notably, people for whom these signals are observed are also prone to exhibit aversion to a sure loss.[41]

Agency Conflicts at Sony

The behavioral influences driving Ibuka's actions represented a threat to the wealth of Sony's other shareholders. Morita sharply criticized Sony's engineers for wasting money in order to indulge their own scientific curiosity, and encouraging Ibuka to pursue a nonprofitable technology. Tensions rose as Morita's planners and accountants began to attend brainstorming sessions that the engineers held to grapple with Chromatron's technical problems.[42]

Ibuka's reluctance to terminate the Chromatron project caused the wealth of Sony shareholders (including Morita) to be sacrificed to the desire of some managers to indulge their curiosity. The traditional manner in which to address the agency conflicts between managers and owners is to use equity in order to align the incentives of managers with shareholders. However, Ibuka was a Sony founder and major shareholder. Being rewarded as a major shareholder did not prevent him from succumbing to the sunk cost fallacy in his actions as a manager. There is no doubt that incentives are important. However, the Sony example illustrates that incentive effects by themselves do not eliminate the impact of behavioral elements. It is a mistake to believe that monetary incentives alone can mitigate behavioral bias.

4.6 CONFIRMATION BIAS AND SUNK COSTS: ILLUSTRATIVE EXAMPLE

Notably, over half of the publicized failures mentioned in Section 4.3 began to display serious symptoms during system development, and a quarter showed these symptoms during initial planning. Downplaying information about project problems

Behavioral Pitfalls: Syntex

Syntex Inc. was a pharmaceutical corporation that was registered in Panama in 1944 and headquartered in Palo Alto, California, until 1995, when it was taken over by Roche Holding Ltd.

In 1977, Gabriel Garay, a senior Syntex researcher with a Ph.D. in pharmacology, led a team that created a new drug, Enprostil. Enprostil was designed to turn off production of stomach acid and thereby heal stomach ulcers.

At the time, approximately 23 million people worldwide had ulcer problems. Enprostil was conservatively forecast to generate sales of $50 million to $100 million a year. Syntex's managers hoped that these sales would help offset the expiration of the patent on its major product, Naprosyn, an anti-inflammatory drug. The patent for Naprosyn was due to expire in December 1993. At the time, Naprosyn accounted for half of Syntex's sales and more than half of its operating profit. This made the Enprostil project highly visible.

After Syntex invested in the research-and-development phase of Enprostil, researchers in Garay's laboratory found that Enprostil tended to make blood platelets clot in the test tube, posing a possible risk of stroke or heart attack. An internal Syntex memo from Garay's laboratory warned that in intravenous form, Enprostil could provoke a blood clot (thromboembolism) that was possibly crippling or even fatal. Moreover, independent researchers found that Enprostil significantly increased damage caused from ingesting alcohol.

The decision maker who bore ultimate responsibility for the Enprostil project was John Fried, the President of Syntex's research division and also the vice chairman of the corporation. Fried characterized Garay's memo as inflammatory, speculative, and irrelevant. He ordered that the memo be rewritten. In 1986, researchers reported that several dogs involved in some Enprostil animal studies had died. Fried stated that he was not surprised by the dog deaths because the drug had been administered rapidly and because the tests had also used other chemicals.

In 1987, researchers reported having discovered the mechanism underlying Enprostil, and that this mechanism was known to cause clotting and spasms in veins and arteries, thereby further raising the danger of possible strokes or heart attacks in patients. Fried commented that the Enprostil team was going around in circles instead of going forward meaningfully. He expressed concern that their efforts were potentially wasting the FDA's time.

In February 1988, the FDA met with Syntex and told them that side effects made it unlikely Enprostil could win broad market approval as a treatment for common ulcers. Shortly afterward, Syntex withdrew its application.

Sources: M. Chase, "A Matter of Candor: Did Syntex Withhold Data on Side Effects of a Promising Drug?" *The Wall Street Journal,* January 8, 1991; "Has Syntex Run Out of Steam? Wall Street Is Impatient with Sluggish Sales and Few New Products," *Businessweek,* July 12, 1993.

is a form of confirmation bias. Consider an example from the pharmaceutical industry, presented in the Behavioral Pitfalls box on the next page.

Behavioral Bias and Agency Conflicts at Syntex

Syntex's John Fried threw good money after bad, trying to beat the odds. And the odds of success are low to begin with. The Tufts Center for the Study of Drug Development reports that for every 5,000 medicines tested, five are tested in humans and one reaches the market. Between 1979 and 1991, the cost of developing a new drug rose from approximately $54 million (in 1976 dollars) to $231 million (1987 dollars).

Like Sony's Ibuka, Syntex's John Fried was a major shareholder in his firm. In addition, he was vice chairman. His financial interests were aligned with shareholders. Yet he decided to throw good money after bad in a losing project.

Corporate Nudges

Errors or biases: Reluctance to terminate failing projects.
Why does it happen? Aversion to a sure loss, regret, and confirmation bias.
How does it happen? People become risk-seeking when facing the prospect of a sure loss. People experience regret, which makes it difficult for them to admit to having made a mistake. People also overweight information that confirms their views and underweight information that disconfirms their views.
What can be done about it? Managers can ask themselves particular questions, or ask others to ask them the following questions:

- Can I clearly define what would constitute success or failure for this project?
- Has my definition of what would constitute success or failure changed since the time the project began?
- Do I have trouble hearing other people's concerns about the project?
- Am I more concerned about the welfare of this project than I am about the organization as a whole?
- If I took over my job for the first time today and found that this project was underway, would I support it or terminate it?

As in the Sony case, the message here is that behavioral biases can dominate financial incentives.

To be sure, firms also suffer from traditional agency conflicts, such as the consumption of perquisites. Syntex's 1992 proxy statement indicates that Paul Freiman, Syntex's CEO at the time, had received perquisites valued at $98,304, approximately 10 percent of his total compensation. These perquisites had tripled in value from the previous year. The financial press noted that Freiman had been making frequent personal trips to Brazil on Syntex's corporate jet. At the same time, he had been in the process of divorcing his wife of 36 years and appearing in public with a woman from Brazil.[43]

As a general matter, granting CEOs personal use of corporate aircraft destroys value. The stocks of firms that have granted this perquisite have underperformed the stocks of firms that have not granted this perquisite by 4 percent a year, a differential far in excess of the associated aircraft costs.[44] Instead the costs are more closely correlated with the CEO's outside interests as measured, say, by long-distance golf club memberships.

In one respect, the actions of both Freiman and Fried caused the wealth of Syntex's shareholders to decline. In another respect, there is a significant difference between the two situations. The appropriate way to reduce agency conflicts of the sort associated with the actions of Freiman is to correct the distortions in his compensation package. However, there are no compelling reasons to think that Fried's actions were the result of distorted incentives.

Summary

Heuristics, biases, and framing effects adversely impact the behavior of managers when they formulate forecasts of project cash flows and make decisions about both project adoption and project termination. The planning fallacy lies at the heart of the issue. Excessive optimism leads managers to establish cash flow forecasts that are upwardly biased. Overconfidence leads managers to underestimate project risk. Managers who do not undertake discounted cash flow analysis for the purpose of capital budgeting, and instead rely exclusively on the affect heuristic, are vulnerable to preference reversal, in that they select low-value projects over high-value projects. The combination of aversion to a sure loss, regret, and confirmation bias leads managers to continue a failing project when they should terminate the project.

Managers display excessive optimism for many reasons. Managers typically exaggerate the degree to which they can control events. They might establish forecast ranges but set expected cash flows at the top end of the range. If the success of a project depends on the conjunction of several events, then anchoring may lead managers to overestimate the probability of the conjoined event that defines success. In forming their own judgments about project success, managers may become anchored on the forecasts of those proposing the project and fail to adjust sufficiently from that anchor.

These issues pertain to the inside view. Managers might be able to mitigate excessive optimism and overconfidence by adopting an outside view with reference class forecasting.[45] However, adopting an outside view does not come naturally to managers.

Behavioral impediments are not the same as agency conflicts. The remedy for agency conflicts involves the alignment of incentives between principal and agent. Behavioral phenomena need to be addressed using debiasing techniques.

Additional Behavioral Readings

Eveleens, L. and C. Verhoef, "The Rise and Fall of the Chaos Report Figures," *IEEE Software,* January/February 2010, pp. 30–36.

Flynn, J., P. Slovic and C. K. Mertz, "Gender, Race, and the Perception of Environmental Health Risks," *Risk Analysis,* vol. 14, no. 6, 1994, pp. 1101–1198.

Flyvbjerg, B. and D. Techn, "From Nobel Prize to Project Management: Getting Risks Right," *Project Management Journal,* vol. 37, no. 3, August 2006.

Graham J. and C. Harvey, "How Do CFOs Make Capital Budgeting and Capital Structure Decisions?" *Journal of Applied Corporate Finance,* volume 15, number 1, Spring 2002.

Graham J. and C. Harvey, "The Theory and Practice of Corporate Finance: Evidence from the Field," *Journal of Financial Economics,* vol. 60, nos. 2–3, 2001, pp. 187–243.

Lovallo D. and D. Kahneman, "Delusions of Success," *Harvard Business Review,* July 2003, pp. 56–60.

Slovic, P., M. Finucane, E. Peters and D. MacGregor, "The Affect Heuristic." In T. Gilovich, D. Griffen, and D. Kahneman (eds.), *Heuristics and Biases: The Psychology of Intuitive Judgment.* New York: Cambridge University Press, 2002.

Key Terms

Explore the Web

www.standishgroup.com
The Standish Group is a consulting firm that conducts studies on the capital budgeting practices of various organizations and posts summary updates of its studies on its web site.

csdd.tufts.edu
The Center for the Study of Drug Development at Tufts University posts key information associated with the development costs for new drugs.

www.citylab.com/work/2013/07/why-mega-projects-end-costing-way-more-expected/6364/
Article entitled "Why Mega-Projects Always End Up Costing More Than Expected," by Eric Jaffe.

www.economist.com/news/business/21601882-bad-project-comes-goodwith-better-yet-store-next-20-years?zid=303&ah=27090cf03414b8c5065d64ed0dad813d
"Eurotunnel: The next 20 years. A bad project comes good—with better yet in store."

Chapter Questions

1. In what way were the situations at Boeing (with the 787) and Airbus (with the A380) similar, and in what way were they different? Discuss this question through the lens of the planning fallacy.
2. In what way were the situations at Boeing (with the 787) and Motorola (with the Iridium project) the same, and in what way were they different? Discuss this question through the lens of the planning fallacy.
3. Despite the growing popularity of cellular phones during the middle and late 1990s, Iridium undertook a $180 million promotional campaign to launch its product. It ran advertisements in *The Wall Street Journal, Fortune* magazine, and 37 airline magazines. It also launched a major direct-mail campaign in 20 markets and in 20 languages. Discuss any behavioral issues associated with Iridium's promotional expenditures.
4. In 1999 Iridium declared bankruptcy and was sold to private investors. Suppose that you were to learn that by the end of 2003, Iridium had gone out of business. How surprised would you be? How would you imagine that the events surrounding Iridium's liquidation took place? Now suppose instead that you were to learn that by the end of 2003, Iridium had turned cash flow positive. How surprised would you be? How would you imagine that the events surrounding Iridium's turnaround took place?
5. Consider Robert Galvin's approach to evaluating the satellite project proposal. The text suggests that in not developing discounted cash flow analysis, Galvin's approach was flawed. In hindsight, Iridium was a failed project for Motorola, and even positive NPV projects can turn out to be failures after the fact. Can you provide a critique of the behaviorally based argument and suggest some reasons why in foresight it might have been entirely rational for Robert Galvin to have proceeded in the way that he did?

6. Consider the contention that excessive optimism and overconfidence are important characteristics of leadership. Might these traits help managers initiate and complete daunting projects that they would otherwise reject or abandon? Discuss this contention.
7. Consider the responses to a survey conducted of geologists working in the mining industry.[46] The survey put the following question to the geologists: "If an economic deposit was discovered tomorrow, how many years would pass before it could be put into production? Consider only typical problems, planning permission, objections, engineering studies, etc." In responding, the geologists provided a range, from 5 to 10 years. Historically, the typical project has taken 10 years. Discuss whether the geologists' responses exhibit any behavioral biases.
8. One of the points made in the discussion about the construction of the Anglo-French tunnel is that engineers designed the tunnels before they designed the trains, so there were many design changes because of health and safety. Are there any behavioral issues associated with these design changes?

Additional Resources and Materials for Chapter 4 Are Available at www.mhhe.com/shefrin2e

Minicase

MGM Resorts International: Las Vegas CityCenter

In 2004, the hotel casino company MGM Resorts International (MGM) (previously MGM Mirage) initiated what would later become the world's largest private sector project. They called it CityCenter, and it would involve a 67-acre complex on the Las Vegas strip with a major casino, condominiums, hotels, shops, restaurants, and entertainment venues. MGM subsequently partnered with Dubai World during the construction phase.[47]

MGM was managed by a very experienced set of professionals, who were quite sophisticated about capital budgeting. These professionals relied heavily on DCF, engaged consultants to assist with cash flow forecasts, and were very detailed in their analyses about a wide range of issues, including contract cost management and availability of labor resources.

In 2004, MGM provided no official budget for Project CityCenter, but its board approved one, which the company suggested would be in the vicinity of $4 billion. This amount excluded the sale of an estimated 1,650 condominiums, which the company envisioned would sell for about $1 billion. Thereafter, MGM referred to its budget as a moving target, raising it to $5 billion in 2005.[48] MGM also added qualifying language stating: "The design, budget and schedule of Project CityCenter are still preliminary, however, and the ultimate timing, cost and scope are subject to risks attendant to large-scale projects."

By March 2006, the budget for Project CityCenter had grown to $7 billion, as reported in the company's 2005 published annual report. This figure excluded the value of underlying land and marketing costs, as well as revenues from sales of condominiums, which were forecasted to be $2.5 billion. The majority of the land value at historic cost was recorded at $40 million. Therefore, they estimated net cost to be $4.5 billion.

Jim Murren, MGM's CFO at the time, attributed $800 million of the $3 billion increase to expected inflation, and $1.2 billion to the company's decision to increase the number of condominiums.

The condominium decision reflected a rapidly growing real estate market. Although construction costs had been rising rapidly across the United States, Murren and CityCenter President Bobby Baldwin were not concerned, with Baldwin having said: "We have a complete, nailed-down design scope."[49] In regard to building materials, MGM was creative—for example, by taking the unconventional step of making large purchases from Chinese suppliers.

The project's primary construction contractor was the Perini Building Company. In respect to design, MGM engaged the services of the highly regarded firms Ehrenkrantz, Eckstut & Kuhn to develop the conceptual master plan for the project and Gensler as executive architect. In all, the company engaged 11 architectural firms for various projects within the overall CityCenter masterplan complex. They commissioned the renowned design architect Cesar Pelli to produce a design for the main hotel and casino building that would be "paradigm-shifting." By their nature, paradigm-shifting projects are highly complex, and laden with uncertainties. A key risk of the project was "scope creep," a tendency for the architectural scope of the project to increase as the architects worked on the project, thereby leading to cost escalation.

In April 2007, MGM revised CityCenter's estimated gross cost to $7.4 billion, and its net cost to $4.7 billion. This increase largely stemmed from the company having decided to expand three of the CityCenter hotels and to add parking spaces. The motivation for the decision was that between 2004 and 2006, revenues from gambling on the Las Vegas Strip had increased by 21.5 percent, and room rates for hotels had increased by 33.2 percent. Moreover, the company raised its estimates of proceeds from condominium sales to $2.7 billion, noting that buyers had already placed $800 million of orders. At the same time, housing estate prices in the United States had peaked in February of 2006, after having been in a speculative bubble since at least 2003 and arguably several years before. As housing prices began to decline, the market for asset-backed commercial paper experienced a run in the summer of 2007.

In October 2007, unanticipated complexity with some of the architectural designs led MGM to increase the CityCenter budget to $7.8 billion from $7.4 billion. The increase stemmed from additional steel being needed for the project's mall, Crystals, designed by world-renowned architects Libeskind and Rockwell.

At this time, foreclosure rates had begun to increase in comparable markets for second residences, such as in Miami; however, MGM executives expressed no concern about the market for CityCenter condominiums, even though more than 2,600 units that were part of the project represented a very large increase in residential housing for the Strip. Based on previous experience, Las Vegas developers developed the belief that increased supply would generate its own demand: if they built it, buyers would come. This belief would lead MGM to place all of CityCenter's condominiums on the market at once.[50]

By the end of 2007, Dubai World had invested $4.3 billion in the venture and their contribution was based on a maximum ("capped") cost of $8.5 billion, including construction for one component of the project, the Harmon Hotel and Condominiums.

In February 2008, MGM revised budgeted costs to $8.7 billion gross and $8 billion net. At this time, the company had begun to experience cancellations at its existing properties, and it predicted a slowdown for the rest of the year. Moreover, as a result of the design process still being in flux, the company had not completed negotiations with its contractors for all of its maximum-price guarantees.

MGM also experienced complaints of unsafe working conditions from workers and inspections by the Occupation and Safety and Health Administration, and retrofitted repairs reported by government inspectors detailed concerns that building towers were structurally unsound and did not meet earthquake resilient building code. In 2008 serious construction defects were found in the Harmon, designed by the prominent architect Norman Foster, which resulted in an indefinite halt to that project. At this stage, the Harmon was half-built. It had originally been conceived as having 47 stories, with the hotel on the lower half and condominiums on the upper half. The developers decided to terminate construction at 25 floors and abandoned the plan for 200 condominiums, leaving it as a 400-room hotel.[51]

In May 2008, MGM revised the project costs to $9.2 billion gross and $8.5 billion net. Moreover, these figures were not inclusive of all costs. When including the cost of the land, estimated fair market value of $1.7 billion, preopening expenses of $200 million, $100 million for additional expenses such as brands and management expertise, training and marketing costs, and research and development, the total estimated cost came to $11.2 billion. Moreover, the company had still not fully negotiated a maximum price agreement with all of its contractors.

By May 2008, the global financial crisis had already begun to unfold. Although the market for asset-backed commercial paper had stabilized, the investment bank Bear Stearns had collapsed in March, from having been overly exposed to mortgage-backed securities. By May, condominium sales had peaked and begun to slide, while revenues from gambling on the Strip had fallen 16 percent from a year earlier.

In respect to the budget revisions, perhaps the most significant issue was the sale of 2,400 condominium units in a collapsed Las Vegas residential market and the leasing of the 450,000-square-foot Crystals shopping mall. Relative to its previous forecasts, MGM could not sell as many units as it anticipated, and was forced to decrease prices on the ones it could sell. Low initial hotel occupancy also presented a major impact on revenue. As for cost overruns and delays, the underlying issues were varied: they were primarily driven not only by changes in design, but also by the rapidly rising costs of concrete, steel, and labor.[52]

In September 2008, the full global financial crisis erupted with the bankruptcy of investment bank Lehman Brothers. As a result, MGM found itself unable to obtain several billion dollars of loan financing it had planned to borrow from a consortium led by Bank of America. The company was forced to rely on its own cash, which made it vulnerable to going bankrupt.

On December 1, 2008, Jim Murren was named Chairman and CEO of MGM. In March 2009, the company's debt was $14 billion, and it indicated that it was considering bankruptcy. Dubai World filed a lawsuit against MGM seeking relief from its obligations. In April, the two partners reached an agreement allowing the project to continue. The consortium of lenders would provide $1.8 billion in loan financing at an interest rate 2 percent higher than originally negotiated, and MGM would be responsible for absorbing any project costs that exceeded $8.5 billion.

In May 2009, MGM announced that it had signed all of the guaranteed maximum price contracts with its contractors, and was confident its budget would remain at $8.5 billion.

In December 2009 CityCenter opened, but without the Harmon hotel, which was not expected to open until late 2010. As part of his statement at the opening in 2009, Murren stated: "And while we now stand on far more solid ground, 2009 still served as a wake-up call.... As a company, we begin every day with a new lease on life and a keen sense of optimism, armed with the lessons of the past."

MGM adapted to the changed economic environment. Unable to fill Crystals completely with high-end retail establishments, it leased out space temporarily to "pop up stores." It rented out unsold condominiums on a short-term basis. Nevertheless, between 2009 and 2012, CityCenter recorded approximately $2.5 billion in impairments related to CityCenter, roughly 25 percent of the project's cost.

Because of its construction flaws, the Harmon Hotel never opened. MGM sued Perini and won the judgment. In 2014, the Harmon was subsequently demolished as a result of the final court order and settlement with Perini.

By 2015, MGM had written down 50 percent of its share of the CityCenter investment.

Case Analysis Questions

1. Consider the issues of project budget, scope, and project timetable. Discuss the extent to which the CityCenter project reflects survey evidence discussed in the chapter about capital budgeting biases associated with the planning fallacy.
2. Consider whether MGM faced issues in the CityCenter project that could be characterized as sunk costs, and if so, whether they exhibited behavior consistent with "escalation of commitment."
3. Compare the CityCenter project with specific projects discussed in the chapter, namely: Sony's Chromatron, Syntex's Enrprostil, Motorola's Iridium, Eurotunnel's Channel Tunnel, Boeing's Dreamliner, and Airbus's A380. Your discussion should indicate whether the main psychological phenomena that surfaced in each project also surfaced in the City Center project, as well as commenting on similarities and differences in the comparisons.

Chapter Five

Inefficient Markets and Corporate Decisions

The main objective of this chapter is for students to demonstrate that they can identify the psychological phenomena that obstruct market efficiency and the associated implications for managers' behavior.

After completing this chapter students will be able to:

1. Differentiate among sentiment and fundamental risk as drivers of expected returns.
2. Explain how the limits to arbitrage can interfere with market efficiency even in the presence of smart money.
3. Describe the implications of the market efficiency debate in respect to catering behavior and market timing for corporate financial decisions involving project selection, earnings guidance, stock splits, and new equity issues.

5.1 TRADITIONAL APPROACH TO MARKET EFFICIENCY

The risk premium for a security is the minimum additional expected return, over and above the risk-free rate, that investors require in order to compensate them for risk. When the additional expected return exceeds the risk premium, investors are said to earn a positive abnormal return.

In the traditional framework, rational investors or smart money constantly monitor markets for abnormal profit opportunities. Therefore, the argument goes, smart money will quickly spot any opportunities that arise and begin to exploit them. Such exploitation, the buying of underpriced securities and selling of overpriced securities, is known as (risky) arbitrage. Notably, arbitrage will eliminate the opportunities as smart money bids up the prices of underpriced securities and bids down the prices of overpriced securities. Therefore, in the traditional view, inefficiencies will be small, short-lived, and unpredictable.

The efficient-market hypothesis evolved from statistical studies of market price movements that concluded that such movements were essentially random and unpredictable. In 1965, Nobel laureate Eugene Fama formalized this observation into the definition of market efficiency. Fama pointed out that in an efficient market, prices correspond to intrinsic (or fundamental) value.[1] However, he subsequently argued that because of the difficulty in computing intrinsic value with precision, it is better to define a financial market as being efficient when it is impossible to earn positive abnormal returns, thereby "beating the market." Of course, when the market prices of all securities coincide with their intrinsic values, investors will be unable to beat the market on a risk-adjusted basis.

In practice, the notion of market efficiency involves an asset pricing model such as the capital asset pricing model (CAPM) or a multifactor model such as the Fama-French model, named for economists Eugene Fama and Kenneth French, who developed it. In its original form, the Fama-French model featured three factors respectively corresponding to the market premium, firm size measured by market capitalization of equity, and the ratio of book-to-market equity (B/M). Subsequently, Fama and French added factors relating to profitability and firm investment, bringing the number of factors to five.[2]

The five-factor model captures historical patterns in realized returns whereby higher realized returns are associated with smaller market capitalization, higher B/M, higher profitability, and lower firm investment. According to the efficient market hypothesis, higher expected returns represent exact compensation for risk bearing, so that higher risk is associated with smaller market capitalization, higher B/M, higher profitability, and lower firm investment.

Notably, some pricing phenomena do not require a risk-based explanation. For example, market efficiency implies that stock splits will not affect the market values of firms because such splits only represent a cosmetic change, with no impact on intrinsic value.

The main message from traditional textbooks is that corporate managers should trust market prices, as far as publicly available information is concerned. This means that managers should not believe that the securities of their firms are mispriced, unless as managers they have private information to the contrary. For example, the traditional approach warns managers to abstain from market timing, issuing new shares because they believe the stocks of their firms to be overvalued, and conversely to abstain from repurchasing shares because they believe the stocks of their firms to be undervalued.

5.2 BEHAVIORAL APPROACH TO MARKET EFFICIENCY

According to the behavioral perspective, valuation errors stemming from psychological phenomena can cause departures from efficient pricing to be large and long-lasting rather than small and short-lived. The valuation errors are known as sentiment, and the inability of smart money to eliminate mispricing stemming from sentiment is known as the **limits to arbitrage**. Market inefficiencies are important, as they present opportunities for corporate managers to engage in market timing and catering. Market inefficiencies are also important to investors, a point which is discussed in Chapter 13—available online.

limits to arbitrage
Smart investors do not fully exploit mispricing because of the attendant risks that the mispricing will become larger before it becomes smaller.

Irrational Exuberance and Stocks as a Whole

irrational exuberance
Excessive optimism and overconfidence causes the stock market to be overvalued.

"**Irrational exuberance**" is a special case of sentiment whereby excessive optimism and overconfidence cause the stock market to be overvalued. The term irrational exuberance was first used in a December 1996 speech by then Federal Reserve Chair Alan Greenspan, and later popularized by economist and Nobel laureate Robert Shiller.

Together with John Campbell, Shiller presented evidence that the stock market is not always efficient.[3] In this regard, Exhibit 5-1 displays the long-run relationship between the price-to-dividend ratio (P/D) and subsequent 10-year excess returns (computed as the difference between the compounded average growth rate and the 10-year bond rate, both in real terms). Extremely high values of P/D are associated with an overvalued stock market, which when corrected over time results in negative returns.

When the stock market is efficient and stocks are riskier than bonds, the risk premium on stocks should always be nonnegative. Given the strong linear relationship in Exhibit 5-1, the evidence suggests that negative returns, as well as risk premiums, are predictable when P/D is sufficiently high.[4]

Sentiment Beta

There are a variety of ways to measure sentiment, one of which is the Baker-Wurgler sentiment index (B-W), named for the economists who developed it, Malcolm Baker and Jeff Wurgler.[5] Baker and Wurgler suggest that when sentiment rises, investors increase the riskiness of their portfolios by holding a higher proportion of stocks and by shifting into more speculative stocks. The primary example of a speculative stock is a company that is young, currently unprofitable but potentially very profitable, has no earnings history, and a highly uncertain future. Notably, these characteristics

EXHIBIT 5-1
Scatter Plot of Price-to-Dividend Ratio for S&P 500 Stocks and Subsequent Ten-Year Excess Returns, for Ten-Year Intervals Beginning in December 1899

Source: Online Data Robert Shiller, **www.econ.yale.edu/~shiller/data.htm**

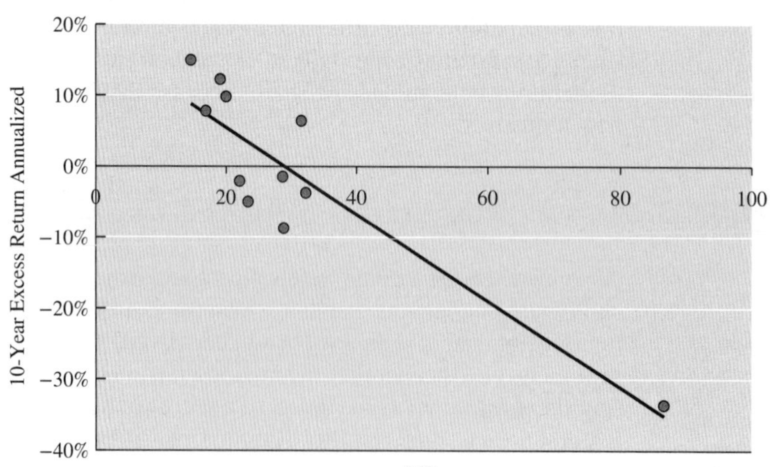

support a wide range of investor valuations. At the other end of the spectrum are stocks of firms that feature a long history of earnings, tangible assets, and stable dividends. These stocks tend to be easier to value, less likely to generate a wide range of valuations, and safer than speculative stocks. In practice, stocks are sorted from safe to speculative according to their total historical volatility.

Baker and Wurgler introduce the notion of "sentiment beta," the sensitivity of a stock's historical return to changes in B-W. When investors become excessively optimistic, stocks with high and positive sentiment betas tend to be overvalued. However, as future events typically fail to live up to inflated expectations, subsequent returns tend to be inferior. Conversely, when investors are excessively pessimistic, stocks with high and positive sentiment betas tend to be undervalued, leading their subsequent returns to be superior.

Evidence provided by Baker and Wurgler indicates that subsequent abnormal returns to high sentiment beta stocks are negative after periods of high sentiment and positive after periods of low sentiment. In addition, the absolute value of abnormal returns is positively related to sentiment beta.

Limits to Arbitrage

Unlike the efficient market hypothesis, which postulates that risk arbitrage by smart money quickly eliminates deviations from market efficiency, the behavioral approach postulates that there are limits to arbitrage. A pertinent example of such a limit involves the restrictions on short selling. Even when the optimism of some investors is counterbalanced by the pessimism of other investors, the higher transaction costs of taking short positions in stocks, relative to long positions, dampens arbitrage activity and results in market prices reflecting optimism.

The behavioral approach emphasizes the importance of costly arbitrage. Economists[6] note that would-be arbitrageurs who trade to exploit mispricing expose themselves to additional risks. The most important risk is that irrational investors push prices further away from fundamentals, even after arbitrageurs take their positions. Professional investment managers are natural candidates for being arbitrageurs. Nevertheless, unless they have long horizons and very deep pockets, these investment managers might not have the patience to withstand mispricing becoming worse before it gets better. This is especially true when their clients mistakenly conclude that the managers lack skill, and head for the exits by withdrawing funds in the face of losses. A related risk stems from liquidity, when a wave of pessimism turns to panic and a preponderance of investors seek to sell at the same time.

Some stocks are more difficult to arbitrage than others. A notable example consists of stocks of young, small companies that are unprofitable or experiencing extreme growth. The returns to such stocks tend to feature high idiosyncratic risk, which can be problematic for professional money managers betting on them, for the reasons mentioned in the previous paragraph. Notably, these companies do not pay dividends for many years, making the task of estimating their intrinsic values more challenging, and subject to greater speculation. These are the kinds of stocks that feature high sentiment betas. In other words, the same securities that are difficult to value also tend to be difficult to arbitrage.

Risk and Sentiment

CONCEPT PREVIEW
Question 5.1

Imagine two stock portfolios, one called "winners" and one called "losers," both formed by sorting all U.S. stocks according to their most recent six-month returns. The winners portfolio comprises the stocks in the top 20 percent, while the losers portfolio comprises stocks in the bottom 20 percent. Suppose that the historical evidence is that in the six months subsequent to forming the two portfolios, the winners portfolio has tended to drift upwards, while the losers portfolio has continued to drift downwards, with the winners portfolio outperforming the losers portfolio by 10 percent a year. How would you explain this difference in returns?

anomalies
Findings that are inconsistent with the joint hypothesis that markets are efficient and risk and return are related through a particular asset pricing model.

momentum
Recent losers tend subsequently to underperform the market, and recent winners tend subsequently to outperform the market.

The factors in multifactor models have evolved through the discovery of **anomalies**. During the 1970s, academic economists concluded that the CAPM, a single factor model, adequately explained expected returns without attendant market inefficiencies. However, a series of studies then found positive abnormal returns associated with a series of variables such as market capitalization (size), B/M (value and growth), **momentum** (short-term drift), and profitability.[7]

Fama and French use the phrase "brute force" to describe their multifactor approach, noting that the framework has no theoretical basis, but instead was developed by them because it captured essential empirical traits in realized return data. In 2008, Fama acknowledged the possibility that size and book-to-market might reflect psychological phenomena, but argued that it is impossible to test whether or not this is the case.[8] In 2013, when he was awarded a Nobel Prize in economics, together with Shiller and Lars Peter Hansen, he repeated his assertion that it is not possible to distinguish between behavioral and rational explanations for how stocks are priced.[9]

Managerial Decisions: Market Timing and Catering

Corporate managers are natural candidates to be arbitrageurs in the securities of their own firms when those securities are mispriced, by engaging in market timing or catering behavior. In this regard, evidence about high returns to insider trading strongly suggests that managers possess information about their own firms that is superior to other investors.[10]

Certainly, managers can manage earnings, thereby producing information to their advantage. There is strong evidence that managers manipulate earnings in order to avoid reporting negative earnings per share (EPS), if they can avoid doing so. For example, EPS is highly clustered around zero from the right, a penny a share, but drops off dramatically when moving left, minus a penny a share.[11] There is evidence that managers are more inclined to manage earnings when compensated with company stock and options.[12] Moreover, they can use earnings guidance to influence analysts' earnings forecasts and recommendations,[13] and investor relations to influence investor perceptions of their firms.

Like other arbitrageurs, corporate managers are subject to the limits to arbitrage. However, some of those limits apply less strictly to them than to professional money managers. When the equity in their firms becomes overvalued, and money managers need to contemplate the trading costs of short selling, corporate managers can issue new shares. In addition, corporate managers tend to have longer horizons on which their performance is evaluated, and less of a need to have deep pockets to deal with redemptions. Subsequent increases in the firm's stock price are unlikely to generate criticism of corporate managers, whereas for money managers who have shorted the stock, the situation is very different.

The traditional efficient market-based advice for corporate managers has been to trust market prices, as there is no value to engaging in risky arbitrage. The behavioral-based advice is more nuanced. In the presence of mispricing, corporate managers who are "sufficiently smart" can add value to their firms through catering and market timing. The caveat is being "sufficiently smart," a concept which entails self-knowledge about vulnerabilities to psychological pitfalls. If strong enough, such pitfalls can outweigh the other advantages available to corporate managers. That said, corporate managers who are near-rational would be well advised to act as arbitrageurs if given the means and the motive.

The remainder of the chapter discusses arbitrage by corporate managers in respect to three types of managerial decisions: investment policy in combination with earnings guidance, stock splits, and undertaking an initial pubic offering (IPO). In each case, the discussion focuses on how market inefficiency, or the perception of market inefficiency, impacts these decisions.

5.3 MARKET EFFICIENCY, EARNINGS GUIDANCE, AND NPV

Financial managers routinely disclose information to security analysts in a process called *guidance*.[14] Among the most important information that managers disclose is the managers' own forecasts of what future earnings per share will be for their firms. For this reason, managers are able to influence stock prices by choosing to disclose information to analysts and investors.

Net present value (NPV), when properly computed, measures incremental intrinsic value. In an efficient market, price equals intrinsic value. This important point, made by Fama, underlies the rationale for encouraging corporate managers to maximize NPV. In an efficient market, maximizing NPV is equivalent to maximizing market value.

When prices are inefficient, maximizing NPV based on cash flows might not be the same as maximizing the market value of the firm. As a result, market inefficiency can present financial managers with a dilemma about whether to cater to investors' biases.

Evidence from a survey of chief financial officers indicates that the majority view earnings rather than cash flows as the key variable upon which investors rely to judge value.[15] Because the market reacts very negatively when a firm misses an earnings target, a strong majority of managers are willing to sacrifice fundamental value in order to meet a short-run earnings target. Survey evidence finds that over

Behavioral Pitfalls: Herman–Miller

During 2000, furniture manufacturer Herman-Miller was evaluating a potential web-based project. The firm had put together a business plan for the project, with projected financial statements over a three- to five-year horizon. An accounting issue arose in connection with the project, because the initial investment had to be expensed rather than capitalized. Therefore the project, despite having positive net present value, would adversely impact net income in the short-term.

The managers at Herman-Miller said to themselves: "Maybe we shouldn't do it this year." Brian Walker, the president of Herman-Miller North America then asked the group: "How would we view this if it was capitalized and not expensed on the income statement?" He reported that members of the group looked at each other and said: "If it were capital and not expense, we'd do it; the problem was [that] it was hitting EPS."

Herman-Miller's CFO, Elizabeth Nickels, described the balancing act her firm faced, in the following terms: "Much of the outside world still looks at EPS, whether you like it or not, and the question is, how do you balance between the two?" Herman-Miller dealt with this balancing act by reevaluating and reprioritizing other expenditures in order to free up capital for the new project.

Walker also offered the following observation, contrasting his firm with Internet firms:

> For dot.coms, it appears that the market has implicitly capitalized a lot of those costs. The market views their negative earnings as investments in the future. It's more difficult for a traditional Old Economy company trying to participate in the New Economy, because when it affects my earnings, it's more difficult for Wall Street to say, "We'll give you a break on this."

Source: G. Millman, "Capital Allocation: When the Right Thing Is Hard to Do," *Financial Executive*, September/October 2000, pp. 29–40.

half of managers would avoid initiating a very positive NPV project if doing so meant missing analysts' target for the current quarter's earnings. In other words, these managers choose catering behavior.

The relationship between investment and earnings can also be direct in that managers can use expenditures on research and development (R&D) to affect earnings. For example, if managers are concerned that the firm's actual earnings will fall below analysts' earnings expectations, they tend to postpone planned expenditures for R&D. Notably, R&D expenditures are expensed rather than capitalized.[16] In this respect, consider the example featuring the firm Herman-Miller that is presented in the nearby Behavioral Pitfalls box.

5.4 STOCK SPLITS

Proponents of market efficiency urge managers to trust market prices.[17] For example, according to the efficient-market view, a firm that splits its stock should not expect to see an abnormal change in its market value of equity. However, it turns out that there is positive drift associated with stock splits.[18]

Firms that split their stocks earn an average abnormal return of 7.93 percent in the first year, and 12.15 percent in the first three years. The three-year effect seems to be concentrated in value stocks. For growth stocks, the effect does not extend beyond the first year. What is especially interesting is that firms that decide to split their stocks tend to feature pessimistic coverage by analysts in respect to earnings forecasts.[19] In addition, firms that announce stock splits are much less likely to experience a decline in future earnings, relative to firms with comparable characteristics.

Example: Tandy's Stock Split

In 1962, the Tandy Corporation purchased RadioShack, a company that specialized in selling high-margin, non-brand-name electronic goods to hobbyists. During the late 1970s and early 1980s, RadioShack sold the most popular personal computer in the world, the TRS-80. Eventually the TRS-80 lost most of its market share to competitors such as IBM and Apple.

Tandy maintained its focus on its loyal base of hobbyists and electronic do-it-yourselfers. However, it simultaneously embarked on a strategy of opening stores, which were quite different from RadioShack, to sell brand-name, big-screen televisions; home appliances; and other items. Although these stores generated large sales, they were highly unprofitable, and Tandy lost money for the first time in its history. In May 1999 Tandy announced a two-for-one stock split. In making the announcement, Leonard Roberts, Tandy's CEO, stated that he believed Tandy's stock price to be undervalued, even though it had increased 81.5 percent since the beginning of the year. He also indicated that he expected that the digital revolution would continue to fuel growth in Tandy's sales and profits, especially for cell phones.

Chuck Hill, the research director for First Call Corporation, which tracks corporate earnings, offered two interesting comments in respect to Tandy's stock split. First, he stated that he believed that Tandy would not have undertaken the split if it had concerns about a downturn in the near future. That statement reflects the general finding that firms that announce stock splits are much less likely to experience a decline in future earnings, relative to firms with comparable characteristics.

Second, Hill suggested that the lower stock prices would generate interest among individual investors, even though institutional investors held 72 percent of Tandy's stock. His reason? The stock price will look cheap even though the intrinsic value of the firm will be unchanged. Hill noted that stock splits often make a difference, even though the logic is questionable.[20] Notably, Tandy's stock outperformed the S&P 500 (by 11.3 percent) one year after the stock split.

The cell phone strategy that Roberts negotiated with carriers provided RadioShack with a share of device sales and also a share of customers' monthly payments. Although it was successful in generating cash flow, signing up new customers turned out to be very time-consuming, and diverted the attention of salespeople from the company's hobbyist customers. RadioShack also initiated an e-commerce strategy, but failed to compete successfully with firms such as Amazon. By 2005, Roberts retired and the company's business began to decline. Cell phone companies began operating their own stores instead of selling through RadioShack. In addition, improvements in cell phones resulted in lower RadioShack sales for items such as voice recorders, GPS devices, answering machines, and camcorders. RadioShack tried to reduce costs by hiring less skilled salespeople, thereby losing business from hobbyists. By 2015, it closed the majority of its stores, declared bankruptcy, and commenced a cobranding agreement with Sprint.

5.5 TO IPO OR NOT TO IPO?

hot issue market
Demand for new issues is relatively high.

initial underpricing
The offer price is too low, resulting in a large first-day price pop.

long-term underperformance
New issues earn lower returns than stocks with comparable characteristics against which they have been matched.

Three Phenomena

IPO decisions take place against the backdrop of three phenomena: a **hot issue market, initial underpricing,** and **long-term underperformance.**[21] In a hot issue market, investor demand for IPOs is high, thereby potentially presenting issuing firms with the opportunity to engage in market timing. To say that a new issue is initially underpriced is to say that the offer price is too low, resulting in a large first-day price pop when the stock is traded publicly for the first time. To say that the stocks of new issues feature long-term underperformance is to say that new issues earn lower returns than stocks with comparable characteristics (size and book-to-market equity) against which they have been matched.[22]

In order to understand these phenomena, and the way they have changed over time, begin with Exhibit 5-2.[23] This exhibit displays two monthly series for the time period 1980 to mid-2015, the number of offerings and the average first-day return to an IPO (in percent). Notice how the number of IPOs occurs in waves, giving rise to so-called hot and cold issue markets.

The first-day return has also been highly volatile over time. In this respect, look at four distinct subperiods: the 1980s (1980–1989), the 1990s (1990–1998), the so-called (dot.com) bubble period (1999–2000), and the postbubble period (2001 to present). The average first-day return was about 7 percent in the 1980s, 15 percent in the 1990s, 65 percent during the bubble period, and 12 percent in the postbubble period.

Exhibit 5-3 displays the general finding about long-term underperformance for the period 1980 to mid-2015. Notice that during the first six months, the returns of issuing firms were higher than the returns of comparable firms that were similar in size and book-to-market equity, but did not issue new shares. However, beginning

EXHIBIT 5-2
Number of Offerings and Average First-Day Returns, 1980 to mid-2015

Source: Jay Ritter's web site, **site.warrington.ufl.edu/ritter/ipo.**

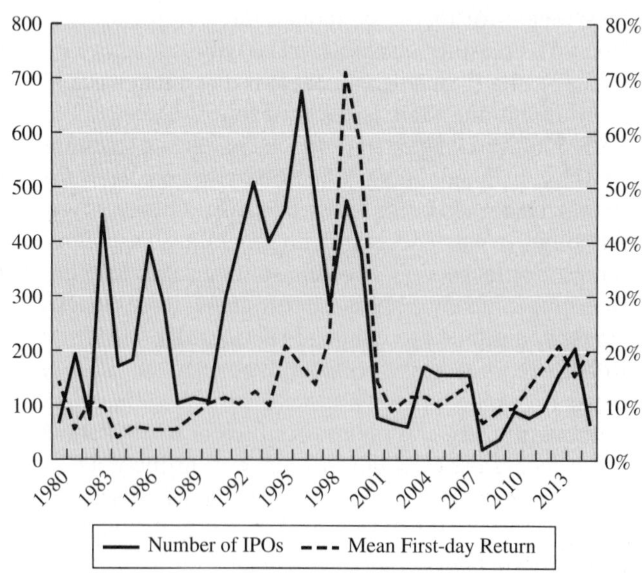

EXHIBIT 5-3
Comparison IPO Returns and Firms Matched by Size and Book-to-Market Equity, 1980 to mid-2015

Source: Jay Ritter's web site, **site.warrington.ufl.edu/ritter/ipo.**

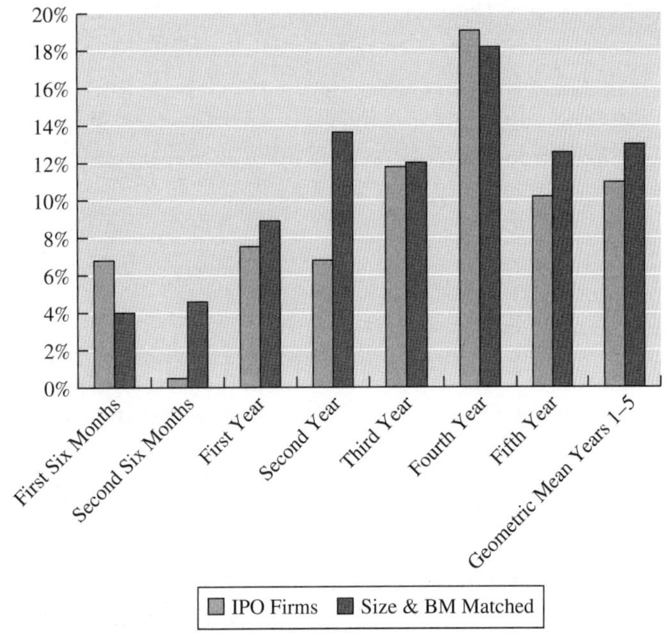

six months after the new issue, the shares of issuing firms began to underperform the shares of similar firms that did not issue new shares. Over a five-year horizon, IPOs underperformed by 2 percent a year (= 0.13 – 0.11). The degree of long-term underperformance has not been steady over time. In the 1980s it was 2.8 percent, and in the 1990s it was 5.2 percent.

IPO Decisions

All three IPO phenomena discussed reflect decisions made by financial executives. Consider the nature of these decisions in relation to the concept of market efficiency.

Hot Issue Markets

Imagine the financial executive of a privately held firm that does not plan on raising external funds for at least two years. When the firm needs external funds, the executive plans to raise those funds through an IPO. Suppose that the current market is a hot issue market. Should the executive move up the firm's plans to take the firm public to try to take advantage of the hot issue market?

The traditional efficient-market based advice is that managers should not try to time markets. In contrast, the typical advice from financial executives is to try to exploit hot issue markets. On May 20, 2004, *The Wall Street Journal* quoted George Rathmann on this issue. Rathmann was the first chief executive officer of biotechnology firm Amgen. He drew an analogy between deciding whether or not to go IPO and deciding whether or not to accept hors d'oeuvres at a cocktail party when the tray comes around. His advice? Take the hors d'oeuvres when the tray comes around, whether you are hungry or not.[24]

Behavioral Pitfalls: The IPO of Palm

Between January 1997 and August 1999, when the equity market rose sharply, 3Com's stock declined in value. In August 1999, about half of the analysts following 3Com were bearish on its stock and expressed widely divergent views about the firm's mixture of businesses.

At the time, 3Com had three businesses: modems and adaptor cards, networking equipment, and personal digital assistants (PDAs). CEO Eric Benhamou considered whether his firm had become unfocused. In September 1999 3Com announced its intention to carve out its PDA Palm division, making it an independent publicly traded company, and refocusing on networking equipment.

In March 2000, 3Com began to separate its handheld organizer division by selling 6 percent of Palm's outstanding shares, mostly in an initial public offering (IPO). As part of the IPO, 3Com sold the shares to an investment banking syndicate, which in turn placed the shares with institutional investors at a price agreed upon by the investment banks and 3Com. (The lead underwriters were Goldman Sachs and Morgan Stanley.)

Between August 1999 and March 10, 2000, the Nasdaq composite index virtually doubled, and peaked at 5132 on March 10. Palm went public on March 2, 2000.

Palm's offer price was $38 per share. At the pricing meeting that established the offer price, 3Com executives realized that there would be severe initial underpricing. However, an offer price higher than $38 would have required refiling with the Securities and Exchange Commission and that would have resulted in a delay.

On March 2, Palm stock opened at $165 and closed the day at $95. When Palm went public, it had fewer than 700 employees. At $165 per share, Palm's valuation was $92.7 billion, placing it in the company of some of the largest firms in the United States, such as Disney and Boeing whose market capitalizations that day were $71.4 billion and $33.5 billion, respectively.

At the close of its first day of trading, Palm was worth $53.4 billion, more than 3Com's value of $28 billion. And 3Com still held 94 percent of Palm. In July 2000, 3Com sold its remaining shares of Palm, and the price of 3Com stock declined from just above $65 to about $15, about the same as it had been in late February, days before the initial Palm IPO.

Why did the market permit Palm's stock to trade as high as it did early on, especially in March of 2000? Was there not a clear profit opportunity there? Indeed there was. However, investors who thought that Palm was highly overvalued at that time could not find shares to borrow in order to short the stock. Therefore the beliefs of excessively optimistic investors set the price of Palm.

In October 2000, *The Wall Street Journal* ran an article describing growing consumer demand for Palm PDAs. At the time, Palm's shares were trading at a forward P/E ratio of 350 and a price-to-sales ratio of about 20. Paul Sagawa, a wireless telecommunications analyst at Sanford Bernstein, rated Palm's shares as "outperform," called it his favorite stock, and described it as cheap because of its enormous upside potential. *The Wall Street Journal* article mentioned that Sagawa's enthusiasm for the stock increased after he purchased a Palm for his wife and watched her use it to keep track of her phone numbers and social appointments.

Eleven months after Palm's IPO, its stock was trading at $21. Palm employees were becoming distracted by the declining stock price, as their stock options were "under water." In this respect, the exercise price on those stock options had been set at the $38 offer price. At that time, 3Com executives concluded that Palm was overvalued. For their part, Palm's executives acknowledged being uncertain how to compute Palm's fair value. And they did rely on P/E and price-to-sales in order to assess Palm's intrinsic value, comparing Palm's ratios to the ratios for other comparable firms. However, they were well aware about hot and cold issue markets. Eleven months after Palm's IPO, the firm's CFO indicated that Palm would not have wanted to raise equity in the conditions prevailing at the time, with Palm's stock down 45 percent from its offer price and the Nasdaq composite down by about the same amount.

The price of Palm's stock went from its all-time high of $165 on March 2, 2000, to $0.60 in August 2002.

The general evidence in respect to fundamental value is that the executives of many Internet firms did not believe their firms were overvalued at the time of their IPOs. Some years after Palm's IPO, former 3Com executives were asked whether in retrospect 3Com had sold overvalued shares to the public. They responded saying that they viewed Palm's shares as being overvalued relative to fundamentals, but undervalued at a $38 offer price relative to what the market was willing to pay in the aftermarket.

As to being overvalued relative to fundamentals, 3Com executives stated that they had the responsibility of maximizing value for their current shareholders at the time, and that it would be irresponsible not to do so, despite the likelihood that the return on Palm stock would be low in the long term.

As the firm struggled, it split itself in two, becoming PalmOne and PalmSource, seeking to focus on its traditional mobile device business as well as developing a new cell phone strategy. However, it failed to compete successfully with Apple's iPhone, Research in Motion's BlackBerry and devices that ran Google's Android software. In particular, Palm was slow to recognize the role of smart phone applications. By 2010, Palm was running out of projects and sold itself to Hewlett-Packard (HP) for approximately $1.2 billion in cash. HP stated that it was interested in Palm's WebOS operating system for smart phones and tablets, as well as its more than 400 patents. Nevertheless, in 2014, HP sold the remnants of Palm's patents to Qualcomm. In 2015, HP sold Palm's brand to the Chinese firm TCL Communication, which planned to revive the firm with a new set of products aimed at what had once been loyal Palm customers.

Sources: See C. Scott, "Smartmoney Daily Screen: Who's Right About 3Com?" September 15, 1999, *Dow Jones News Service;* See "3Com Plans to Spin Off Palm Computing Unit to Focus on Networking," *Dow Jones Business News*, September 13, 1999; See O. Lamont and R. Thaler, "Can the Market Add and Subtract? Mispricing in Tech Stock Carve-Outs," *Journal of Political Economy* 111, pp. 227–268, 2003; See P. Schultz and M. Zirman, "Do the Individuals Closest to Internet Firms Believe They Are Overvalued?" *Journal of Financial Economics*, vol. 59, 2001; Guest lectures presented by former 3Com executives at Santa Clara University, April 29, 2005.

Initial Underpricing

Financial executives' decisions play an important role in the extent of initial underpricing. The IPO offer price is typically determined in a pricing meeting between the firm's executives and the underwriters taking the firm public, just before the stock begins to trade publicly. The existence of initial underpricing suggests that on average, executives agree to an offer price that is too low, that they do not bargain hard enough, and consequently they leave money on the table.

Risk. If markets are efficient, the initial underpricing reflects compensation for risk, not the fact that executives do not bargain hard enough. That is, investors purchasing the shares at the offer price face risk in buying the shares of a new firm. Therefore, they are only willing to purchase those shares if the offer price is low enough.

Psychology and Changing Underpricing. Exhibit 5-4 shows that the magnitude of underpricing increased throughout the 1990s and soared during the bubble period, 1999–2000. Why were executives increasingly willing to leave so much money on the

EXHIBIT 5-4
Amount Left on Table, 1980 to mid-2015

Source: Jay Ritter's web site, **site.warrington.ufl.edu/ritter/ipo.**

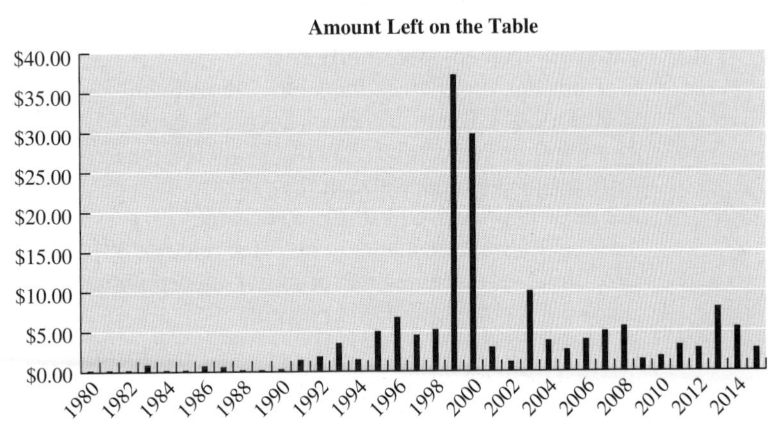

table, especially during the bubble period? There are several possible explanations: changing risk, behavioral phenomena, and agency conflicts. Behaviorists contend that there is no strong evidence that changing risk conditions could explain the dramatic amounts of money left on the table during the bubble period.[25] However, they do suggest that there are strong reasons to suspect that behavioral phenomena and agency conflicts were key.

CONCEPT PREVIEW
Question 5.2

Imagine two people, Ginger and Jane, who have each just received parking tickets that will cost them $50 apiece. As it happens, both Ginger and Jane have won office lotteries for $75. Ginger won her office lottery the month before she received her parking ticket. Jane won her office lottery the same day she received her parking ticket. Both Ginger and Jane feel the pain of their parking tickets.

1. Who do you think feels the pain more intensely? You may answer Ginger, Jane, no difference, or no opinion.
2. Suppose that instead of receiving a parking ticket that will cost her $50, Ginger learns that she missed out on winning $50 in another office lottery because she was absent from work that day. Which do you believe would cause Ginger more pain, receiving the $50 parking ticket or having missed winning $50 in an office lottery?

Concept Preview Question 5.2 offers two lessons. The first lesson is that most people feel that Ginger experiences the pain from receiving her parking ticket more than Jane feels the pain from receiving hers. Presumably, Jane can mentally offset her $50 loss with the $75 lottery win and view herself as $25 ahead at the end of the day. However, that mental operation is much more difficult to do for Ginger, who is less likely to associate the $75 gain with the $50 loss because the gain occurred a month earlier. Therefore, Ginger is likely to view herself as being down $50 at the end of the day because of the parking ticket, instead of up $25.

The second lesson from Concept Preview Question 5.2 is that Ginger feels the $50 loss from the parking ticket more than she feels having lost out on winning $50 in the office lottery. Generally, people experience a cost that is out of pocket more intensely than an opportunity cost.

Consider an IPO example to illustrate the behavioral phenomenon just described.[26] VA Linux Systems (later to become Geeknet, Inc.) sells computers that run the Linux operating system, an alternative to Microsoft's Windows. When the firm planned to undertake an IPO, it filed with the SEC and established a file range for its offer price of $11 to $13 a share. VA Linux went public on December 9, 1999, issuing 4.4 million shares at an offer price of $30 to raise $132 million. That day VA Linux set a new record for initial underpricing, closing its first day at a price of $239.25, for a return of 698 percent.

Based on the difference between its offer price and its stock price at the end of its first day, VA Linux left $920.7 million on the table. Had the offer price been $239.25 instead of $30, the firm would have only needed to issue 551,724 shares

EXHIBIT 5-5
Money Left on Table for VA Linux IPO

Source: Jay Ritter's web site, **site.warrington.ufl.edu/ritter/ipo.**

Midpoint file range in initial prospectus	$12.00
Offer price	$30.00
Price close on first day of trading	$239.25
Number of shares held prior to IPO	35,307,419
Number of shares issued in IPO	4,400,000
Amount raised by IPO	$132,000,000
Number of new shares issued if no underpricing	551,724
Percent of firm retained by initial investors	88.9%
Percent of firm retained by initial investors if no underpricing	98.5%

to raise $132 million, not 4.4 million shares. As a result, the original shareholders ended up owning about 9 percent less of the firm. See Exhibit 5-5.

Was VA Linux's huge first-day return gain predictable? Based on other recent IPOs, a large first-day gain was predictable, although certainly not the record amount set. As Exhibit 5-2 shows, throughout the bubble period the magnitude of underpricing had been large. Several months earlier, on August 11, the share price of Red Hat Inc., a distributor of Linux, tripled on its first day of trading. By the time VA Linux went public, Red Hat shares had risen twentyfold and were trading at $286.25. Andover.net Inc., another firm with a significant Linux component, had gone public a few days before VA Linux, and its share price had more than tripled.

In agreeing to initial underpricing, VA Linux's chief executive, Larry M. Augustin, agreed to owning 2 percent less of the firm than he would have if the offer price had been set at $286.25. As was mentioned, the original investors collectively gave up 9 percent.

Think about the changes to Augustin's personal wealth during the IPO process. When VA Linux went public, Augustin owned 6.6 million shares. Based on the midpoint of the $11 to $13 file range specified in the initial prospectus, he might have expected his shares to be worth $12 each. Therefore, the $30 offer price constituted a mental gain of $18 per share, a total wealth gain of about $119 million. And the record first-day return increased Augustin's wealth by another $1.4 billion.

As in Concept Preview Question 5.2, the money left on the table is not experienced as painfully if it occurs in conjunction with some other gain, and moreover, is framed as an opportunity cost. Although giving up 9 percent of a firm is not small change, it is difficult to imagine a CEO feeling too badly when his personal wealth has just increased on successive days by $119 million and $1.4 billion. Those gains are not only tangible, but also take attention away from the money left on the table because of initial underpricing. Moreover, the amount of money left on the table is an opportunity cost, not an out-of-pocket cost.

Evidence indicates that CEOs who are satisfied with the psychological balance of gains and losses described above use the same underwriter for their first seasoned equity offering as their IPO.

Agency Conflicts and Changing Underpricing. Every year, the publication *Institutional Investor* ranks security analysts. Analysts achieving the highest rank are accorded star status. Notably, investment banks that underwrite IPOs employ analysts, with investment banks employing all-star analysts tending to gain market share in the underwriting business. Presumably this is because firms who choose an underwriter to take them public factor in analyst coverage in the aftermarket (post-IPO).

In exchange for taking a firm public, an investment bank typically charges an underwriting fee that amounts to 7 percent of the gross offering. Underwriters do not charge firms directly for analyst coverage. However, firms might pay indirectly for analyst coverage by agreeing to initial underpricing. That is, a firm might accept a lower offer price in exchange for coverage by an all-star analyst, believing that such coverage will promote higher stock prices in the future.

Underwriters might capture the benefits of initial underpricing indirectly rather than directly. They do so circuitously by allocating hot IPO shares, those that are likely to feature a large first-day return, to clients who will do a lot of business with their firm. To illustrate, consider a real example involving the investment bank Credit Suisse First Boston (CSFB).[27] A CSFB customer received an IPO allocation of 13,500 shares of VA Linux, which he sold on the first day for a profit of $3.3 million. The customer then sold two million shares of Compaq through CSFB, paying a commission of $0.50 a share, or $1 million in total. The customer then repurchased the two million shares of Compaq from another brokerage firm, paying only $0.06 a share in commissions. Overall, the customer paid $1.2 million in commissions, but came out $2.1 million ahead. CSFB captured $1 million of the $3.3 million in underpricing associated with the customer's allocation.

Investment banks extended the process of allocating hot IPO shares to favored customers. The practice came to be called *spinning* and was eventually banned as part of a legal settlement initiated by Eliot Spitzer, then the New York Attorney General. Spinning exploits agency conflicts. An underwriter would spin hot IPO shares by allocating them to the personal accounts of financial executives whose investment banking business the underwriters wished to attract. Investment banker Frank Quattrone of CSFB attracted the most attention for the practice, and the brokerage accounts he set up for corporate executives came to be called *Friends of Frank* accounts.

On March 7, 2003, the *San Jose Mercury News* published a list of 63 executives who had Friends of Frank accounts. The median executive earned $538,000 from his or her account. An agency conflict arises when the executive of a firm that is planning to go public chooses to use CSFB and agrees to initial underpricing in exchange for large future allocations in his or her Friend of Frank account. The executive gains that benefit by imposing the underpricing cost on his or her own firm's investors. For its part, CSFB comes to be known for underpricing, and its Friends of Frank accounts attract a steady stream of executives to provide underpriced IPOs for its revolving-door scheme.

Frank Quattrone was tried for obstructing justice when he forwarded an e-mail message to CSFB employees suggesting that they delete documents. The e-mail was sent shortly after federal investigators began to focus on IPO practices at CSFB. In September 2004, Quattrone was found guilty and sentenced to an 18-month prison term, which he appealed. A year earlier, the National Association of Securities Dealers (NASD, later to be renamed FINRA) had barred him from the securities industry for life. Quattrone's conviction was overturned on appeal, and the NASD also reversed its decision.

Long-Term Underperformance

The stock of VA Linux closed in 2002 at a price of $0.91 per share, providing a dramatic example of all three IPO phenomena. Although proponents of market efficiency suggest that long-term underperformance can be explained by factors such as size and book-to-market equity, Exhibit 5-3 provides evidence that this is not the case.[28] Although size and book-to-market equity explain some of the returns to IPOs, there appears to be a separate new-issue phenomenon. Nevertheless, size appears to be much more important than book-to-market, with especially low long-term returns to firms that have low sales.[29]

Dilemma

The three IPO phenomena present executives with something of a dilemma. Maximizing market value in the short-term might well require going IPO in a hot issue market and paying for all-star analyst coverage by means of initial underpricing. However, doing so might involve exploiting excessive optimism on the part of current investors. If so, then there is reason to expect long-term underperformance, as the market eventually corrects itself.

What then should managers do? Maximize the interests of short-term investors over those of long-term investors as 3Com's CEO suggested, vice versa, or try to balance the two? There is no easy answer to this question, although anecdotes such as the one involving Herman-Miller suggest that managers are prone to strike a balance.

To the extent that market prices revert to fundamental value in the long-term, maximizing long-term value corresponds to the conventional approach based on NPV. To the extent that the impact of size, book-to-market equity, and momentum on expected returns stems from behavioral mispricing rather than fundamental risk, discount rates used for the long-term should be based on a single-factor CAPM approach.

The preceding statements should not be interpreted to mean that managers compute NPV correctly. Doing so requires that managers prepare unbiased forecasts of cash flow, the market risk premium, and risk. The evidence presented throughout this text suggests that managers' forecasts exhibit systematic bias.

Corporate Nudges

Errors or biases: Executives agree to offer prices that are too low.

Why does it happen? Executives exhibit framing bias, emphasizing in-pocket gains over opportunity losses, and agency conflicts.

How does it happen? In the case of large revisions relative to the file range, executives overweight gains relative to the midpoint of the file range in relation to money left on the table from initial underpricing.

What can be done about it? Executives need to identify all the benefits and costs associated with going IPO, and think explicitly about treating opportunity costs in the same way as out-of-pocket costs.

Summary

Market efficiency is a subject of great debate among financial economists. The traditional approach holds that markets are efficient, whereas proponents of behavioral finance hold that in special circumstances market prices tend to be inefficient.

The notion of arbitrage is central to the debate between proponents of market efficiency and proponents of behavioral finance. Traditionalists contend that the actions of arbitrageurs render price inefficiencies small and temporary. Behaviorists contend that arbitrage is limited and that as a result market prices can deviate from intrinsic values substantially and for long periods of time. They note that the degree to which a security is mispriced can reflect its sentiment beta. Securities that are difficult to value and difficult to arbitrage tend to have higher sentiment betas than securities that are easier to value and easier to arbitrage.

Managers appear to behave as if they believe markets are inefficient, leading them to engage in catering behavior and market timing. For example, they indicate that they would reject positive NPV projects if accepting those projects would lower their firm's EPS. They split their stocks, even though doing so has no value when markets are efficient. And they time IPOs to take advantage of hot issue markets.

Behavioral explanations alone do not explain managerial behavior in respect to IPOs. Agency issues also contribute to explaining initial underpricing and long-term underperformance, two other IPO phenomena.

Additional Behavioral Readings

Baker, M and J. Wurgler (2007), "Investor Sentiment in the Stock Market,"*Journal of Economic Perspectives* 21, 2007, pp. 129–151.

Fox, J., "Learn to Play the Earnings Game (and Wall Street Will Love You)," *Fortune,* March 31, 1997.

Lamont, O. and R. Thaler, "Can the Market Add and Subtract? Mispricing in Tech Stock Carve-Outs," Working Paper, University of Chicago, 2000.

Loughran, T. and J. Ritter, "Why Has IPO Underpricing Changed over Time?" *Financial Management,* vol. 33, no. 3, 2004, pp. 5–37.

Key Terms

anomalies, *114*
hot issue market, *118*
initial underpricing, *118*
irrational exuberance, *112*
limits to arbitrage, *111*
long-term underperformance, *118*
momentum, *114*

Explore the Web

http://knowledge.insead.edu/blog/insead-blog/the-buyback-fund-that-gives-back-3777
Description of buyback fund run by Theo Vermaelen and Urs Peyer, INSEAD Professors of Finance.

www.headquartersinfo.com/groupon-headquarters-information/
The web site for Groupon, which is featured in the minicase to this chapter.

www.sec.gov/litigation/litreleases/lr17327.htm
Search for SEC litigation release 17327, documenting the manner in which Credit Suisse First Boston captured a portion of the value generated by initial underpricing.

Chapter Questions

1. In April 2003, analysts at Morgan Stanley and Prudential had set 12-month target prices of $106 and $108 for the firm eBay. At that time, eBay's stock price was $89.22 and the consensus forecast for eBay's EPS was $1.45. Subsequently, eBay split its stock two-for-one. Its actual EPS turned out to be $0.82 (postsplit, corresponding to $1.64 on a presplit basis). On April 30, 2004, eBay's stock price closed above $82 ($164 on a presplit basis), and the consensus analyst EPS forecast for the subsequent 12 months was $1.18 (postsplit). Discuss whether the stock of eBay was efficiently priced in April 2003. (In answering this question, you may wish to refer to the discussion in Chapter 3.)
2. Consider the comments of Brian Walker, the president of Herman-Miller North America, who was quoted in the chapter as having said: "For dot.coms, it appears that the market has implicitly capitalized a lot of those costs. The market views their negative earnings as investments in the future. It's more difficult for a traditional Old Economy company trying to participate in the New Economy, because when it affects my earnings, it's more difficult for Wall Street to say, 'We'll give you a break on this.'" Discuss Walker's remark in the context of the concepts developed in the chapter.
3. For many years, the large retail firm Walmart chose not to provide guidance. The firm's legendary founder, Sam Walton, wrote in his autobiography that he did not care what the market thought. Beginning in 1994, Walmart's earnings announcements generated a string of negative surprises. In the resulting post-earnings-announcement drift, Walmart's cumulative abnormal return relative to the S&P 500 drifted down for the subsequent four years. Walmart's situation changed dramatically in 1998. An article appearing in *Fortune* magazine described Walmart stock as being hot again and noted that the reason stemmed from earnings. The article described Walmart as having applied its "Main Street marketing skills" to its interactions with Wall Street analysts. Discuss what it means to apply Main Street marketing skills.
4. On August 19, 2004, the Internet search firm Google went public, at an offer price of $85 per share. The IPO was unconventional in that Google used an auction to determine its offer price and to sell shares to investors. In this respect, underwriters did not allocate shares to clients. Instead investors registered to participate in the auction and indicated the maximum price they were willing to pay, along with the number of shares they wished to purchase. If a registered investor's maximum price was at least the offer price, the investor paid the offer price, not their maximum price. Google had established its initial file range for the offer price to be $108 to $135 a share. However, based on the interest shown by investors in registering for the auction, the firm's executives reduced the range to between $85 and $95. On its first day, Google stock opened at $100 per share. Were investors who purchased Google shares at $100 irrational, in that they could have paid $85 the day before? Or might there be some other explanation for the 17 percent jump in price when the stock began to trade publicly? Discuss.

www.mhhe.com/shefrin2e

5. In 2004, 55 percent of firms provided guidance to analysts, down from 72 percent in the prior year.[30] Before Google's IPO, the firm's executives announced that they did not plan to issue earnings guidance to analysts. Discuss the pros and cons of such a decision.
6. Discuss whether any of the three IPO phenomena apply in regard to the Palm IPO described in the Behavioral Pitfalls box.
7. Use the ideas developed in this chapter to assess whether Palm and 3Com were efficiently priced on Palm's first day of trading.
8. Analyze the assessment of Palm made by analyst Paul Sagawa.

Minicase

The IPOs of Groupon, Facebook, and Twitter

Groupon grew its business based on a simple idea: to provide an Internet platform that would allow local merchants to offer deals to retail customers in the form of coupons, subject to the number of customers accepting the offer exceeding a minimum threshold. Groupon's revenue stemmed from taking a share of the revenue from these sales. Groupon's coupon-based strategy exploited a psychological issue that behavioral economists call "transaction utility," whereby consumers derive benefit from making a good deal that adds to the benefit called "acquisition utility," stemming from the use of the good or service itself.

Groupon was founded in 2008 and grew rapidly over the next three years, leading many investors to wonder whether it would be as successful as Amazon had in creating an online retail superstore. Executives at Yahoo! and Google thought this possibility to be sufficiently likely that in 2010 they explored acquiring Groupon, with Google offering to pay $5.7 billion, four times more than Yahoo! had offered.

Groupon's board and executives were ambivalent on whether to accept Google's offer. The firm's sales had been approximately $25 million per month, but had quickly doubled. The firm's data scientist suggested that by optimizing its processes, the firm could soon be ten times larger. In the end, Groupon declined Google's offer, and by the second half of 2011, its revenues (not adjusting for return sales) exceeded $400 million per month.

Groupon's IPO took place on November 4, 2011, at an offer price of $20 per share, in which the company sold 5 percent of its shares. During its first trading day, the company's stock price briefly rose above $30, and closed at $26.11, with an implied valuation of approximately $16.5 billion. Groupon's IPO was the second largest of the year for a technology firm, after professional networking firm LinkedIn had gone public in May: LinkedIn's shares more than doubled on its first trading day.

At the time of its IPO, the *New York Times* described Groupon as a firm with momentum but no profits whose offering not only stunned Wall Street but also echoed the dot.com bubble. In this regard, The Times interviewed money manager Josef Schuster at IPOX Schuster, who indicated that investors' willingness to take a risk with Groupon would have a positive spillover effect on other technology offerings.[31] At the same time, Schuster noted that thereafter the risk was to the downside, that he did not buy shares on November 3, that in the short term it would be expensive to short the stock, and that in the short term trading the stock would be popular among short-term traders.

In February 2012, Groupon announced a loss of $37 million on revenue of $506.5 million for the fourth quarter. In reaction, its stock price declined below $20.

At the time of its IPO, Groupon faced criticism about unorthodox accounting practices. In March 2012, it announced that it would have to revise its financial statements—the first it was filing as a publicly traded company—for not having set aside enough reserves associated with customer refunds. The company's auditor, Ernst & Young, characterized the error as a material weakness in its internal controls. The accounting changes reduced stated revenue for the quarter by $14.3 million, and increased the loss by $22.6 million. In reaction, Groupon's share price declined by 6 percent, to $17.20.

The company's CFO issued a statement saying that they were "confident" in the fundamentals of their business. However, in the ensuing months Groupon's actual revenues fell below analysts' estimates and the company's guidance. By November 2012, Groupon's shares were trading around $3. In March 2013, the board fired its CEO. For the next few months, Groupon's share price rose, peaking at approximately $12 in September. Thereafter the share price declined and in February 2016 the stock was again trading close to $3 per share, with an associated market capitalization of approximately $3.2 billion.

In May 2012, social networking firm Facebook prepared for its IPO. As investor interest increased, the firm raised the range of its offer price from $28 to $35 a share to $34 to $38 a share. At $38 a share, Facebook would raise approximately $16 billion and its market capitalization would be approximately $104 billion. This would make Facebook's IPO the third largest in U.S. history, behind Visa (in 2008) and General Motors (in 2010).

Facebook founder and CEO Mark Zuckerberg planned to sell 30.2 million shares as part of the IPO, thereby netting more than $1.1 billion. However, he would continue to hold more than 500 million shares, corresponding to approximately 30 percent of the company.

The venture capital firm Accel Partners was the largest shareholder after Zuckerberg, and planned to sell 49 million shares as part of the IPO, which comprised approximately one-quarter of its holdings of Facebook.

On May 18, 2012, Facebook had its IPO. Although its stock increased 11 percent when it began trading on the Nasdaq, the price fell during the day, and the underwriters found themselves having to provide buying support in order to keep the market price from falling below $38. At the close, Facebook traded at $38.23. The Nasdaq also experienced a series of technical difficulties that day. Traders did not receive confirmations, and some (such as UBS) mistakenly entered multiple trades because they thought that their initial requests did not clear.

Facebook's prospectus listed several risks, one of which was that it lacked mobile advertising, citing this as a risk factor. Several months before, Facebook had begun to experiment with such ads. In this regard, *The Wall Street Journal* quoted money manager Kevin Landis of the technology investment fund Firsthand Capital Management about Facebook's need to engage in experimentation.

The Wall Street Journal discussed whether the absence of a first day price pop for Facebook would generate a ripple effect for IPO valuations over the next few months, especially in regard to social media firms. The *Journal* quoted John Fitzgibbon, president of research site IPO-Scoop.com, who called Facebook's IPO "a sobering experience." *The Journal* also quoted an IPO author and blogger named Tom Taulli as saying that Facebook's failure to "skyrocket and do well" suggests that investors would be less willing to pay for stocks associated with smaller offerings, which in turn would lead to fewer of them going public.

Facebook's stock was fairly flat for the rest of 2012 and the first part of 2013. Thereafter, it began to rise. By the end of 2015, the company's stock had increased 250 percent from the time of its IPO, roughly about the same as for the technology sector.

Twitter is famous for developing a platform in which users could send each other "tweets" of at most 140 characters. The firm's IPO took place on November 7, 2013, when Twitter had yet to generate positive earnings, and on this count it was not alone. In 2013, 64 percent of firms that went public had negative earnings. Twitter set its offer price at $26 a share, its stock opened at $45.10 the next day, peaked at $50.09 a share, and closed at $44.90, slightly below the opening price.

A week after its IPO the variation in analysts' price targets for Twitter stock was wide. On November 27, 2013, the stock closed at $40.90. At that time, the mean price target was $36, the median target price was $34, the standard deviation was $9, and the range was $24 to $54. Three-quarters of the analysts following Twitter provided a target price below the November 27 closing price. Notably, two analysts provided DCF-based free cash flow valuations: Cantor Fitzgerald and Wunderlich. Cantor Fitzgerald's target price for Twitter was $32 and Wunderlich's was $34.

Twelve months later, in October 2014, the S&P 500 was up approximately 6.5 percent for the year. Twitter's stock was down 26 percent. Based on the mean price target, analysts were forecasting that in the next 12 months, Twitter's stock would increase by 14 percent.

Twitter's GAAP earnings and free cash flow were both negative two years after its IPO. Through April 2015, Twitter's stock price ranged between $30 and $70, mostly between $40 and $50. However, in May it began to fall, and in October 2015, the stock traded around $30.

At the time, the median analyst price target for Twitter stock was $36 and the mean price target was above $38, implying a holding return above 16 percent. Shortly thereafter, the firm announced that it would lay off 8 percent of its workforce, and halt a planned expansion. Part of the reason offered for the layoffs was increased competition from firms such as Instagram, SnapChat, and WhatsApp. In February 2016 when the overall market was in decline, Twitter's stock was trading around $15. At the time, the firm announced that user growth had stalled for the first time since the company's IPO, noting complaints from new users about complexity.

Exhibit 5-6 depicts the cumulative returns for the S&P 500 for the period January 2010 through December 2015, along with the cumulative returns to Groupon, Facebook, and Twitter from the times of their IPOs.

Case Analysis Questions

1. Discuss the psychological aspects associated with how Groupon's board and executives analyzed whether or not they should accept Google's offer.
2. Consider the notion of "transaction utility." How does this concept apply to Groupon's business strategy?
3. Compare the IPOs of Groupon, Facebook, and Twitter in respect to hot issue market, initial underpricing, and long term underperformance.
4. Given the details in the minicase, to what extent did Groupon, Facebook, and Twitter engage in either catering behavior or market timing?
5. Discuss the chronology of Twitter through the lens of the Baker-Wurgler sentiment framework.

EXHIBIT 5-6
Comparison IPO Cumulative Returns of Groupon, Facebook, and Twitter Relative to the S&P 500 from the Time of Their IPOs Through December 2015

Source: Center for Research in Security Prices

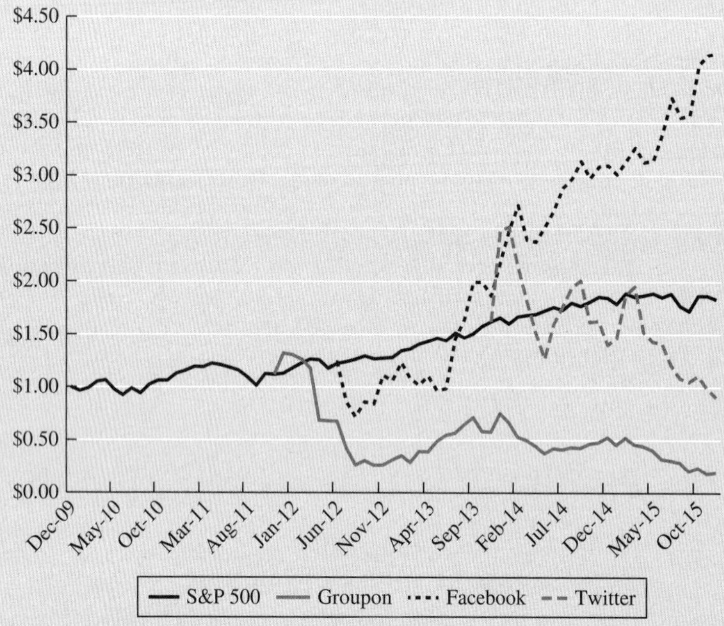

Chapter Six

Perceptions about Risk and Return

The main objective of this chapter is for students to demonstrate that they can identify the manner in which managers, investors, and analysts perceive the relationship between risk and return.

After completing this chapter students will be able to:

1. Identify managers' perceptions about the characteristics that underlie risk and return.
2. Analyze how representativeness leads managers, investors, and market strategists to form biased judgments about the market risk premium.
3. Present evidence that firms' managers rely on the heuristic "one discount rate fits all," which according to the traditional approach to corporate finance, leads to the destruction of value.

6.1 TRADITIONAL TREATMENT OF RISK AND RETURN

Corporate managers make judgments about risk and return in order to estimate the cost of capital for the purpose of making decisions about investment and capital structure, while investors make judgments about risk and return in order to value securities and construct portfolios. This chapter largely focuses on judgments of risk and return by corporate managers, while Chapter 13 focuses mostly on the judgments of investors.

The typical starting point for the analysis of risk and return is the capital asset pricing model (CAPM), which provides a theory for determining the expected return that investors require in order to hold a security. Underlying the CAPM is the notion that investors are risk averse and require compensation in the form of a risk premium for bearing risk. In this respect, the beta of an individual stock measures the amount of risk that justifies compensation in the form of a higher expected return. The main tenet of the CAPM is that the risk premium on a stock is the product of beta and the market risk premium. For individual stocks, this tenet can be expressed in terms of a graph known as the *security market line.* The security market line features a positive linear relationship between beta on the x-axis and expected security return on the y-axis.

Between 1926 and 2015, stocks returned about 10 percent per year, 6.5 percent more than the return on investing in one-month treasury bills. The 6.5 percent figure has served as a reasonable starting point for estimating the market risk premium. That being said, there is no uniformly accepted estimate for the magnitude of the premium. For example, textbook authors Richard Brealey, Stewart Myers, and Franklin Allen express their opinion in the form of a range, believing the market risk premium lies between 6 and 8 percent.[1] The range suggested within the academic literature, including textbooks, is even wider: −10 percent to 20 percent.

Estimates for the market risk premium based on survey evidence vary from year to year. In the 1990s, academics' mean estimate of the market risk premium was 7 percent, but this figure fell to approximately 5.5 percent in early 2001, and over time remained at this lower figure, albeit with some variability. Academics typically use valuation theory to infer the market equity premium, for example by inverting the dividend discount model to solve for the expected return on the market as the sum of the dividend yield and long-term dividend growth rate. Both terms in this sum can be estimated from market data, and then subtracting the risk-free rate.[2]

In 2015, academics in the United States provided a mean estimate of 5.5 percent for the market risk premium, and a mean estimate of 2.4 percent for the risk-free rate. The sum of these two, 7.9 percent, is the mean estimate of the required return on the market. These figures are similar for other developed countries, but higher for less-developed countries such as Brazil and China, where estimates of the market risk premium are 7.5 percent and 8.1 percent respectively.

The CAPM features a single factor to measure risk, the market premium. As it happens, sorting stocks on market beta does not sharply differentiate realized returns across beta-deciles.[3] As discussed in Chapter 5, multifactor models involve additional variables such as size, book-to-market equity, and momentum to explain realized returns. These factors are often structured as the return to specific long-short portfolios, such as the return on small cap stocks minus the return on large cap stocks.[4]

The frameworks for relating risk and return underlie the textbook approach to the cost of capital. A firm's cost of capital is often described as the expected return that its investors collectively require as compensation for bearing the risk of holding the firm's securities. Because interest is tax deductible, the cost of capital is often computed to reflect the after-tax cost of debt. Corporate finance textbooks teach that the cost of capital is the appropriate discount rate to apply to the expected cash flows of a project whose risk level is average for the firm. In this regard, managers are urged to discount expected cash flows of projects with higher-than-average risk at a rate higher than the cost of capital, and expected cash flows of projects with lower-than-average risk at a rate lower than the cost of capital. Moreover, if a project's cash flows comprise several subcomponents of varying risk, then managers are urged to discount the subcomponent flows at discount rates that reflect their respective risk levels.

Survey evidence indicates that for corporate financial managers, the CAPM is much more widely used for estimating the cost of equity capital than any other method. Almost 75 percent of respondents claim to use it.[5] This chapter focuses on the psychological nature of the judgments that corporate managers make about the relationship between risk and return.

6.2 PSYCHOLOGICAL ISSUES ESTIMATING THE MARKET RISK PREMIUM

The CAPM features three key variables: the risk-free rate, beta, and the market risk premium. This section mostly focuses on the psychology underlying the judgments made about the magnitude of the market risk premium. Notably, there is considerable disagreement about its magnitude. A major survey of financial economists that was conducted in 2015 found the range to be 2 to 15 percent, with a corresponding standard deviation of 1.4 percent.[6] To begin the discussion, consider the following Concept Preview Question.

CONCEPT PREVIEW
Question 6.1

The S&P 500 was first formulated as an index in 1926. Consider the 90-year period from 1926 through 2015. Define an up-year as a year when the total return on the S&P 500 was positive. Define a down-year as a year when the total return on the S&P 500 was zero or less. Without consulting historical data, write down your best responses to the following three questions:

1. For what fraction of the years 1926 through 2015 was the total return on the S&P 500 positive?
2. Focus on the years that followed an up-year. Some were up-years, and some were down-years. What fraction corresponded to up-years?
3. Focus on the years that followed a down-year. Some were up-years and some were down-years. What fraction corresponded to up-years?

The S&P 500 goes through periods that are bull markets and periods that are bear markets. Is the S&P 500 "hot" during a bull market and "cold" during a bear market? If the market is truly hot during a bull market, then the S&P 500 is more likely to have an up-year next year if last year was an up-year. Similarly, if the market is truly cold during a bear market, then the S&P 500 is more likely to have a down-year next year if last year was a down-year. On the other hand, if these probabilities do not depend on past outcomes, then past performance provides no guide to future performance.

The S&P 500 featured a positive return in exactly two out of three years during the period 1926–2015. Moreover, two-thirds of the time an up-year followed an up-year. Similarly, two-thirds of the time, actually 65.5 percent, an up-year followed a down-year. In other words, the probability with which an up-year occurred was approximately two-thirds, regardless of whether the prior year was an up-year or a down-year.

The bottom line is that for annual returns, the S&P 500 did not experience hot and cold periods, even though it did give rise to bull markets and bear markets.

Die-Rolling

A good way to gauge your intuition about how randomness works is to do the following exercise. Take out a sheet of paper and prepare two blank columns. In the left column, write down the numbers 1 to 90. Now imagine that your professor takes a pair of dice, selects one of the die, and tosses it 90 consecutive times. Suppose that each time the die turns up 3 through 6, you win $1, and each time the die turns up 1 or 2, you lose $1. Therefore, the probability of winning $1 is two-thirds, and the probability of losing $1 is one-third. In the right column, write down your best sense of a plausible sequence of wins and losses that might occur for you if you played the game for real. For example, if you imagine that you win $1 on the first toss, enter a *W* in the right column beside the 1. Similarly, if you imagine that you lose $1 on the second trial, enter an *L* in the right column beside the 2. After you have entered 90 imagined outcomes, go through the right column and count the number of times a *W* follows an *L* and an *L* follows a *W*. Add 1 to your total and you will have counted the number of runs. Then identify your longest run of consecutive *W*s and your longest run of consecutive *L*s, and write down their respective lengths.

Imagine that you play this game and win $1 five times in a row. Call this a streak (or run) of five. Are you on a hot streak? What is the probability that you will win $1 the next time? Is it two-thirds, or is something different from two-thirds?

The answer is that the probability of winning $1 is two-thirds, the same as the situation if you had lost $1 five times in a row. The past outcome offers no guidance to future performance.

If you were to play the roll-a-die game just described 90 consecutive times, you would expect to experience long streaks when you would win and long streaks when you would lose. On average, the longest winning streak turns out to be 9.5 with a standard deviation of 2.6, and the longest losing streak turns out to be 3.7 with a standard deviation of 1.0. If you counted the number of times a win was followed by a loss, and a loss was followed by a win, the average number would be about 40.5, with a standard deviation of 5.4. That is, on average the number of streaks for the die-rolling game is about 40.

The occurrence of up- and down-years for the S&P 500 is akin to die-rolling. It is striking to see how closely the up-years and down-years for S&P 500 returns resemble die-rolling. The S&P 500 exhibited 40 streaks during the period 1926–2015. The longest streak of up-years occurred between 1982 through 1989 inclusive and was eight years. This may surprise some people, because that interval contains 1987, the year the stock market crashed. However, 1987 was an up-year for the S&P 500 overall, in that it returned 2 percent (including the dividend yield). The longest streak of down-years occurred from 1929 through 1932 inclusive, a streak of four years. In short, the pattern of up-years and down-years in the annual returns to the S&P 500 is absolutely typical of die-rolling.

In respect to returns, between 1926 and 2015, the mean arithmetic return to the S&P 500 was 7.7 percent. The mean return for up-years was 18.6 percent, while for down-years it was −14.0 percent. Following an up-year, the mean return was 7.1 percent, with a standard deviation of 11.4 percent. Following a down-year the mean return was 9.0 percent, with a standard deviation of 12.0 percent. The 1.9 percent difference between the two conditional mean returns is not statistically significant.

The market risk premium is the expected value of the excess return, defined as the market return minus the risk free rate.[7] With three qualifications, applying the same analysis to excess returns as returns on the S&P 500 yields similar results. The qualifications are as follows: First, excess returns are discernably more volatile after down-years than after up-years. Second, an up-year is a bit more likely (approximately 71 percent) after a down-year than after an up-year (for which the probability is 67.2 percent). Third, the mean excess return after an up-year is 5 percent, whereas after a down-year it is 11.5 percent. Given these relationships, it is not surprising to learn that regressions of both S&P 500 returns and excess returns on their respective prior year values leads to slope coefficients that are effectively zero.[8]

Extrapolation Bias: The Hot-Hand Fallacy

Most people do not think of S&P 500 annual returns as being analogous to rolling a die. Most people are unaware of the historical statistics just described. Historical statistics constitute examples of what psychologists call **base rate information.** Base rate information is typically abstract and not readily available. Therefore most people base their judgments about risk and return on information that is more available, such as recent events. Psychologists call this type of information **singular information.**

base rate information
Information pertaining to the general environment.

singular information
Unique information directly related to a situation or object.

Psychologists suggest that people who overweight recent events are prone to extrapolating recent trends when forming forecasts. Therefore, during a bull market such people will expect high returns from stocks. During a bear market, they will expect low returns from stocks. If such extrapolation is unwarranted, the resulting bias is called **extrapolation bias.** Another name for extrapolation bias is the **hot-hand fallacy,** a term arising from basketball.

extrapolation bias, or the **hot-hand fallacy**
Unwarranted extrapolation of past trends in forming forecasts.

Some people who rely on representativeness identify the environment for which recent events are representative as being the underlying environment. During a bull market, people believe that the environment is one in which stock prices naturally go up. During a bear market, people believe that the environment is one in which stock prices naturally go down.

When the true environment is like the die-rolling game, people who are prone to extrapolation bias will make biased forecasts. In regard to the S&P 500 up- and down-years, people who are prone to extrapolation bias will be excessively optimistic during bull markets and excessively pessimistic during bear markets.

Gambler's Fallacy

gamblers' fallacy
The tendency to overweight the probability of an event because it has not recently occurred at a frequency that reflects its probability.

Whereas hot hand fallacy pertains to predictions of unwarranted continuation, **gambler's fallacy** predicts unwarranted reversals. People who are vulnerable to gambler's fallacy begin with a belief such as the probability of an up-year for the S&P 500 being two-thirds. Think about the outcomes over three consecutive years. With the probability of an up-year being two-thirds, a representative outcome over three years will feature two up-years and one down-year.

Representativeness leads people to view three-year outcomes featuring two up-years and one down-year as being more likely than they actually are. This is because representativeness leads people to over-focus on stereotypes. At the same time, representativeness leads people to view sequences that feature long streaks, such as eight consecutive up-years, or four consecutive down-years, as being less likely than they actually are. This is because these sequences are not viewed as representative of a situation where the probability of an up-year is two-thirds.

The key point is that when people are familiar with the base rate for the S&P 500, representativeness will lead them to view long streaks as being unlikely. Therefore, representativeness predisposes such people to be overly prone to predict reversals. Psychologists call this phenomenon gambler's fallacy. Gambler's fallacy gets its name from the tendency of gamblers at a craps table to believe that a 7 or 11 is due, if neither have been rolled recently.

Notice that both hot hand fallacy and gambler's fallacy stem from representativeness. People who commit hot hand fallacy tend to draw inferences about how unknown probabilities might be changing over time from their observations. In contrast, people who commit gambler's fallacy tend to believe they already know the probabilities. On a related matter, psychological studies show that when people are forecasting price movements after a trend, they are generally inclined to predict reversals rather than continuation. That said, predicting whether a trend will continue or reverse is impacted by causal attributes such as news stories that purportedly explain the reason for a past trend. Notably, availability of such news leads to predictions that trends will continue.[9]

6.3 BIASES IN FINANCIAL EXECUTIVES' JUDGMENTS OF MARKET RISK PREMIUM

Since 2000, Duke University has been surveying CFOs about their return expectations. The CFOs' responses provide informative data about their views on the magnitude of future returns, the magnitude of the equity premium estimate, and its relationship to the mean forecast of stock market volatility.

Overview

Survey evidence from the Duke/CFO study suggests that financial executives generally succumb to extrapolation bias when estimating the market risk premium.[10] The higher the market return has been in the prior quarter, the higher their forecasts of the equity premium over the subsequent year.

Survey evidence also suggests that financial executives surveyed are overconfident in respect to risk. Typical market estimates for volatility are in the neighborhood of 20 percent. Financial executives' forecasts of volatility tend to be in the neighborhood of 6 to 7 percent. Remember that overconfidence leads people to be surprised more frequently than they anticipated. Overconfidence leads people to establish confidence intervals that are too narrow.

In regard to optimism, financial executives' estimates for the equity premium tend to be lower than the values provided in many corporate finance textbooks.

Detailed Look

The Duke/CFO survey elicits CFOs' views on returns over the subsequent 12 months and subsequent 10 years. The survey questions begin by mentioning the value of the Treasury rate associated with the length of the forecast horizon. Survey participants are then asked for their best guess about the average S&P 500 return over the relevant horizon, along with two additional guesses, one called the worst case and the other called the best case. The worst case pertains to a 1-in-10 chance that the S&P return will fall below a value provided by the survey respondent. The best case pertains to a 1-in-10 chance that the S&P return will exceed a value provided by the survey respondent.

The estimate of the risk premium is the difference between expected return and the Treasury rate. The time series for the estimated risk premium, volatility, and interest rate are displayed in Exhibit 6-1 for both the one-year horizon and ten-year horizons.[11]

Consider the one-year horizon forecasts. The mean estimate of the CFOs' risk premium over the sample is 3.8 percent. Regression analysis reveals that the CFOs' expected return for the S&P 500 is positively and significantly related both to the risk-free rate and the prior year's return. The contribution of the prior return suggests that CFOs exhibit a touch of hot hand fallacy.[12]

The regression analysis suggests that on average, CFOs act as if they estimate expected return on the S&P 500 by using the following heuristic: begin with *one-third of the risk-free rate*, add a premium of about 4.9 percent, and then add about 2 percent of the prior-year return. Because the risk premium is expected return minus the risk-free rate, the fact that the starting point is only one-third of the risk-free rate instead of the entire risk-free rate implies that CFOs believe that the risk premium is negatively related to the risk-free rate.

The judgments of the surveyed CFOs reflect market-wide sentiment, as measured by the price-to-dividend ratio P/D and Baker-Wurgler index B-W, which were introduced in Chapter 5. Regression analysis indicates that the average CFO-forecasted return is the sum of 0.1 percent of P/D and −1.0 percent of

EXHIBIT 6-1a
Panel A CFOs' Estimates of the Market Risk Premium and Future Volatility for a 1-Year Horizon from the Second Quarter of 2002 (2002Q2) Through the Fourth Quarter of 2015 (2015Q4)

Source: J. Graham and C. Harvey, Duke University, **www.cfosurvey.org**

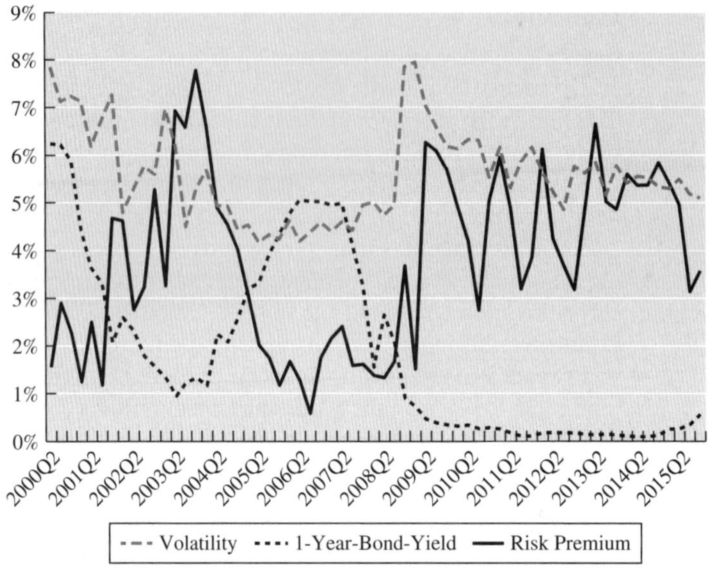

EXHIBIT 6-1b
Panel B CFOs' Estimates of the Market Risk Premium and Future Volatility for a 10-Year Horizon from the Second Quarter of 2002 (2002Q2) Through the Fourth Quarter of 2015 (2015Q4)

Source: J. Graham and C. Harvey, Duke University, **www.cfosurvey.org**

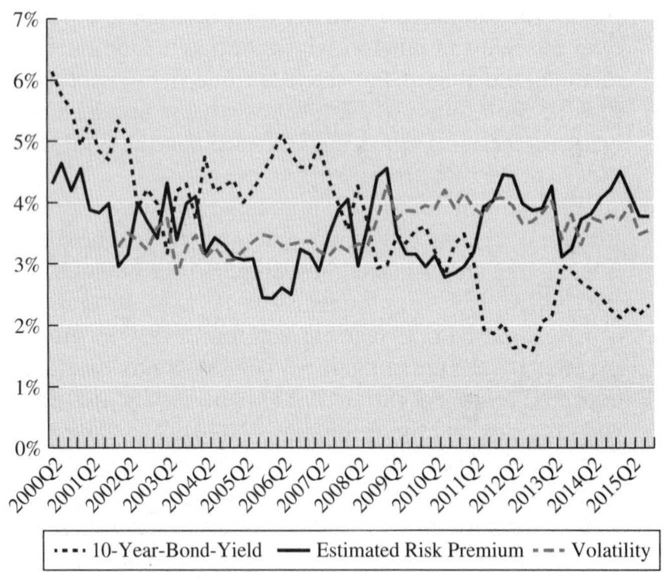

the B-W. The risk-free rate, prior-year return, and own volatility do not enter this regression with statistical significance.

The most striking feature of the CFOs' forecasts is their estimates of volatility, which feature extreme overconfidence. For one-year returns, the mean estimated return standard deviation over the period was 5.2 percent, with a range of 4.2 percent to 8.0 percent. These estimates are much too low: historical volatility for the S&P

500 has been about 19 percent, and for the period 2000 through 2015 was about 15 percent.[13]

For CFOs, the 10-year horizon is important in respect to long-lived projects. The findings for the ten-year horizon are similar in some respects to those for the one-year horizon. The mean risk premium is 3.6 percent, similar to the 3.8 percent for the one-year horizon. The two series are weakly positively correlated. Notably, the CFOs' estimate of the risk premium is roughly two percent below the academics' mean forecast discussed earlier.

Mean forecasted return for the one-year horizon is 5.7 percent and for the ten-year horizon is 7.2 percent. Certainly, the associated forecasted returns are roughly in line with the historical averages for the S&P 500, which for the period 1927 through 2015 featured a 7.7 percent arithmetic mean and a 5.8 percent geometric mean. For the period 2000 through 2015, the arithmetic return on the S&P 500 was 3.8 percent and its geometric return was 2.1 percent.

Perhaps the reason why CFOs' implied risk premiums are significantly lower than those of academics relates to CFOs being overconfident about volatility. In respect to the ten-year horizon, the mean volatility estimate was 3.6 percent, even lower than the volatility associated with the one-year horizon. Certainly, underestimating risk and the associated market risk premium can contribute to overinvestment by firms.

The most notable differences between the one-year forecasts and ten-year forecasts involve the relationship between the risk premium and volatility. While the relationship is not statistically significant for the one-year horizon, it is for the ten-year horizon. A simple regression of the risk premium on the volatility estimate has a slope coefficient of 0.52 with an associated *t*-statistic of 2.37. In this respect, the correlation between the two series is 0.31, and the regression explains roughly 9 percent of the variation in the risk premium.

Setting aside market sentiment, the "as if" heuristic for arriving at forecasted returns is a bit different for the ten-year horizon than the one-year horizon discussed earlier, and it is also stronger. For the 10-year horizon, CFOs forecast returns as if they begin with 51 percent of the risk-free rate, add 7 percent, and then subtract the sum of 47 percent of their volatility estimate and 95 percent of the prior-year return. The correlation between the 10-year interest rate and forecasted volatility is −0.66 in the Duke survey.

There are five notable features about the "as if" heuristic for the 10-year horizon implied by regression analysis.

First, as with the one-year horizon, CFOs' forecasts suggest that they believe that the risk premium is negatively related to the risk-free rate.

Second, the "as if" heuristic regression explains approximately 75 percent of the variation in forecasted returns, which is much higher than is the case for the one-year horizon returns.

Third, the strong negative contribution of past returns reflects gambler's fallacy. In this regard, the estimated risk premium and prior-year returns are negatively correlated.

Fourth, when computing expected returns, volatility enters negatively. In this respect, keep in mind that even though the risk premium and the volatility estimate

Corporate Nudges

Errors or biases: Managers exhibit either hot hand fallacy or gambler's fallacy.
Why does it happen? Reliance on representativeness to combine base rate information and singular information.
How does it happen? Those who exhibit hot hand fallacy overweight recent events and underweight base rates. They form forecasts by asking for which environment is the most recent event representative. Those who exhibit gambler's fallacy overweight base rate information, in the sense that they believe that small samples must be representative of the base rate information.
What can be done about it? Carefully identify both the base rate information and the singular information. Use statistical forecasting techniques, and contrast the outcomes with forecasts based on intuitive judgments. Based on the contrast, ascertain whether the intuitive judgments fail to make appropriate use of either the base rate information or the singular information.

are positively related, when computing expected return, CFOs do not simply add the risk premium to the risk-free rate.

Fifth and finally: forecasted returns and forecasted volatility are negatively related. The correlation coefficient is −0.65, which is statistically significant.

Next consider introducing market sentiment into a regression-based heuristic for the CFOs' forecasted returns over the 10-year horizon. The analysis suggests that the average CFOs' forecast is formed by beginning with 48 percent of the risk-free rate and adding the sum of 3.2 percent, −1.6 percent of the prior-year return, and 0.04 percent of P/D.

Notice two additional features of the heuristic just described. First, the B-W sentiment index does not enter significantly. Second, *in addition* to their forecasts reflecting market sentiment, CFOs' forecasts feature gambler's fallacy.

6.4 EXECUTIVES, INSIDER TRADING, AND GAMBLER'S FALLACY

The manner in which financial executives make personal portfolio decisions about the securities issued by their firms provides additional insights into their thought processes. What do the patterns of their insider trades reveal?

Notably, financial executives appear to be guided by gambler's fallacy in their insider trading activity. That is, evidence of financial executives displaying gambler's fallacy in respect to expected returns for the stocks of their firms can be inferred from insider trading patterns. In this regard, financial executives tend to sell the stocks of their own firms when those stocks have featured high positive appreciation in the previous year. In contrast, executives hold, or even purchase, the stocks of their firms when those stocks have featured low price appreciation in the previous year.

Typically, growth stocks have experienced high price appreciation in the previous year and value stocks have experienced low price appreciation. That is, price appreciation in the previous year is negatively correlated with book-to-market equity. To see the magnitude of the effect, sort stocks into deciles according to book-to-market equity. Then for the period 1992 to 2000, the prices of the bottom decile (growth) stocks appreciated by 80 percent, whereas the prices of the top decile (value) stocks declined by 5 percent. The associated correlation coefficient between price appreciation and book-to-market equity decile was about −93 percent. Therefore, executives appeared to engage in insider selling when the stocks of their firms are growth stocks and engage in holding or insider buying when the stocks of their firms are value stocks.[14]

Executives' insider trading activity does not appear to have been particularly effective. Even though executives' insider trades feature the sale of growth stocks and the purchase of value stocks, those trades fail to earn economically significant abnormal returns. That is, the predictions of reversals implicit in executives' insider trades are unwarranted, in line with gambler's fallacy.

6.5 BIASES IN FINANCIAL EXECUTIVES' JUDGMENTS RELATING TO RISK, RETURN, AND DISCOUNT RATES

As was discussed earlier, approximately three-quarters of financial executives report that they rely on the CAPM to estimate the cost of equity for their firms, which in theory they use to compute the associated cost of capital. At the same time, according to the Duke/FEI survey, between 30 and 40 percent use their firm's historical average arithmetic stock return.[15] Between 30 and 40 percent also report that they take other factors into account, and use a multifactor approach. Of these other factors, the most cited factor is interest rate risk, closely followed by foreign exchange risk, and then business cycle risk. After that come unexpected inflation, size, commodity prices, term structure, and distress. At the bottom lie book-to-market equity and momentum, the variables that academics emphasize. Notably, almost two-thirds of survey participants report that they judge idiosyncratic risk as being somewhat or very important in determining their firm's cost of capital.

The survey evidence is clearly mixed on the extent to which financial executives use textbook finance to make judgments about the cost of capital for their firms. The evidence is less mixed when it comes to how they incorporate project risk and judgments of the cost of capital into hurdle rates. The main finding is that managers generally use a single discount rate for all projects, but are less inclined to rely on a single discount rate when the costs of doing so are high.[16]

Of course, in theory managers discount project cash flows at a rate that reflects the systematic risk of those flows. If those flows comprise a series of components, all featuring different levels of risk, then in theory managers should discount each component separately, using its own discount rate.[17]

The survey asked the following question of CFOs: "How frequently would your company use the following discount rates when evaluating a new project in an overseas market?" The list included

- The discount rate for the entire company.
- A risk-matched discount rate for this particular project (considering both company and industry).
- The discount rate for the overseas market (country discount rate).
- A divisional discount rate (if the project line of business matches a domestic division).
- A different discount rate for each component cash flow that has a different risk characteristic (e.g., depreciation versus operating cash flows).

The ordering of these items actually corresponds to the rating order provided by respondents. The survey found that 59 percent of CFOs use the discount rate for the entire company, that is, a "one size fits all" heuristic. Fifty-one percent indicated that they would use the second highest rated item, a risk-matched discount rate. Notably, the survey authors report that large firms are more likely to use risk-matched discount rates than are smaller firms. Fewer than 10 percent vary the discount rate across component cash flows.

To be sure, the simple heuristic "one discount rate fits all projects" leads to bias. Its application leads to risky projects being favored over safer projects, all else being the same. As in the traditional framework, risk should be defined as being systematic. However, estimating the systematic component of project risk is quite challenging, and availability bias tends to induce managers to focus on idiosyncratic risk as a result.

Discount Rate and WACC

In addition to using a "one size fits all discount rate heuristic," many firms do not actually use their cost of capital (WACC) as that discount rate. Survey evidence indicates the tendency for firms to use a much higher discount rate, on average 15 percent instead of the average WACC of 8 percent. That being the case, the question is why, and what are the implications?[18]

Firms set discount rates above the cost of capital when they ration capital, thereby refraining from undertaking all projects that have a positive net present value (NPV). Why they do so involves a combination of financial constraints, operational constraints, and consideration of idiosyncratic risk. "Operational constraints" encompass scarcity of physical capital, human capital in respect to a sufficiently skilled workforce, and managerial time in respect to organizational bandwidth.

Survey evidence points to operational constraints being more important than financial constraints. More than half of responding CFOs indicate that their firms do not invest in all positive NPV projects, even during normal economic times.[19] Of the reasons provided, operational constraints outnumber financial constraints by about two-to-one.

The evidence indicates that firms that set high hurdle rates have higher cash holdings. In this regard, such firms might be holding higher levels of cash to take advantage of future opportunities, also known as growth options. As discussed in Chapter 3, firms with high growth opportunities have high intrinsic market-to-book equity. The evidence actually indicates that firms with high market-to-book equity set higher hurdle rates, on average, than firms with lower market-to-book equity. However, the relationship is only marginally statistically significant.[20]

One other explanation for firms setting high discount rates could be psychological: managers set high hurdle rates to compensate for excessively optimistic project cash flow forecasts. Notably, fewer than 10 percent of survey respondents strongly agree that they adjust their discount rates upward for this reason. At the same time, the evidence suggests the strong presence of dispositional optimism among entrepreneurs, a feature that is important because historically, the returns to entrepreneurial activity have been inferior.

If entrepreneurs are not just dispositionally optimistic but excessively optimistic, then they will be predisposed to overestimate the returns to entrepreneurial activity. To illustrate, 56 percent of French entrepreneurs initially estimate that there will be "development" in the near future and only 6 percent expect difficulties. However, three years into their ventures, only 38 percent expect development and 17 percent expect difficulties.[21]

At the same time, nonpecuniary benefits can compensate for inferior financial benefits. For entrepreneurs, nonpecuniary benefits come in many forms. Chief among these are **value expressive** activities, meaning activities that allow entrepreneurs to express personal values such as working on "clean technology" projects to improve the environment. Perhaps as a result, entrepreneurs hold poorly diversified portfolios, in that they are more likely to concentrate their wealth in their own private business. Indeed, entrepreneurs are more likely to be married and have larger families than non-entrepreneurs. In respect to planning, entrepreneurs are almost three times more likely to indicate that they never intend to retire. In this regard, people who do not plan to retire work about 3 percent longer per week than people who plan to retire.

Value expressive activities
Activities that allow people to express their personal values.

Summary

In theory, managers use the relationship between risk and return to make capital budgeting decisions and to value securities. The judgments made by firms' managers relate both to the market risk premium and the amount of systematic risk associated with different securities. In practice, the influence of representativeness can be discerned in these judgments, both at the aggregate level and the individual level. In the main, CFOs exhibit hot hand fallacy for a one-year forecast horizon but gambler's fallacy for a 10-year forecast horizon.

CFOs' judgments of the market risk premium are positively related to market sentiment. In this regard, long-term realized returns are negatively related to market sentiment, not positively related. In addition, the relationship between CFOs' mean 10-year forecast of the market risk premium and future volatility is weak, but positive. Nevertheless, the relation between 10-year forecasted returns and volatility is negative.

In their judgments about the risk and return of individual stocks, CFOs state that they largely rely on the CAPM, and do not take into account factors associated with book-to-market equity and momentum. Nevertheless, the majority of CFOs indicate that they do not adjust project discount rates to reflect risk, which runs counter to the prescriptions of the CAPM. Moreover, discount rates are often chosen to be higher than the firm's cost of capital.

Additional Behavioral Readings

Bocskocsky, A., J. Ezekowitz, and C. Stein (2014), "The Hot Hand: A New Approach to an Old 'Fallacy,'" Working paper: Harvard University.

Celati, L., *The Dark Side of Risk Management: How People Frame Decisions in Financial Markets.* London: Prentice-Hall, Financial Times, 2004.

Finucane, M., A. Alhakami, P. Slovic and S. Johnson, "The Affect Heuristic in Judgments of Risks and Benefits," *Journal of Behavioral Decision Making,* vol. 13, 2000, pp. 1–17.

Greenwood, R. and A. Shleifer, "Expectations of Returns and Expected Returns," *The Review of Financial Studies*, vol. 27, no. 3, 2014, pp. 715–746.

Landier, A. and D. Thesmar, "Financial Contracting with Optimistic Entrepreneurs," *Review of Financial Studies*, vol. 22, no. 1, 2009, pp. 117–150.

Shefrin, H., "Investors' Judgments, Asset Pricing Factors and Sentiment," *European Financial Management*, vol. 21, no. 2, 2015, pp. 205–227.

Key Terms

base rate information, *135*
extrapolation bias, *135*
gambler's fallacy, *136*
hot-hand fallacy, *135*
singular information, *135*
value expressive activity, *143*

Explore the Web

www.sloansportsconference.com/?p=13014
Discussion of hot hand phenomenon.

faculty.fuqua.duke.edu/~jgraham/videos.htm
Web site of John Graham at Duke University, with links to several topics pertinent to the discussion in this chapter.

www.cfosurvey.org
Video describing the Duke University survey of CFOs.

www.youtube.com/watch?v=LnX3DxFOdOc
Video with interview given by Robert Shiller.

aswathdamodaran.blogspot.com
Link to Aswath Damodaran's blog.

Chapter Questions

1. During a presentation in February 2001, the CFO of Palm Inc. was asked how frequently her firm assesses and uses its cost of capital. In response, she stated that Palm computes its cost of capital "from time to time." As far as computing the expected

return on individual projects, she stated: "We do try to do this once in a while, but probably not as much as you might think we do." Discuss this remark in the context of the chapter.[22]

2. In 1999, the S&P 500 returned 21 percent, closing out a streak of five consecutive stellar up-years. Then in 2000, the S&P 500 returned −9.1 percent. In 2001, the S&P 500 returned −16.1 percent. At the end of 2001, Wall Street strategists who were interviewed by *Barron's* forecast that the S&P 500 would increase by 21 percent in 2002. In 2002, the S&P actually returned −23 percent. The average strategist's forecast for 2003 was for an increase of 15.3 percent. Do these forecasts reflect any psychological biases?
3. One behavioral school of thought holds that in complex situations where it is difficult to estimate probabilities, simple heuristics are generally better than complicated heuristics. Discuss this perspective in the context of the "one size fits all" discount rate heuristic.
4. Chapter 3 contains a discussion about how the Morgan Stanley analyst team computed a discount rate to use in its free cash flow valuation of eBay stock. Discuss any similarities between the procedure the analysts used and issues described in Chapter 6.
5. The Duke/CFO study on financial executives' forecasts for the 10-year horizon features a negative correlation between forecasts of return and forecasts of volatility. Discuss this property in light of the finding that the correlation between executives' forecasts of the risk premium and volatility forecasts is positive.

Minicase

Elon Musk, Tesla Motors, Risk, and Return

Entrepreneur Elon Musk set himself the lofty goals of making financial transactions over the Internet more secure, combatting global warming by building the first commercially successful electric car, and building a private space company that could help establish a human colony on Mars.

Born in South Africa, he grew up in Canada, and in 1995 at age 26 moved to Silicon Valley. There he cofounded a high-tech firm called Zip2 that provided online publishing for media companies. In 1999, Compaq Computer Corporation purchased Zip2 for $307 million, of which Musk's share was $22 million. He set aside $4 million for personal use, and invested the rest in a startup called X.com.

X.com eventually became PayPal, the online payments firm discussed in Chapter 3. When eBay acquired PayPal in 2002 for $1.5 billion in stock, Musk's share was $165 million. That year he cofounded the space firm SpaceX, and in 2004 invested in Tesla Motors, whose goal was to produce a commercially successful, fully electric car. Tesla had been incorporated in 2003, and in addition to cars planned to design and manufacture highly efficient battery packs, charging stations, and powertrain components. In 2007, SpaceX won a $1.6 billion contract to transport cargo to the International Space Station. A busy person, Musk and his first wife Justine together raised five sons.[23]

Using a factory in Fremont, California, known as Nummi that had once been used by Toyota and General Motors,

Tesla began producing the first fully electric sports car, the Tesla Roadster.

Risk entails the potential for failure as well as success. Tesla presold the Roadsters for a price of $92,000, but was having difficulty getting the cost below $95,000. The firm's bank balance declined through 2008 and was going to need a large cash infusion to survive. Both Daimler and Toyota were considering investing in the firm, but had not yet done so.

Musk faced a choice between investing all of his remaining personal wealth in Tesla, $20 million at the time, or walking away and allowing the firm to fold.[24] Musk's brother, and former partner in Zip2, asked him if it was rational for him to go for broke, and he decided that it was. At that stage, his marriage to Justine had broken up, and he needed to borrow money from friends in order to pay his living expenses. He described that time as eating glass every day and staring into the abyss of death.

In late 2008, Musk became CEO of Tesla in order to implement a strategy that would see the firm complete deals with Daimler and Toyota and allow the firm to move forward on the next phase of his plan, which was to develop a new model, to be called Model S.

This period was not only difficult for Tesla; it was also a very difficult time for the automotive industry. The Great Recession was underway, and demand for cars was declining rapidly. The eruption of the global financial crisis would push General Motors and Chrysler into bankruptcy. After a decade-long decline, Ford Motor Company had just begun a turnaround under a new chief executive, but was forced to delay its plans for returning to profitability.

Under Musk's leadership, Tesla began hiring a workforce, dealing with unions, handling production without the benefit of economies of scale, and setting up its own independent showrooms. It faced a competitive marketplace for electric cars, and began to sell the Roadster with moderate success. Musk commented that although he was no longer staring into the abyss of death, he did continue to eat glass. Although not yet profitable, Tesla went public in June 2010.

Exhibit 6-2 displays the value of investing in the stocks of Tesla and Ford, as well as the S&P 500. The return trajectories begin in January 2004 when Ford was still struggling and Tesla was still private. As can be seen, Ford's stock initially underperformed the S&P 500, but eventually reversed course. The exhibit is constructed so that at the time of Tesla's IPO, investments in Ford, the S&P 500, and Tesla were all worth $1. Thereafter, the exhibit shows that Ford's stock performed similarly to the S&P 500, while Tesla's stock rose dramatically.

EXHIBIT 6-2
Cumulative Returns to Tesla, and Adjusted Cumulative Returns to the S&P 500 and Ford Stock

Source: Center for Research in Security Prices.

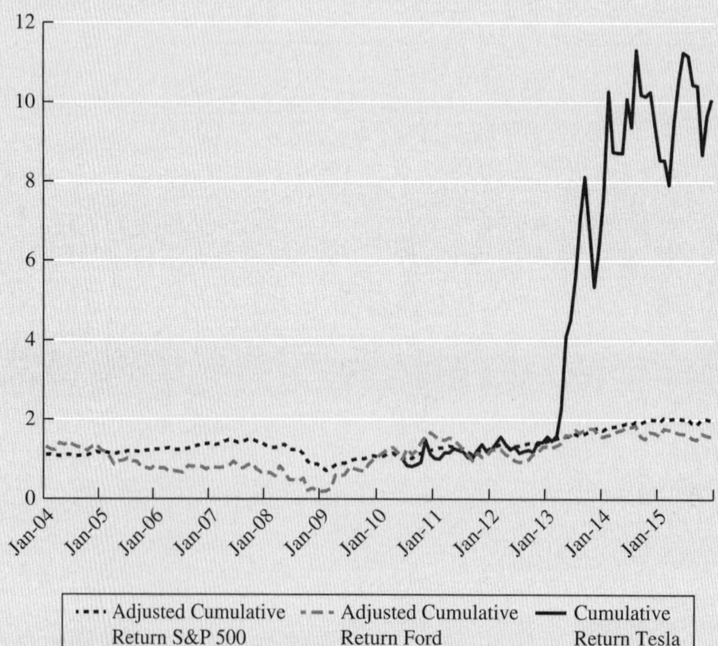

Tesla's second vehicle was the Model S, a fully electric luxury sedan, which it began to deliver on June 12, 2012. The run-up in Tesla's stock price appears to have begun on March 22, 2013. According to a study by Brad Cornell and Aswath Damodaran, there was very little fundamental news generated during the first year of the run-up that would have justified that kind of price increase.[25]

On February 21, 2013, Tesla's stock was trading at $38.54. JPMorgan's analyst team was following the stock, and based on DCF-based free cash flow analysis, its price target was $37.00. Notably, the analysts assigned a recommendation of Neutral to the stock. At the same time, Morgan Stanley's investment team, also relying on DCF-based free cash flow analysis, established a price target of $47.00, and assigned the stock a recommendation of Overweight.

As Tesla's stock began to rise rapidly, both analyst teams began to revise their free cash flow forecasts and associated price targets. On August 8, 2013, when Tesla stock had risen to $134.23, the JPMorgan team changed its price target to $83 and maintained its recommendation of neutral. The day before, the Morgan Stanley team maintained its price target of $109, as well as its recommendation of Overweight. In an interview with CNBC, Musk said that the market's valuation of Tesla was, honestly, more than they had any right to deserve.[26]

Aswath Damodaran developed a DCF-based free cash flow analysis to test whether Tesla's market price could plausibly reflect intrinsic value. To do so, he used assumptions he considered highly optimistic but possible. These related to revenue growth, operating margins, and required investment. In Damodaran's analysis, the terminal horizon begins in year 2024, when the present value of Telsa's growth opportunities are assumed to fall to zero, and Tesla's free cash flows are assumed to grow at 2.5 percent into perpetuity. For September 2013, Damodaran's analysis produced a value of $67.12, when its stock was trading at $168.76.

Damodaran's upwardly biased estimate of Tesla's intrinsic value per share was lower than the price targets for both JPMorgan and Morgan Stanley. The valuation tables are available in Available Resources for Chapter 6, and so it is possible to compare the three DCF-based free cash flow valuations. The three analyses make different assumptions about the discount rate, growth rates, and date that the terminal horizon begins. In respect to the terminal horizon, Damodaran assumes the lowest discount rate, 8 percent, while the others assumed discount rates closer to 11 percent. While the analysts assume a constant discount rate over the entire forecast period, Damodaran assumes that the discount rate is 10 percent in 2014, declines to 9.6 percent in 2019, and then decreases stepwise by 0.4 percent per year until the terminal period.

On his blog, Damodaran wrote that when he posted his $67 valuation (max) for Tesla on his blog, he "learned a lesson about how passionate its stockholders were in defending it, viewing it less as an investment and more as a calling."[27] One of his readers commented that investing in Tesla was an investment in Elon Musk, just as investing in Walmart was an investment in Sam Walton, and investing in Apple was an investment in Steve Jobs.

As can be seen in Exhibit 6-2, Tesla's stock continued to climb after September 2013. In February 2014, Tesla announced its fourth quarter loss narrowed sharply from the prior year, as revenue surged from the sales of its Model S. It also stated that it was expecting a 55 percent increase in sales the following year. In response, Tesla's shares increased by 12.6 percent. The previous day, the stock hit its all-time high when media reported that Musk had met with the head of mergers and acquisitions at Apple.[28] In its report of February 20, 2014, the JPMorgan analyst team stated that they raised their estimates and price target after Tesla had reported modestly better fourth-quarter results.

In September 2015, Tesla introduced its Model X, a crossover. And in April 2016, Musk unveiled a prototype of its Model 3 car for the mass market, which would carry a starting price of $35,000. Although delivery was scheduled only to begin in late 2017, that April Tesla received 400,000 paid reservations.

At the time, Blogger Randy Carlson opined that those who based their valuation of Tesla using traditional techniques were missing the way that investors, and customers, related to Tesla. He pointed out that the previous year, General Motors had introduced its own electric car, the Bolt, which despite its technical advances drew zero customer reservations. In discussing the different reactions, Carlson pointed out that although GM sells 200 times as many cars as Tesla, Musk had communicated a higher-level purpose and message than had GM. That message is about Tesla's raison d'être: an entity created to provide a transportation solution to address the dangers posed by man-made climate change.[29]

While Tesla was experiencing all the excitement surrounding the unveiling of its Model 3, the stocks of GM and Ford were disappointing their investors. Although sales were booming for both firms, GM's stock was trading just above $30, $3 less than what it was the day GM reemerged from bankruptcy in November 2010. Ford's stock price was approximately $13 at the time, close to where it had been three years earlier.

In April 2016, investors appeared to be concerned about the prospects for slowing sales, relating to weaker economic growth in China, which was the world's largest vehicle market, and increased levels of subprime auto loans and buyer incentives in the United States. Notably, Ford's stock was trading at 6.6 times expected 2016 earnings, and for GM, the corresponding figure was 5.6 times.[30] In contrast, the forward P/E for the S&P 500 was 17, while Tesla's forward P/E was 73.7.

In August 2016, a *Wall Street Journal* article pointed out that Tesla's market capitalization of $34 billion was approximately one-third of the capitalization of General Motors and Ford combined. In this regard, the article mentioned Tesla's acquisition of the solar energy firm Solar City, whose largest shareholder was Musk. However, the article's main purpose was to document how in the previous five years Tesla had missed at least 20 of its forecasts, including10 of Musk's timeline goals that were approximately a year late. Quality problems relating to the Model S arose as Tesla increased production levels, and design problems delayed the introduction of the Model X by two years. Notably, Tesla itself attributed "hubris" as the reason for the delay in the Model X, pointing out that the firm had set overly ambitious goals in respect to the car's technological features. The article quoted Musk as saying that he never knowingly set unrealistic goals, while noting that to achieve a good outcome it is important to aspire to a great outcome. The article concluded with Musk stating that investors who believe that Tesla will fail to meet its goals should not purchase its stock.[31]

Case Analysis Questions

1. Based on the information presented in the minicase, and the discussion in both Chapter 2 and this chapter, to what extent does Elon Musk fit the general characteristics of an entrepreneur and a CEO, especially in respect to his attitude about risk and return?
2. Consider the manner in which the readers of Aswath Damodaran's blog responded to his $67 valuation for Tesla, as discussed in the minicase. Analyze the psychological basis for their responses.
3. From the MHHE web site for Chapter 6, download the free cash flow analysis file associated with this minicase. Compare the various cash flow analyses, for both the same point in time in 2013, to identify how the analysts' views differed from Damodaran's views, and then in 2014 to illustrate how the analysts' cash flow forecasts changed as Tesla's stock price climbed. As part of your answer, evaluate the assumptions about risk. In addition, assess whether the different analyses assume that Tesla would experience zero growth opportunities during its terminal horizon.
4. Consider the possibility that the volatility of Tesla's stock has placed some investors in a situation where they are averse to a sure loss. On October 22, 2015, an article on the site seekingalpha.com suggested that this was the case.[32] At that time, Tesla's stock price was approximately $210. The article notes that the first time Tesla's stock price had been at $210 was in February 2014. As can be seen from Exhibit 6-2, 2014 was a very bullish year for Tesla. On September 4, 2014, its share price peaked at an intraday high of $291.42. Thereafter, until the end of May 2015, Tesla's share price declined, falling to an intraday low of $181.40 on May 27, 2015. The article suggests that with Tesla's share price down to the same level it was 18 months before, investors who purchased the stock at a higher share price would be inclined to hold rather than sell. Discuss the argument.
5. On April 19, 2016, an article that appeared on the web site seekingalpha.com discussed the implications of selling Tesla stock short.[33] The article warns short sellers to be cautious in believing that even though Tesla's fundamentals are poor, they should be wary of concluding that its stock price will drop imminently. In this regard, the author points to the sharp increase in the stock after Elon Musk unveiled the Model 3. Discuss this position in the context of Exhibit 6-2.

Chapter Seven

Capital Structure

The main objective of this chapter is for students to demonstrate that they can identify the manner in which biases and framing effects impact the decisions that managers make about capital structure, amount of financing, and capital budgeting.

After completing this chapter students will be able to:

1. Describe the evidence that the primary factors that drive managers' decisions about capital structure are dilution, market timing, and financial flexibility, while traditional considerations such as taxes, costs of financial distress, and information asymmetries are secondary factors.
2. Compute behavioral adjusted present value (BPV) to analyze how corporate managers balance the interests of long-term shareholders and short-term shareholders when making decisions about financing, investment, catering, and market timing.
3. Explain why concerns about dilution and market timing lead to interdependencies between financing and investment policy, with the latter being sensitive to cash flows, causing excessively optimistic, overconfident managers of cash rich firms to adopt some negative net present value projects, and excessively optimistic, overconfident managers of cash poor firms to reject some positive net present value projects.
4. Identify excessive optimism and overconfidence in the psychological profile of executives, and the associated impact of these phenomena on their decisions about financing and investment.
5. Explain why in some circumstances, framing effects can inhibit some firms from fully exploiting their debt capacity.

7.1 TRADITIONAL APPROACH TO CAPITAL STRUCTURE

Traditional corporate finance is built on a set of rationality assumptions, namely that managers are perfectly rational and markets are efficient. With this perspective, the traditional approach to capital structure developed to reflect the following five elements: tax shields, expected costs of financial distress, signaling stemming from asymmetric information, management discipline, and financial flexibility.

Tax shields and expected costs of financial distress lie at the heart of what is known as Modigliani-Miller tradeoff theory. Tradeoff theory focuses on the tradeoff between debt tax shields and financial distress. Because interest paid is tax deductible, capital structure affects the after-tax cash flows to the firm's investors. In this respect, taxes confer a tax shield, typically valued as the product of the corporate tax rate and the amount of debt.

Bankruptcy results in additional direct legal expenses. Moreover, bankruptcy involves the appointment of a court-ordered trustee with the charge of protecting the interests of debt-holders rather than shareholders. As such, a firm operating under bankruptcy incurs indirect costs of financial distress, as the trustee imposes constraints on the decisions of managers.

Notably, firms need not be in bankruptcy to incur indirect costs associated with financial distress. Sometimes the whiff of a possible bankruptcy is enough to induce a firm's customers to flee, its suppliers to insist on cash payment, its employees to begin searching for new jobs, and its managers to cut back on valuable research and development in an attempt to save costs. Firms with sizable tangible assets that can be sold to cover interest and repayment of principal are less at risk than firms whose assets consist mostly of intangibles.

Taking on additional debt typically involves a tradeoff: increased tax shields on the positive side, and increased personal taxes and expected costs of financial distress on the negative side. A firm that chooses its debt-to-equity ratio in order to equate the two effects at the margin is said to choose an optimal capital structure.

Pecking-order theory reflects signalling, and suggests that a firm does not have an optimal debt-to-equity ratio. Instead, the firm follows a pecking order. If it needs additional financing, the firm first uses internally generated equity (cash). Once it exhausts its cash, it resorts to debt financing. If it exhausts its debt capacity, then it moves to new equity as a last resort.

What is the traditional rationale behind the use of a pecking order? The answer is asymmetric information. Potential new shareholders might bid down the price of new equity, out of concern that managers know more than they themselves do and issue new equity when it is overvalued. That is, new shareholders worry that managers who issue new equity are signalling that their firms have unfavorable prospects: this is because existing shareholders extract the most value from the firm having favorable prospects when debt financing is used. For their part, managers do not wish to issue new equity when they perceive it to be undervalued and therefore might only do so once they have exhausted other sources of financing.

The need for financial flexibility stems from managers being aware that taking on high debt levels might make it difficult for them to raise new debt quickly if profitable opportunities occur suddenly. For this reason, the objective of preserving financial flexibility can limit managers' desire to use debt financing.

Absent a concern about agency conflicts, a firm's board can try to motivate managers by taking on high debt levels, thereby putting managers' feet to the fire in respect to making interest payments and repaying principal. For this reason, debt can be used to discipline managers who shirk.

In the traditional approach to corporate finance, managers make financing and investment decisions by maximizing adjusted present value (APV), the sum of net present value (NPV) and the value of associated financing side effects. Traditional financing side effects include tax shields and the flotation costs associated with new issues. Under some conditions, decisions about financing and decisions about investment can be made independently, as one does not impact the other. In this case, investments are made with the goal of maximizing NPV and financing decisions are made to balance the five elements discussed above. However, the independence conditions do not always apply, in which case managers who seek to maximize firm value need to make their decisions about the firms' investment jointly with their decisions about financing. For example, flotation costs of raising new capital might impact whether a firm decides to undertake a new project.

7.2 BEHAVIORAL CONSIDERATIONS PERTAINING TO FINANCING AND INVESTMENT

The traditional approach makes two important assumptions: first, managers are fully rational and second, markets are efficient. In contrast, the behavioral approach relaxes both assumptions, allowing managers to be imperfectly rational and vulnerable to psychological pitfalls, and market prices to deviate from their corresponding intrinsic values. This section discusses a behavioral extension of the traditional framework for analyzing how managers make decisions about financing and investment in the face of their own pitfalls and market inefficiencies.

Economists Malcolm Baker and Jeffrey Wurgler propose the following behavioral extension.[1] Imagine the case of a perfectly rational manager who is operating in a world in which sentiment creates a distortion between the prices and the intrinsic values of the firm's securities, particularly its stock. Set aside agency conflicts, so that in the absence of pricing distortions, the manager would unambiguously choose to maximize the market value of the firm. Critically, in the presence of pricing distortions, the manager faces a quandary. Although he is aware that in the long-term prices revert to intrinsic value, he knows that at the moment he might be able to make decisions that increase the current market value of the firm, even though doing so would reduce its intrinsic, and therefore long-term, value.

Some of the firm's investors will have long-term horizons, but some might have short-term horizons. When the firm's securities are mispriced in the market, managers face a potential conflict regarding whose interests to serve—those of long-term investors or those of short-term investors. The presence of such a conflict means that the manager will have to make an assessment about the relative importance of each. In this regard, the manager will set himself a goal of balancing his estimate of the value V_L of the firm to long-term investors and the value V_S of the firm to short-term investors. To do so, suppose that he seeks to maximize the sum $V_L + aV_S$, where a is a non-negative weighting parameter reflecting the importance of V_S relative to V_L.

BPV, behavioral APV
The inclusion of behavioral elements in the adjusted present value formula to reflect either mispricing or managerial biases.

Call the sum $V_L + aV_S$ **behavioral APV,** or simply **BPV.** The more weight attached to short-term value, the more myopic will be managers' actions. In this regard, managers can vary from each other. Some will focus primarily on long-term value, some will focus primarily on short-term value, and some will aim to balance the two.

Imagine that the manager has three types of decisions to make in respect to maximizing the weighted objective. The first type of decision consists of the firm's investment options, meaning how much new capital (and in what form) the firm should purchase in connection with new projects. The second type of decision involves catering, which consists of actions that increase the current market value of the firm, but not its intrinsic value. The third type of decision involves financing, such as the issuance of new equity, to take advantage of perceived mispricing of the firm's assets. In regard to buying low and selling high, managers buy low when they engage in market timing by repurchasing the shares of their firm when they believe those shares are undervalued and selling new shares when they believe those shares are overvalued.

Long-term value V_L consists of two components: intrinsic value and the benefits of market timing. Short-term value V_S reflects the impact of catering. In the special case where $V_S = V_L$, meaning that short-term value is the same as long-term value, maximizing BPV means maximizing long-term value, as in the traditional approach.

In the traditional framework, managers maximize value by selecting all projects for which APV is greater than or equal to zero. In the behavioral framework, perfectly rational managers evaluate each project by its contribution to BPV. Therefore, even if the expected cash flows from a project feature negative APV, the firm might still undertake it because doing so involves catering, which increases current market value enough to make its BPV non-negative. Notably, catering can amplify the value of market timing, by increasing the current value of new shares being sold.

In regard to financing, take as a starting point the capital structure that the manager would choose were the market to be fully efficient. In this case, selling equity beyond the level associated with the starting point would bring extra costs to intrinsic value in the form of, say, reduced tax shields and additional flotation expenses, which would not be offset by other benefits.

Now consider the benefits that could be had as a result of market inefficiency, which would increase BPV. For the sake of discussion, consider the case when managers perceive that the stock of their firm is overvalued; the undervalued case is discussed below. Given the firm's starting point described above, viewed as its current capital structure and assets, consider how a BPV-maximizing manager would evaluate the implications of selling new equity with an intrinsic value of \$1 but a market value of \$1 + x. Here x is the distortion associated with the market inefficiency.

Selling this equity for \$1 + x results in the original shareholders making a net gain of x. When the market is efficient and x is zero, selling equity involves balancing the traditional elements such as tax shields, costs associated with financial distress, flotation costs, and price changes stemming from signaling, so that selling an additional dollar of new equity brings a net benefit of zero. However, when x is greater than zero, and the net marginal benefit from the traditional elements is zero, then managers can increase BPV by issuing new equity. Keep in mind that x will be associated with short-term value, not long-term value, and so the impact on market-timing-motivated equity issuance will reflect how much weight managers attach to the short-term relative to the long-term. Notice that in the BPV framework, it is natural for investment and financing to be determined jointly, rather than independently.

When managers are imperfectly rational, they will be inclined to misjudge the components of BPV, especially the intrinsic value component. The evidence discussed in this book suggests that at the individual level there is great variation in managers' susceptibility to psychological phenomena. Some managers might be relatively immune while others might exhibit strong excessive optimism and overconfidence. Those exhibiting excessive optimism and overconfidence about the NPV of their projects will be prone to overinvest, so that the true NPV of the marginal project might well be negative, even though managers perceive marginal NPV as being nonnegative. The examples described in Chapter 2 and Chapter 4 aptly illustrate this point.

In addition, psychological phenomena can impact decisions about financing. Excessive optimism and overconfidence lead managers to believe that the market undervalues their equity. Such managers will be inclined to hold less equity than they would otherwise, for example by repurchasing shares. They will seek to balance savings in perceived dilution from lower equity against the additional costs in financial flexibility and expected financial distress, net of benefits from tax shields, managerial discipline, and signaling.

Decisions about capital structure take place in an environment that features considerable variation across markets, firms, and managers. Sentiment is stronger in some industries than in others. Sentiment betas are larger for the stocks of some firms than for others. Relative to long-term value, some managers attach more priority to short-term value than others. Psychological phenomena impact some managers differently than others.

The remainder of this chapter describes how these variations impact decisions about financing and investment. With this in mind, we turn next to the survey evidence about the considerations managers take into account when making these decisions.

7.3 HOW DO MANAGERS MAKE CHOICES ABOUT CAPITAL STRUCTURE IN PRACTICE?

In practice, behavioral considerations combine with traditional considerations to drive the capital structure decisions made by executives. The main behavioral consideration is market timing, meaning buying low and selling high to take advantage of perceived inefficient prices. Executives sell high when they issue equity that they perceive to be overvalued. They buy low when they repurchase equity that they perceive to be undervalued. In this connection, perceptions are key, being unbiased in some circumstances and biased in others.

A good indication that capital structure decisions reflect both traditional considerations and market timing comes from the cover story of the September 2003 issue of *Financial Executive,* the main publication of Financial Executive International (FEI). That story was devoted to capital structure and was based on a series of wide-ranging interviews conducted with chief financial officers, corporate treasurers, consulting experts, and financiers.[2]

Those interviewed for the cover story explicitly state that the theoretical models taught in traditional finance classes are too static to provide them with the framework they need to make decisions about capital structure. Instead the interviewees focused on volatility associated with the future cash flows of their firms, uncertainty about subsequent investment opportunities, and conditions in capital markets. Many indicated that flexibility is key so that their firms can take advantage of opportunities involving investments, acquisitions, or market mispricing.

New Equity: Market Timing

Financial executives explicitly state that market timing is an important consideration in their decisions about issuing new equity. General evidence about the views of financial managers on capital structure comes from a survey of CFOs conducted jointly by Duke University and FEI. Of the executives in 4,400 firms surveyed, 392 responded.

The survey posed the following question to financial executives: "Has your firm seriously considered issuing common stock? If 'yes', what factors affect your firm's decision about issuing common stock?" The survey offered a series of factors from which executives could choose. Executives were asked to respond on a scale from 0 (not important) to 4 (very important).

In responding to this question, executives rated as the second most important consideration "the amount by which our stock is undervalued or overvalued in the market." Notably, 63 percent of CFOs attach a 3 or 4 to the following factor: "If our stock price has recently risen, the price at which we can sell is high." The mean response for this factor was 2.69. That is to say, market timing is a prominent consideration driving capital structure decisions, at least in the short-term.

Empirical evidence suggests that firms tend to issue new equity, and therefore achieve lower debt-to-equity ratios, when their market-to-book ratios are high.[3] This finding suggests that managers issue equity when that equity is most likely to be overvalued. Supporting evidence for this statement comes from a finding that when managers issue new shares, they also tend to engage in insider selling in respect to their personal portfolios.[4] As was discussed in Section 6.6 of Chapter 6, this aspect of managers' behavior appears to be driven by gambler's fallacy. Strictly speaking, managers might not perceive their stocks as being overvalued, but instead perceive their stock prices as high. Some researchers have concluded that issuing equity when the market-to-book ratio is high is no short-run phenomenon, meaning that fluctuations in market value can have very long-run impacts on capital structure.[5]

Number One Consideration, Earnings Dilution

The highest-rated consideration in respect to equity issuance was "earnings dilution." Sixty-nine percent rated this factor as either a 3 or 4, and its mean rating was 2.84. What does this mean? In the traditional approach, expected earnings per share (EPS) is directly related to the debt-to-equity ratio. Therefore, an equity issue would lower the debt-to-equity ratio, thereby driving down expected EPS. And executives might interpret lower EPS as dilution; and of course issuing new shares when earnings growth is low will also typically lead to lower EPS. In the behavioral approach, dilution is associated with market timing, a point taken up later in the chapter.

New Debt: Financial Flexibility and Debt Timing

Consider next the factors that drive financial executives' decisions about new debt. The FEI survey tells us that the top factor is financial flexibility: having enough internal funds available to pursue new projects when they come along. This item had a mean survey rating of 2.59: sixty percent rated it as either a 3 or 4. Not surprisingly, flexibility was also a key theme in the comments of those interviewed for the *Financial Executive* cover story mentioned earlier.

Convertible Debt

The survey finds that more than 55 percent of CFOs who issue convertible debt assign either a 3 or 4 to the statement that convertible debt is an inexpensive way to issue "delayed" common stock. Indeed, 50 percent assign a 3 or 4 to the statement that they issue convertible debt because their stock is currently undervalued.

Convertible debt exhibits at least two behavioral features that make it appear attractive to financial executives.[6] First, the interest rate on convertible debt tends to be less than the interest rate on fixed debt, because debt-holders pay a premium for the conversion feature, so convertible debt appears to be a cheap form of debt financing. Second, because convertible debt converts to equity only when the future stock price rises, it appears to be a cheap form of equity as well. These framing features by no means imply that convertible debt is necessarily a cheap form of financing. That depends on how the debt is priced in the market. Indeed there is evidence that hedge funds trade convertible debt in order to exploit mispricing. In some instances, this trading activity injects considerable volatility into the firm's stock price.[7]

Debt Timing

Executives report that they engage in debt timing, seeking to attempt to time interest rates by issuing debt when they judge that market interest rates are low. In this regard, the survey response of 2.22 is moderately strong, and for large firms with sophisticated treasury departments it is somewhat stronger at 2.40. Notably, executives are more prone to time market rates than their own credit ratings, a feature that is somewhat surprising because executives have private information that is pertinent to their credit risk, but do not have private information about market interest rates.

Target Debt-to-Equity Ratio

The FEI survey indicates that executive decisions about capital structure reflect traditional tradeoff considerations as well as market timing. At the same time, the survey evidence indicates that executives assign tradeoff considerations a lower priority than other competing concerns.

The main survey question that elicited executives' responses asked: "What factors affect how you choose the appropriate amount of debt for your firm?" Among the factor choices that the survey offered CFOs was "maintaining a target debt-to-equity ratio," this being the central issue in tradeoff theory. Just over 50 percent of CFOs assigned either a 3 or 4 (very important) to this factor. In other words, 50 percent indicate that a major feature of tradeoff theory is important. At the same time, this factor is rated fifth.[8]

In answering the question, 57 percent of CFOs attach a 3 or 4 to the firm's "credit rating (as assigned by rating agencies)," and 45 percent mention "the tax advantage of interest deductibility." These were the second- and fifth-highest rated items, respectively. Interestingly, less than 5 percent of CFOs attach a 3 or 4 to the "personal tax cost our investors face when they receive interest income."

There are three behavioral issues that are particularly germane to firms' target debt-to-equity ratios: market timing, aspiration-based risk appetite, and biases such as excessive optimism and overconfidence. The evidence suggests that by and large firms rebalance their capital structures slowly, so that shocks to capital structure are long-lived.[9] Some empirical studies conclude that executives do establish target debt-to-equity ratios and attempt to close half the gap between current ratios and target ratios in less than two years.[10] These studies suggest that market timing is a minor consideration. However, other empirical studies conclude that market timing is a major consideration, so the issue is not settled.[11]

Part of the controversy about market timing and capital structure concerns the interpretation of a finding about the weighted average of a firm's past market-to book ratios, where the weights in question are external financing. If firms issue equity in order to time the market, then this ratio will be higher than it otherwise would be, and likewise the debt-to-asset ratio will be lower than otherwise. The empirical evidence indicates that the two ratios are negatively related to each other. While some argue that the negative relationship reflects market timing, others argue that it reflects growth opportunities.[12]

The role of aspiration-based risk appetite on target debt-to-equity ratios is discussed in Chapter 2. In this regard, the tax benefit of debt has been estimated to be about 9 to 10 percent of firm value, before taking into account the effect of personal taxes. Personal taxes bring the estimate down to 7 percent.[13] Although traditional theory predicts that firms with lower costs of debt will choose to hold more debt than firms with higher costs of debt, the evidence suggests that the opposite is true.

Firms with low expected costs of financial distress use debt conservatively. Large liquid firms in noncyclical industries use debt conservatively. During the early 1990s, the magnitude of unexploited tax shield by U.S. firms was about the same as the overall tax shields. During the early 1980s, the unexploited tax shield was almost three times higher.

Chapter 6 contains a discussion about the confidence intervals financial executives report for their forecasts of the market return, both for a one-year horizon (the short-term) and a ten-year horizon (the long-term).[14] On average, these confidence intervals are too narrow, implying that financial executives are overconfident in the sense of having overly precise beliefs. One of the most important findings from the study of these forecasts is that overconfidence and debt are positively related, a point discussed in greater detail in section 7.7.

Notice that aspiration-based risk appetite and overconfidence impact debt levels in opposite directions. Therefore, caution needs to be exercised in drawing conclusions about, for example, whether firms set target debt-to-equity ratios which are either too high or too low. John Graham, who authored the study about unexploited tax shields speaks of firms that "use debt conservatively," in order to leave open the possibility that it might actually be appropriate for some firms to use debt conservatively.

There is evidence that debt policy is sensitive to prior stock losses, but not gains, with debt-to-assets declining with the size of the loss. Asymmetrically, the ratio of net working capital to assets, which pertains to liquidity, increases with prior stock gains, but not with prior losses.[15]

The Big Five

Big Five
A psychological framework characterizing people's personalities on five traits.

A psychological framework known as the "**Big Five**" characterizes people's personalities on five traits.[16] The traits are openness, conscientiousness, extroversion, agreeableness, and neuroticism, whose first letters spell the word "ocean." Big five scores are typically obtained by asking people to use a five-point scale indicating the degree to which they agree or disagree with statements such as "I see myself as someone who is curious about many different things." This particular statement pertains to openness.

The evidence indicates that for CEOs, openness and conscientiousness are related to choices involving leverage and investment. In this regard openness is negatively associated with leverage and positively associated with the intensity of research and development (R&D). This finding is consistent with CEOs who exhibit curiosity running companies that engage in R&D, and who also behave in accordance with the debt puzzle; that is, companies like Merck discussed in Chapter 2. Conscientiousness is positively related to the ratio of book-to-market equity, suggesting that highly conscientious CEOs are not drawn to innovative cultures that value risk-taking.[17]

Traditional Pecking Order

The traditional pecking-order theory predicts that investors' concerns about being informationally disadvantaged relative to managers will lead managers to prefer internal equity to debt financing, and debt financing to external equity financing. Notably, when large firms engage in substantial investments, they tend to rely on debt financing. However, they do not appear to exhaust their cash reserves before undertaking debt.[18] Therefore, managers do not behave in strict accordance with the predictions of pecking-order theory.

The FEI survey reports little support for the asymmetric-information basis underlying traditional pecking-order theory. To be sure, CFOs are reluctant to issue equity when they believe that their firms' stocks are undervalued. However, the FEI survey finds little evidence to suggest that executives believe that the source of the undervaluation is perceived information asymmetry.

7.4 MARKET TIMING: HOW SUCCESSFUL?

In some situations, the biases afflicting investors are strong enough to create exploitable market inefficiencies, and in addition the biases afflicting corporate managers are weak enough to allow those managers to exploit those inefficiencies through market timing, either by issuing new shares or by repurchasing shares.

To set the stage for the discussion in this section, consider two examples. The first example involves Facebook, which in February 2014 announced that it would issue new shares to acquire the startup WhatsApp, for which it would pay $19 billion, a very high price. Although Facebook's share price initially fell in value by 3.4 percent on the announcement, it recovered by the end of the trading day. Indeed, Facebook's share price continued to climb for several months thereafter, and as a *Wall Street Journal* blog noted, Facebook's stock had become more valuable than J.P. Morgan's stock.[19]

The second example involves General Electric (GE). In 2015, GE initiated a $50 billion share repurchase plan. In March 2016, an article in *Barron's* argued that although some repurchases were intended to exploit short-term timing opportunities, others such as GE were more long-term focused, reflecting the fact that market value lay below fundamental measures of value.[20] By April 2016, the shares of General Electric (GE) had increased by 56 percent since the previous August. Its earnings were beating analysts' forecasts, its dividend yield was 2.9 percent, and its trailing P/E ratio was 20, which a *Barron's* article characterized as "hardly cheap."[21] As for short-term timing, the *Barron's* article specifically cited Motorola Solutions, which during the previous year had repurchased 20 percent of its shares and whose one-year return was about 14 percent.

Perception of Overvalued Equity: New Issues

As was discussed in Chapter 5, IPO volume and stock market valuations are highly correlated with each other, a phenomenon that has been documented for most of the world's major stock markets. In this regard, long-term underperformance of IPOs generally suggests that corporate managers might intentionally time the market by issuing new shares when they perceive their stocks to be overvalued.

As for seasoned equity offerings (SEOs), the historical evidence indicates that recent stock price appreciation leads firms to tilt their financing policy toward equity issuance. The historical evidence also indicates the existence of long-term underperformance, similar in nature to the pattern for IPOs that is displayed in Exhibit 5-3. Exhibit 7-1 is the counterpart for SEOs to Exhibit 5-3 for IPOs.[22] Both exhibits indicate that new issues underperform relative to counterparts that are matched by style, meaning size and book-to-market equity. However, as was mentioned in Chapter 5, underperformance can be nuanced, for example, by being concentrated in a particular style such as "small growth." Therefore caution is in order when interpreting these two exhibits.[23]

Suppose that firms generally issue new equity when the stock market is overvalued. If so, equity returns will tend to be low following periods of high equity issuance because of mean reversion. The evidence suggests that this is the case, both for the United States and international markets. Historically, when the equity share of new financing has been in its top historical quartile, the average *value-weighted* market return over the next year has been negative.[24] In line with the evidence presented in Chapter 6, this finding suggests that managers are impacted by the same waves of sentiment as are investors, rather than managers generally being able to expertly time the market as a whole.

EXHIBIT 7-1
Comparison of Firms Issuing Seasoned Equity to a Style-Matched Sample That Did Not Issue Seasoned Equity. Returns and Firms Matched By Style, 1970–2011

Source: Jay Ritter's web site, site.warrington.ufl.edu/ritter/ipo-data.

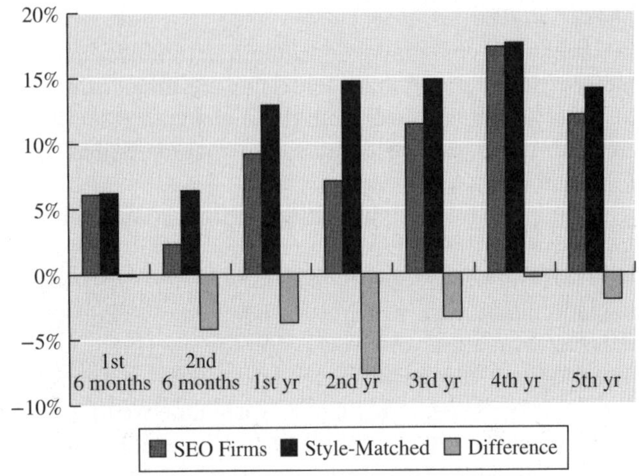

The general finding is that on average, equity issues in the United States underperform the market in the range of 20 to 40 percent over a five-year period. Notably, underperformance appears to apply to new issues, but not rights offerings aimed at existing shareholders, suggesting that overpriced new issues are focused on exploiting new shareholders, as opposed to existing shareholders.[25]

Perception of Undervalued Equity: Repurchases

A separate survey of FEI members, conducted jointly by Duke University, Cornell University, and FEI was structured to investigate financial executives' views about payout policy, meaning repurchases and dividends. Financial executives' views about dividend policy are discussed in Chapter 8, and so here the focus is only on repurchases. Financial executives indicate that they initiate or accelerate share buybacks when they perceive that the stock prices of their firms are low by recent historical standards. In this regard, more than 85 percent of survey respondents indicate that firms engage in share buybacks when they perceive that their company's stock is good value, relative to its true value, making this response the most popular among survey questions relating to repurchases.

Approximately half of the CFOs interviewed for the survey indicate that their firm tracks repurchase timing. Moreover these CFOs state that their firm can beat the market, perhaps by $1 or $2 per share during the course of a year.

In respect to establishing a target for repurchases, just over half of respondents indicate that they view repurchases as a flexible goal. Almost all survey respondents are clear to say that they do not establish a target ratio for repurchases as a proportion of earnings. About a fifth use repurchases to target variables such as shares needed for employee stock option exercises, the debt ratio, and the amount of excess cash. Only a quarter of respondents indicate that they have some kind of rigid target for repurchases. When asked what they would do with the extra funds were they to decrease repurchases, financial executives' most popular response is that they would pay down debt.

Underreaction

In some instances, managers actually announce that they are repurchasing shares because they believe that their firms are undervalued. The evidence supports the idea that managers who repurchase shares are sending the market a clear signal. The average market response to the announcement of an open market repurchase is 3.5 percent.

Notably, investors appear to underreact to repurchases, in that stock prices drift upward when firms repurchase shares.[26] This drift effect comprises the flip side to the drift effect associated with new issues. (As was mentioned in Chapter 5, the market appears slow to adjust to new issues: The stocks of firms with new issues underperform for several years after the offering.)

As to long-run performance, the stocks of firms who repurchase shares and have high book-to-market equity earn abnormal returns of 45.3 percent over four years. When averaged over all firms, the average abnormal return after the initial announcement is 12.1 percent.

The historical evidence suggests that by timing repurchases, firms listed on NYSE/Amex reduced their cost of equity by 1.3 percent a year.[27] Of course, there is considerable variation across firms. For mature firms that rarely raise external equity, the gains are likely to be negligible. But for firms that repeatedly engage in seasoned equity issues and stock-financed mergers, gains on average are considerably larger.

Debt Market Timing

When the debt market is efficient, the cost of debt is equal across maturities, with the yield curve reflecting unbiased expectations about future yields and appropriate compensation for bearing term risk. In this case, financial executives cannot expect to time the market by raising debt when its cost is unusually low.

As was discussed in section 7.3, many financial executives believe they can successfully engage in debt market timing; and they certainly appear to try. In this regard, the finding from the Duke/FEI survey is that CFOs report that they borrow short-term when they feel that short rates are low relative to long rates or when they expect long-term rates to decline. The survey findings also provide moderate evidence that relatively low foreign interest rates impact the decision to issue abroad. Although insignificant, small growth firms are more likely to make this claim. Notably, if covered interest rate parity holds, there is no reason why rational managers with no private information would pursue this strategy.[28]

The general evidence indicates that when spreads are wide, financial executives borrow short term, waiting for spreads to fall in the future.[29] In this regard, the term spread has historically been positively related to subsequent excess bond returns. In addition, debt issues, much like equity issues, have been followed by low equity returns for issuers. In this regard, the shares of both straight debt issuers and convertible issuers have underperformed a size- and book-to-market benchmark over five years. For convertible issuers, the underperformance is a significant 37 percent.[30] If the equity returns were low, then associated deteriorating credit quality would lead debt issues to have low returns as well.[31]

These findings could stem from market timing or could stem instead from financial executives being impacted by sentiment, a feature that was discussed in Chapter 6. If financial executives are excessively optimistic at the same time that capital is cheap, they will tend to raise new debt, new equity, or both when sentiment is high.[32]

7.5 FINANCIAL FLEXIBILITY AND PROJECT HURDLE RATES

Undervalued Equity: Cash-Poor Firms Reject Some Positive NPV Projects

Historically, the firm AutoNation has been the largest seller of used and new cars in the United States. See the Behavioral Pitfalls box about AutoNation nearby. Suppose that AutoNation had a project whose NPV managers perceived to be \$100 million. Imagine that undertaking the project required that AutoNation raise external financing in the amount \$150 million at a time when its managers perceived the market value of their equity to be one-third of the intrinsic value of their equity. Suppose further that AutoNation had no debt capacity and almost no cash. In this case, AutoNation's managers would perceive the intrinsic value of a \$150 million equity issue to be \$450 million, thereby resulting in a \$300 million wealth transfer from old shareholders to new shareholders (\$300 = \$450 – \$150).

According to the Duke/FEI survey, the top factor that financial executives consider in their decision to issue new equity is dilution. In this example, the \$300 million dilution cost outweighs the NPV of \$100 million, leading the net effect on BPV to be –\$200 million. As a result, the managers of cash-poor AutoNation would be wise to avoid issuing equity and to reject the project.

Undervalued Equity for Cash-Limited Firms: Invest or Repurchase?

According to the Duke/FEI survey, the top factor that financial executives consider in their decisions about debt is financial flexibility. Inadequate financial flexibility means that the firm's managers might have to make their decisions about capital structure and investment jointly instead of separately. Just as the traditional approach adjusts project hurdle rates using an after-tax weighted average cost of capital to reflect tax shields, the behavioral approach adjusts hurdle rates to reflect mispricing.

The results from the FEI survey indicate that 75 percent of firms make the decision about repurchase policy after having determined their investment plans. Many financial executives are willing to reduce repurchases in order to fund new projects.[33] Moreover, only about 25 percent believe that there are negative consequences attached to a reduction in repurchase activity.

In the traditional approach, market timing is not a traditional factor underlying the decision either to issue or repurchase shares. However, as the discussion about AutoNation in the Behavioral Pitfalls box nearby demonstrates, in practice financial executives come to learn that market timing is an important consideration in their decisions about capital structure.

Behavioral Pitfalls: AutoNation

In 2003, AutoNation was the largest seller of used and new cars in the United States. In June of that year AutoNation held more than $200 million in cash. Its CFO at the time was Craig Monaghan. Suppose that Monaghan correctly judged that AutoNation's stock was undervalued. What action could Monaghan take to exploit this situation, buy low or sell high? In this case, he would buy low, meaning that AutoNation would engage in a share repurchase.

Although AutoNation could use some of its cash to repurchase shares, should it? The answer depends on the opportunity cost of that cash. At issue is how else that cash could be spent. What projects might not get funded if AutoNation uses cash to repurchase shares?

Between January 2002 and June 2003, AutoNation implemented an $836 million stock repurchase program and repurchased 20 percent of its outstanding shares. Notably the firm makes its decisions about repurchasing shares in conjunction with its operational goal of earning a 15 percent return on its investments. In this respect, the repurchasing decision to exploit market mispricing is treated like an investment project in respect to opportunity costs.

Craig Monaghan states that when he was in business school, he learned the traditional approach to capital structure and capital budgeting. Notably, the traditional approach is premised on market efficiency. However, in practice Monaghan bases his capital structure decisions on market timing, as he describes here:

> Right now we can move from acquisitions to share repurchases to spending on infrastructure. So if we see an opportunity to spend $100 million on an auto dealership, we can do it. Or we can do a stock buyback if the stock goes down . . . My professors at Wharton will tell you that a stock buyback is a wash. But when companies buy back their stock, they are sending a message loud and clear that management and the board have a strong belief that the company has more value and a brighter future than the market is recognizing. . . .

Source: P. Sweeney "Capital Structure: Credibility and Flexibility," *Financial Executive International*, September 2003, pp. 33–36.

In the traditional approach, a firm like AutoNation computes the NPV of its average project by discounting future expected cash flows at its cost of capital. If AutoNation's cost of capital is 15 percent, then it uses a hurdle rate of 15 percent to compute the NPV component of BPV. As long as the firm has adequate cash or access to external capital markets, it can finance all projects that feature nonnegative perceived BPV and can draw on cash holdings or debt capacity to repurchase shares.

A firm with limited cash and debt capacity might have to choose between repurchasing shares and financing investment projects. In this situation, managers should view a share repurchase as akin to an investment project. Those shareholders who do not tender would view a repurchase favorably, as long as engaging in the repurchase does not siphon away funds that would otherwise have been used to finance more valuable projects.

Suppose that AutoNation had limited cash, had no debt capacity, and is undervalued in the market. How would its managers choose between using the firm's cash to repurchase shares and using the firm's cash to finance a new project? The answer is that they base their choice on BPV.

Consider an example. Imagine that the firm's shares are undervalued by 25 percent. Suppose that the project requires an initial investment of $500 million and has an NPV of $100 million. Which decision would create more value for investors, spending \$500 million to repurchase shares or spending \$500 million to fund the project? The value received from the share repurchase is \$625 million (= 1.25 × \$500 million), whereas the value received from the investment project is \$600 million (= \$500 million + \$100 million). Transaction costs aside, repurchasing creates more value.

The point of this example is that repurchasing increases the opportunity cost of the firm's investment projects. Two key variables determine the appropriate adjustment to project hurdle rate: the firm's financing constraints and the impact of the firm's repurchase activity on the price of its shares. Suppose a firm has enough debt capacity to fund half the project with debt and uses its cash to fund the other half. In this case, the project will have a lower hurdle rate than if it is entirely financed with cash. Second, suppose that the firm's repurchasing activities cause its share price to rise dramatically. In this case, its managers might engage in limited repurchase activity, even if they only had mediocre projects available. Hence, the associated hurdle rate would be lower than if the repurchase activity had a lower impact on the market price.[34]

7.6 SENSITIVITY OF INVESTMENT TO CASH FLOW

The authors of the report describing the Duke/FEI survey results conclude that executives make decisions about capital structure by relying heavily on practical, informal rules or heuristics. Managers who rely on rules might adjust their capital structure as a by-product of their investment policy, particularly if they follow a pecking order where they finance first from cash.

The tendency for investment policy to depend on how much cash a firm holds is known as the **sensitivity of investment to cash flow.** The evidence is strong that when firms receive more cash or take on less debt, they invest more.[35] Consider the example presented in the Behavioral Pitfalls box that appears on the next page.

sensitivity of investment to cash flow
Investment depends on how much cash a firm holds.

In 2001, Adaptec CFO David Young also served as national chairman of FEI, the source of the survey data described previously. In this regard, FEI's chairman approached decisions about capital structure at his firm in much the same way as FEI's general membership. Notably, there are three important issues about Adaptec's approach to capital structure.[36]

First, Young tells us that before his tenure as CFO, Adaptec made unwise investments when it was cash-rich and its stock price was high. In this respect, Adaptec is typical when it comes to the sensitivity of investment to cash flow. The evidence is strong that when firms receive more cash or take on less debt, they invest more. Other instances of cash flow sensitivity that have been documented are as follows:

- Firms' acquisition activity increases when they are the recipients of large cash windfalls coming from legal settlements unrelated to their ongoing lines of business.[37]
- Reinsurance companies reduce the supply of earthquake insurance after their capital positions have been impaired by large hurricanes.[38]
- When cash flow increases or leverage decreases in one division of a firm, investments in other divisions of the firm increase significantly.[39]

Behavioral Pitfalls: Adaptec

In 2001, Adaptec was a Silicon Valley firm headquartered in Milpitas, California, that produced and sold networking and storage devices. Adaptec was founded in 1981 and went public in 1986. In 2010, the firm PMC-Sierra acquired Adaptec, and in turn was acquired by Microsemi in January 2016. Microsemi is headquartered in San Ramon, California.

In 1991, Adaptec's debt-to-equity ratio, measured using book values, was close to zero. However, in 1996 Adaptec increased that ratio to 33 percent, and it stayed between 25 percent and 30 percent for the next five years.

David Young was chief financial officer at Adaptec between 2000 and 2003. When he joined Adaptec, Young was already an accomplished executive, having served six years as Vice President and CFO at Datum, a timing and synchronization solutions company; two years as CEO and CFO at Blower-Dempsey, a paper and chemical company; and two years as Vice President and CFO at Alpha Microsystems, a proprietary hardware and software company.

In a presentation made in December 2001, Young was asked about the factors he takes into consideration in determining Adaptec's capital structure. In response, Young mentioned a variety of issues.

The first factor was cash. Young indicated that financial executives spend less time thinking about the debt-to-equity ratios of their firms when they have cash than when they do not. In this respect, he stated: "Cash is king and we live by that motto." At the conclusion of its fiscal year 2001, Adaptec had over $600 million in cash, and therefore did not have to go to the capital markets to raise funds.

The second factor was the current stock price. Adaptec's stock price had steadily climbed during 1999 and rose from about $10 per share, peaking above $50 per share in early 2000. See Exhibit 7-2.

However, as technology stocks fell during the remainder of 2000 and 2001, Adaptec's stock fell below $10. At the time of the discussion with Young, in November 2001, Adaptec's stock price stood at about $14. Young indicated that he did not view the market at the time as appropriate for Adaptec to be issuing new equity. He indicated that the issue of new equity would lead to a "dilution effect" for its existing shareholders because the price of its stock was "so low."

Young mentioned that Adaptec had last gone to the debt market in 1998, with a $200 million convertible issue bearing a $4\frac{3}{4}$ percent coupon rate. He stated that if Adaptec did need to raise $200 million at the time of his presentation, then it would do so in the debt market rather than the equity market. However, were the firm's stock price to be in the $30 to $40 range, then he would be willing to raise funds in the equity market, rather than the debt market.

Young described investments that his firm had made prior to his taking over as CFO. He pointed out that Adaptec had generated a lot of cash during the bull market of the 1990s. He stated: "Adaptec built a large Milpitas campus and a factory in Singapore when they had lots of cash coming in, that's what companies do." He then noted that the company had overinvested in both.

Source: Presentation made by Adaptec's chief financial officer at the time, David Young, on November 9, 2001, at Santa Clara University.

Second, in line with the Duke/FEI survey, market timing was an important consideration for Adaptec in its approach to capital structure. Had the firm a need for external financing in 2001, Young would not have chosen to issue what he perceived to be undervalued equity. Instead, he would have chosen to issue convertible debt.

Third, in line with the Duke/FEI survey, Young made no reference to a target debt-to-equity ratio. Instead, he approached capital structure with a pecking order in mind: cash, followed by convertible debt, followed by external equity as a last resort. However, the basis for the pecking order did not appear to be asymmetric information, but rather his perception that Adaptec's stock was undervalued in the market.

EXHIBIT 7-2
(a) Adaptec Stock Price January 1990–October 2001
(b) Adaptec Net Income (Loss) 1990–2001

Source: Center for Research in Security Prices, Compustat.

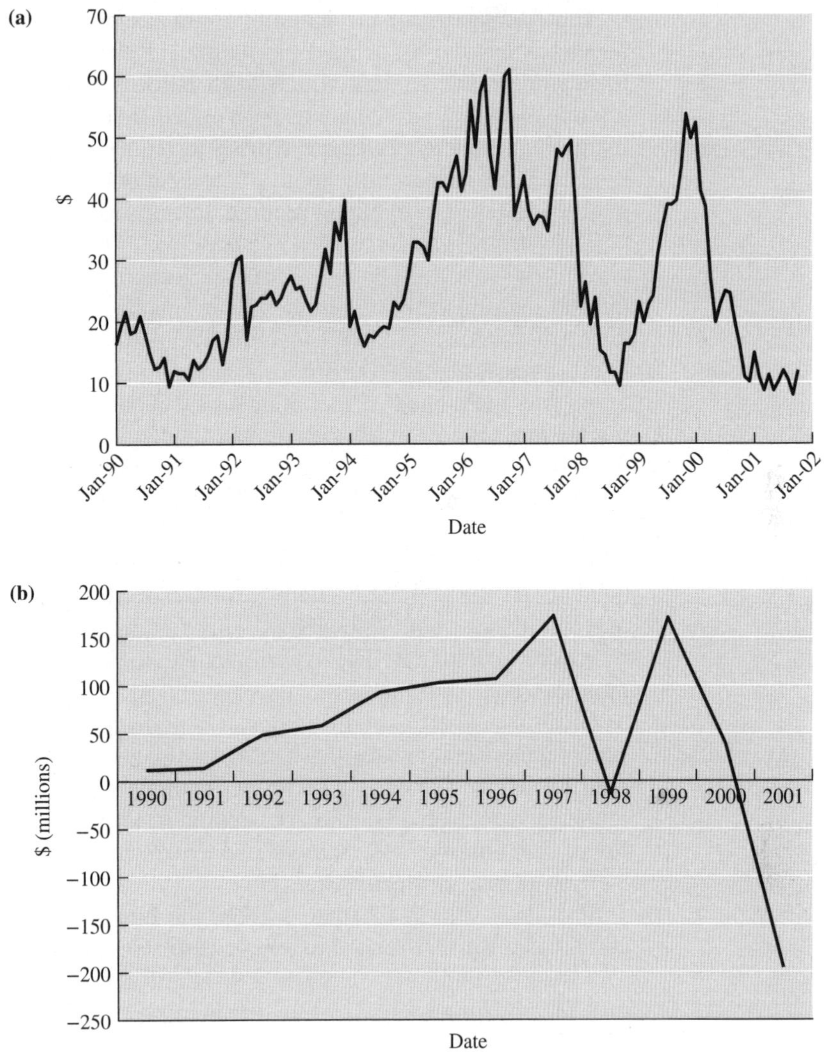

7.7 PSYCHOLOGICAL PHENOMENA AND INTERDEPENDENCIES AMONG FINANCING, INVESTMENT, AND CASH

An important implication of the discussion about BPV in section 7.2 is that behavioral considerations imply that financing decisions and investment decisions are interdependent rather than separable. This means that a firm's choice of capital structure is made jointly with its choice of investment policy. In this respect, financing and investment will reflect executives' susceptibility to psychological phenomena.

The findings from the Duke/FEI surveys provide evidence about both interdependencies and associated psychological phenomena. For example, in respect to interdependency, approximately 75 percent of firms make the decision about repurchase policy after having determined their investment plans. In this regard, many financial executives are willing to reduce repurchases in order to fund new projects.[40] Moreover, only about 25 percent believe that there are negative consequences attached to reducing repurchase activity.

The various Duke surveys, some done with FEI and some done with *CFO* magazine, provide insights about the variation across executives in respect to psychological phenomena, and the impact of these phenomena on corporate policies. Chapter 6 contains a discussion about inferring excessive optimism and overconfidence from executives' forecasts of market returns as well as returns from the projects in their own firms.

As was mentioned in that chapter, CFOs are highly overconfident about their market forecasts, as evidenced by their underestimates of future volatility. Because there is a documented relationship between psychological phenomena and corporate policies, it is important to understand the degree to which indicators such as forecast confidence intervals are robust. Experimental evidence indicates that the width of interval forecasts, as a measure of overconfidence, are positively correlated across the population with responses to the question in Chapter 1 assessing overconfidence about knowledge. This finding suggests that overconfidence is a reasonably stable trait. The experimental evidence also finds that professionals are more overconfident than students.[41]

Given the experimental findings, it is perhaps not surprising that the Duke/CFO survey evidence indicates that CFOs' estimates of internal rate of return (IRR) for their own firm's projects also reflect extremely low estimates of future volatility, relative to reasonable benchmarks. Nor is it surprising that CFOs who are overconfident about market-wide returns also tend to be overconfident about the returns to their own firms' projects.

The discussion in Chapter 4 about the planning fallacy noted that investment activity is positively related to executives' excessive optimism and overconfidence. The specific finding is that a one standard deviation shift in overconfidence (as measured by long-term overprecision in market return forecasts) is associated with a shift of 0.6 percentage points in corporate investment, relative to a mean of 8.7 percentage points and a median of 5.4 percentage points. An increase of one standard deviation in optimism (measured by long-term optimism in market return forecasts) is associated with an increase of 0.9 percentage points in corporate investment.

As was discussed in section 7.3, overconfidence is also an important phenomenon when it comes to debt. The specific finding is that a one standard deviation shift in overprecision is associated with an increase of 1.36 percent in book leverage, measured as the ratio of total debt to total capital employed, relative to a sample mean of 22.3 percent. For long-term overprecision, the effect is approximately half that of short-term overprecision. The results using market leverage are similar to the results using book leverage, although slightly weaker.

The general finding is that excessive optimism and overconfidence are positively related to both leverage and investment activity. This feature is accentuated by the finding that leverage and investment debt levels increase in the years following the start-date of CFOs who are excessively optimistic and overconfident.

The discussion in Chapter 6 emphasized how representativeness induces some decision makers to exhibit hot hand fallacy and others to exhibit gambler's fallacy. The academic literature suggests that corporate executive decisions are prone to hot hand fallacy. An example is investment in the dry bulk shipping industry. The evidence suggests that executives in this industry exhibit hot hand fallacy when they extrapolate exogenous demand shocks. They also exhibit confirmation bias when they partially neglect the way their competitors invest in response to these shocks. As a result, executives overinvest in new ships when their current earnings are high, and experience low subsequent returns as a result.[42]

The presence of hot hand fallacy is a general phenomenon, not confined to the shipbuilding industry. The Duke/CFO surveys ask executives to forecast earnings and capital spending over the subsequent 12 months. Findings from analyzing these data shows that on average, executives' planned investment growth in the next 12 months is a weighted average of their forecasted earnings growth and the change in their fixed assets. The evidence indicates that executives exhibit hot hand fallacy when they extrapolate recent earnings growth in order to estimate long-term earnings growth. As a result they overinvest when recent earnings growth has been high, and underinvest when recent earnings growth has been low.[43]

Excessive Optimism, Overconfidence, and Cash

As discussed above, susceptibility to excessive optimism and overconfidence is important for firms' financing and investment activity. In this regard, the combination of excessive optimism and overconfidence leads the managers of cash-rich firms to undertake negative NPV projects. The discussion of Adaptec in Section 7.6 serves to illustrate this point. However, as in Section 7.5, excessive optimism and overconfidence might also lead the managers of cash-poor firms to reject some positive NPV projects. Taken together, this implies that the investment policy in firms whose executives are excessively optimistic and overconfident will tend to display cash flow sensitivity. The evidence indicates that on balance, these firms overinvest.[44]

It is easy to see why the managers of cash-rich firms undertake negative NPV projects. Excessive optimism and overconfidence leads managers to overestimate future project cash flows and underestimate project risk. As a result, these managers overestimate project NPV. When their firms are fairly valued in the market, the same biases lead them to conclude that their firms are undervalued. However, because they are cash-rich, they have no need for external financing. As a result, they use their cash to fund projects that they perceive to feature positive (or zero) NPV, but which in reality feature negative NPV.

Excessively optimistic, overconfident managers of cash-poor firms also overestimate project NPV and are prone to conclude that their firms are undervalued in the market. However, these managers face a dilemma. In computing BPV, they overestimate both project NPV and the associated financing side effects. In particular, their reluctance to avoid dilution can dominate their desire to fund a positive NPV project. The net result is that excessively optimistic, overconfident managers misjudge fundamental APV to be negative when it is, in reality, positive. As a result, they reject some positive NPV projects when they are cash-poor and have limited debt capacity.

Identifying Excessively Optimistic, Overconfident Executives

press coverage overconfidence indicator
The press uses the words *optimistic* and *confident* to describe an executive.

In addition to the survey-based measures discussed above, there are at least two other indications that a CEO is excessively optimistic and overconfident. The first indicator is press coverage. When press descriptions of a CEO tend to use words such as *optimistic* and *confident,* there is good reason to suspect that the executive is actually excessively optimistic and overconfident. Call this the **press coverage overconfidence indicator.** Concept Preview Question 7.1 sets the stage for the second indicator.

CONCEPT PREVIEW
Question 7.1

Imagine that you are the chief executive officer of a firm that has granted you one million stock options. These options were granted to you seven years ago and will expire in three years time. Your firm has done very well in the last seven years, your current outlook is bright, and your stock now trades at $35 per share. At the same time, your options are said to be deep "in-the-money" and allow you to purchase your firm's stock at a price of $10 per share. Suppose that you face a choice. You can do one of the following:

- Exercise the options today, sell the stock, take the $25 million profit, and purchase other assets for your portfolio.
- Delay exercising your options, hoping the stock price will go up even more.

What would you do if you were the CEO?

The second indication of CEO excessive optimism and overconfidence is that CEOs hold their executive stock options until they are close to expiration. Unlike outside investors, CEOs will be much more exposed to the unique risk associated with their firms, and therefore their portfolios will tend to be undiversified.

There are two main reasons for lack of diversification in CEO portfolios. First, CEO compensation contracts regularly contain large quantities of stock and option grants in lieu of cash compensation. To maximize the incentive effects of these holdings, boards prohibit their CEOs from perfectly hedging against the risk by selling company stock short. Second, the CEO's reputational capital is invested in the firm, so a bad outcome in her firm will not only negatively impact her personal portfolio but will also reduce her outside opportunities.

There are several psychological phenomena associated with the choice in Concept Preview Question 7.1. Because the worst outcome is that the options expire worthless, the two alternatives lie in the domain of gains. Remember from Chapter 1 that risk aversion in the domain of gains leads people who delay exercising their options to expect more than $25 million by accepting the risk of delay. Therefore, excessive optimism and overconfidence can trump the normal tendency to be risk averse in this type of situation and induce executives to delay exercising instead of accepting the sure $25 million.

The duration of a typical executive option is 10 years, and the option becomes fully vested after four years. How long should a CEO delay exercising his or her options, if those options are in-the-money? To answer this question, a CEO must trade the time value of holding the stock options against the costs of being undiver sified. In typical situations, the optimal exercise schedule involves exercising well before the final year.

longholders
Excessively optimistic, overconfident CEOs who delay exercising executive options that are deeply in-the-money well before the expiration date and instead hold their options into the final year.

Excessively optimistic, overconfident CEOs who hold their options into the final year are called **longholders.**[45] A study based on 477 large[46] publicly traded U.S. firms, for the period 1980 through 1994, found that 16 percent held an option at least once until the year of expiration. Further, these options were typically deep in-the-money, the median percentage by which the market price exceeds the exercise price having been 253 percent.

As was mentioned, the investment policies of firms with excessively optimistic, overconfident managers display excessive sensitivity to cash flows. The evidence indicates that firms with longholder CEOs are more likely to rely on internal cash to finance investment than other firms.[47] Longholding figures prominently as one of the key determinants of investment activity, along with cash flow, size of board of directors, and a measure of growth opportunities.[48]

Behaviorists do not say that people never learn, only that they learn slowly. Excessively optimistic, overconfident CEOs make the mistake of holding their executive options too long and end up losing money. Interestingly, a substantial number repeat the mistake. Notably, firms whose investment is especially sensitive to cash flow have CEOs who have repeated the mistake at least once and have lost money on their options at least once as a result.[49] Moreover, for these firms, the sensitivity of investment to cash flow is stable over the tenure of the CEO.[50] The Behavioral Pitfalls box on the next page illustrates the two overconfidence indicators in respect to the CEO of Sun Microsystems Scott McNealy, whose experiences were discussed in Chapter 2. As you read the contents of the box, keep in mind that analysts had been critical of Sun Microsystems decision to invest heavily when it was cash rich but its sales and stock price were in rapid decline.

Assessing Value

CONCEPT PREVIEW
Question 7.2

Consider the two panels in Exhibit 7-2. The top panel displays the stock price between 1990 and October 2001, just before Adaptec's CFO made his remarks. The bottom panel depicts Adaptec's earnings history between 1990 and 2001.

In December 2001, when Adaptec's CFO made his presentation, Adaptec's stock price stood at $14. Based on the information in Exhibit 7-2, how would you judge Adaptec's stock at this time?

1. Overpriced
2. Fairly priced
3. Underpriced

Behavioral Pitfalls: Scott McNealy

Chapter 2 discusses the cover story in the July 26, 2004, issue of *Businessweek* is about Scott McNealy, the chief executive officer of high-technology firm Sun Microsystems. The *Businessweek* article uses the following adjectives to describe Scott McNealy: optimistic, smart, and cocky. Such coverage reflects the first indicator of excessive optimism and overconfidence.

Consider the second indicator. Is Scott McNealy a longholder? In 2004, McNealy received a salary of only $100,000 per year. The rest of his compensation was in the form of executive stock options.

In August 1997 Scott McNealy exercised options to buy 300,000 shares at $4.19. He sold them on the same day for over $46, receiving a gain of about $12.6 million. A spokesperson for Sun said that McNealy exercised the options because they were about to expire after 10 years.

In August 2001 McNealy exercised options to buy 929,088 shares for 74 cents apiece. He sold them for $17.03 each, for a net gain of more than $15.1 million. A spokesperson for Sun said that McNealy exercised the options because they were about to expire, but declined to comment further on the transactions. At the time, McNealy held more than 55 million shares of Sun.

In 2002 McNealy exercised existing stock options for a $25.2 million gain. A Sun spokesman said that most of the options McNealy exercised that year had lost most of their value and were about to expire. McNealy kept most of the shares.

In an interview published on April 1, 2002, McNealy told *Businessweek* that Sun's stock price was highly overvalued when it reached its peak of $64 two years before. In this respect, he sold about $100 million of Sun's stock in the fiscal year ending June 2000. However at that time he did not choose early exercise for the stock options that expired in 2002, which lost most of their value by the time he did exercise them.

Perhaps McNealy suffered from **hindsight bias** in 2002, the tendency to view events as obvious or almost certain when viewed in hindsight when those events were neither obvious nor almost certain when viewed in foresight.

In April 2003, McNealy exercised options to buy 1.6 million Sun shares for 86 cents a piece and sold those shares for about $3.30. A spokesperson for Sun said that the options were to expire in August.

As of May 2003, McNealy owned about 56 million shares of Sun, valued at about $227 million. As of September 2002, he also held 16.4 million exercisable options, according to the company's proxy statement filed with the Securities and Exchange Commission.

Sources: Dan Lee, "Sun Microsystems Chief Executive Gains $3.88 Million on Sale of Shares," *San Jose Mercury News*, May 26, 2003; Gary Strauss, "McNealy's Pay Value: $87M," *USA Today*, October 1, 2002; "Sun Microsystems CEO McNealy Exercises Stock Options," *Associated Press Newswires*, October 8, 2001; Duncan Martell, "Sun Executives Cash in on Options, Sell Shares as Stock Price Doubles," *Austin American-Statesman*, August 30, 1997; "A Talk with Scott McNealy: Sun's Chief on the Post-Enron Economy, HP, and More," *Businessweek*, April 1, 2002, p. 67.

hindsight bias
The tendency to view events as obvious or almost certain in hindsight when they are neither obvious nor almost certain when viewed in foresight.

Adaptec's CFO indicated that the firm's investment policy exhibited cash flow sensitivity. His comments also suggested that Adaptec followed a pecking order that was driven by market timing, in that he judged the stock to be undervalued. Was that judgment reasonable?

In respect to Concept Preview Question 7.2, subsequent events offer a little guidance. Adaptec's stock price and earnings both declined in 2002, as did the S&P 500. However, in 2003, when the S&P 500 returned 28.6 percent, Adaptec's stock price rose by 56.4 percent from $5.65 to $8.84. Still, this was a far cry from the $30 to $40 that in 2001 Adaptec's CFO considered to be fair.

Excessive optimism and overconfidence lead executives to conclude that the stocks of their firms are undervalued. The Duke/FEI survey documents that most financial executives view the stocks of their firms as being undervalued. Only about 25 percent of managers believe that their stocks are correctly valued.

7.8 CATERING AND THE CONFLICT BETWEEN SHORT-TERM AND LONG-TERM HORIZONS

Proponents of behavioral finance suggest that stock returns tend to feature short-term momentum and long-term reversals. This pattern represents a challenge for financial managers. For example, suppose that investors are irrationally exuberant about a firm's prospects and would bid up a firm's stock price if its managers undertook a particular project. If managers believe that the project features negative NPV, should they engage in catering behavior and undertake the project? Or, as was discussed in Section 5.3 of Chapter 5, in the case of the firm Herman-Miller, managers might make a choice between adopting a project that increases long-term value but decreases market value in the short-term.

Consider the case of a firm whose book-to-market equity ratio is low and whose stock price has increased rapidly. From a behavioral perspective, such a firm is

Corporate Nudges

Errors or biases: Managers of cash-rich firms undertake negative NPV projects and hold too little debt, while managers of cash-poor firms avoid issuing external equity and reject positive NPV projects.

Why does it happen? Excessive optimism and overconfidence.

How does it happen? Excessively optimistic, overconfident managers misjudge fundamental APV. They overestimate the NPV of their potential projects as well as the intrinsic value of their firms.

What can be done about it? Executives can check their forecasts of market returns, including confidence intervals, as well as *two* additional indicators for excessive optimism and overconfidence. The first pertains to the financial press to ascertain whether they have been characterized as optimistic and confident. The second is their own exercise policy in respect to stock options. Executives who have been granted executive stock options can ask themselves whether their exercise behavior qualifies them as longholders. One technique to mitigate excessive optimism and overconfidence is to employ the two-step outside view. In the first step of the outside approach, a firm's managers assess how successful managers at other comparable firms have been in making the same types of decisions. In the second step, managers ask themselves if they can honestly identify reasons why they should expect to be more successful than their peers.

likely to earn low returns long-term, not because it is relatively safe, but because its stock is overpriced and its price will revert toward intrinsic value. Therefore, managers who adopt projects for short-term gain effectively act as if they use low discount rates in their capital budgeting analysis. As was discussed in Section 5.5, the executives at 3Com faced a related issue in connection with Palm.

In theory, managers have to decide whose interests they serve, investors who hold the stock for a short period and sell, or investors who plan to hold the stock long-term. There is no easy prescription to offer. As was discussed in Section 7.2, managers need to balance the two competing interests.

As was discussed in Chapter 6, managers generally place little weight on momentum and book-to-market equity when estimating the cost of equity. Therefore, relatively few managers might explicitly consider the tradeoff between serving the interests of investors who plan to hold the stock for a short period and those who plan to hold the stock long-term. From a capital budgeting perspective, the means by which managers estimate the cost of equity might lead them to downplay the gains from exploiting short-term mispricing.

Summary

Survey evidence indicates that dilution and market timing are the top factors that influence financial executives' decisions about issuing new equity. The top factor influencing financial executives' decisions about new debt is financial flexibility. As a group, financial executives also report that they attempt to target values for their firms' debt-to-equity ratios.

The BPV approach to capital structure features managerial biases and framing effects as well as market sentiment., the market, or both. Managers who perceive that the securities of their firm are mispriced will be prone to engage in market timing. Such activity will be tempered by the extent to which the firm is financially constrained, its growth opportunities, and the sensitivity of its market price to new issues or repurchases.

Excessively optimistic, overconfident managers of cash-poor firms are prone to reject positive NPV projects because they overvalue the equity of their firms. Excessively optimistic, overconfident managers of cash-rich firms are prone to adopt negative NPV projects because they overvalue the cash flows from those projects.

Point and interval forecasts of returns provide information about the degree to which executives exhibit excessive optimism and overconfidence. Two additional indicators of CEO overconfidence involve press coverage and options exercise behavior. The behavioral approach to capital structure suggests that firms with excessively optimistic, overconfident managers take on more leverage and invest more than other firms, and their investment policies exhibit excess sensitivity to cash flows. In some circumstances, framing effects can operate in the opposite direction, and inhibit some firms from fully exploiting their debt capacity, a point also discussed in Chapter 2. Empirical studies shows that firms with longholder CEOs have investment policies that are excessively sensitive to cash flows.

Additional Behavioral Readings

Baker, M. and J. Wurgler, "Market Timing and Capital Structure," *Journal of Finance,* vol. 57, 2002, pp. 1–32.

Ben-David, I., J. Graham, and C. Harvey, "Managerial Miscalibration," *The Quarterly Journal of Economics,* vol. 128, no. 4, 2013, pp. 1547–1584.

Graham, J., "How Big Are the Tax Benefits of Debt?" *Journal of Finance* vol. 55, 2000, pp. 1901–1941.

Greenwood, R. and S. Hanson, "Waves in Ship Prices and Investment," *The Quarterly Journal of Economics,* 2015, pp. 55–109.

Malmendier, U. and G. Tate, "CEO Overconfidence and Corporate Investment," Forthcoming in the *Journal of Finance.* 2004.

Stein, J., "Rational Capital Budgeting in an Irrational World," *Journal of Business,* vol. 69, no. 4, 1996.

Key Terms

BPV, behavioral APV, *151*
Big Five, *157*
hindsight bias, *170*
longholders, *169*
press coverage overconfidence indicator, *168*
sensitivity of investment to cash flow, *163*

Explore the Web

www.autonation.com
The web site for AutoNation provides a customer interface for customers to purchase vehicles.

www.cogentco.com/en
The web site for Cogent Communications discussed in the minicase.

www.cfosurvey.org
This web site contains the results from the ongoing survey conducted by Duke University and *CFO* magazine. In addition to the current survey results, see the tabs Past Results and Special Surveys.

Chapter Questions

1. In August 2004, Google went public at a price of $85 per share. One year later, its stock price reached $285, as the firm's earnings consistently exceeded analysts' consensus forecasts. At that time, its forward P/E ratio was 37.5 and its ratio of book-to-market equity was 0.052. In August 2005, Google announced that it planned to issue 14,159,265 new shares in a seasoned equity offering. At the price prevailing at the time, the amount of the new offering would have been about $4 billion. In its SEC filing, Google managers stated that the proceeds for the offering were for general corporate purposes but the firm had no current agreements or commitments concerning material acquisitions. Analysts reacted with a series of speculative comments about what Google's managers might be planning to do with the proceeds of the new issue. Discuss Google's seasoned equity offering in the context of the ideas described in the chapter. In addition, comment on the choice of the precise number Google managers selected in respect to the number of shares in its offering.
2. From January 1990 through March 1993, the stock of Cypress Semiconductor Corp. underperformed the S&P 500 by 26.5 percent on a cumulative basis. Then in April, the firm announced that its board authorized the repurchase of an additional one million common shares of the 37.6 million shares that were outstanding. In making the announcement, Cypress's management stated that they believed their firm's stock to be undervalued.

In response to the announcement, Cypress shares rose 25 cents, closing at $10.125. Over the next year, Cypress's stock outperformed the S&P 500 by 66.4 percent. Over the next four years, Cypress's stock outperformed the S&P 500 by 16 percent on an annualized basis. Is the experience of Cypress Semiconductor typical or atypical of firms that repurchase shares?

3. On December 19, 2000, an article appeared in *The Wall Street Journal* discussing stock price declines that followed share repurchases made by AT&T, Intel, Microsoft, and Hewlett-Packard.[51] The article mentions that Warren Buffett, chairman of Berkshire Hathaway, criticized firms that engaged in share repurchases. In a letter to shareholders, he noted that share repurchases made sense during the mid-1970s, when many stocks traded below their intrinsic value. However, he argued that conditions changed during the bull market of the 1990s, even though share repurchases had become much more frequent. He also suggested that the motivation for share repurchases had also changed and that during the 1990s firms bought back their shares in order to pump up their stock prices. Discuss Warren Buffett's views in the context of the chapter text.
4. The March 11, 2004, issue of *Businessweek* magazine reported that Standard & Poor's had reduced Sun Microsystem's debt rating to junk status. Over the course of the next two days, Sun's stock price fell by 11 percent. Both S&P and the financial analysts covering Sun had been expressing concerns about the firm's profitability and urging the firm to cut costs. In response, Sun's executives stated that the concerns expressed were overblown. They pointed out that the firm had more than $5.1 billion in cash and short-term investments and was hardly on the verge of ruin. Discuss the response of Sun's executives within the context of the chapter material.
5. Imagine that AutoNation is contemplating a project that requires a $350 million initial outlay and features an NPV of $48 million. The firm is all-equity financed and has $150 million in cash that it plans to invest in the project. AutoNation's current market value of equity is $3.4 billion. AutoNation's investment bankers have advised the firm's financial managers that they could raise $200 million of external financing either by issuing new debt at 5 percent or by issuing new equity. If the firm issues new equity, then the new shareholders would come to hold 5 percent of the firm, whose total value, conditional on adopting the project they estimate to be worth about $4 billion. Suppose that AutoNation's managers have concluded that their firm is overvalued in the market. Specifically, they have concluded that the minimum which new shareholders should demand for the $200 million is 5.3 percent of the firm. In this respect, the managers estimate that the intrinsic value of the firm would be about $3.8 billion if they adopt the project. Assume that flotation costs are zero. Suppose that the corporate tax rate is 35 percent, the risk of financial distress is low enough to be ignored, and that the firm can borrow at an interest rate of 5 percent. Compare the BPV of the project if financed with debt to the BPV of the project if financed with equity. Which is the better way to finance the project, with debt or with equity?
6. Imagine that Adaptec is contemplating a project that requires a $3.75 billion initial outlay and features an NPV of $466 million. The firm is all-equity financed and has $1 billion in cash that it plans to invest in the project. Adaptec's current market value of equity is $6.68 billion. Adaptec's investment bankers have advised the firm's financial managers that they could raise the $2.75 billion by issuing new equity. However, Adaptec has no capacity for debt. If the firm issues new equity, then the new shareholders would

come to hold 28.5 percent of the firm, which is conditional on adopting the project they estimate to be worth $9.569 billion. The investment bankers have computed the NPV of the project to be about $227 million, not the $466 million computed by Adaptec's managers. Adaptec's managers have concluded that their firm is undervalued in the market and that its intrinsic value would be about $13 billion if it adopts the project. In addition, the managers have concluded that the new shareholders merit 21.2 percent of the firm for their $2.75 billion investment. Nevertheless, the investment bankers have made it clear that unless Adaptec's managers agree to give up 28.5 percent of their firm, they will not be able to raise the $2.75 billion. Assume that flotation costs are zero. Suppose that Adaptec has no debt capacity and has to rely on external equity. What value of BPV would the managers of Adaptec compute if they adopted the project and financed it with equity?

7. In 2011, Millard Drexler, the CEO of fashion retailing firm J. Crew, together with two private equity firms, TPG and Leonard Green & Partners, did a $3 billion leveraged buyout. The strategy left J. Crew with approximately $15 billion of debt on its balance sheet. TPG had backed J. Crew in 1997, for which it earned a 700 percent return. In 2015, as part of a downturn in fashion retail, the company's same-store sales were declining and its profits were falling. As a result, it laid off 10 percent of its employees. At the same time, Drexler, with over forty years of experience in the industry, was honored with a special industry award by the Council of Fashion Designers of America, which described him as "the Merchant Prince." The decline in J. Crew's revenues stemmed from a combination of at least three different factors. The first is the general economic downturn. The second was that the firm had lost ground to competitors, such as Ann Taylor and Old Navy, for clothing known as "athleisure wear." The third is that J. Crew focused on high-priced, higher-end clothing at a time when its low-price competitors were increasing the quality of their products. In commenting on the firm's prospects, Drexler sent out an e-mailed statement to say that he continues "to have confidence" in the company's future growth, and that the company is "making the adjustments necessary to deliver the products its customers want."[52] Use the ideas developed in Chapter 7 to analyze whether psychological phenomena were prominent in the experience of J. Crew between 2011 and 2015.

8. Solar energy firm Solyndra manufactured cylindrical solar panels that, while expensive to produce, were easy to install on the roofs of commercial buildings. The firm was founded in 2004. In March 2009, Solyndra had raised approximately $650 million in private equity financing as well as $535 million in debt that was guaranteed by the U.S. government as part of a program to encourage clean energy. At the time, Solyndra had a single manufacturing facility, but was planning to build a second. Later that year, Solyndra filed an IPO registration statement, which it later withdrew after investment bankers expressed concern about declining prices for electricity. Nevertheless, the firm built a second, larger facility. *The Washington Post* quoted a former engineer at the firm as saying that after receiving the loan guarantee, Solyndra spent money "left and right," and that the cash infusion "made people sloppy."[53] Notably, the firm built its second facility, despite growth in unsold inventory at its first facility. Moreover, Solyndra's profit margin at the time was negative and worsening. In 2011 the firm filed for Chapter 11 bankruptcy. Using the concepts developed in Chapter 7 and earlier chapters, analyze the decisions made at Solyndra.

www.mhhe.com/shefrin2e

Minicase

Cogent Communications and PSINet

In 1999, entrepreneur David Schaeffer founded the networking firm Cogent Communications, and thereafter served as its Chairman, Chief Executive Officer, and President. Schaeffer initially wrote a business plan under the premise that the Internet was going to be the only network that mattered. At the time, most of the networks that carried Internet traffic were telephone and cable television networks, but their architectures were inefficient for carrying Internet traffic. Schaeffer's plan was to construct a global network to deliver the Internet efficiently that worked like a cheap office network, essentially built around nothing more than routers manufactured by Cisco Systems along with some fiber optic cable. He estimated that constructing such a network would cost approximately $2 billion.

Cogent initially raised $26 million from six venture capital firms, which led many large equipment manufacturers to offer the firm generous vendor financing deals. Schaeffer accepted an offer from Cisco whereby for every $1 of Cisco gear that Cogent purchased, Cisco would lend Cogent $1.40. As a result of this arrangement, Cogent had a $409 million credit line.

In the autumn of 2000, an economic downturn in the wake of the collapse of the dot.com bubble led many network firms to experience financial distress. In 2001, drawing on its credit line, Cogent acquired the assets of the firm NetRail. In early 2002, Schaeffer merged his firm with Allied Riser, which wired large office buildings with fiber optic cable, effectively trading 13 percent of Cogent for $132 million in net cash and 100 percent of Allied Riser's fiber network.

In April 2002, Cogent acquired PSINet, a firm in bankruptcy, with an interesting history. PSINet went public in 1995 and raised $46 million. Shortly thereafter, PSINet began to serve business customers, establishing 100,000 business accounts in 27 countries. The firm undertook a strategy to run one of the world's largest networks, linked to a massive number of PSINet-owned web-hosting centers.

At the time, PSINet's debt load increased 36-fold, from $112 million to $4 billion. Its annual interest obligations went from being $5 million in 1997 to being $400 million in 2000. In April 1998, for the first time in its history, PSINet issued debt that was below investment grade (junk), selling $600 million in bonds paying 10 percent.

The firm then made a series of large investments: It spent $34 million for new headquarters, purchased a corporate jet, and agreed to pay $90 million in order to have the new Baltimore Ravens football stadium bear its name.

The cover story in the May 28, 2001, issue of *Forbes* magazine describes how PSINet's CEO, William Schrader, and its board of directors assessed the firm's financing strategy.

"We knew we were going to be heavy on the debt side, light on the equity side," says William Baumer, a board member and an economist who heads the University of Buffalo's philosophy department. "The assessment was that the debt markets are wide open, the equity markets not as good, and if we are successful here, we won't have any trouble retiring this debt." Schrader insists Wall Street would have been cool to additional stock offerings, despite PSINet's lofty price. "Wall Street says when you can raise equity," he claims.

In the two years leading to the peak of the technology bubble in March 2000, PSINet's stock price rose from $7 to $60. Between 1997 and 2000, PSINet made 76 acquisitions.

After a period of very rapid growth in the second half of the 1990s, the telecommunications sector began a sharp decline in the autumn of 2000. On May 1, 2001, PSInet began to default on its $400 billion debt. It missed a $20 million interest payment and announced that it would likely seek bankruptcy protection. Its stock fell to 18 cents a share and was delisted, as the firm did file for bankruptcy.

PSINet's CEO and founder, William Schrader, resigned in May 2001. The *Forbes* story contains an interesting description of Schrader, stating that "implacable self-confidence helped Bill Schrader transform a few leased phone lines into a sprawling global network."

In 2002, when Cogent was considering acquiring PSINet, then still in bankruptcy, PSINet's secured creditors and unsecured creditors were in a protracted negotiation about the terms of settlement. At the time, PSINet had $4.3 billion in debt, of which $3.7 million was unsecured, and $300 million in cash. Cogent offered to buy the firm for $10 million and shut down the business, which both groups of creditors accepted.

Cogent CEO Schaeffer made a complicated deal with the unsecured creditors. Once he had control of PSINet, he took physical possession of its assets and placed the most valuable components into a series of warehouses. He then offered to provide these to secured creditors instead of selling them; however the secured creditors refused the offer. That refusal allowed him to petition the bankruptcy court to declare the assets abandoned goods, a tactic which removed them from the bankruptcy proceedings. As a result, the secured creditors effectively found themselves to be unsecured creditors. The court then distributed the $300 million in cash on a pro rata basis, and the unsecured creditors paid Cogent $40 million, an amount that covered the $10 million purchase price and a severance agreement with employees of PSINet, as Schaeffer only retained 53 of PSINet's 9,000 employees.

By the end of 2004 Cogent had purchased 13 distressed firms, which collectively had deployed $4 billion of fixed assets. At the time Schaeffer had spent only a quarter of the $2 billion he had originally estimated he would need.[54]

For the next decade, Cogent pursued a business strategy in which it served two types of customers. The first type consisted of corporate customers located in skyscrapers where Cogent owned fiber optic lines. These customers purchased dedicated Internet access service for $700 per month, accounting for just over half of the firm's revenues, but only 3 percent of its traffic. The second type consisted of customers who purchased bandwidth by the megabit, not by the connection. Cogent emerged as the price leader in that market, selling at half of the price of their next-closest competitor, allowing them to secure 20 percent of global Internet traffic. According to Schaeffer, by 2013, the size of Cogent's second business was $165 million, operating in a total addressable market of $1.5 billion.

In 2001, the going rate for high-capacity data transport was $300 per megabit per second. When Cogent entered the market, it charged $10, driven by Schaeffer's conviction that success in this sector would come from achieving high volumes to exploit economies of scale. Over the subsequent seven years, as prices fell to an average of $20 per megabit, Cogent kept reducing its price, and in 2008 advertised itself as the "home of the $4 megabit."[55]

Speaking at a Barclays Growth Conference in November 2013, Schaeffer mentioned that Cogent was under-leveraged, had generated free cash for the previous six years, had bought back 15 percent of its "float," and had plowed back earnings in order to grow its expanding network. In addition to growing its dividend, and because it was less leveraged than its peers, Schaeffer stated that the firm's policy was to increase leverage and also pay out an additional $10 million to investors every quarter either through a buyback or a special dividend, at the discretion of management.

In respect to achieving a target leverage ratio, Schaeffer noted that he measured leverage as the ratio of net debt-to-trailing 12-month EBITDA, where net debt is defined as debt minus cash. He then stated that the target value for the ratio is 2.5, while the current value of the ratio is 1.6.

Exhibit 7-3 contains several panels depicting key time series, such as Cogent's free cash flows, its cumulative returns relative to the S&P 500 from 2002 through 2015, its cumulative returns relative to the S&P 500 from 2010 through 2015, leverage ratios, and its net income and taxes paid. Exhibit 7-4 displays a table from Cogent's November 215 8-K filing which shows the computation of its leverage ratio as of September 2015.

Case Analysis Questions

1. Based on the information presented in the minicase, how would you characterize PSINet CEO William Schrader's susceptibility to psychological phenomena?
2. Discuss the extent to which PSINet's financing and investment decisions conform to the BPV framework presented in the chapter.
3. In your view, how similar is the personality of Cogent Communications CEO Dave Schaeffer to the personality of PSINet CEO William Schrader?
4. Discuss the extent to which Cogent's financing and investment decisions conform to the BPV framework presented in the chapter.
5. Analyze the ratio that Cogent Communication uses to measure leverage, and compare it to common textbook ratios measuring leverage.

EXHIBIT 7-3

Panel A: Free Cash Flow Series for Cogent Communications, 2000–2015

Sources: Compustat, Center for Research in Security Prices.

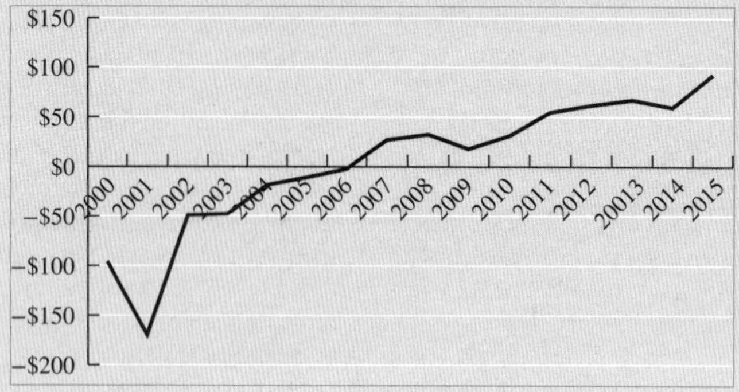

Panel A

Panel B: Cumulative Returns and Market Capitalization (in $ millions) for Cogent Communications, 2002–2015

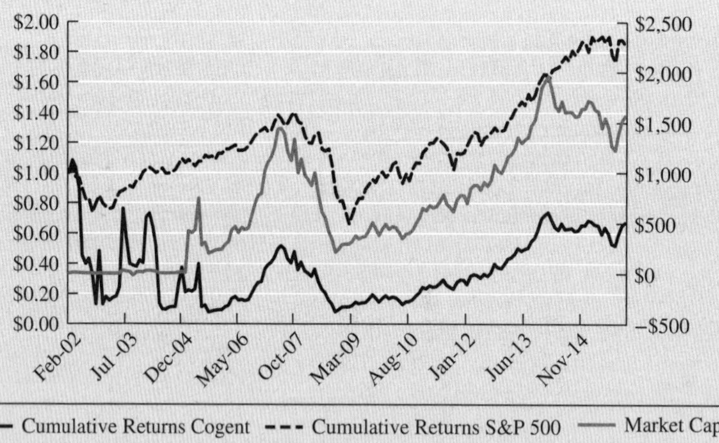

Panel B

Panel C: Cumulative Returns and Market Capitalization for Cogent Communications, 2010–2015

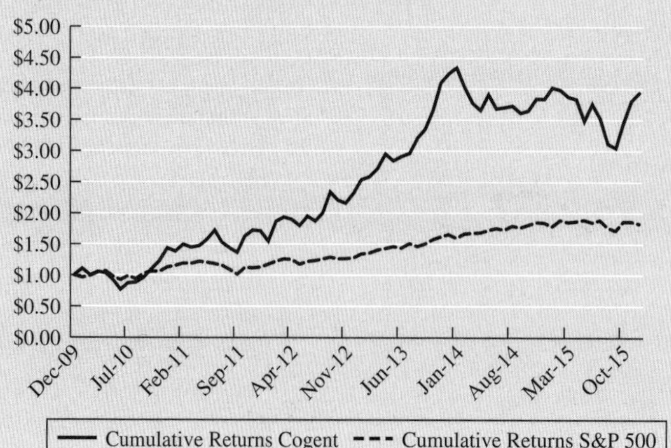

Panel C

EXHIBIT 7-3
(Continued)

Panel D: Total Liabilities to Assets, Book Value and Market Value, Cogent Communications 2002–2015

Panel D

Panel E: Net Income and Income Taxes Paid, Cogent Communications 2000–2015

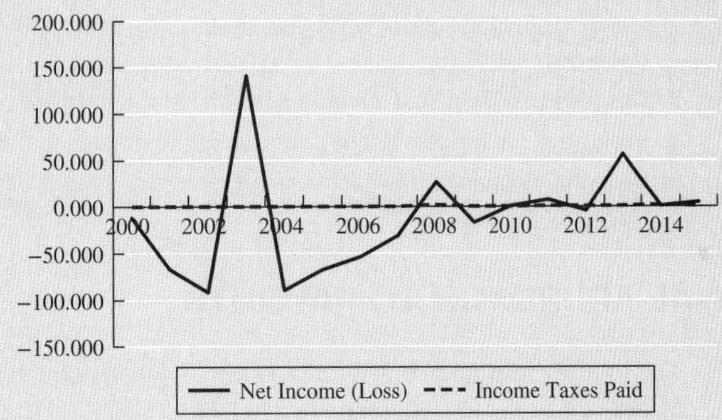

Panel E

EXHIBIT 7-4
Cogent Communications' Calculation of Net Leverage Ratio

Source: Cogent Communication's SEC filing of form 8-K, November 5, 2015. **www.sec.gov /Archives/edgar/data/1158324 /000110465915076009 /a15-22291_1ex99d1.htm**

($ in 000's)—unaudited	**As of September 30, 2015**
Cash and cash equivalents Debt	207,290
Capital leases—current portion	7,670
Capital leases—long term	123,207
Senior unsecured notes	200,000
Senior secured notes—par value	250,000
Note payable	15,508
Total debt	596,385
Total net debt	389,095
Trailing 12 months EBITDA, as adjusted	130,439
Net Leverage Ratio	2.98

Chapter Eight

Dividend Policy

The main objective of this chapter is for students to demonstrate that they can identify the manner in which heuristics, biases and framing effects impact the behavior of managers, investors, and market prices in respect to dividend policy.

After completing this chapter students will be able to:

1. Explain why framing effects lead some investors, finding cash dividends attractive, to employ dividend-based heuristics.
2. Identify conditions under which managers cater to investors' preference for cash dividends.
3. Describe heuristics that managers use to set the dividend policies of their firms.
4. Explain how managers use dividend policy to engage in behavioral signaling.
5. Describe the manner in which managers view dividends differently from share repurchases.

8.1 TRADITIONAL APPROACH TO PAYOUTS

The traditional framework for analyzing dividend policy was developed by Merton Miller and Franco Modigliani and is known as MM.[1] The basic premise of the MM framework is that investors are immune to framing effects, so that value is based on cash flows no matter how these flows are framed.

MM suggests that when taxes and transaction costs are set aside, dividend policy is irrelevant. According to this theory, if there are tax disadvantages to dividends, firms should choose low or zero payout rates. The MM argument for dividend irrelevancy assumes that investors are immune from framing effects. MM points out that if investors desired dividends, and firms were not paying dividends, then investors could create homemade dividends by selling shares.

There is no single traditional view about what constitutes appropriate dividend policy. Some follow MM and advocate minimizing dividend payouts. Others advocate dividend payouts because of issues that MM does not take into account, such as agency conflicts. In this respect, zero dividend payouts might make sense if investors could trust managers to avoid adopting projects that benefit the managers but carry negative NPV from the perspective of shareholders.

There are other reasons why firms might pay out dividends: Managers often know more than investors. For example, think about what happens when managers, as insiders, have good projects, with high NPV, but regular investors lack the inside information to assess the value of these projects properly. In that case, managers with high-NPV projects might choose to pay a dividend, in order to signal that they can afford the tax-related penalty.

Notably, there is a tax penalty attached to cash dividends. Dividends are taxed immediately as ordinary income; however, capital gains can be deferred until they are realized. Of course, if firms plow back all their earnings instead of paying dividends, then investors receive their wealth in the form of capital gains instead of dividends and only pay tax when they sell the stock. The benefits of deferred taxation discourage dividend payouts.

Is there an alternative to paying the cash out to shareholders, an alternative that avoids double taxation? Indeed yes, namely share repurchase: The firm can simply repurchase shares on an intermittent, irregular basis. However, repurchases need to be intermittent and irregular. Otherwise they will be treated as dividends and subject to tax.

In the absence of transaction costs, a share repurchase offsets a new issue of the same magnitude. Setting aside tax considerations, the argument developed by MM makes clear that the same relationship holds in respect to dividends and new issues. In this respect, share repurchases have identical cash flow implications as dividends, meaning that the two can be considered as a substitute means for distributing cash to shareholders.

8.2 DIVIDENDS AND INVESTORS: PSYCHOLOGY

Two phrases capture the key psychological phenomena associated with dividends, namely "bird-in-the-hand" and "widows-and-orphans stock." Consider each in turn.

Dividends and Risk: Bird in the Hand

Over the years, articles appearing in *Barron's* and *The Wall Street Journal* have used the phrase "bird in the hand," which comes from one of Aesop's fables, in connection with dividends. The articles in these columns have consistently emphasized that people attach value to a bird in the hand, and that dividends represent a bird in the hand in respect to being a much surer bet than capital gains.With that said, consider the following question.

CONCEPT PREVIEW
Question 8.1

1. Imagine that you face the following choice. You can accept a guaranteed $1,500 or take a risk. If you take the risk, the outcome will be determined by the toss of a fair coin. If heads comes up, you win $1,950. If tails comes up, you win $1,050. Would you accept the guaranteed $1,500 or take the risk?
2. Imagine that you took a risky decision that resulted in a gain of $1,500 for you, and you pocket the money. Now you have the opportunity to take a second risk. If you take the second risk, the outcome will be determined by the toss of a fair coin. If heads comes up, you win $450. If tails comes up, you lose $450. Would you accept the second risk?

Typically more people say they are willing to accept the second risk in part 2 of Concept Preview Question 8.1 than to accept the risk in part 1. Yet, in terms of incremental cash flows, the two risks are identical. Therefore, people who respond differently to the two parts of the question exhibit frame dependence. Apparently, people prefer to experience gains separately rather than together. This is part of a general phenomenon known as **quasi-hedonic editing,** which was mentioned in Chapter 4 in connection with prior losses. When people's behavior conforms to quasi-hedonic editing in respect to gains, they are more willing to take risks when they can experience gains separately rather than together, and/or are able to integrate small losses into larger gains.

quasi-hedonic editing
People prefer to experience gains separately rather than together, but integrate small losses into larger gains.

The main point is that people are more willing to accept risk when the payoff is decomposed into a certain prior gain and an uncertain outcome than when the payoff is not decomposed. In this respect, the total return on a stock can be decomposed into a dividend yield and a capital gain (or loss). In the traditional framework, investors only care about after-tax total return: the decomposition is irrelevant. This is not so in the behavioral framework.

In the case of dividend-paying stocks, cash dividends play the role of the certain prior gain. Some people are more willing to accept risk when their payoffs are framed as packages of a safe component, such as a dividend, and a risky component, such as an uncertain capital gain. This is the reason why a dividend is sometimes described as "a bird in the hand," as contrasted with "two in the bush."

Self-Control and Behavioral Life Cycle Hypothesis: Widows and Orphans

When the press speaks about "widows and orphans" in connection with dividends, they are usually referring to the manner in which retirees depend on dividend income. In this regard, see the example in the nearby Behavioral Pitfalls box. An important question to ask as you read the contents of the box is whether there is some pitfall underlying a connection to the reliance on dividend income.

In 2006, *The New York Times* feature "Sunday Investing" quoted several investment professionals in respect to dividends. An equity fund manager was quoted as saying that the attractiveness of dividend-paying stocks would soar because of retiring baby boomers "looking for income." A J. P. Morgan Asset Management strategist was quoted as saying that retirees view dividends as preferable because they need not "touch the principal."[2]

In the traditional MM argument, investors can always create homemade dividends to fund consumer expenses by selling a portion of their stock holdings. In practice, older retired investors are reluctant to do so. The behavioral explanation for this reluctance is known as the **behavioral life cycle hypothesis.**

behavioral life cycle hypothesis
Over the course of their lives, people use framing-based rules to cope with potential self-control problems that cause inadequate savings.

In the aggregate, people are challenged by the task of saving adequately for retirement.[3] Many fail to save adequately because the allure of current consumption overpowers their desire to delay gratification. People often use framing techniques to help themselves face this challenge. One of the most important techniques involves **mental accounting,** the separation of information into manageable pieces, through the maintenance of separate accounts. In the previous subsection, dividends and capital gains can be thought of as being separated into distinct mental accounts.

mental accounting
Mentally separating information into manageable pieces, by maintaining separate accounts.

Behavioral Pitfalls: Widow-and-Orphan Stocks

Consider an example to introduce the concept of a widows-and-orphans stock. In January 2003, Microsoft Corporation announced that after a two-for-one stock split it would pay an annual dividend of 8 cents per share, beginning in March. The March dividend was the first in Microsoft's history and amounted to a total payout of $870.6 million at a time when Microsoft held $43.4 billion in cash and cash equivalents. Eight months later, it announced that it would double its dividend payout.

On July 20, 2004, Microsoft announced that it would pay a special dividend of $32 billion in December 2004, would double its regular dividend to $3.5 billion, and would repurchase $30 billion in stock over the subsequent four years. The $32 billion payout would be a record. In response to the announcement, the price of Microsoft stock rose 5.7 percent in after-hours trading. Notably, Microsoft had the largest cash holdings of any firm, $56.4 billion.

In a front page story, the July 21 issue of *The Wall Street Journal* stated that Microsoft was seeking to broaden its investor base and was moving in the direction of the old AT&T model, that is, a *widows-and-orphans* stock in respect to regular dividend income and low risk.

In May 2003 the individual tax rate for both dividends and capital gains was reduced to 15 percent. Before that, dividends had been taxed as ordinary income, at a top rate of 38.6 percent, and capital gains had been taxed at 20 percent. The previous tax differential had imposed a penalty on investors who favor cash dividends over capital gains.

With the differential eliminated, firms increased their payouts, thereby indicating that dividend policy is important and responsive to economic conditions. In May 2004 *The Wall Street Journal* reported that firms in the S&P 500 paid out record-level dividends. Indeed, 75 percent of firms in the index, 376 in total, were paying dividends, up from 351 in 2002. The firms that paid out the most in dividends were Citigroup, General Electric, and Exxon Mobil. Notably, 119 firms in the index raised their payouts, among those being Wal-Mart, Coca-Cola, and Harley-Davidson. Only three reduced their payouts. Among those, Winn-Dixie Stores was the only firm to suspend its dividend.

An article that appeared in *Barron's Online* on July 17, 2003, pointed out that investors no longer viewed dividends as negative and passé, as they did during the 1990s dot-com bubble.

Sources: See Karen Talley, "S&P 500 Companies Are Poised to Pay Record-Level Dividends," *The Wall Street Journal*, May 19, 2004; See "Dividend Mania: New Corporate Contagion?" *Barron's Online*, July 17, 2003.

People who behave in accordance with the behavioral life cycle hypothesis establish mental accounts for their wealth and adopt spending rules that are tied to their associated account balances. Broadly speaking, the mental accounts correspond to (1) current income, (2) liquid assets, (3) home equity, and (4) future income.

If dividend income is allocated to current income, then people tend to treat that income as "spendable." In this respect, retired individual investors use dividends to mimic pension income, Social Security checks, and the paychecks of yesteryear. That is why dividends are labeled as "income." However, equity is typically held in an asset account. Retired investors who adopt the heuristic "don't dip into capital" essentially prohibit themselves from spending out of their asset accounts.

self-control
The act of exercising control over one's impulses, usually to delay gratification.

Many older, retired stockholders will not dip into capital as a way of exerting **self-control.** They seem to worry that if they allow themselves to sell stock in order to finance consumer purchases on a regular basis, they will be raiding their nest egg and killing the goose that lays their golden eggs.[4]

Additional insight into the psychology associated with dividends can be found in Chapter 13, which is available online. The discussion includes a summary of advice that individual investors have received over the years about the importance of dividend income, pertaining both to the bird in the hand effect and to the widows and orphans effect.

Behavioral Pitfalls: Cisco Systems

In November 2002 the shareholders of Cisco Systems voted on a proposal that Cisco initiate a cash dividend and rejected the proposal by a margin of 10-to-1. At the time, Cisco held $21 billion in cash, and it had been generating cash flow from operations at the rate of $4 billion per year. Cisco's board of directors had authorized share repurchases up to $8 billion, and Cisco had repurchased about $3 billion during the prior 14-month period.

Cisco's board and managers opposed the proposal to initiate a cash dividend. Institutional investors also objected, stating instead their preference for share repurchases. At the same time, individual investors had been pressing for dividends at Cisco's annual shareholder meeting.

Consider the comments made by Lionel Stevens, a 71-year-old retired airplane-maintenance worker, who owned roughly 1,000 Cisco shares. Mr. Stevens' views about cash dividends were quoted in *The Wall Street Journal*. He said: "You know you're getting something. Growth is fine, but at the moment, it's not doing me much good."

The article in *The Wall Street Journal* quoting Mr. Stevens went on to make an interesting observation.

> Analysts, investors and executives said decisions about paying dividends involve judgments about investor psychology and who can put the cash to better use. Paying a dividend would make Cisco more attractive to value investors; managers of some mutual funds are limited to investing in stocks that pay dividends. At the same time, some investors might view a dividend as a statement that managers expect slower growth.

To what psychological phenomena is this quotation referring? Does the issue involve agency conflicts as well as behavioral phenomena? If so, Cisco's managers apparently resented the implication. And the vote cast by Cisco's institutional investors indicated that they trusted the firm's management.

Source: Scott Thurm, "Companies: Cisco Systems' Shareholders Reject Proposal for Dividend," *The Wall Street Journal*, November 20, 2002.

Institutional Investors

Individual investors have a larger average ownership in non-dividend-paying stocks than in dividend-paying stocks. However, the reverse is true for institutional investors, whose ownership in dividend-paying stocks is about twice as large as in non-dividend-paying stocks.

Nevertheless, institutional investors have a much different perspective on the attractiveness of dividends than do individual investors. Among institutional investors, pension funds and banks find dividends attractive mainly because of stricter "prudent-man" rules, rather than because of a sizeable payout. However, the evidence suggests that institutional investors favor repurchases over dividend payouts.[5] When a firm increases its dividend payouts, institutions tend to decrease their holdings. The Behavioral Pitfalls box nearby illustrates the differences between individual and institutional investors.[6]

The discussion in Chapter 13 describes evidence that individual investors spend their dividends rather than reinvest them. Notably, institutional investors also refrain from reinvesting most dividends. For mutual funds, dividend reinvestment is only 2 percent as common as zero percent reinvestment; and for institutional investors, the comparable figure is 10 percent. Low reinvestment rates are consistent with investment professionals seeking to satisfy prudent man constraints rather than targeting desired portfolio weights for dividend paying stocks.[7]

8.3 SURVEY DATA DESCRIBING HOW MANAGERS THINK ABOUT DIVIDENDS

Consider the factors that drive managers' decisions about dividends. The discussion begins with a historical perspective.

Changing Payout Policies: Some History

Companies pay out cash to shareholders in three distinct ways: (1) cash dividends, (2) share repurchases, and (3) liquidating dividends to the shareholders of a target firm that has been acquired. Large corporations typically pay out a substantial percentage of their earnings in the form of dividends and repurchases. During 1999, U.S. corporations paid out more than $350 billion in dividends and repurchases and over $400 billion in liquidating dividends. In the early 1970s, dividends dominated repurchases as a form of payout. Corporations paid out more than $10 in dividends for every $1 spent repurchasing shares.

During the 1980s this situation began to change, as corporations increased the frequency with which they repurchased shares. See Exhibit 8-1, which displays the historical yield series for both dividends and total payouts (the sum of dividends and repurchases). In 1990, dividend payouts were only twice as large as share repurchases. For corporations with positive earnings, dividends amounted to roughly 25 percent of earnings. Starting in the early 1980s, most corporations initiated their cash payments to shareholders in the form of repurchases rather than dividends. The percentage of firms doing so went from 27 percent in 1974 to 81 percent in 1998.

Between 1973 and 1996, individuals received more than half of the dividends that corporations paid out. Moreover, these individuals were in high tax brackets (40 percent) and therefore paid substantial taxes on these dividends.

EXHIBIT 8-1
Dividend Yield and Payout Yield 1971–2003

Sources: Franklin Allen and Roni Michaely, "Payout Policy." In George Constantinides, Milton Harris, and René Stulz (eds.), *North-Holland Handbooks of Economics;* Jacob Boudoukh, Roni Michaely, Matthew Richardson, and Michael Roberts, "On the Importance of Measuring Payout Yield: Implications for Empirical Asset Pricing," Working Paper, New York University, 2003.

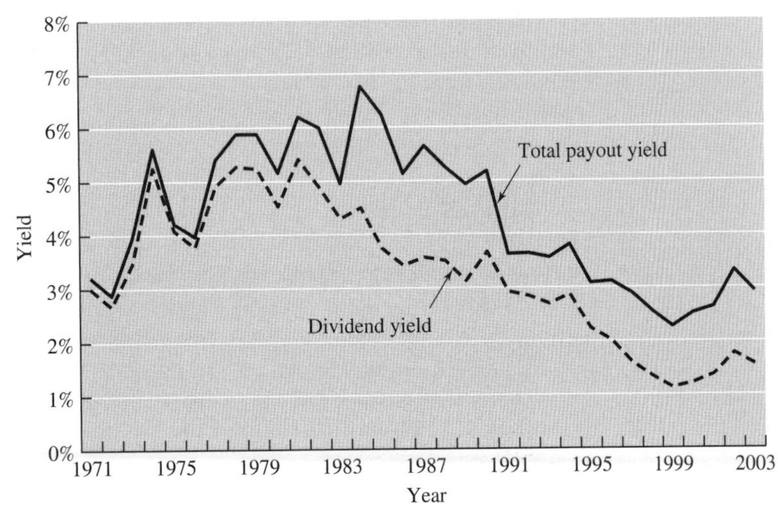

Corporations smooth dividends relative to earnings. Between 1972 and 1998, aggregate earnings fell five times. However, aggregate dividends fell only twice, once in 1992 and again in 1998, and the decline was much smaller than for earnings. However, repurchases are more intermittent and irregular in their timing. Therefore, repurchases are more volatile than dividends. Between 1972 and 1998, aggregate repurchases fell seven times.

Dividend increases occur much more frequently than dividend decreases. During 1999 there were 1,703 dividend increases or initiations. In contrast, there were only 135 decreases or omissions during the same period. At the same time, it appears that corporations might have become less reluctant to omit dividends. Between 1989 and 1992, the average number of omissions was 302. Between 1993 and 1998, the average had grown to 1,087.

Notably, the market reacts positively to announcements of repurchases and dividend increases and negatively to announcements of dividend decreases. The effect is asymmetric: The price impact associated with a decrease in dividends is considerably stronger than the impact associated with an increase in dividends.

Survey Evidence

What are the factors that in practice determine corporate dividend policy and investors' differential attitudes toward payouts? In a classic 1956 article, John Lintner sought to understand how managers think about dividends by asking them directly, in interviews.[8] In doing so, he discovered that they establish long-run target payout ratios, yet smooth dividends in the short-run. He reports that managers are particularly concerned about having to rescind a dividend increase.

Lintner conducted his survey over a half century ago. Do CFOs still follow the heuristics identified by Lintner? The answer to this question is the subject of a recent survey of financial managers.[9] Apparently, little has changed in respect to what CFOs regard as the important factors in a company's dividend decisions. The factor most frequently cited is maintaining consistency with the firm's historic dividend policy, which was mentioned by over 80 percent of respondents. This was closely followed by stability of future earnings, and a sustainable change in earnings.

CFOs and Dividend Policy

CFOs are explicit, indicating strong agreement with the following statements[10]:

- We try to avoid reducing dividends per share.
- We try to maintain a smooth dividend stream from year to year.
- We consider the level of dividends per share that we have paid in recent quarters.
- We are reluctant to make dividend changes that might have to be reversed in the future.
- We consider the change or growth in dividends per share.

The authors of the survey updating Lintner's study conclude by stating that

> Weak support for the modern theories of payout policy points to the third dimension revealed by our surveying and interviewing hundreds of financial executives. Due to the complexity and high dimensionality of the optimal decision-making process, executives tend to employ

decision rules (rules of thumb) that are fairly straightforward, in response to a handful of widely held beliefs about how outsiders and stakeholders will react.[11]

Dividend Heuristics

What are the rules of thumb, or heuristics, that executives follow when setting dividend policy? The authors of the study state the following:

> There is a severe penalty for cutting dividends, meet investors' expectations about the magnitude and form of payout (these expectations are set according to the firm's tradition and the stability of earnings), do not deviate far from competitors, maintain a good credit rating, it is good to have a broad and diverse investor base, maintain flexibility, and an important portion of investors price stocks using earnings multiples, so do not take actions that reduce earnings. These rules of the game are consistent with the informal rules[12] that . . . most affect debt policy, such as the desire for flexibility and a good credit rating, and equity policy, such as earnings per share and stock price appreciation.

Dividend Targets

Consider the findings that lead the study authors to these conclusions. One of the survey questions poses the following question to CFOs whose firms have paid dividends for the prior three years: "What do you target when you make your dividend decisions?" The most frequent target is dividends per share, a response that drew just under 50 percent. This was followed by the dividend payout ratio (about 25 percent), and growth in dividends per share (also about 25 percent).

Dividends as a Conveyor of Information

Consider whether CFOs consciously use dividends to convey information. Do they use dividends to affect investors' perceptions about the riskiness of their firm? The survey results are illuminating. Over 75 percent of respondents believe that dividends convey information about their firm to investors, and over 80 percent state that there are negative consequences to reducing dividends. About a third believe that paying dividends, instead of plowing back earnings, makes a firm's stock less risky. Given the strength with which these views are held, it is no surprise that just over 60 percent would rather raise funds to finance new investment projects than reduce dividends to finance those projects.

Attracting Investors

Presumably, CFOs set dividend policy with investors in mind. In the survey results, just under 50 percent mention that they set their policy in order to attract institutional investors to hold their stock, or to influence institutional investors. Is this because CFOs believe that paying dividends serves as a disciplinary device to reduce agency cost, by reducing managers' ability to choose negative net-present-value projects? About 30 percent cite "attracting institutional investors because they monitor management decisions." Yet, fewer than 15 percent cite "paying out dividends to reduce cash, thereby disciplining our firm to make efficient decisions."

Just over 40 percent mention that they set policy in order to attract individual (retail) investors. In this last respect, fewer than 30 percent mention the tax penalty associated with dividends, which is very interesting indeed.

Signaling

Some academics suggest that firms could use dividends as signals. Signaling theory is similar to a ceremony associated with the Native American celebration known as a *potlatch*. In Native American communities, blankets were important commodities that took many hours to produce. Yet, in some ceremonies, the members of one tribe would sometimes make a display by burning their own blankets in front of the members of some other tribe. Why? They did this in order to signal their wealth, meaning they were wealthy enough to burn blankets and not suffer unduly.

In the traditional signaling theory of dividends, cash payouts play the same role as burning blankets. Managers who can afford to pay the cash out as a dividend, despite the associated cost to investors from tax-inefficient distributions, foregone profitable investment, and/or costly external finance, will do so because their firm has highly profitable projects.

Do CFOs see themselves as using dividends as a signal? In particular, do they see dividends as the analogue of potlatch, burning blankets to show that they can afford the loss? As it happens, very few claim to use dividends in this way. Fewer than 10 percent indicate that they pay dividends to show they can afford to bear the costs of external funding or of passing up profitable investments, in order to make their firms look better than competitors.

Fewer than 20 percent of CFOs indicate agreement with the following statements:

- We pay dividends to show that our firm is strong enough to raise costly external capital if needed.
- We pay dividends to show that our stock is valuable enough that investors buy it even though they have to pay relatively costly dividend taxes.
- We pay dividends to show that our firm is strong enough to pass up some profitable investments.

Dividend Initiation

Consider firms that do not yet pay dividends but might initiate payouts. What are the main factors that their CFOs see as important to the decision? The following items were cited by over 40 percent of respondents:

- Increasing earnings per share.
- The influence of our institutional shareholders.
- Our company having extra cash/marketable securities.
- Having fewer profitable investments available (e.g., as our industry matures).

Fewer than 30 percent cited the attraction of retail investors or the undervaluation of their stock. As for using dividends as a disciplining device, fewer than 10 percent cited this issue.

What Has Changed Since 1956?

Some things have changed since Lintner conducted his survey in 1956. The evidence indicates that relatively fewer firms currently target the dividend payout ratio. Instead, more target the current level of dividends or the dividend growth rate. Notably, executives indicate that these targets are quite flexible through time.

8.4 DIVIDEND POLICY AND INVESTORS' TASTES

Dividend policy is partly a marketing decision, involving market segmentation. Investors arrange themselves into dividend clienteles. Managers need to think about their shareholders in the same way that they think about their customers. Like customers, investors have needs that are psychologically based. Just as customers react favorably or unfavorably to a firm's product or service, investors react favorably or unfavorably to a firm's dividend policy.

Through experience, financial managers have developed a set of heuristics to guide their dividend decisions. In particular, they smooth dividends. Think about the marketing implications of smoothing.

For widows and orphans, personal consumption expenses have a regular, predictable pattern. Therefore, investors relying on dividends to fund personal consumption expenses will want dividends to have a regular, predictable pattern. If a firm's shareholders hold its stock because they like dividends, then managers may find it in their interest to smooth dividends relative to earnings.

During a bear market, investors seeking a bird in the hand might also favor stable dividend payouts because they are more tolerant of risk when they can frame total return into a stable dividend and a risky capital gain. A stable dividend payout can meet these investors' needs. However, during a bull market, changes in investors' perceptions of risk and return lead investors to regard dividends as passé. Managers cater to investors' needs when they choose their payout policies to reflect the degree to which investors favor dividends.

To illustrate this last point, consider an article that appeared in *Barron's* on April 23, 2001, with the title "Bird in the Hand." The article reports that during the dot.com bubble, individual investors had moved away from dividend-paying stocks, mentioning the unfavorable tax treatment of dividends along with the fact that dividend-paying companies might have had few opportunities for growth and capital appreciation. However, the article goes on to say that investors were reversing themselves after the bubble collapsed. In this regard, the article notes that somehow the combination of steady cash income and the opportunity for capital appreciation suddenly seemed like not such "a bad idea."[13]

Citizens Utilities Company

Between 1956 and 1989, Citizens Utilities Company offered two classes of shares, one that paid cash dividends and one that paid stock dividends. By charter, the payouts from the two shares had to have the exact same pretax value. Because of special Internal Revenue Service exemptions, the regular stock dividends were not taxable as ordinary income. Therefore, on an after-tax basis, the class paying stock dividends was superior to the class paying cash dividends. Yet, the cash dividend class actually traded at a premium over the stock dividend class.[14] This phenomenon is consistent with the idea that investors view the attractiveness of cash dividends as something special.

The case of Citizens Utilities suggests that investors' preference for cash dividends can lead to pricing effects in the market. Therefore, managers who understand that investors have a special preference for cash dividends might cater to this preference through their payout policy.

Catering and Price Effects

By catering dividend policy to investors' needs, managers might impact the short-term price of their stock and therefore the value of BPV. As was discussed in Chapter 7, BPV is the sum $V_L + aV_S$, where value V_L is the value of the stock to long-term investors, V_S is the value of the stock to short-term investors, and a is a non-negative weighting parameter reflecting the importance to managers of V_S relative to V_L.

Consider how paying an extra dollar of dividends might impact the firm. First there are costs related to taxes and financing, which enter through V_L. When maximizing BPV, managers need to be sure that they can compensate for these costs through benefits associated with incremental V_S: these benefits come from generating a higher stock price and market timing activity to exploit possible overvaluation.

One way to gauge whether or not the stocks of dividend-paying firms are priced differently from the stocks of non-dividend-paying firms is to compare their book-to-market ratios.[15] If investors favor cash dividends, then we would expect the stocks of dividend-paying firms to have higher market values and therefore lower book-to-market equity than those of non-dividend-paying firms. Moreover, we would also expect that the difference in these ratios would change over time, with the differential being wider during the bear market of the 1970s than during the bull market of the 1990s.

As it happens, this is the way things have worked. Indeed, the magnitude of the book-to-market equity differential turns out to be correlated with the price differential between the two classes of shares offered by Citizens Utilities. The evidence supports the idea that many managers initiate dividend payments in an effort to cater to investors' demand for cash dividends. Initiations rise when the book-to-market equity differential widens.

Dividend increases occur after past earnings have improved, and stock prices respond positively to announcements about dividend increases.[16] However, future earnings are at best weakly related to past dividend changes. The strongest link seems to be that firms that increase dividends are less likely to suffer future earnings decreases than firms that maintain dividend payouts. Changes in dividends signal the past rather than the future.[17] That is, managers engage in unwarranted trend extrapolation.

There is longstanding evidence that the share price reaction to dividend cuts is larger in magnitude than the reaction to dividend increases, with the difference roughly being a factor of two. Notably the relationship between share price reaction and the magnitude of the change in dividend per share is highly nonlinear. In particular, changes around zero are much more important than are larger movements. On average, the market reacts to small cuts in dividends of up to $0.025 by increasing 76 basis points for each $0.01 change. In contrast, the market reacts to small increases in dividends up to $0.025 with a market reaction of 36 basis points. For the next increments, the pattern is similar but the reaction per $0.01 of dividend change drops off quickly.[18]

Consider how the market reacts to a firm's announcing a dividend omission.[19] Most firms that omit dividends are prior losers. Following the announcement, prices drift for at least a year, suggesting underreaction. The reaction to dividend initiations, not surprisingly a price rise, also features drift. But the strength of the effect is half as large as it is for dividend omissions. In this respect, remember that psychologically losses loom at least twice as large as gains.

Behavioral Signaling

The survey evidence discussed earlier is clear on the fact that managers seek to set smooth dividend payouts at levels that will enable them to limit the risk of having to reduce those payouts. In this regard, almost 90 percent of survey respondents state that they believe that there are negative consequences to reducing dividends. In addition, 80 percent believe that dividend policy conveys information to investors. At the same time, almost all survey respondents strongly reject the idea that they use dividends to engage in traditional signaling activity. Very few endorse the idea of signaling through taxes. And in a subgroup of financial executives chosen to discuss the signaling issue specifically, all clearly stated their firms do not contemplate increasing dividends in order to separate themselves from their competitors.

Behavioral signaling
Managers establish dividend policy in terms of dividends per share, which they seek to stabilize over time, with intermittent increases, but minimal decreases and omissions.

Consider therefore a behavioral variant of the traditional signaling framework, where dividend policy does convey information from managers to investors without firms treating dividends as akin to burning blankets. With **behavioral signaling**, managers simply seek to maximize BPV in markets where many of their investors employ reference points associated with either consumption, as in the case of self-control, or to measure gains and losses for quasi-hedonic editing purposes.[20] This means that managers need to take into account that because of loss aversion, these investors react more strongly to losses relative to their reference points more intensely than gains of comparable magnitude. With this in mind, managers will want investors to interpret dividend payout policy as a signal, but primarily to increase stock price rather than to separate themselves explicitly from competitors.

In the behavioral signaling framework, managers will come to learn which variables investors tend to use as reference points, and manage dividend policy accordingly. Such learning might take some time. As was mentioned earlier, in Lintner's survey managers sought to stabilize either dividend payout ratios or dividend yields. However, in recent surveys, managers focus much more on dividends per share. For managers, there is no inherent direct advantage to any of these insofar as defining payout policy. However, there is a clear advantage from catering to investors who have a distinct preference for one policy target over the others.

Among individual investor dividend clienteles, older retired investors have a natural reason to focus on dividends per share. They mostly consume their dividends, pay attention to their consumer budgets, and dislike having to cut consumption. Those in other clienteles who reinvest their dividends might find dividends per share to be a more salient reference point than dividend payout ratio and dividend yield, both of which generally give rise to variable dividends per share. In this regard, the original research in prospect theory emphasized a property known as subcertainty, which stipulated that people value what they perceive as a sure thing disproportionately more than an almost-sure thing, no matter how close "almost" is to "always."

Once managers understand that many of their investors set dividends per share as a reference point, they can exert some control over the precise value of that reference point. Recent dividend payouts per share serve as the most likely candidate for generating that precise value. Believing that this is the case, managers can set payout policy in a way that makes reference points as salient to investors as possible, and to manage their variation over time to maximize BPV, all the while being aware that the policy they set influences both V_S and V_L. While catering mostly focuses on V_S, instituting a highly variable dividend policy for investors with behavioral preferences can reduce the value to them of holding the stock long-term. In this regard, the *Barron's* article "Bird in the Hand" mentioned earlier makes the point that reports that tobacco stocks had been replacing electric utilities as reliable dividend payers because of deregulation in the market for electricity.

In view of the preceding discussion, BPV-maximizing managers who think about catering behavior in which they raise the level of the next dividend per share in order to increase V_S must take into account their ability to avoid having to reduce dividends per share thereafter, which would decrease V_L. Because of loss aversion, "better safe than sorry" is a maxim that applies. In a sports betting analogy with a game between teams A and B, a loss-averse person who would not bet on team A winning might well refuse to bet against team B winning either. Hating to lose leads people to avoid betting unless the probabilities and payoffs are sufficiently attractive. By the same token, investor loss aversion will lead BPV-maximizing managers to keep dividends per share constant over time unless they feel very confident that by increasing the next dividend per share they will not have to reverse the decision at some time in the future.

Consider some of the decisions that managers actually make in order to accentuate the salience of dividends per share as a reference point. Many boards appear to think of setting and communicating dividend policy in easily recalled dollar amounts. The most common threshold unit for defining dividend per share is twenty-five cents. This is followed by ten cents, fifteen cents, five cents, and twenty cents, with notable spikes at multiples of five cents. Non-round values are rare.

For changes in dividends per share, the modal increase is exactly to the next threshold. However, for the most part, changes in quarterly dividends cluster at zero exactly; or in other words, firms mostly maintain dividends per share, and most only consider changing the level on an annual basis.

Long streaks generate stronger reference points, therefore suggesting that patterns in announcement effects should be more pronounced in series with longer streaks. The evidence bears this out. On average, the longer a streak has been, the longer it is likely to continue. After a streak has lasted for several years, the probability of its continuing from the prior quarter is almost 90 percent. For example, in the long streak sample, the market reaction to dividend cuts is 106 basis points per $0.01 change in dividends just below zero, stronger than the unconditional reaction of 76 basis points. Similarly, in the long streak sample the market reaction to a dividend increase is 54 basis points, which is stronger than the 36 basis points mentioned earlier.

From a reference point perspective, special dividends and repurchases are different from ordinary dividends. Certainly a firm cannot commit to repurchasing shares at the same constant price every quarter; and receiving a cash payout with a repurchase requires an investor to tender shares. In addition, managers would be hard-pressed to specify repurchase programs in salient and memorable terms, even if they are structured to be financially equivalent to dividends.

Corporate Nudges

Errors or biases: Individual investors do not treat money as fungible.
Why does it happen? Mental accounting associated with the widows and orphans effect and the bird in the hand effect.
How does it happen? People attach mental tags to dollars depending on their sources or uses, and use spending rules that are based on mental accounting.
What can be done about it? For corporate managers, the choice of dividend policy should reflect the manner in which shareholders treat dividends. Managers of firms whose shareholders rely on dividends to fund consumption expenses need to understand behavioral signaling, and that as a result, they too might need to treat money as if it is not fungible. For example, managers might need to rely on external financing to fund new projects instead of reducing the dividend.

Summary

Policies regarding dividends and repurchases, relate to framing. In the traditional MM approach, people are assumed to be impervious to framing effects. In the behavioral approach, mental accounting and hedonic editing framing effects lead individual investors who regard dividends as attractive to employ dividend-based heuristics. Older, retired investors find dividends attractive because they view dividends as a replacement for wage and salary income. Young, employed investors find dividends attractive because regular dividends make it easier for them to tolerate stock market risk.

When it comes to dividend policy, psychological phenomena matter a lot, as managers have developed heuristics to meet investors' psychological needs. Those heuristics involve smoothing of dividends per share around numerical values that are salient and memorable. In following these heuristics, managers convey information to investors, and in this sense dividend policy serves a signaling function. However, behavioral signaling is different from traditional signaling in that the latter emphasizes incurring costs with the intent to distinguish the firm from its competitors.

Share repurchases are not psychologically equivalent to dividends. In this respect, managers also think about share repurchases differently than they think about dividends. Share repurchases need not be regular, whereas dividend payouts entail much more of a commitment to regularity.

Prices are impacted by changes in dividend policy and share repurchases. Many of these impacts give rise to price inefficiencies, notably drift effects. Markets underreact to both dividend omissions and dividend initiations, and the strength of the price impact is twice as large in the case of omissions. Markets also underreact to share repurchases. In addition to catering to investors' general psychological needs in respect to dividends, managers also engage in catering activities that serve to increase the short-term stock prices of their firms.

Additional Behavioral Readings

Allen, F. and R. Michaely, 2003. "Payout Policy." In G. Constantinides, M. Harris, and R. Stulz (eds.), *North-Holland Handbooks of Economics,* vol. 1A, 1B, 2001. North Holland, Amsterdam.

Baker, M. and J. Wurgler, "A Catering Theory of Dividends," *Journal of Finance,* vol. 59, 2004, pp. 271–288.

Graham, J. and A. Kumar, "Dividend Preference of Retail Investors: Do Dividend Clienteles Exist?" *Journal of Finance,* vol 6, 2006, pp.1305–1336.

Shefrin, H. and M. Statman, "Explaining Investor Preference for Cash Dividends," *Journal of Financial Economics,* vol. 13, June 1984, pp. 253–282.

Key Terms

behavioral life cycle hypothesis, *182*
behavioral signaling, *191*
mental accounting, *182*
quasi-hedonic editing, *182*
self-control, *183*

Explore the Web

www.conedison.com
The web site for the utility firm Consolidated Edison discussed in this chapter.

www.frontier.com
The web site of Frontier Communications, formerly Citizens Utilities, a firm discussed in this chapter.

www.apple.com/about
The web site for Apple, whose dividend policy is the subject of the minicase for this chapter.

www.bp.com
The web site for British Petroleum, whose dividend policy is the subject of one of the chapter questions.

Chapter Questions

1. On July 23, 2002, an article entitled "Investors Appreciate Dividends Again, See Them as Safer Bets in Bear Market" appeared on *Associated Press Newswires*.[21] The article described two reasons why financial planners have routinely recommended that investors hold dividend-paying stocks, especially in bear markets such as the period 2001–2002. First, retired investors who use quarterly dividends to augment their income find dividends to be more attractive during bear markets. Second, investors search for a bird in the hand, which dividends represent. In this respect, dividends provide investors with the ability to be patient and wait out the market decline. The article quotes Steve Wetzel, a professor of finance at New York University's School of Continuing Education and a certified financial planner, and Arnie Kaufman, editor of Standard & Poor's newsletter *The Outlook*. Discuss both reasons mentioned, in the context of the chapter text.
2. Ashland Inc. is an oil services and diversified chemical company that is located in Covington, Kentucky. In 2002 Ashland Inc. was paying an annual dividend of $1.10 per share and was planning to keep its dividend payout steady. However, the firm's chairman, Paul Chellgren, noted that he was receiving more inquiries about its dividend policy from investors than at any time in his 28 years with the firm. He also noted that during the bull market of the 1990s, investors had asked him why the firm did not eliminate its dividend, since it was no longer important. Discuss Ashland's experience with investor communications in the context of the chapter text.
3. An article that appeared in *The Wall Street Journal* in February 2001 described the experiences of several investors who held dividend-paying stocks.[22] The article mentions two investors, Wayne Denny and George Gleghorn. Wayne Denny was 72 years old at the time of the article and had been living off $35,000 a year of annual dividends. His portfolio included AT&T, Edison International, and J.C. Penney Co. The point of the article was that all three firms had omitted their dividends during the past year. George Gleghorn was 73 at the time and had long preferred safe stocks that pay regular dividends. He too had invested in the California utility Edison International, as well as Pacific Gas and Electric. However, in the wake of deregulation in the electricity-generating industry, both stocks had fallen by more than 50 percent in the previous six months, and the two firms had omitted their dividends. Discuss the experiences of investors like Wayne Denny and George Gleghorn in the context of the chapter text.
4. In 1996, Kodak paid a cash dividend of $1.60 per share. At year-end 1996, Kodak shares were trading at about $80 per share. Between 1997 and 2001, Kodak paid $1.76, and in 2002 raised its dividend to $1.80. Yet, despite the stable dividend payout, the price of Kodak stock steadily fell, reaching $27 in 2003. At that time, the firm announced its intention to reduce its dividend to about $0.50 per share, in order to invest $3 billion in digital technology purchases. Investors reacted to the announcement by bidding down Kodak shares by 14 percent. On October 21, 2003, *The Wall Street Journal* reported that some of Kodak's larger shareholders attempted to persuade Kodak executives to abandon their plan.[23] Discuss this issue in the context of the chapter text. Although Kodak eventually declared bankruptcy in 2012, discuss this question from the perspective of 2003, trying to avoid hindsight bias.
5. On January 31, 2005, an article appeared in *The Wall Street Journal* comparing the relative performance of stocks in the S&P 500 that pay dividends with stocks in the S&P 500 that do not pay dividends.[24] Between the end of the bear market in October 2002 and the date of the article, January 2005, nondividend payers rose by 63 percent, whereas dividend payers rose by 52 percent. Notably, dividend payers have tended to outperform

nondividend payers when the market is soft, but not when the market is strong.[25] Based on these patterns, the article contends that the change in the tax treatment of dividends that was made in 2003 did not change investors' preferences for dividend-paying stocks. Discuss this contention.

6. Analyze whether there are any behavioral issues in Cogent Communications' dividend policy, which is described in the minicase for Chapter 7.
7. Analyze whether there are any behavioral issues associated with CFO Judy Lewent's views about Merck's dividend policy in respect to the Vioxx incident discussed in Chapter 2.
8. In December of 1998, energy firm British Petroleum acquired American-based Amoco and became BP-Amoco. BP's stock was listed on the London Stock Exchange and also traded on U.S markets through an American depositary receipt (ADR). Before the merger, Amoco's dividend policy for the previous four years had been to increase dividends by \$0.025 every year, but maintain a quarterly dividend within each year. For its part, for the previous two years, BP had increased dividends by £0.0125 semiannually. As a result of the merger, BP fixed dividend increases in dollar terms. For several years thereafter, BP increased its dividends at the rate Amoco had followed, \$0.025 each year, but maintained the common policy in the United Kingdom of making semiannual payments. Based on the material in the chapter, discuss BP's decision to adopt Amoco's recent policy for dividend growth. In addition, analyze how investors in the United States might regard dividend policies associated with ADRs, where dividend policy is established in terms of a foreign currency subject to foreign exchange volatility, but which nevertheless pays U.S. investors in dollar amounts.

Additional Resources and Materials for Chapter 8 Are Available at www.mhhe.com/shefrin2e

Minicase

Apple

Steve Jobs, the visionary founder and CEO of Apple, died in October 2011. Under Jobs's leadership, Apple had introduced major innovative products such as the iPod in 2001, the iPhone in 2007, and the iPad in 2010. These innovations propelled Apple from nearly failing to having the highest market capitalization among U.S. firms. Tim Cook, who had headed Apple's operations, succeeded Jobs as CEO. Two-and-a-half years after Cook had become CEO, Apple's annual revenue had grown by about 58 percent, and its profits had grown by about 40 percent.

At the time, Apple's CFO was Peter Oppenheimer, who in 2012 oversaw Apple's first dividend payments in over a decade, as well as a more aggressive share-repurchase program. Notably, Apple limited both of those programs because it held almost 80 percent of its cash overseas for tax reasons. The company paid a quarterly dividend of \$2.65 a share (\$10.60 annualized), amounting to \$10 billion in cash per year. At the time, Apple indicated it would periodically discuss updating its dividend but did not specify a timeframe. Its board of directors also authorized a \$10 billion share repurchase program, to begin in 2013.

In February 2013, hedge fund manager David Einhorn of Greenlight Capital, which held Apple stock, appeared on CNBC and Bloomberg proposing that the company issue preferred shares with a 4-percent dividend yield.[26] Apple responded with a press release, noting that its board had been having active discussions about returning additional cash to shareholders.

Security analyst Bill Choi from Janney Capital Markets wrote to say that although Apple might be considering issuing preferred shares, he thought it more likely that Apple would simply increase the dividend payout ratio on its existing shares. He also stated that he thought that Apple's financial condition would support a 4 percent dividend, which would likely expand the firm's shareholder base.

In April 2013, Apple issued $17 billion in bonds, at the time the largest corporate bond offering on record.[27] It did so to return more capital to shareholders without having to incur repatriation taxes on its overseas holdings of cash.

In September 2012 Apple shares peaked above $700. From then through the end of February 2014, the stock returned –16.5 percent while the S&P 500 returned 33.1 percent. Analysts covering Apple were disappointed and the percentage of those issuing buy recommendations fell from 94 percent to 69 percent. Its 30 top shareholders reduced their Apple holdings from 36 percent to 30 percent during this period, down from a peak of 40 percent in 2009. According to Morgan Stanley, this kind of reduction was anomalous for large-cap tech stocks.

In March 2014, sentiment about Apple was on the low side. Investors were questioning the firm's growth potential, especially after it reported its first annual decline in earnings in over a decade, largely because iPhone sales were lower than expected for the quarter that ended the previous December.[28] Fund managers began to view Apple as less of a growth stock, and more as value stock, trading at a lower market-to-book ratio with large dividend payouts and repurchases. Still, activist Carl Icahn was pressuring Apple to distribute more of its $159 billion of cash, the largest such holding among all nonfinancial firms. A decade earlier, Apple's cash holdings were only about $5.5 billion.

A book entitled *Haunted Empire: Apple after Steve Jobs* by *Wall Street Journal* writer Yukari Kane compared Cook to Jobs. In March 2014, she gave an interview to the *New York Times,* where she expressed the opinion that Apple was struggling to cope with the loss of its visionary founder, whose thumbprint was all over its innovative products, and whose presence was an integral part of its identity.[29] She pointed out that Apple had defined success for itself as being exceptional and making insanely great products. Yet in the time since Cook became CEO Apple had not introduced new products that could be so described.[30]

A related *Wall Street Journal* article also compared the two CEOs. The article noted that Jobs was an intuitive decision maker who immediately knew what he liked and what he disliked. This allowed him to be comfortable at making snap decisions, but these sometimes led to erroneous judgments.[31] In contrast, the article noted that Cook is more thoughtful, taking extra time to mitigate errors. For her part, Kane stated that she regards Cook as more systematic and analytical than Jobs had been, and that Apple will be financially well managed under his leadership.

In March 2014, Apple also announced that its CFO Peter Oppenheimer would retire in June, to be replaced by Luca Maestri.[32] Under Oppenheimer's leadership, Apple was planning to repurchase up to $60 billion and to return a total of $100 billion, including dividends, to shareholders through 2015.

As for Maestri, for the two previous years he had served as CFO of Xerox, where he sharply increased its share repurchases from zero in 2010 to $700 million in 2011 to $1.1 billion in 2012. A Xerox director who worked with him on the finance committee described him as being shareholder-friendly in respect to payouts, whether dividends or repurchases.[33] Barclays analyst Ben Reitzes characterized Maestri as championing shareholder return and supporting consistent plans for returning capital.

In April 2014, Apple surprised analysts with its earnings announcement for the fiscal second quarter ending March 29, beating their consensus forecast of $10.18 a share on revenue of $43.53 billion. Instead, Apple reported a profit of $10.22 billion, an increase of 7 percent from the previous year. Apple said it sold 43.7 million iPhones in the second quarter, which greatly exceeded analysts' expectation of 38.2 million units.

At the same time, Apple raised its dividend about 8 percent, increased its stock repurchase plan from $60 billion to $90 billion, and indicated that it would split its stock 7-to-1.[34] Taken together, Apple's new target for returning capital to shareholders by the end of 2015 would increase by about $30 billion to about $130 billion. Exhibit 8-2 displays the time series of dividend per share on Apple stock, adjusting for the 7-to-1 stock split.

Cook stated that the planned increase in repurchases reflected Apple's executives' view that its stock was undervalued, saying the decision indicated "how much confidence" its executives had "in the future of the company." He also stated that they decided on the stock split "to make Apple stock more accessible to a larger number of investors."[35] In this regard, Oracle Investment Research analyst Laurence Balter noted that Cook's remark essentially applies to retail investors. A report on CNN noted that Apple's dividend offers a yield that is appealing "to the widow and orphan crowd."[36]

EXHIBIT 8-2
Dividend per Share, Dividend Yield, Apple Stock, 2012–2015, Adjusted for 7-to-1 Stock Split

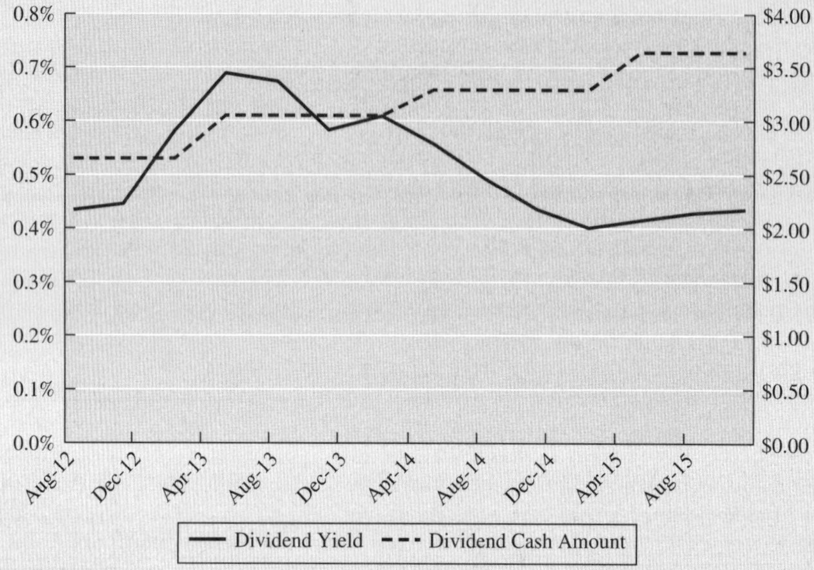

In its announcement, Apple reported that its cash holdings had decreased to about $151 billion from about $159 billion three months earlier. The announcement mentioned that Apple had repurchased $14 billion of its shares in February after its stock price declined as a result of a negative earnings surprise the previous quarter. The firm also indicated that it would issue more debt to fund returning capital to shareholders, rather than pay higher taxes as a result of repatriating profits from abroad.

A week later Apple issued $12 billion of debt of varying maturities at yields that were mostly within a percentage point above comparable U.S. Treasury debt. Apple's debt was rated double-A-plus, the second-highest rating. The head of U.S. investment-grade credit at Invesco, Chuck Burge, stated that Apple's bonds were "an attractive alternative" to treasuries and that "Apple is a brand name everyone knows about."[37] Measured by its market capitalization of $512 billion, Apple continued to be the most valuable U.S. firm.

In September 2014 Apple announced an updated version of the iPhone, a smart watch called the Apple Watch, and a payment system called Apple Pay that would compete with conventional debit and credit cards.[38] The updated iPhone and Apple Pay were positively regarded by investors, but the Apple Watch less so. Immediately after the products were introduced, Apple's stock price increased by 4.8 percent.

In January 2015, Apple's iPhone sales exceeded the consensus analysts forecasted by 12 million. Relative to a year earlier, its earnings had increased from about $13 billion to $18 billion, and its revenue had increased from $57.6 billion to $74.6 billion. Most importantly, iPhone sales surged in China, Hong Kong, and Taiwan. According to research firm Canalys, Apple became the top smart phone maker in China. Apple's share price increased by more than 5 percent on the announcement, providing additional momentum after having gained more than 50 percent in the prior year.[39]

In February 2016, Apple continued to have the highest market capitalization, with Google parent Alphabet being $15 billion behind, in second place.[40]

Case Analysis Questions

1. What are the main issues that the traditional approach emphasizes in respect to Apple's dividend policy?
2. What are the main issues that the behavioral approach emphasizes in respect to Apple's dividend policy?
3. Drawing on the discussion in Chapters 5 and 7, as well as this chapter, analyze Apple's policy in respect to debt, repurchasing shares, and splitting its stock.
4. In January 2004, a multifactor regression analysis of Apple's stock return, based on five years of past

EXHIBIT 8-3 **Factor Regressions for Apple's Stock Return**

	January 2004		February 2004	
	Coefficients	***t Stat***	***Coefficients***	***t Stat***
Intercept	0.02	0.86	0.01	1.54
Excess Return on the Market	1.26	2.72	1.00	4.03
Small-Minus-Big Return	0.54	1.29	0.00	0.00
High-Minus-Low Return	−0.58	−1.11	−0.45	−1.06
Momentum Factor	−0.28	−1.03	−0.25	−1.47

monthly returns, indicated that only the excess return on the market was statistically significant. Factor loadings related to size, book-to-market equity, and momentum were not statistically significant. At the time, the regression coefficient for the excess return on the market was 1.26. In February 2014, the same multifactor regression produced similar results, except that the regression coefficient for the excess return on the market had fallen to 1.0. Exhibit 8-3 summarizes the regression results. How do these findings relate to the information provided in the minicase?

5. Discuss whether there are any behavioral issues in the minicase that have not arisen in connection with any of the preceding questions.

Chapter Nine

Agency Conflicts and Corporate Governance

The main objective of this chapter is for students to demonstrate that they can identify key psychological phenomena that serve to obstruct good corporate governance.

After completing this chapter students will be able to:

1. Explain how overconfidence prevents corporate boards from putting compensation systems in place that align the interests of managers and shareholders.
2. Explain the role of prospect theory casino effects in aligning the interests of shareholders and managers.
3. Describe how aversion to a sure loss can interfere with the alignment of the interests of investors and the interests of auditors engaged to provide opinions primarily about firms' financial statements, and relatedly firms' internal controls.
4. Analyze how, because of aversion to a sure loss and overconfidence, stock option–based compensation can exacerbate agency conflicts.

9.1 TRADITIONAL APPROACH TO AGENCY CONFLICTS

Agency theory is used to study the structure of compensation contracts that principals offer to agents engaged to act on their behalf. In the corporate governance setting, shareholders are the principals, the board of directors is charged with representing the interests of shareholders, and the firm's managers are the agents.

In order to identify the main issues in agency theory, consider the film, and later well-known successful musical, *The Producers*. The plot of *The Producers* features Broadway producer Max Bialystock developing a scheme to defraud investors. Bialystock raises a large amount of money from investors by selling more than 100 percent of a new show—25,000 percent actually—and enlists a meek accountant named Leo Bloom to produce a flop that will enable him to hide his actions. In Bialystock's plan, the show fails, enabling him to apologize to investors for having lost their money, which he then proceeds to keep.

The plot of *The Producers* has three key features. First, there is a principal–agent relationship involved, where principals (the investors) entrust their money to an agent (the producer), who is supposed to take an action on their behalf. Second, there is an inherent conflict of interest between the principals and the agent. Third, the agent is better informed than the principals. Only a successful show would reveal the producer's true action. Of course, in the film and musical, Bialystock's show turns out to be a hit despite his best efforts. But as they say, that's show business.

The plot of the producers serves to highlight the conflicts of interest and information asymmetries between corporate executives and investors. The executives are supposed to act as agents of the shareholders, with a fiduciary interest to act in their best interests. But executives know more than shareholders know. The combination of information asymmetries and inherent conflicts of interest give rise to agency conflicts.

Rational principals offer contracts to rational agents that combine positive rewards and penalties, so-called carrots and sticks, with three goals in mind. The principal's first goal is to offer the agent a contract that is at least as attractive as the agent's next best alternative, in order to induce the agent to participate. This goal is known as the **participation constraint.** The second goal is to set the differential between the carrot-and-stick components so as to induce the agent to represent the interests of the principal. This goal, the alignment of managers' interests and investors' interests, is known as the **incentive compatibility constraint.** The third goal is for the contract not to be unduly generous to the agent. This goal is known as the **nonoverpayment constraint.**[1]

participation constraint
The principal offers attractive enough terms to the agent to induce the agent to participate.

incentive compatibility constraint
The principal chooses the carrot-and-stick differential, in terms of pay for performance, so as to induce the agent to represent the interests of the principal.

nonoverpayment constraint
The principal does not overpay the agent.

In the traditional approach, company stock and associated stock options are typical instruments used in connection with incentive compatibility. However, incentive compatibility typically prevents managers from diversifying away all the unique risk of their firms, especially career risk. Managers who bear such risk might react by behaving in too risk averse a fashion, to the detriment of investors. In theory, managerial risk aversion can be countered by using stock options. This is because options reward managers for favorable outcomes but do not penalize them for unfavorable outcomes.

9.2 PAYING FOR PERFORMANCE IN PRACTICE

The evidence about how well the traditional approach to agency conflicts applies in practice is mixed. The most influential academic studies on executive compensation conclude that CEO pay varies far too little to be consistent with traditional theory.[2] These studies, published in 1990, indicate that most corporate boards do not structure salaries, bonuses, and stock options so as to provide either large rewards for superior performance or large penalties for poor performance. Executive pay has featured too narrow a carrot-and-stick differential, resulting in low variability in respect to corporate performance. The frequency with which CEOs are dismissed for poor results is low. And corporate stock options do not appear to play a major role in aligning the interests of executives and investors. Some evidence points to the relative strength of shareholder rights as being key.

Low Variability

For the median CEO in the 250 largest companies, a $1,000 change in corporate value corresponded to a change of just 6.7 cents in salary and bonuses over two years. Accounting for all monetary sources of CEO incentives—salary and bonuses, stock options, shares owned, and the changing likelihood of dismissal—a $1,000 change in corporate value corresponded to a change in CEO compensation of just $2.59. In this regard, the value of shares owned by the median CEO changed by 66 cents for every $1,000 increase in corporate value. At the median, stock options added another 58 cents worth of incentives.

What does the $2.59 mean when it comes to bad decisions? Consider a CEO who makes a wasteful investment, such as purchasing a new aircraft for the firm's executive fleet, which benefits him but diminishes the market value of the company by $10 million. The total wealth of this CEO, if he is representative, would decline by only $25,900 as a result of the misguided investment. Is this a large penalty or a small penalty? Given that the average compensation of CEOs was $20,000 a week, the penalty is small.

Dismissal

As to dismissal, the CEOs of poor-performing firms are only 6 percent more likely to leave their jobs than CEOs of companies with average returns. In respect to the $2.59 mentioned, by affecting dismissal prospects, a $1,000 change in corporate value translates into an estimated median change of 5 cents in CEO wealth.

Stock Options

During the 1990s, corporations in both the United States and Europe increased their use of executive stock options and employee stock options. Shares allocated to employee incentive plans in the 200 largest U.S. firms increased from 6.9 percent in 1989 to 13.2 percent in 1997. In 2001, 29 percent of CEOs received option grants that had a face value at least eight times their annual cash compensation.

Compensation consultants point out that during the 1990s CEO pay increased by between 400 and 600 percent, mostly driven by the granting of stock options. At the beginning of the 1990s, for the typical company, the value of stock options was approximately 5 percent of the value of stock outstanding, a figure which over the course of 10 years increased to 15 percent.[3] Notably, by the end of the 1990s, stock options comprised approximately 98 percent of executives' long-term incentives.

There is mixed evidence about whether firms offering stock options to their employees perform better than those that do not.[4] A study of 200 firms whose stocks trade on the Nasdaq suggests that executive and employee stock options do lead to increased firm value, principally because they aid in employee retention and serve as a substitute for cash compensation in cash-strapped firms. Less clear is whether stock options serve to align the incentives of executives and employees with those of shareholders.

Despite their increased popularity at the time, the use of stock options has been controversial. Investment legend Warren Buffet has been a long-time critic of the manner in which firms use stock options. He suggests that although options can be appropriate in theory, in practice their use has been capricious, inefficient as motivators, and very expensive for shareholders. The manner in which options are recorded in financial statements was also a long-running subject of debate, whether as footnotes or expensed.

Some academics argued that the simultaneous increase of overall executive compensation and grants of executive stock options did little to improve the sensitivity of equity-based incentives to performance.[5] Furthermore, the associated literature noted that CEOs had been able to increase their proportion of overall executives' compensation, and by 2010 the average CEO's "pay slice," meaning their share of the total compensation paid to the top five executives, was approximately 35 percent. In respect to performance, the evidence suggests that higher values for CEO pay slice are detrimental to shareholder interests. Specifically, relative to their industry peers, firms featuring higher CEO pay slices have lower values of Tobin's q. A related strand of the academic literature suggested that making CEO compensation too dependent on stock options, as happened in the lead-up to the financial crisis, was detrimental to shareholder interests.[6]

Compensation consultants have suggested that particular measures did eventually induce corporate boards to replace stock option compensation with restricted stock. These measures include the Sarbanes-Oxley Act (discussed below), the "say on pay" provision of the Dodd-Frank Act that provided shareholders with advisory votes on executive compensation, and accounting changes that eventually did require stock option grants to be expensed on firms' financial statements. In 2011, options as a percentage of total compensation had decreased to 18 percent, while stock and stock-like instruments had increased to over 40 percent.

In 2012, most CEOs of Fortune 500 companies earned between $9 million and $12 million a year, which was three times the amount earned by the next-highest paid executive, and more than 200 times the amount earned by the average worker. Some academics suggest that CEO compensation is excessive and reflects board members exhibiting undue loyalty to CEOs.[7]

However, not all agree with this view. A study of executive compensation and governance in U.S. firms, which was published in 2014, argued that average executive pay has been positively correlated with firm performance and firm size. The author of the study points out that executive pay contracts reflect significant equity incentives, increase reliance on restricted stock, and stock options that still serve as an important component of overall compensation. The study suggests that compensation committees on corporate boards are generally independent, do not exhibit excessive loyalty, and that there is little evidence that CEO compensation is too high. In this regard, the study notes when it comes to "say on pay," shareholders generally endorse executive pay plans, with few such resolutions failing.[8]

Shareholder Rights

An important aspect of corporate governance is shareholder rights. Provisions that move away from one share, one vote and put antitakeover provisions in place contribute to weak shareholder rights. The evidence indicates that firms with stronger shareholder rights are associated with higher firm value, higher profits, higher sales growth, lower capital expenditures, and fewer corporate acquisitions. In this regard, an index known as the Gompers-Ishii-Metrick (GIM) index rates firms on corporate governance.[9] In the same vein, the California Public Employees' Retirement System (CalPERS) has taken an activist position in respect to corporate governance, maintaining a focus list of firms with poor investment records and poor corporate governance. Over time, the company Institutional Shareholder Services (ISS), whose focus is corporate governance and responsible investment, has gained influence in respect to shareholder activism. In 2016, ISS was following more than 13,000 companies around the world. The opinions it expressed about those companies increasingly impacted the proxy votes cast by institutional shareholders.

9.3 PSYCHOLOGICAL PHENOMENA

A key lesson from the previous section is that arrangements between principals and agents often fall short in respect to paying properly for performance and avoiding overpayment. The point of the chapter is to identify the psychological factors that lead to this state of affairs, such as overconfidence, prospect theory, risk aversion, time preference, and relative incomes.

From the Mouths of Directors

In 2001, *Fortune* magazine interviewed a group of high-ranking corporate directors in respect to executive compensation.[10] In exchange for remaining anonymous, most offered candid comments suggesting serious difficulties with executive compensation. The nearby Behavioral Pitfalls box provides a vivid example. Interviewees' candid remarks characterized directors as being overconfident in their ability to oversee directors and deal with compensation consultants, which one interviewee described as amateurs competing against professionals. Interviewees' comments mention susceptibility to a better-than-average effect associated with attempting to pay a disproportionate number of CEOs compensation in excess of the median. In addition, interviewees point out that directors have difficulty dealing with managers' tendency to resist a low reward for poor performance, but seek a high reward for good performance that stems from external factors rather than their own efforts. Psychologically, this feature corresponds to a combination of self-interest and **self-attribution bias**. Self-attribution bias is the tendency for people to take credit for positive outcomes and to blame others or bad luck for negative outcomes.[11] The Additional Resources to this chapter contains select quotations from directors making these points.

self-attribution bias
The tendency for people to take credit for positive outcomes and to blame others or bad luck for negative outcomes.

Prospect Theory and Stock Option-Based Compensation

There are three important behavioral phenomena associated with stock options being used to compensate employees, especially executives. First, excessively optimistic, overconfident employees will overvalue their firms, thereby overvaluing the stock options they are granted. Second, many employees have a preference for the small probability of a large payoff, what some call a **casino effect.** Third, stock option compensation increases the propensity to engage in accounting fraud, a point taken up in Section 9.6.

casino effect
Preference for the small probability of a large payoff.

Behavioral Pitfalls: Granting a CEO the Authority to Overpay

[T]here was a case at [a] company about five years ago in which I took a strong stand regarding a guy who ran a major division. He was the architect of some terrible deals for the company. . . . All of his projections for his division were wrong. He underestimated what capital expenditures needed to be. He was way off on growth.

So the comp committee has a meeting to talk about bonuses—and if there was ever a person who didn't deserve one, it was this fellow I'm talking about.

Nevertheless, the CEO came into the meeting and recommended that this guy get a pretty good-sized bonus. And I said, "How can you do this? This guy's poor decisions have cost the company billions of dollars. If you're going to pay for performance, you have to have both a carrot and a stick. Basically, this guy should be kicked out of the company. But if he's going to be around, you've got to send a message not only to him but even more importantly to the organization that if someone screws up, they don't get a bonus."

Well, I think the committee sort of agreed with me. But ultimately the others said, "We've got to let the CEO have the authority to run his organization," which I actually think is a bunch of crap. So what happened—and I think this was mainly because of my bitching and complaining—is that the CEO cut this fellow's bonus by half. That meant he ended up getting a reasonable amount for costing the shareholders billions.

Source: C. Loomis, "Executive Pay: This Stuff Is Wrong," *Fortune,* Monday, June 11, 2001.

Overvaluing Options

The evidence suggests that firms pay their employees in options whenever employees are excessively optimistic about the prospects of their firms.[12] In this regard employees are especially apt to purchase company stock for their 401(k) and ESOP plans at market prices, after their company stock has performed well. Moreover, when upper-level executives believe that their firm's stock is overvalued, they appear to grant more options to rank-and-file employees.

Casino Effect

A comment made by one of the directors quoted in the *Fortune* magazine article introduces the concept of *casino effect.*

> What's going to happen this year about compensation, generally? I think bonuses will go down—sharply. Companies may award more options to make up the downdraft. They'll say, "I gave good ol' George $2 million in options last year. This year the stock is down 75%, so I'll give him four times as many options." That'll fit what most people want. They say, "You can fiddle with my bonus, but don't cut out my options"—because they know there's the big casino waiting out there.

As was discussed in Chapter 1, psychologists Daniel Kahneman and Amos Tversky documented that people tend to overweight low probabilities attached to extreme events and to underweight high probabilities associated with moderate events.

According to prospect theory, people often act as if they are risk averse when facing the possibility of only gains, and risk seeking when facing the prospect of only losses. Kahneman and Tversky suggest that the overweighting of low probabilities reverses this behavior pattern: People purchase lottery tickets, thereby seeking risk in respect to gains (casino effect), and purchase insurance policies to reduce risk in respect to losses.

Risk Aversion and Impatience

Section 9.1 makes the point that incentive compatible contracts often require that agents bear risk. Therefore, because of the participation constraint, all else being the same such contracts require that more risk-averse agents need to be better compensated than less risk-averse agents. The "all else" in the last sentence includes psychological phenomena such as excessive optimism and overconfidence. Certainly these phenomena can counteract and even offset the impact of risk aversion.

The behavioral approach distinguishes between mild versions and extreme versions of psychological phenomena such as excessive optimism and overconfidence. Risk-averse managers who exhibit mild versions require less performance-based compensation to overcome their innate aversion to risk. However, managers with extreme versions prefer greater performance-based compensation.[13]

Consider the question of how averse to risk executives actually are? And depending on the answer to that question, to what extent is the average compensation package for very risk-averse CEOs different from CEOs who are less risk-averse?

First things first: how can we categorize people by degree of risk aversion? In this regard, how would you answer the following Concept Preview Question, which one of the Duke studies asked of CEOs and CFOs?

CONCEPT PREVIEW
Question 9.1

Suppose you are the only income earner in your family. Your doctor recommends you move because of allergies. You have to choose between two possible jobs, whose salaries are both fully indexed for inflation. The first job (a) features a 100 percent chance of paying you your current income for life. The second job (b) features a 50 percent chance of paying you twice your current income for life, and a 50 percent chance of paying two-thirds of your current income for life. Given these two alternatives, which job would you choose, (a) or (b)?

If you chose job (a), then answer the following supplementary question. Suppose that the choices you face are not between (a) and (b), but instead are between (a) and (c), where job (c) offers you a 50 percent chance of paying you twice your current income for life and a 50 percent chance of paying you four-fifths of your current income for life. Given these two alternatives, which job would you choose, (a) or (c)?

If you chose job (b), then answer the following supplementary question. Suppose that the choices you face are not between (a) and (b), but instead are between (a) and (d), where job (d) offers you a 50 percent chance of paying you twice your current income for life and a 50 percent chance of paying you one-half of your current income for life. Given these two alternatives, which job would you choose, (a) or (d)?

How people respond to Concept Preview Question 9.1 provides an indication of their overall aversion to risk. There are four possible ways to answer the overall question, and they are:

(b) over (a) and (d) over (a);
(b) over (a) and (a) over (d);
(a) over (b) and (c) over (a); and
(a) over (b) and (a) over (c).

Notably, the degree of risk aversion increases as we go down this list from top to bottom. We can call the four categories: very low risk aversion, moderate risk aversion, high risk aversion, and very high risk aversion.[14]

Separately from the Duke study of CEOs and CFOs, other groups have answered Concept Preview Question 9.1. Exhibit 9-1 displays how various groups vary by risk aversion. The group at the left is drawn from the general U.S. population. Moving left, the next groups respectively consist of undergraduate finance majors, an international group of risk managers, investment professionals, CFOs, and CEOs. Although there is some variation in the character of these groups, one of the most important differences is that CFOs and CEOs feature much greater proportions of people who exhibit very low risk aversion, and much lower proportions of people who exhibit very high risk aversion. Not surprisingly, older CEOs tend to be less risk tolerant than others, and they also tend to be male. In regard to very low risk aversion, CEOs stand out from all the other groups.

According to agency theory, as described in Section 9.1, incentive compensation consists of a fixed salary and a variable performance-related component such as a bonus. The Duke study asked CEOs and CFOs about the structure of their compensation by administering the following questions:

> If all options were vested and exercised, what percent of your company's common stock would you own? (e.g., 5 percent)

EXHIBIT 9-1 **Risk Aversion Histograms for Different Groups**

Source: B. Barsky, F.T. Kimball, M. Juster, and M. Shapiro, "Preference Parameters and Behavioral Heterogeneity," *Quarterly Journal of Economics*, 1997; J. Graham, C. Harvey, and M. Puri, "Managerial Attitudes and Corporate Actions," *Journal of Financial Economics*, 2013; H. Shefrin, *Behavioral Risk Management*, 2016

	General Population	Undergraduate Finance Majors	Risk Managers	Investment Professionals	CFOs	CEOs
Very low risk aversion	12.8%	13.1%	12.2%	12.5%	30.2%	44.8%
Moderate risk aversion	10.9%	34.4%	34.1%	32.7%	37.7%	32.3%
High risk aversion	11.6%	32.8%	31.7%	22.1%	20.4%	11.9%
Very high risk aversion	64.6%	19.7%	22.0%	32.7%	11.7%	11.0%

On average, what is the approximate target percentage of your total compensation that is in the form of:

_________% Stock and option compensation
_________% Bonus
_________% Salary
_________% Other

The responses by the participants in the Duke survey to these questions indicate that performance sensitive compensation (stock, options, and bonuses) comprise approximately 35 percent of total compensation for the average executive in the sample. Salary comprises approximately 57 percent, but is a bit smaller at 5 percent for larger, public firms.

CEOs' and CFOs' responses to the above questions and to Concept Preview Question 9.1 indicate that relative to others, the odds are 217 percent higher that a very risk-averse CEO is mostly compensated by salary and 59 percent lower to be compensated mostly with performance-related incentives.[15] On average, CEOs with very high risk aversion receive approximately 65 percent of their compensation as salary, whereas the corresponding figure for CEOs with very low risk aversion is approximately 55 percent, with the proportions for the other two categories being between 56 and 58 percent.[16] Relatedly, the responses also indicate that the same pattern holds for young, tall, and male CEOs. As for CFOs, only the least risk-averse among them receives a distinctly lower portion of their compensation in the form of salary, approximately 61 percent in contrast to the others for whom the corresponding figure is between 65 and 68 percent.

Next, consider the issue of patience. Executive stock options tend to have expiration times that are 10 years from the time the options are first granted. Theoretically, all else being the same, executives who are very impatient will demand a high return to defer gains, and therefore are much more likely to be compensated with a proportionately smaller performance component in the form of stock or stock options or bonus.

To identify people who are very impatient, the Duke survey asked respondents the following question: Would you rather win $10,000 now or win $13,000 a year from now?

A person who would rather win $10,000 today implicitly discounts the future at 30 percent per year, suggesting great impatience.

Based on the responses of the CEOs and CFOs who participated in the Duke study, CEOs tend to be more impatient than CFOs in the sense that there is a significantly larger proportion of CEOs with a high rate of time preference as compared to CFOs. Most importantly, the odds that the average highly impatient CEO's compensation package will be heavily weighted in stocks, stock options, and bonus are 36 percent less than other CEOs.

That CEOs and CFOs are less averse to risk than others is not especially surprising. In a sense, it is cheaper for boards to hire risk-tolerant CEOs, as they demand less compensation for bearing the risk that incentive compatibility requires that they do. Likewise, it is plausible that impatient CEOs will tend to have less of their compensation in a form requiring them to wait to be paid.

Relative Incomes

Why does the magnitude of CEO pay relative to others, especially the general workforce, generate intense emotion? Part of the issue is reference point-based. In this regard, consider the following question.

CONCEPT PREVIEW
Question 9.2

Consider that you might live in one of two hypothetical worlds:

In world A, you earn $110,000 per year, while others earn $200,000.

In world B, you earn $100,000 per year, while others earn $85,000.

If you could choose between living in either of these two worlds, which would you choose?

Concept Preview Question 9.2 focuses attention on income, not just in absolute terms, but relative to others. A majority of people care about relative income. Typically, more than 55 percent of people answering this question choose world B, despite the 10 percent reduction in standard of living.[17]

People are competitive creatures, who care where they place in social pecking orders. Survey evidence documenting levels of happiness find that for the most part, it is relative income that determines happiness, not absolute income. Of course, for people living in poverty, absolute income is indeed important. However, once some income threshold is reached, it is relative income that dominates as a driver of happiness.[18] Indeed, neuroscientific research finds evidence of biochemical processes in the nervous system and testosterone levels that relate to relative positioning; and there is also evidence indicating that relative positioning and health are positively related.

The academic literature contains longstanding survey evidence about the importance of relative salaries within firms. This evidence suggests that how a firm's employees view their own salaries depends to a great extent on what they think other people in the firm are earning. Most importantly, perceptions of relative position have large effects on morale, having to do with feelings about status and respect.[19]

The comments of the compensation consultants discussed earlier include comments about relative income and morale. These comments point out that the paying of large bonuses to top executives not only reduces morale in organizations, but also reduces employees' willingness to share with management information about problems and possible solutions.

9.4 INCENTIVES, ACCOUNTING, AUDITING, AND PSYCHOLOGY

Section 5.3 in Chapter 5 discusses evidence that CFOs believe that investors care more about earnings per share than cash flows. In the context of the BPV framework, this belief would motivate CFOs to manage earnings as part of a catering strategy.

Earnings Management

The evidence suggests that firms take psychological factors into account when managing earnings. To do so, they appear to use heuristics involving a prioritized list of threshold reference points, namely positive earnings, past reported earnings, and analysts' expectations. In this regard, wherever possible, managers will use discretionary items to meet or exceed the highest possible threshold. As a result, the distribution of announced earnings per share (EPS) tends to cluster around reference points from above, especially at zero, but not from below.[20] Such behavior is consistent with the idea of catering when investors exhibit loss aversion in connection with these reference points.

As with dividends, an issue discussed in Chapter 8, EPS also appears to cluster around salient round numbers, such as multiples of five or ten cents—at least for positive earnings. For negative earnings, these patterns do not hold, perhaps because managers seek to distract investors' attention from poor results.[21]

The evidence indicates that firms in which the composition of CEOs' compensation feature a high proportion of stock and options, and therefore are sensitive to stock prices, are more likely than others to manage earnings.[22] Moreover, firms with high accruals tend to earn low subsequent returns, suggesting that the executives of such firms are successful at temporarily increasing their firms' stock prices.[23] Chapters 5 and 7 contain discussions about new equity issues. There is evidence that the underperformance of these issues is greatest for firms that are most aggressive in managing pre-issue earnings.[24]

Auditing

Both loss aversion and aversion to a sure loss are central features of prospect theory. According to prospect theory, people behave as if they seek risk when facing the prospect of what they perceive to be a sure loss. Aversion to a sure loss can wreak havoc with the traditional incentives normally relied upon to resolve agency conflicts. To see how this can happen, consider the issues associated with the auditing services upon which corporate boards and investors depend.

Managers, as agents, release financial statements in order to report the financial results of their firms to the owners, or principals. How do the principals monitor managers to verify that these results are accurate? The conventional way is for managers to hire the services of a professional external auditor to perform an audit and then provide an opinion about whether the financial statements are in conformity with generally accepted accounting principles.

In theory, auditing firms serve the interests of investors. Auditors examine the financial statements of firms and decide whether or not they can offer clean opinions on the integrity of those statements. However, auditors receive their fees from the firms they audit, not investors. As a result, auditors face a potential conflict of interest in serving the needs of investors. They are vulnerable to being "bribed" by unscrupulous firms in order to issue clean opinions.

Notably, auditing firms are partnerships, not corporations. Hence, auditing partners are personally liable for the actions of their firms, a feature that allows for a

Behavioral Pitfalls: Arthur Andersen

During the twentieth century, Arthur Andersen was one of the largest and most respected accounting firms in the world. However, a series of events took place in the 1980s and 1990s that led to the firm's demise in 2002.

For years, accounting firms performed consulting services as well as auditing services. By developing expertise in the effect of technology on business strategy, the consulting group at Arthur Andersen, known as Andersen Consulting, became especially profitable during the 1980s. Notably, the consulting division had become much more profitable than the auditing division, a fact that created considerable resentment on the part of the consultants. The resentment stemmed from the fact that Andersen pooled the profits from its two divisions before sharing them, thereby leading the consultants to subsidize the auditors. Indeed, in 1989, the consultants managed to alter the profit-sharing rule, in their favor.

The change in sharing rule left the auditors facing a different economic environment. Because of competition, growth in the demand for auditing services was slowing. Audit fees were declining. The salaries accountants earned were lagging behind those of attorneys, investment bankers, and especially consultants.

The auditing division at Andersen responded to the changing circumstances in a number of ways. They began a separate consulting group of their own, Arthur Andersen Consulting, to compete directly with sister division Andersen Consulting. In this respect, the firm began to urge accounting partners to sell consulting and other services, in addition to traditional auditing.

The auditing division's colleagues at Andersen Consulting were not amused. In 1997, the partners at Andersen Consulting voted to split off completely from Arthur Andersen to become Accenture. In the wake of their departure Arthur Andersen instituted a policy known as "2X." Under 2X, for every dollar of auditing work, partners were required to bring in twice the revenue in nonauditing work.

Most firms hire accountants as employees to perform internal audits that complement the activities conducted by external auditors. One of Andersen's initiatives was to encourage clients to engage Andersen for both internal and external auditing services. Among the list of Arthur Andersen's audit clients were Boston Market, Sunbeam, Waste Management Inc., WorldCom, and Enron. At each of these firms, a major scandal ensued.

After Enron's difficulties became public, Andersen employees tampered with documents. On June 14, 2002, the firm was found guilty of obstructing justice and was subsequently dissolved. In June 2005, the conviction was overturned, but the company did not rise from the ashes.

Source: K. Brown and I. J. Dugan, "Sad Account: Andersen's Fall from Grace—Pushed to Boost Revenue, Auditors Acted as Sellers and Warred with Consultants," *The Wall Street Journal*, June 7, 2002.

large stick to be wielded in the carrot-and-stick framework. The traditional view holds that auditing firms have reputations for integrity to protect. According to the conventional wisdom, this reputation is sufficiently valuable so as to deter dishonest behavior on the part of auditors. In other words, the conventional wisdom holds that it is in the auditors' best interests to issue honest assessments rather than issue clean opinions in cases that do not merit them.

Another aspect of the firm's choice of auditor involves signaling. A firm that seeks to communicate that its financial statements are indeed clean might engage the services of an auditor with a high reputation who also charges high fees. The theory stipulates that firms who face accounting problems would not have an incentive to use such an auditor, and therefore the choice of auditor in and of itself sends a strong signal to investors. Now read the nearby Behavioral Pitfalls box about Arthur Andersen in respect to signaling, paying special attention to the policy known as 2X.

Think about policy 2X in the context of prospect theory. Did 2X amount to a shift in reference point? Given the departure of the consulting division, did 2X shift Andersen's auditors from perceiving themselves to be in the domain of gains to perceiving themselves to be in the domain of losses? Does attitude toward risk depend upon whether a person perceives him- or herself to be in the domain of losses as opposed to the domain of gains?

These are important questions. If the answer to all of them is yes, then prospect theory suggests that policy 2X placed Andersen's auditors into the domain of losses. As a result, aversion to a sure loss induced them to take actions that were bad bets on average but offered the possibility of large payoffs.

Conflicts of Interest

At the time Arthur Andersen decided to take on the roles of both internal and external auditor, Arthur Levitt chaired the Securities and Exchange Commission (SEC). He raised concerns that practices of this sort would jeopardize the quality of audits, because it introduced a potential conflict of interest. In retrospect, that concern was justified. In respect to Enron, Andersen hired the firm's entire team of 40 internal auditors and subsequently engaged in a series of aggressive reporting practices that created friction between the Andersen group responsible for Enron and Andersen's own Professional Standards Group. Ironically on October 15, 2001, the evening before Enron was due to announce its third-quarter earnings, Andersen accountants indicated that they could not approve the financial statements that Enron wished to release. Several weeks later, Enron declared bankruptcy.

9.5 SARBANES-OXLEY AND COSO

Fraud is an extreme example of agency conflict, where behavior crosses from being unethical to being illegal. Since 2000, a succession of corporate scandals with varying degrees of fraud made clear that compensation in the form of stock and stock options could not be counted upon to align the interests of investors and managers. Among the firms involved in fraudulent activities were Coca-Cola, IBM, Sunbeam, Cendant, Xerox, Lernout & Hauspie, Parmalat, Enron, WorldCom, and HealthSouth.

Sarbanes-Oxley (SOX)

In the wake of these financial scandals, Congress passed the Sarbanes-Oxley Act of 2002, directing the SEC to require that the chief executive officer and chief financial officer of every publicly traded firm certify, under oath, the veracity of their firm's financial statements. The first test of the rule came on August 14, 2002, when many firms were scheduled to file their quarterly financial statements with the SEC. An unusual number of firms chose to restate earlier results in connection with their filings.[25] Nevertheless, according to *The Wall Street Journal,* in the first year after its enactment, several firms were in violation. The list included HealthSouth, Qwest Communications, Gemstar-TV Guide, and Footstar Inc. However, the SEC sanctioned only one firm, HealthSouth, for violating Sarbanes-Oxley.[26]

COSO

Many firms use what is known as a COSO framework for structuring their internal controls. COSO is a voluntary private sector initiative whose focus is effective internal control, enterprise risk management (ERM), and fraud deterrence. COSO stands for the Committee of Sponsoring Organizations of the Treadway Commission.

In the COSO framework, internal control is defined as "a process, effected by an entity's board of directors, management and other personnel, designed to provide reasonable assurance of the achievement of objectives" in the following categories:

- Alignment of strategic goals with mission of organization
- Effectiveness and efficiency of operations
- Reliability of financial reporting
- Compliance with applicable laws and regulations

COSO specified five components as being necessary for an internal control system to be effective. The five components are intended to support the firm's attempt to achieve its mission, execute its strategies, and accomplish related business objectives. Comprising the five components are:

1. Control environment, which includes integrity and ethical values, and commitment to competence.
2. Risk assessment, which includes assessing objectives, managing risk, and identifying change.
3. Control activities, which includes policies and procedures, and security.
4. Information and communication, which includes the quality of information and the effectiveness of communication.
5. Monitoring, which includes separate evaluation and reporting of deficiencies.

9.6 FRAUD AND STOCK OPTIONS: ILLUSTRATIVE EXAMPLE

In theory, granting stock to executives serves to align their interests with those of shareholders. In theory, executive stock options serve to counteract executives' reluctance to accept risky projects that would benefit shareholders. An implicit assumption in traditional theory is that market prices are efficient. In practice, prices might be inefficient, and the use of stocks and stock options can provide managers with perverse incentives to engage in catering by fraudulent means.

Excessive optimism and overconfidence already counteract managers' undue caution. Indeed, the granting of stock options might serve to induce managers to accept risky projects that feature negative net present value. Moreover, excessively optimistic, overconfident managers who are unethical will be prone to underestimate the chances that fraudulent behavior on their parts will be discovered. Indeed, stock and stock option compensation can actually amplify agency conflicts when managers find they can manipulate the market value of their firms. The general evidence indicates that firms that were found to have engaged in fraud are more

Behavioral Pitfalls: HealthSouth

HealthSouth was founded in 1984. At year-end 2001, HealthSouth was the largest U.S. provider of outpatient surgery, diagnostic imaging, and rehabilitation services. A Fortune 500 firm, its stock belonged to the S&P 500 Index. Based in Birmingham, Alabama, HealthSouth had almost 1,700 facilities and 51,000 employees in all 50 states as well as abroad.

In 2002 HealthSouth was investigated for an accounting fraud that prosecutors suspect began as early as 1986. According to the complaint filed by the SEC, between 1999 and the second quarter of 2002, HealthSouth overstated its income by $1.4 billion. It did so by making false journal entries that overestimated the amount of third-party insurance reimbursement and underestimated expenses.

The SEC accused HealthSouth executives of having engaged in insider trading by selling substantial amounts of HealthSouth stock while they knew that the firm's financial statements grossly misstated its earnings and assets. As part of their compensation, HealthSouth's executives received options on 3.6 million shares of HealthSouth stock. Five former HealthSouth chief financial officers pled guilty to the SEC charges.

The SEC charges included securities fraud and insider trading. HealthSouth's founder and CEO was Richard Scrushy. Specifically, the SEC alleged that Scrushy induced HealthSouth executives to manipulate the firm's stock price until he could sell off large blocks of stock worth $25 million. The SEC claimed that since 1991 Scrushy sold "at least 13.8 million shares for proceeds in excess of $170 million," based on knowledge of HealthSouth's "actual financial results and the impact that disclosure of those results would have."

CEO Scrushy also enjoyed numerous perquisites such as a fleet of 12 corporate jets facetiously referred to as "Air Birmingham," and a helicopter that was used to transport Scrushy from HealthSouth headquarters to the nearby Birmingham airport, to take Scrushy and his family to his luxury family compound, or to take Scrushy's wife shopping in Atlanta.

HealthSouth's auditor, Ernst & Young LLP, was a top tier accounting firm. HealthSouth appears to have engaged in numerous practices that were intended to deceive its auditors.

In 2001 HealthSouth paid Ernst & Young $1.16 million in auditing fees. It also paid an additional $2.39 million in "audit-related fees" for what HealthSouth called "pristine audits," where Ernst & Young junior-level accountants visited HealthSouth facilities in order to check whether magazines in waiting rooms were orderly, toilets and ceilings were free of stains, and trash receptacles had liners.

Sources: J. Weil, "What Ernst Did for HealthSouth—Proxy Document Says Company Performed Janitorial Inspections Misclassified as Audit-Related," *The Wall Street Journal*, June 11, 2003; L. Vaughan-Adams,"HealthSouth Paid Ernst & Young More to Check Its Toilets Than to Audit Its Accounts," *The Independent—London*, June 12, 2003; K. Frieswick, "How Audits Must Change: Auditors Face More Pressure to Find Fraud," *CFO Magazine*, July 1, 2003; J. Piotrowski, "Noose Tightens: Link to Scrushy Alleged in Criminal Case," *Modern Healthcare*, April 28, 2003.

prone to use stock option-based compensation than firms that were not found to have engaged in fraud. The propensity to commit fraud appears to be related to corporate governance. The propensity is higher in firms featuring high institutional holdings and large blockholders, where CEOs are more likely to be dismissed for poor performance. The propensity is reduced if the board features a high proportion of independent outside directors.[27]

Consider the example about HealthSouth presented in the above Behavioral Pitfalls box. Far from aligning the interests of managers and investors, stock options provided HealthSouth's executives with a motive to exploit shareholders. They did so by using fraudulent financial statements, despite having engaged a top-tier auditing firm, Ernst & Young LLP.[28]

The fraud committed by executives with large holdings of HealthSouth stock enabled them to sell their shares at grossly inflated prices. Exhibit 9-2a displays how HealthSouth's stock performed between 1986 and 2002, relative to the S&P 500.

EXHIBIT 9-2 **(a) HealthSouth versus S&P 500, Cumulative Returns, Sept. 1986–Dec. 2002; (b) HealthSouth Return on Equity, 1986–2001**

Sources: Center for Research in Security Prices, Compustat.

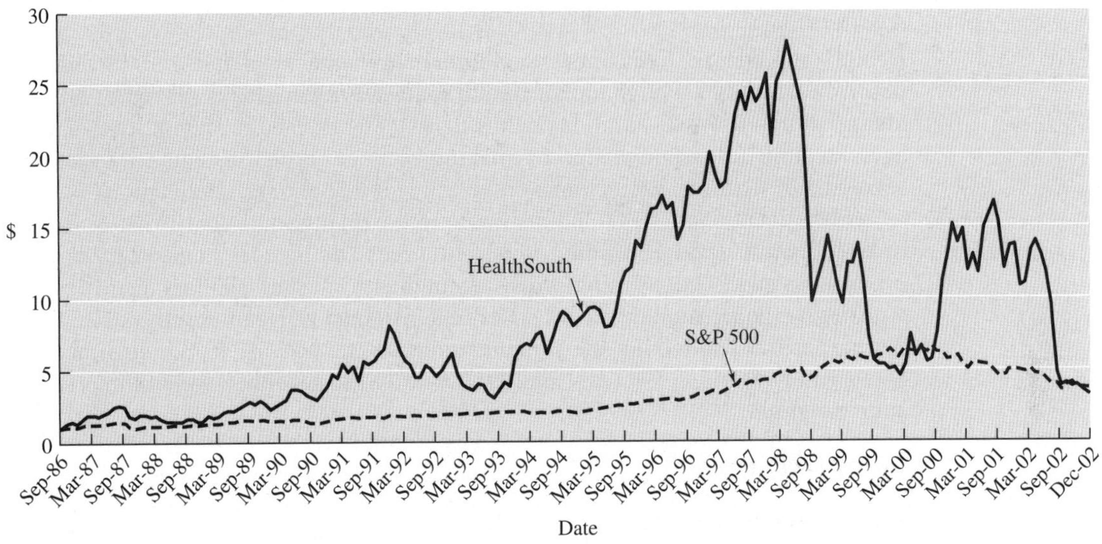

(a)

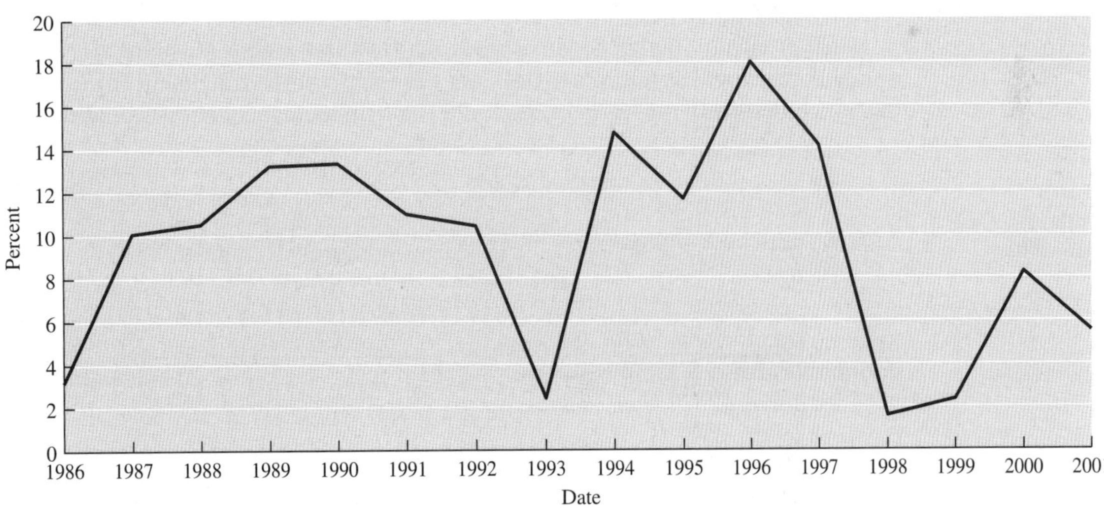

(b)

Exhibit 9-2b displays the time path of HealthSouth's return on equity for this period, derived from its accounting statements. A comparison of the two graphs suggests that the firm's stock price was largely driven by its financials.

Auditors

HealthSouth appears to have engaged in numerous practices that were intended to deceive its auditors. For example, HealthSouth was aware that Ernst & Young did not question fixed asset additions below a particular threshold. HealthSouth's managers exploited this knowledge by making random entries in their balance-sheet accounts for fictitious assets that were worth less than the threshold amount.

As was mentioned, the relationship between HealthSouth and Ernst & Young involved two fees, $1.16 million in auditing fees and an additional $2.39 million for "pristine audit" consulting where accountants checked sanitary facilities. Interestingly, the accountants were specifically trained at HealthSouth facilities for the purpose of conducting the pristine-audit program. Ernst & Young's motto is Quality in Everything We Do. Notably, Richard Scrushy conceived of the pristine-audit program.

Signs of Disease?

Were there any signs that HealthSouth was not especially healthy? There were certainly some major dips in Exhibit 9-2. However, the stock outperformed the S&P 500 on a cumulative basis for most of the period. Until recently, it had not been fashionable for analysts and managers to look at free cash flows. Exhibit 9-3 displays HealthSouth's free cash flows during the period. It portrays a less healthy picture than Exhibit 9-2.

Much of HealthSouth's negative free cash flow in Exhibit 9-3 stems from continued borrowing. High leverage does not necessarily force fraudulent firms to fail in short order. Only on April 1, 2003, did the firm announce that it would default

EXHIBIT 9-3
HealthSouth Free Cash Flows, 1986–2001

Source: Compustat.

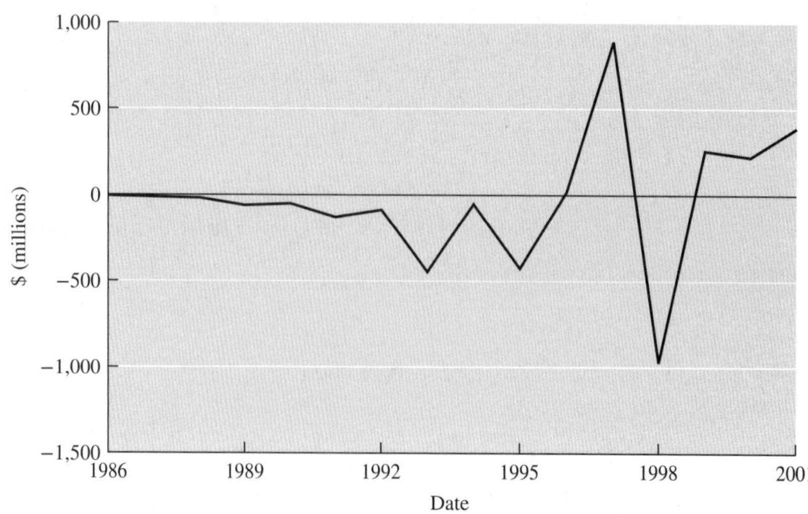

on a $350 million bond payment and was dismissing its CEO Richard Scrushy. In December 1998, HealthSouth's market value of equity was about $12 billion. Its long-term debt was about $3 billion, and it paid $143 million in net interest. By the end of 2001, its net interest paid rose to about $215 million. The firm had increased its debt sharply in 1993 and continued to maintain a debt-to-asset ratio in the range of 40 to 60 percent for the latter half of the 1990s. Apparently there was enough cash flow to enable HealthSouth to perpetuate its fraud for many years without failing.

In a conversation that was secretly taped on March 18, 2003, by one of HealthSouth's chief financial officers, Scrushy comments on the role of bank debt in respect to the firm's fraudulent financial statements. The CFO had indicated a concern about going to prison for "signing these phony financial statements." In his reply to the CFO, Scrushy stated[29]:

> When they get you is when you go into bankruptcy. That's when they come in on you. They don't come in on a company that's paying their bank debt down. They don't come in on a company that's doing good. They come in on a company that's screwed up. And we're, we're seeing a healthy day right now in stock. We're seeing that. I just hate to go down there and just give the keys to them.

In his trial, Scrushy maintained his innocence and insisted that the executives who over time served as HealthSouth's chief financial officers had perpetrated the fraud of their own volition, and not at his direction as they had alleged.

At the outset of his trial, Scrushy began to preach regularly at fundamentalist churches in and around Birmingham, and appeared daily on a morning television religious program. Before his trial began, he also joined an African-American church, but was careful not to preach in churches attended by the six African-Americans who sat on his jury. Nevertheless, the prosecution suggested that Scrushy's preaching activities were an attempt to influence jurors indirectly, a suggestion that Scrushy's defense team denied. In June 2005, the jury acquitted Scrushy on all charges.

Nevertheless, in 2006 Scrushy was arrested, tried, and convicted on a separate set of counts that involved money laundering, extortion, obstruction of justice, racketeering, and bribery in connection with the office of Alabama's governor. For this, he was imprisoned and released in 2012. During his incarceration, a second trial involving the HealthSouth fraud took place. This was a civil case brought by shareholders, which led to Scrushy being found guilty and fined $2.87 billion. After being released from prison, Scrushy became a public speaker, claiming to have been the victim of his executives, the media, and the government.[30]

9.7 ETHICS AND CHEATING

Deliberately engaging in accounting fraud is both illegal and unethical, and ethical issues lie at the heart of many principal–agent conflicts, as the HealthSouth case makes clear. There are important psychological issues associated with the degree to which people behave ethically. One of the best ways to begin thinking about the issue is through student cheating.

CONCEPT PREVIEW
Question 9.3

a. During the past year, have you cheated on an assignment, test, or exam?

b. Indicate the extent to which you agree or disagree with the following statement: "When it comes to doing what is right, I am better than most people I know."

Strongly agree____ Agree____ Disagree____ Strongly disagree____

Incidents of student cheating have increased over time. The Josephson Institute of Ethics has been polling students since 1992. In their 2002 study, they reported that of the 12,000 students that they polled, 74 percent admitted to cheating on an exam at least once in the past year.[31] This rate was the highest ever achieved in the survey's 10-year history. Although the rate dropped to 62 percent in the 2004 survey conducted two years later, the general pattern has continued over time. Similar findings for college students are reported by the Center for Academic Integrity, based at Duke University.

How endemic is dishonesty? Students even cheat in courses about ethics. In 2015, Dartmouth University charged 64 students with cheating in a sports ethics course. In another incident that occurred at Carleton University in Ottawa, Canada, students cheated by passing off as their own an essay they had downloaded from the Internet. In commenting on the issue, an associate dean at Carleton indicated that in addition to being disappointed, he was surprised that the students believed they would not be caught.[32]

Being surprised is the hallmark of overconfidence, and in this case the associate dean was overconfident. The 2002 Josephson Institute survey found that 95 percent of those surveyed thought they could get away with dishonest behavior. Moreover, cheating seemed to be worse at religious schools than at nonreligious schools, and the incidence of cheating was higher among varsity athletes.

The Josephson Institute survey does not confine itself to cheating. The 2002 study found that during the year just under 4 of every 10 adolescents acknowledged stealing from a store, and 93 percent confessed that they had lied to their parents or relatives. In the 2004 study, these figures declined to 3 out of every 10, and 82 percent respectively, but the general pattern has persisted over time. For example, the 2008 report showed that during that year 64 percent cheated on an exam, 42 percent lied to save money, and 30 percent stole something from a store.

Students are the executives of the future. How will they behave when they become executives? In this respect there is cause for concern. Many of the 25,000 students responding to the 2004 Josephson survey were highly cynical about the ethics of successful people. Two-thirds of young males and half of young women believe that "in the real world, successful people do what they have to do to win, even if others consider it cheating." Half the young men and one-third of the young women agree with the following statement: "A person has to lie or cheat sometimes in order to succeed."

Why Students Cheat

Why do students cheat? The Josephson study indicated that the drive toward academic excellence has become a negative excuse for cheating. For example, honors students might justify ethical lapses as a necessity for keeping up with rigorous studies. In other words, a student cheats in order to achieve a particular grade goal, not necessarily in order to avoid a failing grade. This is a reference point issue and relates to prospect theory. If the probability of missing a goal and ending up in the domain of losses is high, aversion to a sure loss can be particularly strong.

Although some people are simply unethical at their core, most people like to view themselves as good and decent. At the same time, self-deception is strong. In the 2002 Josephson Institute report, 76 percent of those surveyed agreed with the following statement: "When it comes to doing what is right, I am better than most people I know." In other words, the overconfidence, better-than-average effect applies in the ethical dimension, even among those who engage in cheating. For varsity athletes and student leaders and honors students, over 80 percent perceived themselves to be better than their peers.

Most people want to be able to look at themselves in the mirror and feel proud of their accomplishments rather than shame. Yet, somehow they wind up sliding down the slippery slope leading to unethical behavior. A major reason is aversion to a sure loss, coupled with self-delusion.

Ethics and Psychology: Why People Cheat

Accounting fraud and the subsequent bankruptcy of Enron in 2001 constituted the first among a series of major corporate financial scandals in the United States that unfolded at the beginning of the twenty-first century. Enron's CFO Andrew Fastow pled guilty to a long list of charges for having instituted a series of practices at Enron that enriched him at the expense of Enron's shareholders.

Was Andrew Fastow a villain through and through? Notably, Fastow was regarded as a model citizen in his Houston community, known for being a major benefactor to Houston's art museums, fund-raising for its local Holocaust Museum, and being a cofounder of a synagogue. People recognized Fastow for personal acts of kindness, such as delivering flowers to the house of a banker after his son's baptism. One of Fastow's closest friends, Robert Lapin, was quoted as saying: "The Andy Fastow I know is one of the most thoughtful and generous people in Houston."[33] When one of Lapin's three children was diagnosed with a rare disease, Lapin says that Fastow was one of the first to call and offer to help.

A *Businessweek* article about Fastow indicates that old high school friends recall Fastow as "popular and well-liked, though extremely ambitious." And that ambition may serve as the key link between behavioral factors and unethical behavior. Being ambitious typically means setting high reference points when it comes to goals. When someone sets their reference point very high, the result is that many reasonable outcomes get internally coded in the domain of losses. And what do we know about behavior in the domain of losses? In the domain of losses people act as if they are risk-seeking, being willing to accept bad bets, meaning bets that pay off poorly on average.

Does Andrew Fastow have a dual personality? Or was he operating in the domain of gains in his personal life, but in the domain of losses in his professional life? Behavioral studies find that attitude toward risk is contextual. Whether people act as if they are risk averse or risk seeking depends on the particular problem at hand and how they frame the problem.

In July 2002, the telecommunications firm WorldCom (now MCI) became the largest corporate firm to go bankrupt in U.S. history. In yet one more case of control fraud, WorldCom's CFO had misclassified more than $3.8 billion of expenses as capital expenditures, in order to report positive earnings instead of losses. WorldCom's chief executive officer, Bernard Ebbers, was tried and convicted of having oversight for WorldCom's fraud. Like Fastow, Ebbers was active in his religious community, serving as a deacon in his church. However, he was also ambitious.

The Josephson Institute data makes clear that most people are predisposed to cheat. Indeed, it is actually easy to structure environments in which most people cheat. The evidence shows that when people are provided with an environment featuring the illusion of anonymity, thereby inducing them to think that they are less likely to be caught cheating, they cheat more. Amazingly, people do not even need to be told that their identities are hidden: Just making the room a bit darker, or, amazingly, providing people with sunglasses, tends to induce more cheating.[34]

Psychological research indicates that people crave respect from their social groups, or, if you like, their in-groups.[35] Therefore, when some in-group members engage in observable cheating, the incidence of cheating by other in-group members increases.[36] Cheating and power are connected, especially when finance is involved: increased power is associated with increased cheating.[37] Cheating tends to be more frequent in situations in which wealth is amply abundant.[38]

People give in to temptation when their impulses to cheat are stronger than their moral compasses. For most, resisting the temptation takes self-control, and self-control takes effort. Neurologically, exercising self-control is a mental task in which our brains need to be fed sufficient glucose to fuel the job. However, when tired, people cheat more because they lack the fuel to fight their instincts. Only those very high in moral identity appear able to resist the temptation to cheat, even when feeling tired.[39]

The academic literature suggests that there are interventions that can nudge people to cheat less frequently. Simply brightening a room can have a positive effect. So can asking people to recall past instances of immoral behavior on their part. So too can asking people to reflect on how being caught would embarrass their loved ones, lead them to lose social standing, and damage their careers.

One of the most powerful interventions is by addressing people's self-image. Most people who cheat do not think of themselves as "cheaters," and instead deal with cognitive dissonance by limiting the degree to which they cheat.[40] Cognitive dissonance and self-deception can be very powerful forces. In this regard, think about Enron's Andrew Fastow and WorldCom's Bernie Ebbers, two cases discussed above.

Self-deception is a kind of "blind spot." Academics working in the area of behavioral ethics identify particular "blind spots" that people have.[41] Typical blind spots are to think that ethical issues only apply to others, to experience ethical fading when during deliberations ethical considerations come to be downplayed, dangerous rewards such as those described earlier in the chapter, and motivated blindness where people find it in their self-interest to ignore unethical behavior by others. The blind spot framework is useful for analyzing the mixed behavior of Andrew Fastow. It can also provide insight into the curious fact that books on ethics tend to be stolen from libraries more than books on other topics, especially by faculty and graduate students in philosophy departments.

In 2009, the Josephson Institute released the results of a formal large-scale study that specifically examined life-cycle issues associated with ethical beliefs and ethical behavior. The study concluded that new generations are more likely to lie and cheat than preceding ones. In this regard, young people tend to be considerably more cynical than their elders, believing it necessary to lie or cheat in order to succeed. Notably, those who believe dishonesty is necessary are more likely to actually lie and cheat. Most importantly, the study concludes that relative to noncheaters, cheaters in high school are far more likely as adults to lie to their spouses, customers, and employers, and to cheat on expense reports and insurance claims. There is no evidence from the study that issues related to religion play any role in the findings.[42]

Corporate Nudges

Errors or biases: Managers behave unethically.
Why does it happen? High ambition coupled with aversion to a sure loss.
How does it happen? Ambitious managers set high goals for themselves, thereby predisposing themselves to aspiration-based risk taking. Failing to meet an aspiration is typically painful, and managers lack the willpower to exercise self-control.
What can be done about it? Establish aspiration points with a contingency plan for how to face ethical dilemmas if forced to deal with the strong possibility of experiencing failure. Make decisions in a bright room. When facing difficult circumstances, ask people to recall past instances in which they exhibited immoral behavior. Ask people to reflect on how being caught would embarrass their loved ones, lead them to lose social standing, and damage their careers. In this regard, remember that most people do not beat the odds. The executives at Enron, WorldCom, Arthur Andersen, and HealthSouth did not meet their ambitious goals, but instead lost their honor, their good names, and the respect of their communities. Many served prison terms. Most importantly, ask people to write down on paper whether they view themselves as cheaters.

Summary

Incentive-based compensation lies at the heart of good corporate governance. A corporation's board of directors needs to ensure that executive compensation is enough to attract and retain talented managers, that compensation packages serve to align the interests of managers with shareholders, and that managers are not overpaid.

The empirical evidence indicates that in practice, executive compensation displays too little variability in respect to pay for performance, insufficient dismissal, and excessive payment for executives. Directors' own comments reveal that the members of corporate boards have been overconfident in their ability to structure incentives appropriately without overpaying executives. Directors also suggest that their tasks are made that much more difficult by overconfidence on the part of executives.

In traditional theory, employee stock options are used to align the risk attitudes of managers and shareholders. In the traditional approach, the inability of managers to diversify their portfolios as well as shareholders leads managers to be more risk averse than shareholders. However, managers who behave in accordance with prospect theory might find the risk characteristics of stock options attractive because of its casino effect. In this respect, stock options might also induce risk-seeking behavior because of the tendency to overweight low probabilities. Moreover, firms appear to pay their employees in options when the latter are inclined to overvalue those options.

The combination of aspiration-based risk taking and overconfidence can also induce ambitious, unethical managers to manipulate accounting information in order to exercise their stock options when the stock is overpriced. In this respect, a combination of behavioral phenomena and agency conflicts affected some accounting firms. Those events were the catalyst for the passage of the Sarbanes-Oxley Act.

Likewise, the global financial crisis was the catalyst for the passage of the Dodd-Frank Act, with its provision for "say on pay." The combination of regulatory changes and real-world events appear to have dampened the growth of performance-based compensation measures, and shifted emphasis from stock options to restricted stock.

Additional Behavioral Readings

Bebchuk, L., M. Cremers, and U. Peyer, "The CEO Pay Slice," *Journal of Financial Economics*, vol. 102, no. 1, 2011, pp. 199–221.

Fahlenbrach, R. and R. Stulz, "Bank CEO Incentives and the Credit Crisis," *Journal of Financial Economics*, vol. 99, 2011, pp. 11–26.

Gompers, P., J. Ishii and A. Metrick, "Corporate Governance and Equity Prices," *Quarterly Journal of Economics*, vol. 118, no. 1, February 2003, pp. 107–155.

Graham, J. R., C. Harvey, and M. Puri, "Managerial Attitudes and Corporate Actions," *Journal of Financial Economics* vol. 109, 2013, pp. 103–121.

Jensen, M. and K. Murphy, "CEO Incentives—It's Not How Much You Pay, But How," *Harvard Business Review*, no. 3, May–June 1990, pp. 138–153.

Jensen, M. and K. Murphy, "Performance Pay and Top Management Incentives." *Journal of Political Economy*, vol. 98, 1990, pp. 225–264.

Key Terms

casino effect, *204*
incentive compatibility constraint, *201*
nonoverpayment constraint, *201*
participation constraint, *201*
self-attribution bias, *204*

Explore the Web

www.healthsouth.com
The web site for the firm HealthSouth, updating its experiences from events in 2003.

www.ey.com
The web site for Ernst & Young.

www.brookings.edu/~/media/research/files/papers/2013/3/18-executive-compensation-polsky-lund/download-the-full-paper.pdf
Andrew Lund and Gregg Polsky discuss their paper "Can Executive Compensation Reform Cure Short-Termism?"

Chapter Questions

1. In July 2003 Samuel Waksal, the founder of ImClone Systems Inc., began a seven-year prison term. In December 2001 Waksal received word that the Federal Drug Administation (FDA) was about to issue a negative report on ImClone's cancer drug Erbitux. Although this knowledge was material information, and Waksal was an insider, he sold some of his ImClone shares and disclosed the information to his daughter, advising her to sell her ImClone shares. Martha Stewart, celebrity and chief executive of Martha Stewart Living Omnimedia, had once been a stockbroker and served on the board of directors of the New York Stock Exchange. She was also a friend of Samuel Waksal. A day before the FDA made its negative announcement about Erbitux, Martha Stewart sold 3,928 shares of ImClone stock at a price of about $60. In an interview with *The New Yorker* author Jeffrey Toobin, she indicated that the sale constituted about 0.03 percent of her assets.[43] On June 4, 2002, Martha Stewart was indicted and charged with nine counts of fraud, perjury, and obstruction of justice. In her defense she claimed that she had an informal stock loss order arrangement with her broker, at a price of $60. In March 2004 a jury found her guilty on all counts, and she served a prison term as a result. By design, the products and services sold by Martha Stewart Living Omnimedia are strongly identified with Martha Stewart the person. In this respect the personal actions of Martha Stewart affected the financial performance of Martha Stewart Living Omnimedia. On August 11, 2003, Martha Stewart Living Omnimedia announced that its quarterly earnings per share had fallen to 2 cents, from 14 cents the year before. An article that appeared in the June 16, 2003, issue of the *Chicago Sun-Times* asked the following question: "Why did this woman who already possesses enormous wealth and the devotion of countless numbers of fans put it all at risk to avoid taking a piddling loss on a single stock?" Martha Stewart was not actually charged with insider trading but with having lied to prosecutors about it when interviewed by them. Therefore, instead of being culpable for a civil offense (her trade) and a fine, she left herself open to being found guilty of a criminal offense, which brought with it the risk of prison time. Discuss any behavioral phenomena that might have played a role in the behavior of Samuel Waksal and Martha Stewart.
2. On May 20, 2004, *The Wall Street Journal* ran a front page story entitled "Biotech's Dismal Bottom Line: More Than $40 Billion in Losses." The article makes several points. First, the majority of biotechnology firms have produced losses, with the result that the return to investments in the biotechnology sector between 1981 and 2004 lies below the return from holding Treasury bills. At the same time, a few biotechnology firms, such as Amgen and Genentech have been spectacularly successful. The article quotes one investor

www.mhhe.com/shefrin2e

who likens biotechnology stocks to a lottery. Despite its track record, in 2003 U.S. biotechnology firms succeeded in issuing almost $4 billion in new equity. The article mentions that venture capitalists also provided funding to biotechnology start-ups hoping to earn a profit when these firms go public. Discuss whether there are any behavioral phenomena involved in the issues raised in the article.

3. Discuss any agency conflicts associated with HealthSouth's pristine-audit program.
4. Eleanor Bloxham is the founder and CEO of the Value Alliance Company and the Corporate Governance Alliance, and is a respected authority on matters involving corporate governance and valuation. In 2012, during an interview, she stated that she would rank executive compensation at or near the top in the hierarchy of corporate governance issues. As justification, she stated that compensation policy drives the way that executives think about all the capital allocation decisions they make. She also pointed out that Tim Cook, the CEO of Apple, held stock options worth nearly $400 million. She suggested that this might be problematic for boards that use Apple as a peer when setting pay levels for their own executives. Assess her perspective on these issues.
5. When the Internet firm eToys went public in May 1999, its CEO Toby Lenk's stockholdings were worth $850 million on the first day the company's stock traded on the New York Stock Exchange. Lenk is quoted as having said to his CFO that day that they would live to regret the run-up, but still decided to build capacity to support $500 million in sales. In the context of catering and the BPV framework, discuss what Lenk might have meant when he invoked the possibility of experiencing regret at some future time.
6. Michael Jensen developed some of the seminal ideas underlying agency theory. He suggests that at the time the market value of Enron peaked at approximately $70 billion, its intrinsic value was approximately $30 billion. He describes Enron as having been "a good, viable business" and "a major innovator." In this respect, he asserts that its senior managers' attempt to defend the stock's $40 billion of overvaluation was a mistake that effectively destroyed $30 billion of intrinsic value. He notes that Enron's executives faced a choice. On the one hand, they could have worked to help the market lower its expectations of the company. On the other hand, they could have tried to use accounting manipulations to fool the market. In this respect, Jensen asserts, Enron's managers gambled with their critical asset, the firm's reputation for integrity. Discuss the psychological issues associated with Enron's decision task, as described by Jensen.[43]
7. In 2016, automobile manufacturer Volkswagen was charged in the United States for having installed software that engaged antipollution technology in diesel cars not at all times as regulations required, but only when undergoing emission tests. The firm apparently installed these so-called "defeat devices" out of an inability to meet U.S. clean-air standards legally. As a result, different Volkswagen diesel cars emitted between 9 and 38 times the legal limits of nitrogen oxide. The decision to do so was made more than a decade earlier, and was first discovered by U.S. regulators in 2014. Volkswagen was slow to acknowledge the problem publicly, and when they did so stated that responsibility was isolated to a small group of engineers. However, in 2016, the lawsuits brought forward by several states charged that higher-level executives early on had been informed about the installation of the devices. The firm eventually admitted to having installed disabling devices on at least 11 million cars globally, with 8.5 million in Europe and a half million in the United States. In a settlement with U.S. authorities, Volkswagen agreed to pay $4.3 billion in U.S. civil and criminal fines. Six of the firm's executives were indicted. In addition, Volkswagen set aside approximately $18 billion to address claims from vehicle owners, environmental regulators, U.S. states and dealers. Use the concepts developed in Chapter 9 to analyze the defeat device issue at Volkswagen.

Additional Resources and Materials for Chapter 9 Are available at www.mhhe.com/shefrin2e

Minicase

Hertz

In 2013, the car rental company Hertz paid its senior executives a base salary, performance-based bonuses, and performance-based equity. For the CEO, fixed salary was 10.5 percent of total compensation, performance-based cash was 20.4 percent, performance-based equity was 60.5 percent, and the rest fell into a category called "Other." Compensation for other senior executives featured a bit more fixed salary, 19.8 percent, with corresponding lower percentages for performance-based components. Of the CEO's total compensation, 81 percent was directly influenced by the firm's financial and operating performance, while for other senior executives the percentage was 70 percent.

During 2013, Hertz's compensation committee conducted an annual review of the risk profile of the Corporation's procedures and Internal Audit Department. The review concluded that:[44]

> for all employees, the Corporation's enterprise-wide compensation policies and practices, in conjunction with the Corporation's existing processes and controls, do not incentivize employees to take unnecessary risks, or pose a material risk to the Corporation, particularly in light of the following factors:
>
> - our use of different types of compensation programs, such as equity- and cash-based plans, that provide a balance of long- and short-term incentives;
> - our claw-back policies, which allow us in certain circumstances in the event of a financial restatement, to seek the recovery of annual incentive awards, long-term incentive performance-based compensation awarded to many of our employees, including all of our senior executives;
> - our use of a variety of financial and strategic performance objectives to help ensure that the Corporation's overall business strategy is properly promoted.

In its 2013 year-end Form 10-K, Hertz reported that during its fourth quarter it discovered "certain out-of-period errors" which totaled $46.3 million. The company indicated that although the errors were not material in any given period, once aggregated, they would be material to the fourth quarter of 2013, when they were discovered. As a result, the company suggested that it might be restating some past financial results. Separately, at this time, Hertz had a new CFO, Thomas Kennedy, who replaced Elyse Douglas: she had resigned on October 1 in order to avoid having to relocate because the company was moving its main headquarters.

In June 2014, Hertz warned that its current quarterly filing would be late and that its financial statements for 2011 could not be relied upon. Hertz's board instructed that the financial statements for 2011 be restated, along with the financial statements for 2012 and 2013, as these might reflect the earlier errors.

In June 2014, the company also disclosed that it identified a material weakness in internal control over financial reporting. As a result, the company indicated that it expected to receive an adverse opinion on its internal control over financial reporting from its auditor PricewaterhouseCoopers (PwC). For years, PwC had issued clean audit opinions on Hertz. Notably in inspection reports, the Public Company Accounting Oversight Board (PCAOB) had faulted PwC for not challenging the internal controls of its clients around allowances for doubtful accounting.

According to Hertz, accounting errors occurred in four specific areas: capitalization and timing of depreciation; allowances for doubtful accounts in its Brazilian operations; allowances for uncollectible amounts associated with damaged vehicles; and restoration obligations connected with facility leases. General reaction at the time suggested that some errors were more of a surprise than others. In particular, doubtful accounts, uncollectible amounts, and future costs associated with restoring leased property tend to involve a fair amount of uncertainty and estimation. On the other hand, depreciation is more straightforward.[45]

PwC did indeed provide an adverse opinion of Hertz's internal controls. By July 2015, Hertz had announced a $78 million loss for 2014, disclosed problems in 15 separate accounting areas, and its restatements indicated that since 2011, the firm had earned $110 million less than had previously been announced going back to 2011. As a result, the firm dismissed its CEO, CFO, general counsel, and chief accounting officer, along with a host of other senior-level executives. Notably, and unusually, Hertz identified its former CEO Mark Frissora as the leading cause for the restatement being necessary.

In its form 10-K, filed July 16, 2015, Hertz stated that Frissora's "management style and temperament created a pressurized operating environment at the company, where challenging targets were set and achieving those targets was a key performance expectation." Hertz's 10-K also stated: "There was in certain instances an inappropriate emphasis on meeting internal budgets, business plans, and current estimates. Our former chief executive officer further encouraged employees to focus on potential business risks and opportunities, and on potential financial or operating performance gaps, as well as ways of ameliorating potential risks or gaps, including through accounting reviews."[46]

A member of Financial Executives International (FEI), who had been a CFO and former treasurer, commented that the situation at Hertz reflected what he called "the classic fraud triangle," featuring "pressure, opportunity, and rationalization."[47]

Frissora resigned in September 2014, citing personal reasons. Hertz paid him a severance package featuring a cash payment of approximately $10.5 million, in addition to other benefits. After leaving Hertz, Frissora became President and CEO of Caesars Entertainment Corp. in Las Vegas.

In its July 2015 10-K filing with the SEC, Hertz described several control problems that resulted in accounting misstatements. These included control deficiencies related to the control environment, risk assessment, information and communication, and[48] monitoring. The COSO chair at the time, Robert Hirth, pointed out that this list represents four of the five components of effective internal control emphasized by the COSO internal control framework.[49]

Case Analysis Questions

1. How would you assess the review conducted by Hertz's compensation committee in 2013?
2. With reference to the Hertz minicase, what psychological phenomenon or phenomena were involved in the fraud triangle?
3. How would you use the COSO internal control framework to assess the internal control environment at Hertz?
4. In what ways was the situation at Hertz, as described in the minicase, similar to that of HealthSouth, and in what ways was it different?

Chapter Ten

Mergers and Acquisitions

The main objective of this chapter is for students to demonstrate that they can identify the manner in which heuristics, biases and framing effects adversely impact the behavior of managers when they make decisions about mergers and acquisitions (M&A).

After completing this chapter students will be able to:

1. Explain why excessive optimism and overconfidence lead the managers of acquiring firms to overpay, thereby experiencing the winner's curse.
2. Use the press coverage measure and longholder measure to identify executives who are prone to engage in acquisitions.
3. Explain why the managers of target firms who are excessively optimistic, overconfident, and trust market prices can destroy value for their shareholders.
4. Identify the manner in which reference point heuristics impact valuation judgments and other decisions by executives and board members in respect to acquisition activity.

10.1 TRADITIONAL APPROACH TO M&A

In the traditional approach to M&A, prices are efficient. Therefore, the market prices of both the acquiring firm and the target firm coincide with their fundamental values, under the assumption that both remain stand-alone firms. However, a merger between the acquiring firm and the target firm holds the potential for synergy. In theory, the shareholders of the acquiring firm will capture this synergy through the acquisition of the target, by paying the current market value plus a warranted premium for the target. Therefore managers of the acquiring firm will only go forward with the acquisition if the value of the synergy is positive. Moreover, since wealth is fungible and all assets are priced correctly, the shareholders of both firms will be indifferent to the combination of cash and equity used to finance the acquisition.

The traditional equation that an acquiring firm would use to evaluate a potential acquisition involves the premium the acquiring firm pays over and above market value, the estimated synergy from the merger, and associated financing side effects. The equation is:

$$APV = -\text{premium} + \text{synergy} + \text{financing side effects}$$

where APV is the adjusted present value of the acquisition decision and the acquirer moves forward if APV ≥ 0.

10.2 THE WINNER'S CURSE

winner's curse
The winning bid in an auction results in the winner overpaying.

hubris hypothesis
Firms experience the winner's curse in mergers and acquisitions because of hubris.

When the winning bid in an auction leads the winner to overpay, the winner is said to experience the **winner's curse.** Because overconfident managers suffer from hubris, winner's curse in acquisitions stemming from overconfidence is known as the **hubris hypothesis.**[1]

The study of the winner's curse dates back to the early 1970s. In a 1971 article, three petroleum engineers raised the specter of the winner's curse.[2] They suggested that oil companies who had participated in government oil lease auctions for rights in the outer continental shelf had earned low returns in the 1960s. Thereafter academics began to study whether oil companies had failed to adjust their bids in order to anticipate the winner's curse.

The winner's curse extends to M&A activity. A study by KPMG International of the 700 largest acquisitions during the period 1996 through 1998 found that over half destroyed value. Acquisition activity peaked at $1.8 trillion in 2000, more than triple the level in the mid-1990s. Between 1995 and 2000, the average acquisition price in the United States rose 70 percent, to $470 million.

Between 1991 and 2001, the shareholders of acquiring firms lost $216 billion. Interestingly, a disproportionate share of these losses can be traced to very large losses by a few acquirers during the period 1998 through 2001. Many of the large-loss acquirers had been active acquirers prior to their large-loss acquisitions and the market values of their firms had been increasing.[3]

A *Harvard Business Review* article appearing in 2011 provided a 70-to-90 percent range for failure rates associated with M&A.[4] Notably, the article described a number of reasons for failed mergers, including overpayment by the acquiring firm.

The Behavioral Pitfalls box on page 229 illustrates some historic examples of M&A activity that featured the winner's curse.

10.3 OPTIMISM, OVERCONFIDENCE, AND OTHER PSYCHOLOGICAL PHENOMENA IMPACTING ACQUIRING EXECUTIVES

The evidence suggests that excessively optimistic, overconfident CEOs are described as such in the press and wait too long before exercising their executive stock options.[5] Firms whose executives qualify as excessively optimistic and overconfident, in terms of both press coverage and the longholder measure, are 65 percent more likely to have completed an acquisition than firms whose executives do not

Behavioral Pitfalls: Examples of Winner's Curse

In 1991, AT&T purchased computer firm NCR for $7.6 billion. Robert Allen was the CEO of AT&T from 1988 through 1995 and oversaw AT&T's acquisition of NCR. On announcing AT&T's intention to acquire NCR, Allen stated: "I am absolutely confident that together AT&T and NCR will achieve a level of growth and success that we could not achieve separately. Ours will be a future of promises fulfilled."

Despite Robert Allen's assertion of confidence, the market's reaction to AT&T's acquisition announcement was negative. AT&T completed the deal, and its computer operations subsequently lost $3 billion over the next three years.

In 1994 media firm Viacom agreed to purchase Paramount for $9.2 billion. By all accounts, Viacom overpaid for Paramount by $2 billion, despite strong signals from the market that this was the case.

What makes the overpayment especially interesting is the extent to which Viacom CEO Sumner Redstone's interests were aligned with shareholders. Redstone owned more than 75 percent of Viacom's cash flow and voting rights.

In 1999 Cisco Systems made its largest acquisition, paying $6.9 billion in stock for Cerent Corp., a small networking firm that had yet to show a profit, was expecting to raise about $100 million in an IPO, and had fewer than 300 employees. At the time, Cisco's market capitalization was about $225 billion, and it was the second largest firm trading on the Nasdaq. In other words, Cisco shareholders exchanged 3 percent of one of the world's most valuable firms for a small start-up that had yet to show a profit.

The telecommunications firm WorldCom engaged in 17 acquisitions using $30 billion of debt, and in 2002 became the largest firm to declare bankruptcy in U.S. history.

In 2002, the market concluded that $10 billion of investments in the personal computer business that Intel had made under its CEO Craig Barrett had generated little value. Indeed the firm's CFO Andy Bryant was quoted in *The Wall Street Journal* as saying: "I don't know of anything that we purchased that was worth what we paid for it."

Sources: N. Deogun and S. Lipin, "Deals & Deal Makers: Cautionary Tales: When Big Deals Turn Bad—Some Hot Mergers Can Come Undone for Many Reasons," *The Wall Street Journal,* December 8, 1999; S. Wollenberg, "Viacom Head Confident of Handling Paramount," *Associated Press, Los Angeles Daily News,* February 22, 1994; S. Thurm, "Joining the Fold: Under Cisco's System, Mergers Usually Work; That Defies the Odds—Ms. Gigoux's SWAT Teams Oversee the Integration of Newly Acquired Units—'The Borg' of Silicon Valley?" *The Wall Street Journal,* March 1, 2000; D. Clark, "Change of Pace—Big Bet Behind Intel Comeback: In Chips, Speed Isn't Everything—Semiconductor Giant Focuses on Products That Power Today's Wireless Gadgets—A Longer Life for Laptops," *The Wall Street Journal,* November 18, 2003; P. Hietala, S. Kaplan, and D. Robinson, 2003. "What is the Price of Hubris? Using Takeover Battles to Infer Overpayments and Synergies," *Financial Management* vol. 32, no. 3, 1–32.

so qualify. This tendency is compounded when the firm is generating positive cash flow, but mitigated when the board of directors has fewer than 12 members.

Excessively optimistic, overconfident executives press on with an acquisition, even when the reaction in financial markets is negative. A case in point is AT&T's acquisition of NCR mentioned in the Behavioral Pitfalls box above. During a news conference to explain the rationale for the merger, a skeptical technology analyst asked AT&T executives if they could name a single high-technology merger between large firms that had turned out successfully. The question effectively prompted the executives to adopt an outside perspective rather than an inside perspective (as discussed in Chapter 4). One executive mumbled that he could not name a single successful merger among large high-technology firms, but the merger went ahead nonetheless.

The market appears to recognize when the executives of acquiring firms are optimistic and overconfident. The market discounts optimistic bids by roughly eight basis points during a three-day window around the announcement of the acquiring firm's bid, beginning with the day before the bid and ending the day after the bid.[6]

Cash flow is important. When firms are financially constrained, excessively optimistic, overconfident executives choose not to go to the capital markets in order to

Behavioral Pitfalls: Optimistic, Overconfident CEOs and Acquisitions

The financial press describes some CEOs as being excessively optimistic and overconfident, but not others. For example, *The Wall Street Journal* has used both *optimistic* and *confident* as adjectives to describe Wayne Huizenga, the founding CEO of Blockbuster Entertainment Group, the video-rental chain. At the same time, there are many CEOs for whom such attribution has not been made, such as J. Willard Marriott, the former CEO of the hotel chain Marriott International.

Excessively optimistic, overconfident CEOs are more prone to engage in acquisitions than CEOs who are not. During 14 years at the helm of Cook Data Services, Wayne Huizenga conducted six acquisitions. In contrast, during the 15 years Willard Marriott was at the helm of Marriott International, he did not conduct a single acquisition.

Sumner Redstone, the CEO of media firm Viacom, had a history of communicating confidence in the face of declining value. In acquiring Paramount, for which in 1994 he overpaid by $2 billion, Redstone took out several billion dollars in debt. He subsequently told the press that he was "confident" that the combined firm would generate sufficient cash to handle the debt. In this respect, Viacom paid $5.5 billion in cash.

Shortly after completing the Paramount deal, Redstone merged Viacom with Blockbuster. Redstone told the press that he was confident about the Blockbuster deal and stated that Huizenga, Blockbuster's chairman, is "as turned on as I am today by what we have wrought."

After the acquisition, Blockbuster turned out to be a major financial disappointment for Viacom. In January 2003, Redstone was commenting on Blockbusters' weak sales, telling investors he was confident that for global media and entertainment, the year would mark a "threshold to the next level of breakthrough financial performance." Later that year, in November, at an investor conference he explained why despite the fact that Paramount had had a mixed year, he was confident Viacom could bring in a "breakout year" in 2004.

It did not turn out that way. In 2004, Viacom announced that it would record a $1.3 billion charge to reflect a reduction in the value of the Blockbuster brand, and spent months trying to sell the chain. Unsuccessful in that attempt, Viacom spun out Blockbuster. A decade earlier, it had paid $8.4 billion to acquire Blockbuster. Then in a 1999 public offering it sold a fifth of its holdings for $465 million, and finally it spun off the remaining 81.5 percent, thereby netting $738 million, tax-free.

As for Huizenga, after selling Blockbuster to Viacom, in 1995 he took control of Republic Industries (later AutoNation). Two years later, Republic's stock lost half its value, and Huizenga explained to stockholders why he was "confident that Republic stock would come back." And it did, from time to time, but with more than twice the volatility of the S&P 500.

Sources: J. Friedman, "Viacom Set to Sell Off Blockbuster," *Marketwatch*, February 10, 2004, http://www.marketwatch.com/story/viacom-plans-blockbuster-sell-off-loses-385-million; S. Schaefer, "M&A Flashback: Sumner Redstone Cuts Viacom's Losses on Blockbuster," *Forbes*, February 10, 2016, http://www.forbes.com/sites/steveschaefer/2016/02/10/ma-flashback-sumner-redstone-cuts-viacoms-losses-on-blockbuster/#55b336c47b61; "Viacom, Dis get bullish: Investors Hear Moguls Tout Gains," *Hollywood Reporter*, November 4, 2003; "Redstone Confident in B'buster: Viacom CEO Predicts Industry Is Poised for a Turnaround," *Hollywood Reporter*, January 9, 2003; H. S. Byrne, "Wheeler Dealer: Wayne Huizenga May Be the Ultimate Car Salesman, After All," *Barron's*, June 23, 1997; S. Wollenberg, "Viacom Head Confident of Handling Paramount," *Associated Press, Los Angeles Daily News*, February 22, 1994; P. Hietala, S. Kaplan, and D. Robinson, 2003. "What is the Price of Hubris? Using Takeover Battles to Infer Overpayments and Synergies," *Financial Management* vol. 32, no. 3, 1–32.

secure the funds needed to conduct an acquisition. Instead they act as if the market undervalues the equity and/or risky debt issued by their firm. That is, the optimism-overconfidence effect is most pronounced for firms that have ample internal resources to finance acquisitions and for which the resulting acquisitions destroy value.

Most of the acquisitions conducted by excessively optimistic and overconfident CEOs stem from diversifying mergers, CEOs' attempts to acquire firms operating in different industries. In this regard, a study conducted by McKinsey & Co. found that executives of acquiring firms overestimate revenue synergies in 70 percent of cases, with the corresponding amount for cost synergies being 40 percent. The McKinsey report pointed out that upwardly biased estimates of synergies occur because executives underestimate customer-defection rates, make poor assumptions about market growth and competitive realities, and are excessively optimistic about the prospects for opportunities to engage in cross selling.[7]

As was mentioned in Chapter 2, the affect heuristic often induces executives to make acquisitions. The March 2005 issue of *CFO Magazine* points out that some executives base their acquisition decisions on intuitive judgment, intent on doing particular deals no matter what. These executives either fail to undertake formal valuations or else tweak the numbers to support the decision that they wish to make.[8] For some illustrations of value destructive acquisitions, see the Behavioral Pitfalls box on page 230.

Psychological Drivers of Risk in M&A

Managers who are overconfident about their knowledge will establish overly narrow confidence intervals and therefore underestimate risk. Managers of acquiring firms who underestimate risk are susceptible to overestimating synergy, and therefore vulnerable to experiencing the winner's curse.

Notably, survey evidence indicates that managers most apt to undertake acquisitions are those with the highest tolerance for risk.[9] These managers are 67 percent more prone to be active acquirers than managers who are less tolerant of risk. Notably, the effect of risk tolerance dominates that of dispositional optimism. As for CFOs, those who are the least risk tolerant are associated with the highest acquisition activity, and are 159 percent more prone to be active than the most risk tolerant. This suggests that acquiring CEOs who are the most risk tolerant might prefer having CFOs who are low in risk tolerance in order to provide some counterbalance. This feature is all the more interesting because the evidence indicates that CEOs are least likely to delegate responsibility for M&A decisions, although those who have recently completed multiple M&As are more likely to delegate more in order to deal with distraction.[10]

Sensation seeking is related to risk tolerance. Activities such as flying private planes and mountain climbing generate thrills. The evidence indicates that relative to others, firms with CEOs who are private pilots are more prone to engage in acquisitions and to have higher leverage. In addition, there is evidence that younger CEOs are more tolerant of risk and more apt to engage in acquisitions than their older counterparts. As a result, younger CEOs are prone to make risky acquisitions, and the more overconfident among them are especially vulnerable to experiencing the winner's curse.[11]

In line with the behavioral approach, framing issues are germane in respect to acquisition activity. Historically, just over 8 percent of firms with negative prior returns have become acquirers, about 4.5 percent the rate of firms with non-negative prior returns. Moreover, the proportion of deals concluded by firms with negative prior returns is about 30 percent more likely to be value destructive than deals concluded by firms with prior nonnegative returns. Here value destruction is measured by market reaction. In the case of public acquisitions, managers receive immediate feedback from markets after announcing their intentions. If the market reaction to an M&A announcement is sharply negative, then investors are signaling their judgment that the deal is value destructive.[12] Call these *bad acquisitions,* and likewise call *good acquisitions* those for which the market reaction to the M&A announcement is sharply positive. Call all other acquisitions *neutral.*

M&A announcements are akin to couples announcing that they have become engaged. Deal completion is akin to their becoming married. The evidence indicates that for bad acquisitions, long-term buy and hold abnormal returns are negative both from the time of the engagement and the time of the marriage.[13] At the same time, markets do not appear to be perfectly efficient. For good acquisitions, buy and hold abnormal returns are positive from the time of the engagement announcement, but negative from the time of the marriage. This finding suggests that markets form unrealistically high hopes about good acquisitions. Indeed, for event windows beginning a month after deal completion, neutral acquisitions actually achieve better performance than both bad and good.

The evidence indicates that acquisitions in which the acquiring firm has a pilot CEO are riskier than other acquisitions. Similarly, both bad and good acquisitions are riskier than neutral acquisitions, but markedly so for bad acquisitions. Engaging in a bad acquisition is associated with a 13.7 percent increase in the variance of daily stock returns in the next fiscal year; and the more negative the announcement returns associated with bad acquisitions, the higher the risk. This finding is notable because acquisitions are generally associated with lower risk, not higher risk. At the same time, risk is also higher for good acquisitions as well as bad acquisitions.

Moreover, the finding about higher risk holds true regardless of whether risk is measured as systematic risk, idiosyncratic risk, or total risk. In addition, the statement holds true if risk is measured as cash flow volatility using quarterly earnings for the subsequent three years. In other words, there is a fundamental basis for the risk being higher: it is not an event purely driven by investor uncertainty.[14]

Reference Point-Based Heuristic Effects on Deal Negotiations

The discussion in Chapters 2, 3, and 6 suggest that because computing the intrinsic value of a firm with precision is typically difficult, interval estimates make more sense than point estimates. Because of this indeterminacy, price proposals that are part of M&A negotiations between the boards of the acquiring and target firms can reflect heuristics which depend on psychological influences such as salience, reference points, and anchoring effects.

Reference point effects
Offer prices are anchored to peak prices at salient horizons.

Reference point effects can apply either to stock prices or to the proportions of combined companies eventually held by shareholders of the two firms. The evidence indicates the presence of clearly discernable reference points involving peak prices for the target over various horizons, most notably the 52-week high, and also the 13-week high and 26-week high. For example, target firm boards that are judging a potential acquirer's offer often compare the offer to the recent high for the target's stock.

Peak-end rule:
People's judgments of an experience strongly reflect that experience at its peak or at its end.

In terms of evidence, histograms of offer prices display spikes at the following horizons: 13 weeks, 26 weeks, 39 weeks, 52 weeks, and 104 weeks. For these spikes, the anchors are so strong that there is no adjustment, in the sense of anchoring and adjustment. In general, peak prices are one of several factors influencing offer prices. Holding constant a variety of bidder, target, and deal characteristics, for 52-week highs of a typical size, a 10 percent increase in the 52-week high is associated with a 3.3 percent increase in the offer premium. This pattern is consistent with the **peak-end rule,** whereby people's judgments of an experience strongly reflect that experience at its peak or at its end.[15]

10.4 THEORY

In order to understand the manner in which excessive optimism and overconfidence impact executives' decisions about merger and acquisitions activity, consider a theoretical example. The example sets the stage for the discussion of several acquisition cases later in the chapter. The example proceeds in segments, beginning with the case of rational managers and efficient prices. Later segments allow for excessively optimistic, overconfident managers and inefficient prices.

Symmetric Information, Rational Managers, and Efficient Prices

Suppose that an acquiring firm is considering the purchase of a target firm. For sake of illustration, assume that the market value of the acquiring firm is \$2 million and the market value of the target firm is \$1 million, where both are valued as stand-alone firms. However, let there be \$850,000 in synergy from a merger of the two firms, so that the value of the combined firms is \$3,850,000 (= \$2,000,000 + \$1,000,000 + \$850,000).

Consider the case when prices are efficient, meaning that the market prices of the firms, both pre- and postmerger, coincide with fundamental values. Suppose too that information is symmetric, meaning that the managers of both the acquiring firm and the target firm are equally well informed.

CONCEPT PREVIEW
Question 10.1

Put yourself in the position of the manager of the acquiring firm.

1. What is the maximum amount you should be willing to pay to acquire the target firm?
2. If your firm is the only bidder, what is the least amount you should expect to pay in order to acquire the target firm?

If the acquirer is the only firm bidding for the target firm and all managers are rational, then the acquirer can obtain the target by paying a hair more than the market value of \$1 million. In this case, the acquirer's managers will do the shareholders of their firm a service by acquiring the target as long as the synergy value is greater than zero. In respect to Concept Preview Question 10.1, the maximum the managers of the acquiring firm should be willing to pay for the target firm is \$1.85 million, the sum of the target's market value as a stand alone firm and the synergy. The least amount they should expect to pay is \$1 million. Ignoring financing side effects, the APV associated with the acquisition will be \$85 million minus the premium. For simplicity, consider the case when the premium is zero, and focus on the form of financing.

The acquirer might offer the shareholders of the target firm a combination of cash and shares in the combined entity. These shares represent some fraction of the value of the combined firm. For example, the acquirer might offer the target's shareholders \$400,000 in cash together with \$600,000 in shares of the combined firm. With a cash payout to the target's shareholders, rather than to the target itself, the value of the combined firm would fall by $400,000, the value of the cash payout. Therefore, the value of the combined firm would fall to $3,450,000.

In this case, the fraction of $3,450,000 that the acquirer offers the target's shareholders must equal $600,000. That is, the fraction offered must be 17.39 percent ($600,000/$3,450,000). In this case, the shareholders of the target firm end up with $1,000,000 in value, ($400,000 in cash and $600,000 in stock), while the shareholders of the acquiring firm end up with $2,850,000 (82.61 percent of $3,450,000). Not surprisingly, the shareholders of the acquiring firm end up with the original value of their firm plus the synergy from the combination.

Notice that in this scenario, the acquiring firm's shareholders end up with a value equal to the original value of the firm as a stand-alone, plus the value of the synergy, regardless of the cash portion of the payment to the target's shareholders. It is the magnitude of the value, not its form, that is critical.

Excessive Optimism and Overconfidence When Prices Are Efficient

Recall that people tend to be excessively optimistic when they believe they exert a lot of control over the outcome. Of course, managers do believe they exert a lot of control over corporate outcomes. Consider what happens when the acquiring firm's managers are excessively optimistic and overconfident about their abilities, but the target firm's managers are rational. As previously, assume that prices are efficient.

What BPV Implies

Although the BPV counterpart to traditional APV features the same type of variables as APV—namely synergy, premium, and financing side effects—the BPV framework incorporates the effects of psychological phenomena. In this regard, estimated synergy and financing side effects place an upper limit on the magnitude of any premium the acquiring firm should pay. However, if excessive optimism and overconfidence lead the acquiring firm to overestimate synergy, then the acquiring firm might overpay. Moreover, excessive optimism and overconfidence might also cause the acquiring firm managers to believe that their firm is undervalued, a perceived financing side effect. Consider the impact of both issues on how the managers of a potential acquirer view a possible acquisition.

In the preceding example, suppose that the acquiring firm's managers believe that their firm is worth $1 million more than the market's judgment of $2 million. Suppose too that the acquiring firm's managers overestimate the amount of synergy by $100,000. How will the excessive optimism of the acquiring firm's managers impact the criterion they use to decide whether or not to proceed with the merger?

The acquiring firm's managers will have to balance two conflicting concerns. First, they will worry that because the target firm's shareholders do not appreciate what the acquiring firm's managers perceive to be the true value of the acquirer, the target firm's shareholders will demand too large a share of the combined entity. In this respect, there may be little the acquiring managers can do, except to accept that this will be part of the price that they pay for acquiring the target. Specifically,

dilution cost
The value that acquirers believe that the target's shareholders receive because the acquiring firm's stock is undervalued in the market.

if the target firm's shareholders receive the fraction of 17.39 percent of the combined entity, then the acquiring firm's managers perceive them to be receiving an additional $191,290 that is unwarranted. Call this amount the **dilution cost**, and for the moment assume that it is the only perceived financing side effect. Second, the acquiring firm's managers need to decide whether the amount of synergy that they perceive in the merger will justify the price to be paid.

In formal terms the acquiring firm's overconfident managers will go through the same kind of logic as their rational counterparts (described earlier). However, instead of pursuing the merger as long as the true synergy value is positive, they will pursue the merger as long as the perceived synergy ($950,000) exceeds the dilution cost ($191,290).

Acquirers who overestimate the dilution cost relative to the synergy might forego value creating mergers. In 2000, Blockbuster CEO Wayne Huizenga, discussed earlier in a Behavioral Pitfalls box, declined an opportunity to purchase Netflix for $50 million, when it was a new DVD-by-mail business. In 2016, Netflix's market capitalization was $38 billion.

As in the preceding discussion, the acquiring firm's managers can offer to pay for the target through a combination of stock and shares. Recall that rational managers of an acquiring firm do not care about how payment is divided between cash and stock. However, overconfident managers who represent the interests of the acquiring firm's shareholders will care. Why? Because by paying in cash, the acquiring firm's managers perceive no dilution cost, whereas when they pay in stock they do perceive there to be a dilution cost.

What will the acquiring managers do as a result of the asymmetry between the two forms of payment? They will prefer to pay as much as possible in cash, in order to minimize the perceived dilution cost. That is, they will follow a pecking order.

When overconfident managers decide to pursue a merger, they believe that because of the dilution cost, they will not be able to appropriate all the synergy for the acquiring firm's shareholders. There are at least three other reasons that may lead to the acquiring firm's shareholders not being able to capture the entire synergy. First, if the acquirer has a competitor who is also interested in acquiring the target, then the bidding pressure may force the acquirer to increase its bid. Second, if the managers of the target are themselves overconfident, they may demand more than the market value in order to agree to the takeover. Finally, other issues such as the impact on earnings per share (EPS) might lead the managers of the acquiring firm to agree to pay more than they would otherwise.

Inefficient Prices, the Acquisition Premium, and Catering

The preceding discussion concerns the actions of an overconfident management operating in an efficient market. How is the situation changed for a manager, overconfident or rational, who operates in an inefficient market?

Overvalued Acquirer

The heart of this issue is managers' perceptions of mispricing. In the preceding discussion, managers of the acquiring firm perceive their firm to be undervalued, and it is this perception that drives their behavior. However, suppose they were to perceive their firm to be overvalued.

In this case, the pecking order needs to be reversed. Now, the manager of the acquiring firm would want to engage in market timing and purchase the target firm using overvalued equity in its own firm, rather than cash.[16]

There is a long history of catering in M&A activity. During the 1960s, investors became convinced that corporate diversification was value creating, and as a result investor demand for conglomerates rose dramatically, peaking in 1968. During the period July 1965 to June 1968, the average return to a portfolio consisting of the 13 leading conglomerates was 385 percent. In contrast, the return to the S&P 425 was only 34 percent.[17] At the time, only diversifying acquisitions featured a positive announcement effect, with the announcement effect for other acquisitions being negative; and during the period July 1968 through June 1970 conglomerates experienced a "diversification premium" of 36 percent.[18] Consistent with catering, the volume of conglomerate mergers accelerated in 1967, peaking in 1968.[19] Also consistent with catering, the subsequent performance of conglomerates was poor. During the period July 1968 through June 1970, the conglomerates described above lost 68 percent, three times the magnitude of the loss on the S&P 425. In this regard, the diversification premium became a diversification discount of 1 percent during the period 1969 through 1971, and 17 percent during the period 1972 through 1974, persisting well into the 1980s.[20]

The main features associated with catering activities associated with conglomerates during the 1960s have generally persisted thereafter. Merger volume and stock prices have been positively related. In addition, stock acquirers have earned negative long-run returns while cash acquirers have earned positive long-run returns.[21] There is evidence that acquirers have tended to be more overpriced than targets.[22] Not surprisingly, offers for targets that have been undervalued were met with greater hostility than others, and overpriced acquirers have paid higher premiums. Notably, although during high-valuation periods investors have reacted positively to acquisition announcements, the subsequent returns to mergers that occur during those periods have been very poor.[23]

Overvalued firms need not cater by using their stock to make acquisitions. They can also issue new shares, which involve fewer costs associated with financing side effects and integration. At the same time, M&A activity can serve to obscure the fact that the acquiring firm's shares are overvalued. In this respect, the acquisition is distracting, and there is an important psychological literature identifying inattention effects associated with distraction.[24]

Overconfident Acquirer and Overconfident Target

If the target firm's managers are overconfident, they will be prone to overvalue their firm relative to the market. In this case, they may require a premium above the market value before being willing to accept the acquiring firm's bid. As will be seen in the examples discussed later in the chapter, premiums are common and sometimes very large.

Asymmetric Information and the Winner's Curse

In the preceding example, the managers of a firm worth $2 million consider acquiring a target firm whose market value is $1 million. Suppose that in confidential discussions, the managers of the potential acquirer learn that the target firm has developed a new technology whose value is not reflected in its current $1 million market capitalization. The acquirer also learns that the new technology would be the only basis for the value of the combined firms to exceed $3 million.

The managers of the target firm explain that they are trying to decide whether they should develop the new technology themselves or instead be acquired and let the acquiring firm develop the new technology. They have done a careful analysis to assess how much the new technology is worth, and they have shared some information with the managers of the acquiring firm, enough for the latter to estimate that the value of the new technology is $850,000.

Because the target managers have only engaged in partial disclosure, the acquiring firm's managers have established a value range centered on $850,000. The low end of the value range is $0, and the high end of the value range is $1.7 million. Moreover, the acquiring firm's managers believe that any value in this range is as likely as any other. They have concluded that were they to be fully informed, they would share the same value for the new technology as the managers of the target firm.

CONCEPT PREVIEW
Question 10.2

The acquiring firm's managers typically make value-based decisions in a risk-neutral manner. Risk neutral means that they do not require a risk premium. Put yourself in the position of a manager in the acquiring firm. What is the maximum price you would pay to acquire the target firm?

The absolute maximum that a risk-neutral bidder answering Concept Preview Question 10.2 should consider paying for the target is $1.85 million, the sum of the market value and the expected value of the synergy. However, that does not mean that a risk-neutral bidder should be willing to pay that amount. Indeed, if the acquiring firm offered to pay $1.85 million and the target firm's board accepted the offer, the acquiring firm should be concerned. Why?

The target firm's managers and board know the true value of the new technology. Suppose that the value of the new technology were to be $500,000, less than the $850,000 estimate. In that case, the intrinsic value of their firm would be $1.5 million. The target firm's board would be only too happy to sell the firm for $350,000 more than its intrinsic value. In this situation, the acquiring firm would overpay, thereby experiencing the winner's curse.

Of course, the new technology might be worth more than $850,000. However, if this were the case, the target firm's managers would reject the $1.85 million offer. The target firm managers would rather develop the new technology themselves.

Because the target firm will only accept offers in which the acquiring firm overpays, the acquiring firm should offer no more than $1 million. That is the lesson of the example: Assume the worst when the other party is better informed.

10.5 AOL TIME WARNER: THE DANGER OF TRUSTING MARKET PRICES

In January 2000, the Internet service provider America Online (AOL) announced its intention to acquire the media conglomerate Time Warner. The purchase price, $165 billion in AOL stock, set an acquisition record. The merger between AOL and Time Warner illustrates excessive optimism, overconfidence, inefficient prices, and the winner's curse on a grand scale.

Strategy and Synergy

The goal of merging AOL and Time Warner was to create a distribution channel whereby Time Warner's media products would be delivered to millions of consumers via Internet broadband. Time Warner brought media products and a television cable network to the combination. As the dominant Internet service provider (ISP) at the time, AOL brought an installed base of AOL subscribers to the combination.

Time Warner's products were known the world over: CNN, HBO, *Time* magazine, *Fortune* magazine, *People* magazine, *Sports Illustrated*, Warner Brothers, Warner Music Group, *Entertainment Weekly*, Looney Tunes, and Cartoon Network. In 2000, CNN was available to one billion television viewers. Time Warner magazines had 30 million subscribers.

AOL was an Internet service provider that packaged Internet access with e-mail and other services. By 2000, AOL had more than 20 million members, and its subscriber rolls were growing at the rate of 50 percent. However, most of these members accessed AOL using low-speed dial-up rather than high-speed cable. High speed is a necessary ingredient for broadband delivery. Notably, Time Warner operated the second largest cable television network in the United States, with 13 million subscribers.

Time Warner had the content to be delivered via the Internet, along with the required bandwidth. AOL had the Internet expertise along with a huge subscriber base. The potential synergy seemed obvious to Time Warner CEO Gerald Levin who had been frustrated in his attempts to bring an Internet focus to Time Warner. The potential synergy also seemed obvious to AOL's CEO Steve Case who felt that AOL had only one main asset, its subscribers, and was vulnerable to a competitive threat from Microsoft.

Valuation

The combination of AOL and Time Warner occurred at the height of the technology stock bubble. Notably, the market's initial judgment of the overall merger was favorable, with the shareholders of Time Warner benefiting at the expense of the shareholders of AOL. On the day of the announcement, the value of the combined companies rose by 11 percent, or $27.5 billion. In this regard, Time Warner stock increased by 39 percent ($32 billion), while AOL stock declined by 2.7 percent ($4.5 billion). Close-to-close, from the day prior to the announcement to two days after the announcement, Time Warner's stock went from $64.75 to $79.625, while AOL's stock went from $73 to $60.25, while the S&P returned –0.6 percent.

In January 2000, the market capitalization of AOL was $185.3 billion, over twice as large as the $83.7 billion market capitalization of Time Warner. A similar statement applies to P/E, where earnings are measured before taxes, interest, depreciation and amortization (EBITDA). With the peak of the bubble not two months away, was AOL overvalued at the time?

Analysts' views at the time suggested considerable confusion about the valuation question. Some suggested that by merging with a large traditional firm such as Time Warner, AOL's P/E would decline in consequence. In this regard, then-Merrill Lynch analyst Henry Blodget asked whether the market would value the new entity using a "traditional valuation" or whether it would instead use "an Internet valuation."[25] In this regard, coverage in the financial press noted that AOL's share price had fallen more than 30 percent from a 52-week high, reached just a month before.[26]

An opinion piece in *Fortune* magazine suggests that AOL could not have been priced at intrinsic value in January 2000.[27] Why? The answer depends on residual income (the portion of earnings that remain after investors have been paid the cost of capital) because the present value of the residual income stream implied by its market valuation was far larger than any firm at any time had ever produced. Moreover, AOL's actual residual income at the time was close to zero.

At the time of the merger announcement, AOL had approximately 65 percent of the combined market value of the two firms, and 20 percent of the cash flow. AOL's CEO was Steve Case, and Time Warner's CEO was Gerald Levin. Did Steve Case knowingly purchase AOL with overvalued stock? And correspondingly, did Gerald Levin and Time Warner's shareholders trust market prices?

Steve Case

Steve Case did not trust market prices. At age 33 in 1991, years before the dot.com bubble, he had become AOL's CEO and in 1995 its chairman. AOL's internal memos indicate that Case judged that dot.com stocks, including the stock of AOL, were overpriced and that he sought to exploit the overpricing.[28] Moreover, he expected that Internet stocks would collapse in the not too distant future and sought to protect AOL shareholders by acquiring a more mature firm.[29] Case eventually offered 45 percent of a combined AOL Time Warner to Time Warner shareholders, a nice round number. Levin had sought 50 percent to make it a merger of equals, but settled for 45. Under the terms of the deal, Levin would be chief executive of AOL Time Warner, while Case would be its chairman.

Gerald Levin

Gerald Levin trusted market prices. During a press conference to announce the merger Levin stated: "Something profound is taking place. I believe in the present valuations. Their future cash flow is so significant, that is how you justify it."[30]

Ted Turner

Ted Turner, the creator of CNN, was a major shareholder in Time Warner. He owned 100 million shares that he acquired through the sale of CNN to Time Warner three years before and held an operating role overseeing his former holdings. Turner was a very colorful figure. At first he apparently opposed the merger of AOL and Time Warner, asking: "Why should I give up stock in a $25 billion company for shares of this little company?"[31]

However, Turner's financial advisers apparently trusted market prices and persuaded him to back the deal, arguing that the merger would increase the value of his holdings. In his own colorful way, he announced his support at a news conference saying[32]:

> Shortly before nine o'clock last night, I had the honor and privilege of signing a piece of paper that irrevocably cast a vote of my 100 million shares for this merger. I did it with as much or more excitement and enthusiasm as I did on that night when I first made love some forty-two years ago.

For a brief time, the merger of AOL and Time Warner increased Ted Turner's wealth by $4 billion. However, he subsequently lost $7 billion in the next two years as the market value of the combined firm declined. In February 2003, Turner announced his resignation as vice chairman of AOL Time Warner.

Publicly, Turner expressed regret at having sold CNN and his Turner Broadcasting organization to Time Warner in 1996. It is rare for executives to admit to being overconfident, but Turner is uncharacteristic in many ways. He stated[33]:

> At the time, I owned nine percent of Time Warner, and I figured Jerry (Levin) thought that he bought me, but I thought I bought them. But nine percent is not fifty-one. I guess I got a little overconfident.

Asset Writedown

In April 2002, AOL Time Warner wrote down $54 billion in goodwill, a charge to its earnings that reflected the decline in the value of the combined firm. Among Time Warner's various businesses, which ones had generated disappointing cash flows?

AOL

Looking back 12 months from the end of the third quarter of 2002, the operating profit for most of AOL Time Warner businesses experienced positive growth. Publishing had grown by 26 percent, networks had grown by 16 percent, and the music business had grown by 10 percent. However, AOL's operating earnings fell by 30 percent.[34]

What had happened? In 2002, total revenue for America Online declined by approximately 6 percent, to about $8.9 billion. Its advertising revenue declined to $1.6 billion, from $2.6 billion in 2001. A chief factor was the collapse of many dot-com firms, who advertised and sold their products through AOL.

In addition, the rate at which new subscribers were signing up with AOL began to fall. Between 1995 and 2000, the subscription rolls had grown at a compound annual growth rate of 50 percent. However, the rate of growth slowed to 24 percent in the first half of 2002 and then to 8 percent in the second half of 2002, when AOL had 35.3 million members.

EXHIBIT 10-1 **AOL Time Warner, Market Capitalization, Jan. 2001–Dec. 2002**

Source: Center for Research in Security Prices.

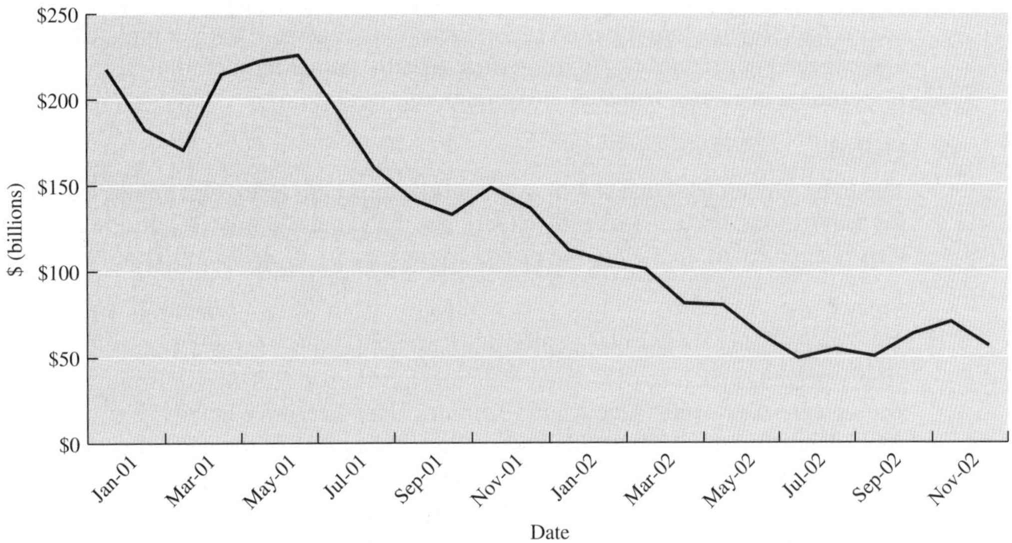

On September 18, 2003, AOL Time Warner dropped the "AOL" from its name. A press release announcing the name change stated: "We believe that our new name better reflects the portfolio of our valuable businesses and ends any confusion between our corporate name and the America Online brand name for our investors, partners and the public."

What's in a name? The change elicited an interesting reaction. At the time, Harris Funds owned 42 million shares of AOL Time Warner stock, primarily in its Oakmark funds. Henry Berghoef, director of research at Harris Associates, stated: "I'm not going out to buy more stock because of a change of name," but then added: "As silly as it sounds, it is healthy psychologically."[35] Psychologically? Might he be referring to salience, availability bias, and the affect heuristic?

Expectations and Accounting

Exhibit 10-1 depicts the market capitalization of AOL Time Warner from the time of its merger through December 2002. From its peak value, the firm had lost roughly 80 percent of its value. Part of the loss stemmed from false expectations.

In seeking support from analysts for the merger, AOL had forecast that earnings would grow by 30 percent. Apparently, those forecasts appeared unrealistic to the person in charge of investor relations at Time Warner. Her name was Joan Nicolais, and she seems to have voiced her concern, preferring instead to provide realistic guidance to Wall Street analysts. The financial press reported her saying that AOL was "basically an elaborate spin machine," whose numbers did not add up. Not surprisingly, Nicolais did not play the investor relations role for a combined AOL Time Warner. That post went to an AOL executive.[36]

In July 2002, *The Washington Post* ran an article alleging that in order to increase the earnings that it would report prior to the merger being completed, AOL had engaged in accounting improprieties. Shortly thereafter, both the SEC and the Department of Justice launched investigations.

Hubris

The hubris hypothesis states that overconfident executives exhibit hubris, overpay for acquisitions, and subsequently experience the winner's curse. Is hubris a characteristic anyone has applied to the principals in the case of AOL and Time Warner?

Steve Case

The adjective *hubris* has frequently been applied to Steve Case. Examples include article headings such as "Doomed Relationship Forged in Hubris," from the *New Zealand Herald,*[37] and "Alec Klein Examines How Executive Hubris Destroyed the AOL-Time Warner Merger," from the *Star-Tribune*.[38] A *Businessweek* editorial stated:

> AOL's merger with Time Warner was, in retrospect, unreal. Distributing entertainment and news over many digital platforms—computers, cell phones, and handhelds—was Case's grand vision. Way too grand, it turned out. His hubris extended to the merger itself. The two corporations had vastly different cultures and didn't mesh.[39]

Gerald Levin

The New York Times did not paint a flattering picture of the executives at Time Warner, stating: "If Case was guilty of hubris, then the Time Warner management team was guilty of ignorance and credulity, industry analysts and academics say."[40] However, Gerald Levin did exhibit hubris, in that he felt no need to consult other executives before agreeing to the merger. Initially, Levin had insisted on a 50-50 split so that the combination would qualify as a merger of equals. However, on his own, without even consulting his board, he agreed to a 45-55 split, thereby leading to an AOL takeover of Time Warner.

Aftermath

In January 2003, Steve Case was pressured to resign as chair of AOL Time Warner. He did so and was replaced by Richard Parsons, Time Warner's chief executive. In 2005, Case resigned from the firm's board. That year, he also wrote a *Washington Post* article arguing that AOL should be split from Time Warner.[41] He argued that the merger failed because the two firms were never integrated, with Time Warner having slowed AOL's progress in building upon its existing social networks and developing Internet telephone service. Case also compared AOL to Apple as they were at the time, suggesting AOL had the same opportunity for recovery as Apple. Several months later, on the Charlie Rose television show, he stated that he regretted having done the deal. In 2009, Time Warner spun off AOL. At a *Business Insider* conference in 2010, hosted by CEO Henry Blodget, Case stated that although the merger had been "a good idea," it was "poorly executed" and for that he blamed himself and his team. He also said that he thought that broadband and digital music would become extremely important, and that AOL needed to diversify.[42]

10.6 HEWLETT-PACKARD AND COMPAQ COMPUTER: BOARD DECISIONS[43]

In 1999 Carleton (Carly) Fiorina, at age 45, became the chief executive of Hewlett-Packard (HP). In May 2002, HP acquired Compaq Computer in a takeover that featured considerable drama. The family foundations established by founders Hewlett and Packard both opposed the merger and actively fought it in a proxy battle. This acquisition offers important lessons about the psychological aspects of executive thinking.

In 1999, HP was involved in three broad business segments: (1) enterprise computing and services for businesses, (2) personal computers (PCs), and (3) imaging and printing. Board members and executives concurred that that HP's enterprise computing business was losing the ability to respond effectively to changing customer requirements and that regaining this ability would require significant new investment. They also concurred that HP's operating margin on PCs was at best breakeven, compared to a 7 percent margin for industry leader Dell Computer.

As for imaging and printing, this was the HP's most profitable business: Ink-jet and laser printers and the steady revenue stream from consumables, such as ink and toner cartridges, produced 93 percent of total imaging operating profits and 118 percent of overall operating profits. However, the board judged that remaining competitive in imaging and printing required continued investment for growth and tighter linkages with enterprise information technology.

The Merger Alternative

Although HP's board began to consider a wide range of alternatives such as exiting the PC business and spinning out the image and printing division, its members focused on a major acquisition. One of the HP board's primary goals was to acquire a firm that would enable it to confront industry leader IBM more effectively. In 2001 IBM was gaining strength, as was PC leader Dell Computer, whereas HP was losing momentum. HP had missed its earnings target for the fourth quarter of fiscal 2000 and subsequently provided guidance for lower future earnings. In this respect its managers were operating in the domain of losses, at least psychologically.

HP's board discussed both Eastman Kodak and Apple Computer as possible acquisition candidates, but in the end rejected both. It also sought, unsuccessfully, to acquire the accounting firm PricewaterhouseCoopers (PwC).

In June 2001, Fiorina contacted Michael Cappellas, the CEO of Compaq Computer, in order to explore the possibility of licensing some Compaq technology. Those discussions evolved from a conversation about licensing to a dialogue about a possible merger. During July, HP asked both McKinsey & Co. and Goldman-Sachs to evaluate such a merger.

Psychological Basis for the Decision to Acquire Compaq

On July 19, 2001, Fiorina raised the merger issue with the other eight members of HP's board. Only three expressed interest. HP director Sam Ginn raised doubts about becoming more deeply involved in the PC business. He pointed out that both HP's computer business and Compaq's computer business were not especially profitable. The consultants at McKinsey responded to his concerns by saying that even a small profit in PCs would translate into a decent return on invested capital.

Outside director Patricia Dunn took an outside view. Dunn was vice chair of Barclay's Global Investors, HP's third largest shareholder. She noted that history has produced many unsuccessful technology mergers and asked what would make the odds of this one any better? The consultants at McKinsey responded by citing $2.5 billion a year in cost savings, which led her to feel more positively about a possible combination.

Nevertheless Fiorina managed to induce HP's board to support her proposal to acquire Compaq. She did so through her use of framing, handing each director a sheet of paper with the following three questions[44]:

1. Do you think the information-technology industry needs to consolidate, and, if so, is it better to be a consolidator or a consolidatee?
2. How important is it to our strategic goals to be Number 1 or Number 2 in our chief product categories?
3. Can we achieve our strategic goals without something drastic?

Consider whether Carly Fiorina's questions appealed to the directors' natural tendency to be overconfident? Did she frame the issue for them in a way that placed them in the domain of losses? In speaking about drastic action, did she induce them to be risk seeking?

The directors slept on Fiorina's questions. The next morning their positions began to change. Sam Ginn indicated that his main goal was to compete with IBM and that merging with Compaq would help. Phil Condit, the CEO of Boeing Co. at the time, stated that although mergers are difficult, focused acquirers are able to make them successful.

Valuation

In September 2001, HP and Compaq signed a merger agreement. Their joint press release indicated that the deal would consist of a stock-for-stock merger whereby one share of Compaq stock would be equivalent to 0.6325 of an HP share. The merged firm would have about $87 billion in sales and 145,000 employees.

Before the acquisition announcement on September 3, the last closing price on HP's stock was $23.21. On September 24, the stock closed at $18.87, and two days later it closed at $17.70. Before the announcement, Compaq's stock price closed at $12.35, and after the announcement its stock price fell to $11.08 on September 4, and then to $10.35 two days thereafter. During this period, the return on the S&P 500 was −1.5 percent.

Consider how HP's executives and board assessed the value of the merger in order to arrive at the terms of exchange. The calculation began with net income.

According to First Call, the firm known for tracking corporate earnings and earnings estimates, analysts were predicting that HP's net income for calendar year 2003 would be $2.4 billion and that Compaq's net income would be $588 million.[45] They perceived the after-tax synergies to HP shareholders for the year to be $1.6 billion,[46] an amount that would be offset by a loss of $364 million in after-tax revenues stemming from the merger.[47]

Taking these amounts together resulted in a net income projection of $4.2 billion for 2003. Given the terms of the merger whereby one share of Compaq stock would be equivalent to 0.6325 of an HP share, HP shareholders' portion of the $4.2 billion net income was $2.728 billion. This represented a 13 percent increase over the $2.4 billion net income forecast for HP as a stand-alone firm.

HP's goal was to achieve $2.5 billion in synergies per year in four key areas. The largest area was head-count reduction: $1.5 billion in synergy was expected to come by reducing head count by 10,000 by 2002 and 15,000 by 2003. The other three areas were procurement, the closing of manufacturing facilities, and the closing of administrative facilities.

Upon completing the merger, HP set up a team to integrate the two companies successfully. One of the co-leaders of the integration team was Jeff Clarke, who had been CFO of Compaq. Prior to joining Compaq, Clarke was with Digital Equipment, which Compaq had acquired in 1998. Compaq's integration of Digital was executed poorly, and as a result, the firm's board fired CEO Eckert Pfeiffer. Clarke understood where the integration had failed, and worked to make HP's integration of Compaq successful.

Notably, in August 2002, HP reported that it was exceeding the plan. It expected to hit its $2.5 billion target one year ahead of plan and to achieve a synergy gain of $3.0 billion in fiscal year 2004.

HP placed a value of $21.2 billion on the expected synergy stream. Exhibit 10-2 illustrates how HP arrived at this value, beginning with the $2.5 billion described in the preceding paragraph.

Implicit within Exhibit 10-2 is the assumption that the merger between HP and Compaq would produce $1.5 billion in after-tax cost savings every year into perpetuity. McKinsey suggested that the cost savings stream be capitalized using a P/E ratio of 20, in that HP had historically traded at about 20 times earnings. The resulting value of $29.4 billion was discounted back to the announcement date using a discount rate of about 15 percent, to arrive at a figure of $21.2 billion.

EXHIBIT 10-2 **Valuation Table Used by HP and Compaq to Value the Synergy From Combining the Two Firms**

Note: Values given in $(billions).
Source: Company Media Relations, Hewlett-Packard.

Synergies	Impact of Revenue Loss	Net Synergies	After-Tax Net Synergies (26% tax rate)	Future Value of Net Synergies at 20 × P/E	Present Value of Net Synergies at 20 × P/E
2.5	0.5	2.0	1.5	29.4	21.2

On September 4, 2001, the first trading day after HP and Compaq announced their merger, HP offered to pay a premium of $2.1 billion over the average market value of Compaq stock during the preceding month. On September 4, the premium actually amounted to $1.2 billion, or 6.9 percent of the September 4 value of Compaq's stock. HP's market capitalization was $35.3 billion on that day, and Compaq's market capitalization was $17.7 billion. Shares outstanding for HP were $1.94 billion, and for Compaq $1.7 billion. In the view of HP's board and executives, the share-exchange ratio of 64/36 implied Compaq's fair share of the synergy amounted to $7.6 billion, more than the premium HP was paying.

HP's Board Accepts Reality

Two years after the HP–Compaq merger closed, the printing unit contributed 30 percent of HP's revenue and 80 percent of its profit. Some analysts actually assessed HP's printer business to be more valuable than the firm as a whole. Despite achieving the promised cost savings, the merger failed to improve the firm's competitive position in its other businesses.

From the time the merger went into effect in May 2002 until March 2004, HP's stock performed about as well as competitors Dell and IBM. However, in April 2004, HP began to miss key performance targets that CEO Fiorina had set during the firm's merger with Compaq. Between May 2002 and January 2005, the firm's stock returned 7 percent, less than the 15.8 percent returned by the S&P 500. In contrast, IBM returned 18.3 percent and Dell returned 55.5 percent during this period. See Exhibit 10-3.

EXHIBIT 10-3 **Cumulative Returns for HP, IBM, Dell, S&P 500, May 2002–Jan. 2005**

Source: Telerate.

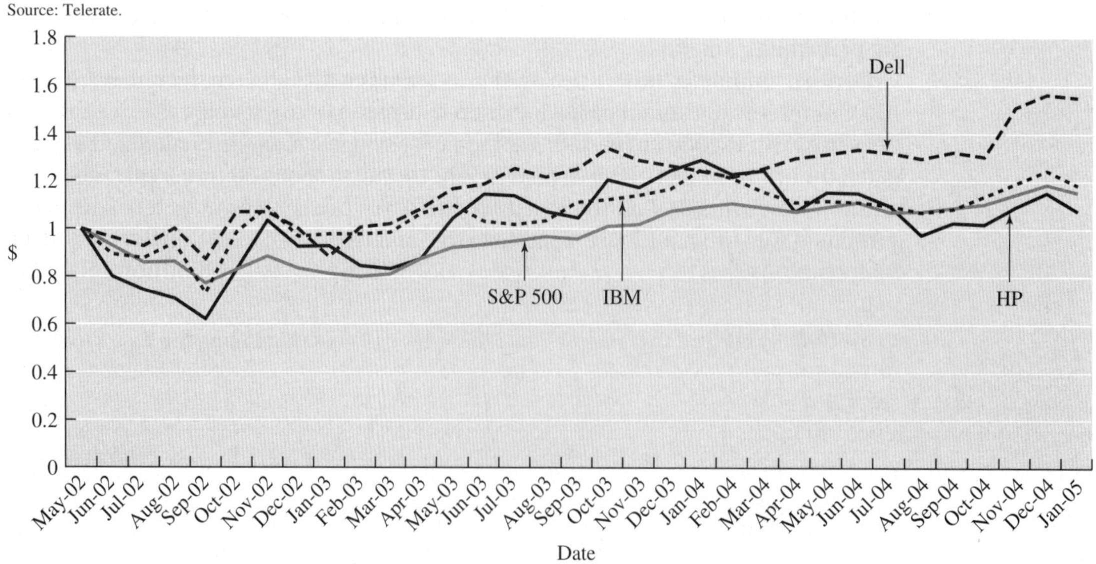

In February 2005, *The Wall Street Journal* characterized HP's business services group as second-tier, relative to industry leader IBM, and noted that its computer division was losing its battle against Dell.[48] That month, HP's board dismissed Carly Fiorina as CEO of HP and named independent director Patricia Dunn as nonexecutive chair.

Aftermath

HP replaced Fiorina with Mark Hurd, who had been CEO of NCR Corporation. Four months after joining HP, Hurd began restructuring HP in order to reduce its costs, with the intention of making the firm more competitive with Dell and IBM. He also made a series of acquisitions, which included software firm Mercury Interactive, services firm Electronic Data Systems Corp, and both 3Com and Palm, thereby moving HP into smartphones and networking equipment.

Hurd's strategy began to have some success. In September 2005, HP CFO Robert Wayman spoke to an FEI chapter meeting to say that the negative judgment of the HP/Compaq merger might have been premature.[49] In 2006, HP passed Dell as the world's largest maker of PCs, and passed IBM as the world's largest technology firm by revenue. HP's PC business continued to improve, and in 2008 Dell's share of the global PC market began a steady decline.

Five years after becoming CEO of HP, Hurd was forced to resign as a result of an ethics controversy involving his expense account and an associated charge of sexual harassment from a person outside the firm. He was replaced by Léo Apotheker. Over time, PC sales would fall, and in 2011 Apotheker announced that HP planned to spin off the $40 billion-revenue PC unit. However, the announcement alienated HP's PC partners, customers, and investors. Several months later, HP replaced Apotheker with Meg Whitman, former CEO of eBay, who promptly reversed the spin-off decision.

During Apotheker's year as HP's CEO, the firm's market value plummeted by 50 percent. A major reason was Apotheker's decision to make what he thought would be a transformative acquisition, purchasing the British software firm Autonomy for $11 billion. The acquisition turned out to be value destructive, not only in hindsight, but also in foresight. Neither Apotheker nor the board chair appear to have read a critical due diligence report on Autonomy, prepared by the accounting firm KPMG, which warned that Autonomy's rapid growth in sales was not "organic," but instead stemmed from its acquisitions. After acquiring Autonomy, HP quickly realized its mistake, and wrote off $8.8 billion related to the acquisition.

In May 2012, Whitman announced that HP would lay off 8 percent of its workforce in order to save approximately $3 billion by the end of 2014. The firm also indicated that it planned to take a $1.2 billion write-down on the Compaq brand. In 2014, HP announced that it planned to split itself into two companies, a PC and printer company to be called HP Inc., and a corporate IT company to be called Hewlett Packard Enterprise.

In respect to HP's PC division, two factors contributed to low profitability. The first was the rise of tablets, which limited the demand for PCs, and the second was low-cost competition from PC-manufacturers in Asia. Moreover, even though HP's printer business continued to be profitable, the increased use of tablet PCs had reduced the demand for printers.[50] In May 2016, Hewlett Packard Enterprise announced that it would sell its enterprise services business to Computer Sciences Corporation in an all-stock deal. Shareholders of HP Enterprise and Computer Sciences would each own half of the combination.

In a 2015 article for *The New York Times,* columnist James Stewart took a retrospective look back at the decisions to acquire both Compaq and Autonomy. He ended his article by noting that although both decisions were bad, at least HP wrote off Autonomy quickly, whereas Compaq lingered for almost a decade.[51]

Summary

As a general rule, the more optimistic and overconfident executives are, the more they engage in acquisitions and the more they leave their investors vulnerable to experiencing the winner's curse. In situations where the market value of a firm roughly measures its intrinsic value, excessively optimistic and overconfident executives overestimate the synergy from acquisitions but believe their own firms to be undervalued. As a result, these executives favor paying for target firms using cash instead of stock.

A longholder is an executive who holds his or her stock options until very near expiration. Executives who are excessively optimistic and overconfident according to press coverage and the longholder criterion are especially prone to engage in acquisitions and prefer to pay in cash instead of stock. Moreover, they tend to discount the negative market reaction to their acquisition announcements, instead pursuing what the market judges to be bad acquisitions.

Acquirers who always trust prices leave themselves vulnerable to the winner's curse during times when investors are irrationally exuberant about target firms. WorldCom's acquisitions serve as an example. Targets who always trust prices and accept payment in the form of the acquirer's stock leave themselves vulnerable to seller's remorse stemming from catering, the flip side of the winner's curse. Time Warner provides such an example.

Acquiring firm executives who participate in acquisitions often do so when they perceive themselves to be operating in the domain of losses. HP's acquisition of Compaq illustrates this phenomenon. The HP–Compaq example also serves to illustrate the psychological phenomena that guide the thinking of executives and directors. However, executives need not view themselves as being in the domain of losses to make acquisitions that increase risk. CEOs who are younger than average and have less than average tenure in their positions are prone to making risky acquisitions, especially if they seek thrills by other means, such as flying private planes.

Valuation is subjective, and for that reason executives rely on heuristics that feature psychological phenomena such as anchoring on recent stock price highs, especially the 52-week high.

Additional Behavioral Readings

Anders, G., *Perfect Enough: Carly Fiorina and the Reinvention of Hewlett-Packard,* New York, Penguin, 2003.

Cain, M. and S. McKeon, "CEO Personal Risk-Taking and Corporate Policies," *Journal of Financial and Quantitative Analysis* 51, 2016, pp. 139–164.

Durfee, D., "A Question of Value," *CFO Magazine,* March 1, 2005.

Malmendier, U. and G. Tate, "Who Makes Acquisitions? CEO Overconfidence and the Market's Reaction," *Journal of Financial Economics* 89, no. 1, 2008, pp. 20–43.

Roll, R., "The Hubris Hypothesis of Corporate Takeovers." In R.H. Thaler (ed.), *Advances in Behavioral Finance,* New York: Russell Sage Foundation, 1993, pp. 437–458.

Key Terms

dilution cost, *235*
hubris hypothesis, *228*
peak-end rule, *232*
reference point effect, *232*
winner's curse, *228*

Explore the Web

www.viacom.com
The web site for Viacom.

www.timewarner.com/corp
The web site for Time Warner.

www.yahoo.com
The web site for Yahoo!, the subject of the Chapter 10 minicase.

Chapter Questions

1. Under the purchase accounting method, an acquirer that pays more than the fair value for a target amortizes the difference over time on its income statement. In the 1990s, mergers between equally sized firms qualified for treatment as a pooling of interests, in which case no amortization was required. John McCormack, a senior vice president at the consulting firm Stern Stewart, is quoted as follows[52]:

   > The accounting model, in brief, says that the value of a company is its current earnings per share multiplied by a standard, industry-wide P/E ratio. . . . Take the case of Bernie Ebbers of WorldCom. I used to think he was brilliant until I heard him explain in a public forum why it was really important to have acquisitions created under the pooling-of-interests accounting method rather than the purchase method. These accounting effects have absolutely no effect on future cash flows, but they will definitely affect EPS. And if you had been persuaded by your investment bankers, as Bernie apparently was, that the value of MCI-WorldCom shares was your earnings per share multiplied by your industry P/E ratio, then you might have believed pooling accounting was important.

   Discuss John McCormack's statements in the context of heuristics and biases, and relate the discussion to the market valuations of AOL and Time Warner.

2. In the chapter discussion of the merger between HP and Compaq, HP director Sam Ginn initially voiced doubts about the deal. However, the McKinsey experts retorted that even a slim profit in PCs would mean a decent return on invested capital. Do you detect any agency conflicts in this exchange?

3. HP director Patricia Dunn works in the banking industry, where consolidation mergers have worked out well in the long run but are vulnerable in the first two years. She responded positively to the McKinsey consultants' statements that a merger between HP and Compaq would produce significant cost savings. Discuss her perspective.

4. HP executives indicate that they use traditional discounted cash flow (DCF) analysis to evaluate investment projects and that the firm's cost of capital is about 12 percent. Consider Exhibit 10-2 which shows how McKinsey consultants proposed that HP value the cost savings stream stemming from its merger with Compaq. On October 15, 2003, HP's forward P/E ratio was 16.1, less than its historical value that stood around 20. HP executives suggest that the lower P/E ratio reflected continued investor uncertainty about whether or not the merger would be successful. Discuss the manner in which HP executives valued the expected cost savings stream when evaluating the merger. In particular address the following questions: Was the technique HP executives used the same, or comparable, to traditional DCF analysis? Do you believe that HP paid a reasonable premium for Compaq? Are there any valuation implications attached to HP's P/E ratio being at 16 rather than 20?
5. Identify any psychological phenomena that were germane in HP's acquisition of Autonomy.
6. A traditional counterargument to the behavioral position described in the chapter is that the chapter arguments only focus on problematic acquisitions. For example, consider consumer products firm Colgate-Palmolive. In 1984 Reuben Mark became CEO of Colgate-Palmolive, taking over from Keith Crane. Like Wayne Huizenga, articles appeared in *The Wall Street Journal* over the years describing Mark as *optimistic* or *confident*. Unlike Wayne Huizenga, no such attribution appears to have been made to Keith Crane, at least in the financial press. Moreover, according to the longholder criterion, Reuben Mark is excessively optimistic and overconfident, but Keith Crane was not. During 11 years at the helm of Colgate-Palmolive, Reuben Mark conducted several acquisitions, of which two were large. Mark also divested businesses where Colgate-Palmolive was not a leader. In contrast, Keith Crane did not conduct a single acquisition. Both Huizenga and Mark conducted acquisitions uniformly throughout their tenures. Neither concentrated acquisition activity in the final years of his option's duration. For example, Mark held an option that expired in 1992. Indeed, between 1990 and 1992 he conducted two acquisitions. However, between 1985 and 1988 he conducted three acquisitions. Colgate-Palmolive appears to have thrived under Mark's leadership. The March-April 2003 issue of the publication *Financial Executive* reports that Colgate-Palmolive's five-year return on equity (ROE) was 71.9 percent, much higher than the industry ROE of 46.5 percent and 12.2 percent for the S&P 500. Does the experience of Colgate-Palmolive not present evidence that contradicts the behavioral position?
7. What insights are to be gleaned from the comments Steve Case made at various times about AOL's acquisition of Time Warner?
8. On February 23, 2000 MGM Grand, Inc. announced its intention to acquire Mirage Resorts, Inc. Over a three day window beginning the day before the announcement, MGM Grand's market value fell by more than 3 percent on a risk-adjusted basis. Prior to the acquisition, Mirage had been the casino earnings leader in in Las Vegas, followed by MGM Grand. At the time MGM Grand was anxious to grow, as it faced increased competition in the casino market. Analysts judged that the deal was a good one because MGM Grand's management had a better reputation for cost-containment and attention to the bottom line than did Mirage Resorts. Because of a competitive bid from competitor Harrah's, MGM Grand was forced to increase its bid for Mirage from $17 per share to $21 per share. Notably, Mirage's stock price had been $11 the previous year. To finance the deal, MGM Grand incurred a debt of $2 billion, believing that it could increase its earnings and free cash flow from its gaming returns. Shortly after the acquisition, MGM

Grand began to seek other expansion projects, and subsequently acquired 55 acres of prime real estate on the Las Vegas Strip for its City Center project, as described in the minicase to Chapter 4. Apply the concepts and ideas discussed in Chapter 10 to analyze MGM Grand's acquisition of Mirage Resorts.

Additional Resources and Materials for Chapter 10 Are Available at www.mhhe.com/shefrin2e

Minicase

Yahoo!

Yahoo! was founded in January 1994 by Jerry Yang and David Filo, then graduate students at Stanford University. The firm grew quickly during the 1990s by offering the most user-friendly way to view the World Wide Web, and in so doing became an important revenue-generating portal. Yahoo! users had access to chat rooms, classified ads, and e-mail. They could follow sports, play games, view movies, follow real estate, keep their calendars, share files, engage in auctions, shop, and maintain an address book.

Three of the main ways that firms generate revenue from operating Internet firms are: selling ads, enabling transactions, and selling products that use the Internet. Yahoo! generated revenue by selling ads that were displayed alongside its content. By 1997, its ad revenues were $70.4 million, and in the next year they increased to $203 million. Under the leadership of its CEO Tim Koogle, Yahoo!'s share price soared during the dot.com bubble, peaking at $118.75. In the aftermath of the bubble bursting, its stock price declined to $8.11 and Koogle left.

From 2000 through 2007, the firm expanded its activities into new areas. Examples are dialup service to compete with AOL, Internet search, social networking, and photo sharing. Throughout its existence, it grew and entered new businesses mostly by making acquisitions, such as the photo sharing firm Flickr. In 2002, Yahoo! added ads to search results. That year the firm's revenue was $953 million. In 2003, its revenue was more than $1.6 billion and in 2004 it was $3.5 billion.

Exhibit 10-4 displays the time series of Yahoo!'s market capitalization, which peaked at $128 billion, $20 billion more than that of Berkshire Hathaway, Warren Buffett's firm. The firm expanded globally, especially in Asia. In 2005, Yahoo! invested $1 billion to acquire a 40-percent stake in the Chinese Internet firm Alibaba, which was little known at the time.

Despite its growth, then-CEO Terry Semel was unable to set a clear strategic direction for the company. Semel had unsuccessfully sought to remake Yahoo! as a media company. Moreover, as Yahoo! had grown into a mammoth portfolio of unfocused Internet services, other Internet firms were focused on single products that would successfully compete with Yahoo! services. These were eBay in auctions, Google in search, Craigslist in classified ads, and eventually Facebook in social media. This intensified competition, and lack of a clear focus by Yahoo!, resulted in a decline in Yahoo!'s revenue growth and earnings.

Beginning in 2005, Yahoo! and Microsoft engaged in discussions about a possible merger. These discussions continued through 2007, but were unsuccessful. During the prior decade Microsoft had not been particularly innovative, despite attempts to be so. For example, it sought to develop a significant upgrade to its core product line, the Vista operating system, but Vista was late to be delivered and had far fewer features than its customers expected.[53] The firm also offered e-mail and search, but neither was sufficiently innovative enough to become an industry leader. The lack of innovation was reflected by the firm's P/E. Between August 2006 and February 2008, Microsoft's trailing P/E ratio averaged about 20, at a time when its cost of capital was approximately10 percent.

In 2007, Jerry Yang replaced Semel as CEO. Still, Yahoo! found that it was unable to compete successfully

EXHIBIT 10-4 **Yahoo!'s Market Capitalization ($ billions), April 1996–June 2015**

Source: Center for Research in Security Prices.

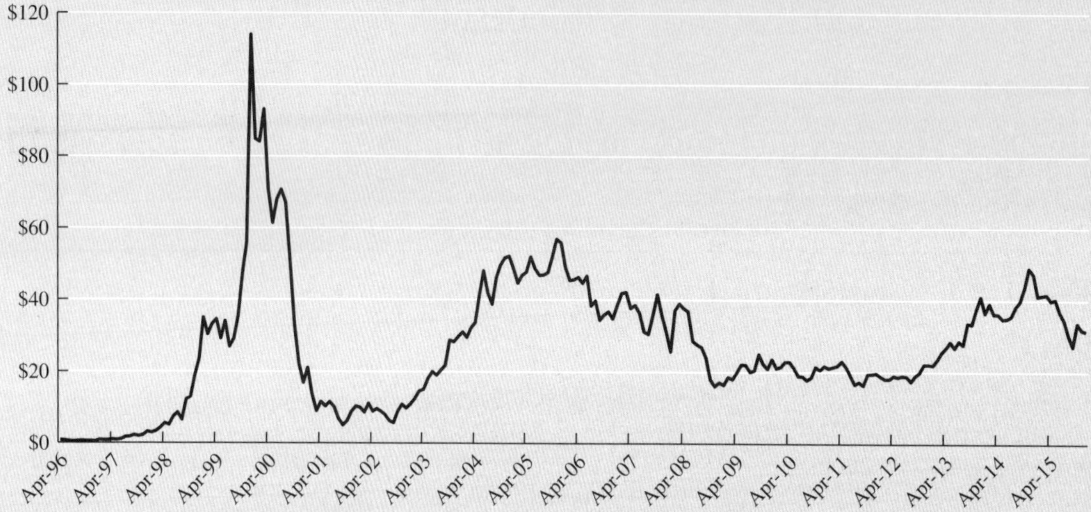

with industry search leader Google; and although it attracted 130 million monthly visitors to its portal, it continued to have difficulty converting the majority of them to paying customers. As a result, on January 29, 2008, Yahoo! announced that it would lay off 1,000 employees, amounting to about 7 percent of its workforce of 14,300.

On January 31, 2008, after markets closed in the United States, Microsoft made an unsolicited offer of $31 per share in order to acquire Yahoo!'s stock, in what Microsoft called a $44.6 billion deal, financed by cash and stock in equal parts. The offer price of $31 amounted to a 62 percent premium, as Yahoo!'s shares had just closed the day at $19.18, up from $19.05 the day before. According to Microsoft, combining the search operations of the two companies and sharing the cost of R&D would lead to synergies of at least $1 billion.

Prior to the announcement, Microsoft's stock closed at $32.60, up from $32.20 the day before. The number of shares of Microsoft stock issued and outstanding was 9,306,980,000 and the number of basic shares of Yahoo! stock issued and outstanding was 1,337,165,000, although the number of Yahoo! diluted shares issued and outstanding was 1,405.486,000.

On February 1, 2008, Microsoft's stock closed at $30.45 per share and Yahoo!'s stock closed at $28.38. On February 5, two trading days later, Microsoft's stock closed at $29.07 per share and Yahoo!'s stock closed at $28.98. From the day before Microsoft's announcement through February 5, the return on the S&P 500 was −3.0 percent. At the time, Microsoft's equity beta was 0.31.

Press coverage of Microsoft's offer made explicit mention of Yahoo! stock's 52-week high, noting that the $31 offer was the 52-week high of $34.08 that had been reached less than four months earlier. One article suggested that boards of target companies typically demand that acquirers pay at least the target's 52-week intraday high.[54]

Yahoo!'s board rejected Microsoft's offer. On February 22, 2008, the board stated that they believed Yahoo!'s shares to be worth more than Microsoft's offer. They based their belief on a number of factors, including Yahoo!'s leading position in the portion of the online ad market known as display advertising, which includes graphical ads such as banners. In this regard, Yahoo!'s web site properties, which range from news to online dating, accounted for 18.8 percent of all display ads seen by U.S. users in November 2007, well above that of Microsoft (6.7 percent) and Google (1.0 percent). The board also mentioned the benefit of the firm's holdings in Asia, such as Alibaba and Yahoo! Japan.[55]

A group of Yahoo! shareholders sued the firm for rejecting the offer. Although activist investor Carl Icahn made a failed proxy bid to take over the firm, in August 2008 he gained a seat on Yahoo!'s board, and continued to argue for a Microsoft partnership. Two Detroit public pension funds accused Yahoo!'s board of introducing a strong antitakeover provision by instituting an expensive plan to retain employees. Yang responded by saying that the firm needed time to explore alternatives, and in fact entered into discussions with AOL Time Warner and News, Corp.

For its part, Microsoft's CFO Chris Liddell noted that Microsoft would have to borrow for the first time in its history. Through the end of 2007, it held $21 billion of cash, which meant that it would have to raise some of the $22.3 billion it had offered to pay in cash for Yahoo!. Given the resistance from Yahoo!'s board, Microsoft was considering the possibility of offering to pay for Yahoo! completely in cash.[56]

At the time, analysts confidently estimated that a combined Microsoft-Yahoo! would generate at least $30 billion in EBITDA—earnings per year, before interest, taxes, depreciation and amortization. As a result, they anticipated that Microsoft's debt would receive a high rating, almost triple-A, and in consequence need to pay a 4.75 percent annual coupon on its debt. Relatedly, Microsoft's corporate tax rate was approximately 30 percent during this period.

Media coverage of the proposed acquisition was generally negative. Some suggested that it had the feeling of being an "AOL-Time Warner 2.0," and would require that Microsoft's then-CEO Steve Ballmer do a better job of selling his case.[57] For Yahoo! shareholders, the recommendation was simple: take the money and run.[58]

When *The Wall Street Journal* interviewed Ballmer, they asked him point blank why he thought he could combine two slow-moving companies into an "accelerant." Ballmer responded by describing the base of talent, assets, and leadership within both companies, despite not having "the market-leading position." *The Journal* noted that although Ballmer believed that he could convert many more of Yahoo!'s users into paying customers, he had failed to do so with Microsoft's own counterpart, MSN.

Instead, *The Journal* hypothesized that by combining Yahoo!'s search engine with that of Microsoft, the size of the combined firm and user base might allow them to compete head-on with Google. However, *The Journal* also went on to say that putting two also-rans together rarely produced a winner, noting that although HP's acquisition of Compaq was doing well at the time, Dell was in decline. Ballmer pointed out that he did not see HP's acquisition of Compaq in quite this way, but instead as an example of a successful integration.[59]

As time passed in 2008, Microsoft began to lose interest in acquiring Yahoo!, although it continued to express interest in its search business. Although Yang was not enthusiastic about ceding control of the business, many Yahoo! shareholders believed that a search deal of some type would have been in the best interest of the firm. In January 2009, Icahn was successful in inducing the replacement of CEO Yang with an outsider, Carol Bartz.

In July 2009, Microsoft and Yahoo announced that they had agreed to form a partnership in Internet search and advertising with the intent of competing more effectively against Google. Under a ten-year agreement, Microsoft would provide the underlying search technology for Yahoo! web sites. The agreement furthered Bartz's interest in focusing Yahoo! on its strengths as a producer of topic-based web media sites, such as finance and sports, with the goal of achieving leadership in online display web advertising.

The agreement provided Microsoft with access to Yahoo!'s search technology, and provided Yahoo! with a significant increase in annual revenues, almost 90 percent of the search-generated ad revenues from its own sites for the first five years of the agreement, which was much higher than was standard in the industry. Ballmer stated that Bartz had bargained hard, getting the lion's share of the revenue without any of the cost. As for Ballmer, he described getting what he wanted, namely "an opportunity to swing for the fences" in respect to search.

In September 2009, Yahoo's share price was about $15. Appearing on CNBC, Bartz was asked whether she would have accepted Microsoft's offer, had she been CEO in January 2008. Her reply: "Sure. You think I'm stupid?"

In November 2010, and about two years after Bartz took over as CEO of Yahoo!, its stock was underperforming, and revenue was flat. Speaking at a *Fortune* event, Bartz pointed to the fact that the economy was still in recession, but confessed that she misjudged just how difficult it would be to achieve the agreement with Microsoft, address other business issues at Yahoo!, and deal with personal issues such as recovering from knee-replacement surgery. When asked to grade her performance as CEO, she said that a year before, she would have given herself a B−, but her then-current assessment was Pass. In September 2011, Yahoo!'s board fired Bartz.[60]

Yahoo! continued to drift as a business, and its share price tended to hover around $15. It remained a very large portal that aggregated content from all across the Internet, but lacked a presence in social media and mobile, two rapidly growing segments. Yahoo! was still seen as unfocused and unlikely to survive with the migration of display advertising to social media and mobile devices. Display advertising made up 34 percent of Yahoo!'s total revenues and in 2011, its share of the global display ad business slipped below 5 percent from being over 6 percent in 2008.

Some analysts argued that Yahoo!'s real value was not in its core business but in its 40 percent stake in Alibaba and its 35 percent stake in Yahoo! Japan. Analysts estimated that the stake in Yahoo! Japan was worth $6.7 billion at the time, while its stake in Alibaba ranged from $9 billion to $12 billion. Taking tax liabilities into account, they estimated Yahoo!'s core business to be valued at a bit more than $5 billion. A common criticism was that Yahoo! had failed to exploit the potential of Flickr, whose photo sharing core and social media features carried the potential for Yahoo! to accomplish what Facebook accomplished.

In July 2012, Yahoo! hired Marissa Mayer as CEO, after having fired former CEO Scott Thompson for falsifying his résumé. Mayer had spent her previous career at Google, where she was responsible for the look and feel of Google's search homepage, Gmail, Google Images, and Google News.

Weeks before Mayer was hired, Yahoo! sold half of its 40 percent stake in Alibaba back to the firm for $7.1 billion, and in September announced it would return $3 billion to shareholders. As part of the arrangement, Alibaba agreed to hold an IPO before the end of 2014. At that point, Alibaba had attracted a lot of positive attention, which meant that investors could invest in Alibaba stock indirectly by investing in Yahoo! stock. As a result, Yahoo! stock had a stable base during the first two years of Mayer's tenure as CEO.

In seeking to change Yahoo!, Mayer invoked Steve Jobs as an example of someone who took a failing Apple in 1997 and instilled a start-up mentality that produced a stream of new, highly successful, innovative products. During her first year as CEO, Mayer made major changes to the firm's homepage, directed a redesign of Yahoo! Mail, and invested in updating Flickr. She also recognized that Yahoo! had underinvested in delivering content on mobile devices, and began an initiative to produce a stream of apps she hoped would be well received. Ultimately, she would describe the essence of her strategy using the acronym MAVEN, standing for mobile, video, and native advertising. Native advertising frames ads to mimic the form of a user's content.

In May 2013 Yahoo! announced that it would acquire the blogging site Tumblr in a deal valued at $1.1 billion. The acquisition was intended to help Yahoo! better connect with an online user base that was younger and more active than its traditional user base. Notably, Yahoo! needed to outbid Facebook by several hundred million dollars in order to secure Tumblr. Yahoo!'s CFO Ken Goldman noted that Tumblr was a long-term investment requiring patience on the part of investors.

Firms such as Yahoo! earn advertising revenue associated with delivering content. When Mayer worked for Google, before joining Yahoo!, she pointed out that traditional producers of media content, such as magazine publishers, were losing competitive advantage as their products came to be distributed in piecemeal fashion by online search firms and social networking firms.

From a marketing perspective, Yahoo! had a middle-American brand and focused on a mass audience. Mayer sought to introduce content that would appeal to a more affluent, sophisticated clientele. She engaged a slate of expensive journalists to create a series of new "digital magazines." She closed down Shine, Yahoo!'s web site for women, which brought in annual revenue of $45 million.

Mayer also hired former CBS News anchor Katie Couric to interview experts on topics like health and parenting. Although editors positioned videos of these interviews prominently on web pages, few users chose to view them. Despite the evidence that viewers were not clicking on these videos, in the middle of 2013, Mayer concluded a contract with Couric as Yahoo!'s "global anchor," in which Couric would receive $5 million per year.[61]

Yahoo!'s users did not resonate to the new strategy. In the second quarter of 2014, the firm's display advertising revenues decreased by 7 percent. Yahoo!'s new and updated apps failed to generate great enthusiasm among users. Neither did the digital-magazine strategy; and Yahoo!'s share of the search business fell to 10 percent instead of growing to 20 percent as Mayer had hoped.

In September 2014, Alibaba conducted its IPO, and its stock price closed at $93.89 per share from its offer price of $68. In contrast, Yahoo!'s stock price declined, suggesting that the value of Yahoo!'s core assets might be very low, or even negative. A week later, activist investor Jeffrey Smith, who ran the fund Starboard Value, published an open letter calling for Yahoo! to divest itself of its Alibaba assets, return the money to shareholders, and subsequently merge with AOL. Under pressure in October 2014, Mayer claimed to have "great confidence in the strength of our business," despite Yahoo!'s revenue having decreased in five of the past six quarters. In June 2015, Verizon completed a $4.4 billion acquisition of AOL, which had assembled a sophisticated set of advertising technologies for both online and traditional media.

The pressure on Yahoo! continued to grow, and in March 2016, Starboard Value was working to nominate a new slate of directors that, if elected, could fire Mayer, bring in new management, and change the direction of the company.

Appearing on the television program *Charlie Rose,* Mayer argued that she needed three more years to complete her strategy of focusing on MAVEN.[62] She pointed that because of the condition in which she found Yahoo! at the time she joined, she had needed to stabilize its legacy business. She then noted that aspects of her strategy, such as mobile, were advancing more rapidly than she expected. She also called some strategic moves, such as acquiring Tumblr, one of her "big bold bets," for which some have paid off and some have yet to pay off.

In April, Yahoo! settled its dispute with Starboard, agreeing to give Smith a board seat, and to bring three other new directors with him who would oversee an auction process to sell the firm.[63] In July, Verizon emerged as the top bidder, agreeing to pay $4.8 billion to acquire Yahoo!'s core Internet business, but not its $41 billion investment in Alibaba, its holdings of Yahoo! Japan, and its portfolio of patents. The terms of the agreement specified that should Mayer be terminated, her severance package would be $57 million.

Verizon's acquisition of Yahoo! and AOL earlier provides it with the potential to earn additional advertising revenue. Such revenue would stem from the provision of content over its wireless networks to it mobile phone customers, thereby enabling Verizon to compete with firms such as Google and Facebook. General reaction to the deal announcement was unenthusiastic. Sprint's CEO noted that no telecommunications company had successfully entered the content business. T-Mobile's CEO described the deal as a "slippery slope," and *Fortune* magazine's comments were critical. During July when the deal was being negotiated, Verizon's stock price declined by −0.9 percent while the S&P 500 increased by 3.3 percent. In the three-day window beginning with the day before the deal announcement, Verizon's stock declined by 0.9 percent while the S&P 500 declined by 0.4 percent.[64]

Case Analysis Questions

1. Which psychological phenomena might have been at play in leading Microsoft to make the offer it did to acquire Yahoo!?
2. Which psychological phenomena might have been at play in leading Yahoo!'s board to reject Microsoft's offer?
3. Discuss the discussion of reference point heuristics in the press coverage of the Microsoft offer, and indicate whether the comments in the press are consistent with the actual merger talks between the two firms.
4. Estimate the value of the synergy associated with the projected cost savings of $1.5 billion per year, assuming that the stream of cost savings would begin a year after the acquisition announcement, and would last into perpetuity. Compare your answer to the size of the dollar premium associated with how much more Microsoft is offering to pay for Yahoo! than its market value on January 31, 2008.
5. Had Microsoft acquired Yahoo!, would the acquisition have been classified as a bad merger? The technical definition of a bad acquisition can be found in the endnotes to this chapter.
6. Identify behavioral issues associated with Microsoft's decisions about capital structure and capital budgeting.
7. Discuss whether there are any behavioral issues associated with whether Microsoft pays for Yahoo! using 100 percent cash, or instead 50 percent cash and 50 percent stock.
8. Which psychological phenomena might have been at play in the negotiations between Carol Bartz and Steve Ballmer?
9. Financial economist Aswath Damordaran was quoted in *The New York Times* about the dangers of the Steve Jobs effect, whereby CEOs seek to emulate Jobs's success in taking Apple from being close to failure to being extremely successful by developing new revolutionary products.[65] He points out that there are many failed firms that sought to accomplish what Apple accomplished. Discuss the relevance of Damodaran's perspective for Yahoo!
10. The minicase makes reference to some of the examples discussed in the chapter. Discuss the connection between

the minicase and the other examples with reference to how the examples are mentioned in the minicase.

11. In September 2016, between the time that Yahoo! and Verizon negotiated the terms of their deal and the completion of the deal, Yahoo! announced its discovery that in 2014 a "state-sponsored actor" had breached its user database, which included names, email addresses, encrypted passwords, birth dates, telephone numbers, and security questions for approximately 500 million users. Then in December 2016, based on information provided by law enforcement investigating the 2014 breach, the firm announced that it had experienced an even more serious breach, in 2013, involving approximately a billion users. These types of breaches are potentially dangerous for users, in respect to its implications for their connections to their financial services and social media profiles. By some accounts, the average time it takes organizations to identify breaches is 191 days, the average time to contain a breach is 58 days after discovery, and the cost to remediate a data breach is $221 per stolen record. Yahoo! had previously experienced breaches in 2010 when the Chinese military successfully breached its system, along with those of other firms such as Google, and in 2012 when more than 450,000 Yahoo! user accounts were compromised. Although Google responded to the 2010 breach by investing heavily in cybersecurity, Yahoo! executives invested less heavily, partly because of a fear that their users would find that extra security measures would make using Yahoo!'s platform harder to use, which would result in users abandoning its platform. Conflicts over the strength of the firm's security measures, between Yahoo! executives and its cybersecurity team, resulted in many security engineers leaving the firm. The timing of the September 2016 announcement raised the question of whether the 2014 breach conformed to the legal definition of a "material adverse change" (MAC), which would lead to a renegotiation of the terms of the Yahoo!-Verizon deal. Verizon's reaction at the time was that they did not understand the full implications of the announcement, but would evaluate the possibility of renegotiating the terms of the acquisition agreement. Both breaches damaged Yahoo!'s reputational capital for offering secure web services. Yahoo!'s reaction to the 2014 breach was that because the original passwords had been encrypted, the risks were low, and that they notified their users to reset their passwords. Their reaction to the 2013 breach was less sanguine. After the announcement of the 2013 breach, Verizon stated that it was continuing to evaluate the associated implications, in respect to renegotiating the terms of the acquisition. Discuss any psychological issues associated with the data breaches described above.

Chapter Eleven

Financial Management and Group Process

The main objective of this chapter is for students to demonstrate that they can identify the manner in which biases and framing adversely impact the behavior of managers or directors when they work together in groups.

After completing this chapter students will be able to:

1. Explain why groupthink, poor information sharing, and inadequate motivation underlie suboptimal decisions made by groups engaged in judgmental tasks.
2. Assess the contribution of poor group process in the governance of firms that experienced major financial crises, especially during the global financial crisis.
3. Describe the manner in which group process can amplify the risk attitudes of individual group members.
4. Identify corporate nudges that groups can take to improve group process.
5. Explain what corporate culture means, and apply the concept to examples, including those related to the global financial crisis.

11.1 TRADITIONAL APPROACH TO FINANCIAL MANAGEMENT

The traditional textbook approach to financial management focuses on techniques associated with a set of themes. Examples of key themes are pro forma forecasting of financial statements, cash budgeting, present value analysis, agency theory, and real options, all of which are related to the broad tasks of corporate financing, investment, and governance.

The traditional approach emphasizes numerical techniques. Technique is important. That said, the techniques taught in regular courses in corporate finance make up only part of what comprises financial management. Real financial management is more than corporate finance. Real financial management features the integration of corporate finance and management, focusing on the manner in which human beings work together in groups to make financial decisions within organizations.

One way to think about financial management is as a set of specific processes. These processes relate to the setting of corporate goals, the preparation of plans for how to achieve these goals, the establishment of incentives to motivate the workforce to achieve goals, and the sharing of information as time unfolds and operations take place.

Good financial management involves bringing people together in groups to do each of these processes well. More than that, good financial management involves connecting these processes so that they are mutually reinforcing. The process for goal setting needs to focus on activities that are value creating, and which are folded into the pro forma financial statements that are developed in the process for planning. The process for establishing incentives, both short-term bonuses and long-term equity sharing, needs to identify clear criteria that tie rewards to actual performance relative to planned performance. The process for information sharing needs to highlight progress in achieving goals relative to plans, with transparency in respect to how performance impacts compensation and non-pecuniary rewards.

Corporate culture
How clearly a corporation articulates its values, and the degree to which those values are shared within the corporation.

Corporate processes take place within corporate cultures. **Corporate culture** is a bit amorphous as a concept, but generally refers to how clearly a corporation articulates its values, and the degree to which those values are shared within the corporation. Key aspects of corporate culture involve the degree to which the workforce contributes to goal setting, the amount of training in business skills as well as operational skills, and how a bonus plan and company stock plan strengthen the degree to which values are shared within the organization.

Culture is important, and impacts the degree to which people enjoy their work experiences, effectively a non-pecuniary reward. In turn, the degree to which people enjoy their work experiences impacts the profitability of the firms for which they work. The evidence indicates that since 1984, annual stock market returns for companies listed in *Fortune* Magazine's "100 Best Companies to Work For in America" exceeded their peers by 3.8 percent.[1]

Trust is an important part of culture, and connected to the degree to which people share the same values, believe they share the same values, and cooperate in achieving common goals when working in groups.

Notably, traditional corporate finance textbooks do not include material on group process. Yet group process is critical to the effectiveness of corporate financial decisions. The major decisions about corporate governance take place in board meetings. The major decisions made by managers take place in managerial meetings.

Effective groups exploit potential synergies from bringing together people with different skills, perspectives, and values. Effective groups are said to experience process gains. In theory, the key to process gains is the constructive use of individual differences among group members.

11.2 PROCESS LOSS

Despite the potential for process gain, many groups are unable to exploit potential synergies and instead experience process loss. The source of this loss is typically psychological, in that group psychology often leads people to make different decisions when they operate as part of a group than when they act as individuals.[2]

accuracy
Groups outperform individuals when it comes to intellectual tasks, but do worse than individuals when it comes to judgmental tasks.

polarization
Group processes tend to accentuate attitudes toward risk.

unwarranted acceptance
Group discussion tends to induce group members to accept a decision too readily.

illusion of effectiveness
Unwarranted confidence in the decision.

Behavioral studies have identified three important features about group behavior.[3] The three features are known as accuracy, polarization, and unwarranted acceptance. A brief description of each follows:

1. **Accuracy:** Groups tend to outperform individuals in particular types of tasks known as intellectual tasks. An intellectual task is a problem with a "correct" answer that once identified, group members would readily acknowledge as being correct. In this respect, an intellectual task is sometimes called a *eureka problem.* Although groups tend to outperform individuals on intellectual tasks, the same is not true for judgmental tasks that are more subjective in nature.
2. **Polarization:** Groups often become polarized in respect to risk tolerance. For example, if at the individual level the members of a group are slightly risk seeking, group discussion typically amplifies the degree of risk-seeking behavior.
3. **Unwarranted acceptance:** Group discussion leads the members of a group to accept a decision readily. However, such acceptance is often unwarranted, producing a phenomenon akin to collective overconfidence known as the **illusion of effectiveness**.

11.3 GENERAL REASONS FOR GROUP ERRORS

Three main factors underlie group inaccuracy and unwarranted acceptance: groupthink, poor information sharing, and inadequate motivation. This section describes these concepts in general terms, and Section 11.4 provides some corporate examples of process loss.

Groupthink

Think about the concept of confirmation bias described in Chapter 1 and Chapter 2. Confirmation bias is the tendency to overweight evidence that confirms a hypothesis or view but underweight evidence that disconfirms that view. The discussion of confirmation bias in these two chapters pertained to individuals. However, a collective form of confirmation bias also affects groups, leading to the phenomenon known as **groupthink.**[4]

groupthink
The drive for achieving group consensus overrides the realistic appraisal of alternative courses of action.

A group exhibits groupthink when the drive for achieving group consensus overrides the realistic appraisal of alternative courses of action. The following conditions are especially conducive to the emergence of groupthink:

- The group dynamics feature amiability and esprit de corps.
- A powerful, opinionated leader leads the group.
- Group members operate under stress.
- Group members are strongly influenced by a desire for social conformity.
- There is no explicit decision-making procedure.

An article that appeared in *Fortune* magazine describes some key reasons why CEOs fail and concludes that the answer is bad execution.[5] The *Fortune* article describes groupthink at General Motors during the failed tenure of CEOs Roger Smith and Robert Stempel. The article notes that committees and policy groups essentially became time-consuming formalities where outcomes were rarely in doubt and serious deliberation was an infrequent occurrence. In contrast, Alfred P. Sloan, the legendary president and chief executive officer of General Motors from 1923 to 1946, articulated a different philosophy. Sloan charged his executives with the task of developing disagreement about major decisions, in order to gain a better understanding of the likely consequences.

Degree of CEO delegation is an issue related to groupthink. How much CEOs delegate depends on a combination of factors, such as: their personalities, own expertise, incentives, and their firm's circumstances. CEOS who are particularly knowledgeable about an area such as finance, or whose executive pay is primarily incentive-based, delegate less. When a firm's divisional managers have proven records of success, CEOs delegate more. When the firm is in the midst of making an acquisition, an important decision, CEOs delegate less in respect to the acquisition itself. However, when the firm is engaged in multiple mergers and acquisitions, and CEOs become distracted, they delegate more in respect to capital structure and internal capital allocation. Likewise, CEOs delegate more when their firms are large or complex. In this regard, companies rely on several decision rules when allocating capital. These include not just rankings by net present value, but also timing of cash flows, financial constraints, and the "gut feel" of senior management.

Vulnerability to groupthink is also related to participation in social networks, especially by corporate board members and CEOs who belong to the same non-professional organizations such as golf clubs and charities. Connectivity can foster groupthink when connected directors share the CEO's perspective or cognitive biases, by dint of having the same background and moving in the same social circles. In addition, connected directors might be motivated by an interest in preserving social ties with the CEO. The evidence suggests a negative relationship between social connectivity and firm value when measured by Tobin's Q, with the effect being strongest when shareholder rights are weak. For example, firms with closely connected directors are less likely to initiate earnings restatements that are internally prompted. In line with the discussion of the winner's curse in Chapter 10, firms with boards closely connected to the CEO are apt to make more frequent acquisitions: the merger bids of these firms destroy $407 million of shareholder value on average, $293 million more than the bids of other firms. In contrast, when connectivity occurs as a result of the acquiring firm and target firm sharing a common director, the acquiring firm tends to pay a lower acquisition premium, thereby benefitting the shareholders of the acquiring firm. Likewise, when one "acquirer director" and one "target director" serve on the same third board, the evidence suggests that the combination features greater value creation.[6]

Poor Information Sharing

poor information sharing
Group members fail to share enough information with other group members.

People are often ineffective when it comes to sharing information within groups, a phenomenon known as **poor information sharing.**[7] One behavioral study analyzed information sharing about job candidates. Relevant information was distributed across group members to see if they would find a way to share the relevant information. The key finding in the study is that people refrain from sharing relevant information with others in their groups, even when the members of the group share a common goal.

In the study, groups made different choices according to how the information was distributed across members of the group. The group task involved ranking job candidates, although the same principles apply to ranking project proposals during capital budgeting. There were two versions of the task. In the first version, all group members received identical information about all candidates. This information strongly suggested that one particular candidate, call him Mr. A, dominated the other candidates. In this situation, most groups chose Mr. A.

In the second version of the task, information about candidates was distributed across members of the group, rather than shared. Collectively, the group had the same information that was available in the first version of the task. However, in order that the individual members come to possess full information, the group had to find a way to share the distributed pieces among themselves.

The information was initially distributed so that most group members perceived that some other candidate, Ms. B, was the dominant choice. When the group came together to discuss candidates, they soon focused on the fact that Ms. B appeared to be the best candidate. They did exchange information. However, the information that members offered was information that supported the choice of Ms. B. That is, the group experienced confirmation bias.

In order to arrive at the correct choice, Mr. A, the group would have needed to find a way to put forward disconfirming evidence in respect to the choice of Ms. B. However, doing so is counterintuitive for most people.

A pertinent example of poor information sharing involves the manner in which knowledge about terrorist threats to the United States was shared within the FBI and between the FBI and the CIA, prior to September 11, 2001. In the spring of 2002, poignant examples were provided during testimony in hearings conducted by the Senate Intelligence Committee and the Senate Judiciary Committee.

Corporate Nudges

Errors or biases: Groupthink.

Why does it happen? Desire for conformity leads to collective confirmation bias.

How does it happen? Members of groups become reluctant to share information or offer arguments to counter proposals made by other members of the group.

What can be done about it?

1. Ask group members to refrain from stating personal preferences at the outset of the discussion.
2. Explicitly cultivate debate, disagreement, and the sharing of information, as opposed to discouraging these behaviors by characterizing them as dissent and unnecessary criticism.
3. Designate one member of the group to play devil's advocate for each major proposal.
4. Regularly invite outside experts to attend meetings, with the charge that they challenge the group not to behave like meek conformists who, in the drive for consensus, value unity over truth.

Behavioral Pitfalls: Ford

In September 2006, Alan Mulally became Ford Motor Company's CEO. At that time the company was in distress, and had been in decline for about a decade. Its debt was at "junk" status, and in 2006 it experienced a $12.7 billion loss, a company record.

When Mulally arrived, in the knowledge that a serious restructuring of Ford was necessary, he learned that the firm's finance team had been working on a plan to raise new debt. Realizing that a large cash infusion would provide an important buffer for a restructuring, he led the initiative to raise $23.6 billion in new debt. To do so, he pledged Ford's brand name Mustang and its logo as collateral, and sold off assets including its prestige brands such as Aston Martin, Jaguar, Land Rover, and Volvo.

The global financial crisis negatively impacted many firms, including Ford. As a result of the crisis, car sales in the United States decreased from 16.5 million units in 2006 to 10.5 million in 2009. Ford's competitors General Motors and Chrysler both required emergency loans from the U.S. government, and even so, both eventually filed for bankruptcy protection. However, Ford did not require emergency funding, and it did not go bankrupt. Indeed by the end of 2010, it was the most profitable automobile manufacturer in the world.

On July 1, 2014, Mulally retired from Ford. When interviewed about how he had managed to turn Ford around, he said that the biggest change he made was cultural. Mulally pointed out that his earliest challenges involved persuading managers to work together, rather than engaging in internal rivalries. This issue surfaced at the regular Thursday managers' meetings, which he instituted in order to share information about progress in meeting the firm's business plans. In this regard, he discovered that he needed to induce people to address problems head-on instead of shunning responsibility. The culture he found when he arrived at Ford featured little sharing of information and a fear of disclosing weakness, pretending failures did not exist. Mulally states that the first indications of successfully changing the culture came when managers arrived at meetings with evidence of failures and requests for help.

Mulally created the concept known as "One Team" to eliminate silos and turf battles within the firm. "One Ford" became a slogan to be repeated in every conversation, meeting, email, and interview. Notably, some employees began to carry a card with one side displaying the firm's business plan, and the other side displaying its culture and expected behaviors. For example, Mulally wanted to build a culture where everyone felt included and part of the team, where everyone's contribution is respected, and where everyone should participate. To achieve this goal, he encouraged Ford managers to stop berating employees when problems surfaced and instead ask those employees what they could do to help out. Mulally contends that this behavioral change proved to be more efficient in respect to problem solving.[8]

Inadequate Motivation

social loafing
Group members reduce their contributions, instead relying on others to exert the requisite effort.

Inadequate motivation leads to a free-rider agency conflict known as **social loafing.** In this regard, some members of the group might choose to reduce their level of effort, relying on the efforts of others to generate group benefits. In other words, individuals who work in groups might not work as hard as individuals who work alone. Setting incentives to deal appropriately with social loafing is difficult when the link between effort and outcome is weak and when responsibility within the group is diffused.

11.4 THE GLOBAL FINANCIAL CRISIS: EXPERIENCES OF DIFFERENT FIRMS

Effective processes lie at the heart of strong corporate cultures and good financial management. Ford Motor Company, described in a nearby Behavioral Pitfalls box, describes the case of a company that turned its situation from unfavorable to favorable by changing its processes and culture. Other examples are discussed in the Additional Resources to this chapter, including Enron and WorldCom, whose failures prompted the passage of Sarbanes-Oxley. The Additional Resources to Chapter 11 is especially important for its discussion about organizational changes that are much more systemic than corporate nudges.

At its heart, the global financial crisis reflected unsound financial management stemming from ineffective processes and weak corporate cultures. This section describes group process issues that surfaced in several select firms, and which illustrate some of the main points. The examples illustrate a variety of psychological phenomena, such as excessive optimism, overconfidence, aspiration-based risk taking, confirmation bias, groupthink, and opaque framing.

Financial Instability Hypothesis

The global financial crisis fits the description of a conceptual framework called the financial instability hypothesis (FIH), which was developed by the late economist Hyman Minsky. According to the FIH, during economic expansions, feelings of euphoria can lead households, firms, and governments to become excessively leveraged, with shadow banks supplying ever-increasing amounts of the associated debt, which they provide through innovative financial products. In addition, the form of financing shifts with repayment of principal, and even interest, becoming evermore reliant on asset appreciation rather than cash flows produced by the assets underlying loans. Minsky applied the labels "speculative finance" and "Ponzi finance" to debt having this feature. As a result, increased debt tends to fuel asset pricing bubbles, which expand and then suddenly burst, producing defaults on debt obligations and generating a financial crisis and economic instability.

In the lead-up to the global financial crisis, household debt levels in the United States did rise dramatically, especially during the economic recovery that followed the bursting of the dot.com bubble in 1999 and 2000. The asset pricing bubble at the heart of the crisis was housing, and the associated financing involved a series of innovative products involving mortgages. Many of these products depended on housing price appreciation to support repayment of principal and interest. During the housing bubble, the proportion of subprime mortgages increased dramatically, as did loan-to-value ratios, as well as the proportion of mortgages that required limited documentation and allowed for zero down payments.

Commercial banks, such as Citibank, and shadow banks, such as Lehman Brothers, played critical roles in financial innovation involving mortgage-related products. However, the role of shadow banks increased significantly during the lead-up to the crisis. Financial firms purchased mortgages and bundled them into pools, which they then used to create mortgage-backed securities with capital structures. In addition, these firms manufactured collateralized debt obligations (CDOs), which applied capital structures to pools of tranches from mortgage-backed securities. As housing prices increased, peaked, and then began to fall, the proportion of high-risk mortgages in the pools backing these assets rose.

Notably, insurance firm AIG sold protection against mortgage default, and rating agencies S&P and Moody's assigned excessively generous ratings to CDO tranches, in many cases triple-A. The actions of both were critical features that allowed financial institutions to sell these innovative products to investors around the world.

Problematic Group Process and Psychological Phenomena at Financial Firms

The Financial Crisis Inquiry Commission (FCIC) characterized the global financial crisis as a colossal failure of risk management.[9] The FCIC report states that the greatest losses from the crisis were experienced by arrangers of CDOs such as Citigroup, Lehman Brothers, Merrill Lynch, and UBS, by financial guarantors such as AIG, and by ratings agencies such as Moody's and S&P. The report explains that these entities placed excessive faith in their quantitative models, retaining exposure to what they erroneously believed to have been the least risky CDO tranches. The Commission's report provides strong evidence of problematic group processes and vulnerabilities to psychological pitfalls that underlay the decisions made by financial firms in the lead-up to the crisis. Below are some examples.

Citigroup

In July 2007, Citigroup CEO Charles Prince made a comment that for many characterized the asset pricing bubble dynamic when he said "as long as the music is playing, you've got to get up and dance. We're still dancing." Indeed, earlier that year the Corporate Library downgraded Citigroup's grade to a D, citing high governance risk and executive compensation that was poorly aligned with shareholder interests. By September 2007, Citigroup had become the systemically most risky financial firm in the United States. According to the FCIC, Citigroup's investment bank paid traders on its CDO desk for volume, but without regard for later losses. Its risk managers granted exceptions to the firm's established risk limits, allowing for increased exposures. Notably, some within the organization raised alerts about doing deals based on limited documentation mortgages that failed to meet the bank's standards, even notifying board member Robert Rubin, who is a former Treasury secretary. There is no evidence that these alerts were acted upon, except to demote those who voiced concerns. One Citigroup banker told the FCIC: "A decision was made that: 'We're going to have to hold our nose and start buying the stated product if we want to stay in business.' "[10] Notably, Citigroup, a $1 trillion commercial bank whose deposits were insured by the Federal Deposit Insurance Corporation (FDIC), chose to expose itself to very significant CDO-based risk. As the FCIC points out, while its competitors did likewise, few were as aggressive in this regard, and few incurred the magnitude of losses that Citigroup did.

AIG

AIG is a major insurance firm, and because it took on very large risk associated with selling protection against mortgage defaults, the company required the largest government bailout when the financial crisis erupted. AIG failed to put a process in place to monitor the changing nature of the mortgage pools for which they sold protection. Rather than subprime mortgages comprising 10 percent of the pools on which they sold protection, the actual percentages were between 80 and 90 percent. That is like selling auto insurance to young drivers at the lower premiums normally charged to middle aged drivers. Moreover, the head of AIG's financial products division, Joseph Cassano, was regarded as having a crude feel for financial risk but a strong tendency to bully those who challenged him. When those within his group expressed concern about taking on more subprime mortgage risk, Cassano pointed to the triple-A ratings from Moody's and S&P, and dismissed their concerns as exaggeration.

Moody's and S&P

Moody's and S&P rate credit risks. In the lead-up to the global financial crisis, they engaged in a battle for market share by relaxing the criteria they used to rate the riskiness of mortgage-related products. The decision to relax these criteria met with some resistance within these firms. At S&P, the head of the Residential Mortgage Backed Securities group expressed his strong concern that a proposal for the rating firm to confer directly with investors, issuers, and investment bankers, if adopted, would lead to agency conflicts in which the firm would lose its independence. His concerns went unanswered, and those within the firm who fought the proposal were systematically excluded from meetings.

Lehman Brothers and Merrill Lynch

The bankruptcy of investment bank Lehman Brothers in September 2008 was the tipping point that converted an economic downturn into a full-fledged financial crisis and subsequent Great Recession. Lehman's bankruptcy stemmed from the decrease in value of its large holdings of mortgage-related securities, as a result of rising defaults associated with falling house prices and a weakening economy. Prior to the downturn, the decision to assume so much risk created an internal debate within Lehman about how aggressive it should be. On one side of the debate were the head of fixed income, Michael Gelband, and the firm's chief risk officer, Madelyn Antoncic. Both warned Lehman's senior management, especially CEO Richard Fuld, against the firm taking on excessive risk in order to compete aggressively against other investment banks. As a result of the conflict, Antoncic was reassigned within the firm, and Gelband left due to what the bank called "philosophical differences."

During the time housing prices were in a bubble, Lehman Brothers was very profitable, indeed more profitable than most of its competitors, such as Merrill Lynch. Merrill Lynch's CEO Stanley O'Neal set for himself the aspiration of beating Lehman, and Goldman-Sachs as well. To do so, he had his firm invest heavily in all mortgage-related activities, from origination, to bundling mortgages into mortgage backed securities, to manufacturing CDOs, to selling mortgage-related products to investors. This was a very high-risk strategy. As was the case at Lehman, instead of increasing resources in risk management to address the higher risk, Merrill actually reduced its risk management activities. Moreover, O'Neal did not tolerate dissent, and took offense easily. As a result, his executives were fearful if they needed to deliver bad news to him. He rarely asked for input when making a decision, and he did not tolerate being challenged once he had made his decision.

UBS

The Swiss-based bank UBS is one of the most interesting cases because the firm engaged in a self-study of what went wrong, which they posted on their web site. As with

Merrill Lynch, UBS was focused on closing the competitive gap between its own position and the position of the market leader. To assist in this effort, it engaged the consulting firm Oliver Wyman, which suggested that UBS develop a strategy involving fixed-income securities related to U.S. subprime residential mortgages. Notably, members of UBS's investment banking division were so focused on their goal that they did not assess the risk. They failed to assess the quality of the underlying assets for the securities they held—but not only that. The bank's CDO business substantially added to its subprime positions, even in the face of an internally generated outlook for that market, which was pessimistic. The self-study report notes that the investment bank's senior management did not sufficiently challenge each other in relation to the development of their various businesses; and it criticizes analysts for a lack of clarity when presenting complex data. As for compensation, the report criticizes the bank's undue focus on short-term profitability, as well as the absence of risk adjustments when judging performance.

Compensation, the last item mentioned, is the theme of Chapter 9, which described psychological phenomena associated with problematic incentive schemes. In this regard, some commentators have noted that there were virtually no prosecutions of individuals for behavior related to the global financial crisis, pointing to problems in the criminal justice system that focus on corporations rather than individual decision makers within those corporations.[11]

Summary

Financial management combines corporate finance and management, focusing on how people work together in groups to make financial judgments and decisions. Examples of corporate financial judgments are risk assessment and valuation. Examples of corporate decisions are budgeting, merger and acquisition activity, capital structure, and bonus plans. Corporate processes, and more broadly corporate culture, define the environment in which these judgments and decisions are made. Financial management is not just a piecemeal collection of skills for making judgments and decisions about the individual elements that constitute corporate finance. Financial management is an integrated approach that focuses on the human elements underlying these group processes. Identifying process loss and lessons for how to mitigate it lie at the heart of how lessons from behavioral corporate finance can increase value.

In theory, group process adds synergistic value to the efforts of the individual group participants. In practice, three factors lead this synergy to be less than maximal, and sometimes negative. First, although synergy is positive for tasks that are intellectual, it is typically negative for tasks that are judgmental. Second, group process often leads to polarization in respect to risk attitude. Third, group discussion typically leads its members to feel more effective than warranted, a form of group overconfidence known as the illusion of effectiveness.

There are three main reasons why judgmental tasks feature negative group synergy: groupthink, poor information sharing, and inadequate motivation. Ineffective group processes plagued many of the financial firms whose activities were at the heart of the global financial crisis. Instituting effective group processes is not easy and requires continual investment on the part of the firm. Effective group processes within firms feature an integrated approach to strategic and financial planning, goal setting, compensation, and monitoring. Effective processes distinguish firms with strong corporate cultures from those with weak corporate cultures; or to put it another way, superior financial management from inferior financial management.

Additional Behavioral Readings

Russo, E. and P. Schoemaker, *Winning Decisions: Getting It Right the First Time,* New York: Doubleday, 2002.

Stack, J. and B. Burlingham, *The Great Game of Business: The Only Sensible Way to Run a Company.* New York: Crown Business, 1992, 2013.

Surowiecki, J., *The Wisdom of Crowds: Why the Many Are Smarter Than the Few and How Collective Wisdom Shapes Business, Economies, Societies and Nations.* New York: Doubleday, 2004.

Whyte, G., "Escalating Commitment in Individuals and Group Decision Making: A Prospect Theory Approach," *Organizational Behavior and Human Decision Processes,* vol. 54, 1993, pp. 430–455.

Zak, P., *The Moral Molecule: The Source of Love and Prosperity.* New York: Dutton, 2012.

Key Terms

accuracy, *259*
corporate culture, *258*
groupthink, *259*
illusion of effectiveness, *259*
polarization, *259*
poor information sharing, *260*
social loafing, *262*
unwarranted acceptance, *259*

Explore the Web

fcic.law.stanford.edu/report
The web site for the findings of the Financial Crisis Inquiry Commission.

www.toshiba.com/tai
The web site for Toshiba, which is the subject of the Chapter 11 minicase.

Chapter Questions

1. In May 2002, Hewlett-Packard acquired Compaq Computer in a takeover that featured considerable drama. In deliberating the acquisition, HP director Walter Hewlett, son of founder William Hewlett, suggested that the decision was not the right choice. He was concerned that the gap between the corporate cultures of the two firms was too wide to bridge, and he was troubled by the heightened focus on the PC business, a highly competitive business where HP was not a low-cost leader. Hewlett opined that doubling down on PCs with Compaq would divert resources from HP's enterprise business, thereby hurting the firm's ability to compete with IBM and Dell. He argued instead that HP should essentially become a printer firm, focusing on its strongest business. Nevertheless, Walter Hewlett reluctantly voted for the acquisition of Compaq as a member of the HP board. However, as chairman of the William and Flora Hewlett Foundation, he actively opposed the merger during a subsequent proxy battle. When Walter Hewlett's term on the board of HP expired in 2002, he was not invited to rejoin. Discuss these events in light of the concepts described in the chapter.

www.mhhe.com/shefrin2e

2. In 2001 the chief executive of AOL Time Warner, Gerald Levin, sought to acquire AT&T's cable business, the only cable business larger than the one already owned by AOL Time Warner. In doing so, he did not consult the firm's board, let alone its chairman Steve Case. Apparently, Case objected to Levin's approach, and Levin resigned in December 2001. Discuss Levin's approach to decision process in the context of judgmental tasks involving groups.
3. What are the main psychological challenges that Ford CEO Alan Mulally faced in respect to Ford's regular Thursday managers' meetings, and how do these relate to issues of process and culture at the firm?
4. In respect to the experiences of financial firms in the lead-up to the global financial crisis, for each firm identify the most important psychological phenomena that destroyed value, and wherever possible link these phenomena to specific processes.
5. The financial instability hypothesis holds that firms take on excessive debt during periods of euphoria. Discuss the behavioral basis for this perspective, drawing if necessary from discussions in previous chapters.
6. Problem 7 in Chapter 9 pertains to Volkswagen's having installed "defeat devices." In describing the issue, media reports pointed to Volkswagen's corporate culture, which according to the New York State Attorney General's Office "incentivizes cheating and denies accountability comes from the very top." The Attorney General's Office notes that the firm's conduct "reflects a corporate culture that had no regard for the law, no respect for the American people and no regard for the environment or peoples' health." Using the ideas developed in this chapter, analyze the characterization of Volkswagen's culture, which the *New York Times* described as "confident, cutthroat, and insular."[12]

Additional Resources and Materials for Chapter 11 Are Available at www.mhhe.com/shefrin2e

Minicase

Toshiba

The global financial crisis adversely impacted a great many firms. One example is the Japanese conglomerate Toshiba. Toshiba is over 140 years old, and consists of many different businesses and divisions whose products include refrigerators, nuclear power plants, electric power lines, iPhone parts, personal computers, and hard drives. Over the years Toshiba came to be well regarded for the quality of its products and the quality of its corporate governance. As with many Japanese firms, it was also respected for its social values, wherein it chose not to terminate losing projects in order to preserve jobs for some of its workforce.

Beginning in 2008, two shocks negatively impacted Toshiba's business. The first was the economic downturn associated with the global financial crisis, and the second was the combination of an earthquake, tsunami, and nuclear disaster that occurred in 2011. Nevertheless, the firm managed to report respectable earnings in the wake of these shocks.

In 2014, Japanese Prime Minister Shinzo Abe initiated policies to attract more foreign investors to Japan, in an attempt to stimulate the country's economy. One of his key provisions involved changes in corporate governance, such as requiring publicly traded companies in

Japan to have at least two outside independent directors on its board. Toshiba met or surpassed most of these policies by, for example, having four outside directors on its 16-person board.[13]

In April 2015, an investigation by financial regulators found accounting inaccuracies at Toshiba. Initially these were thought to involve tens of millions of dollars of bookkeeping discrepancies, but isolated to a single division. Toshiba then hired a committee of independent experts, who reported in July 2015 that the discrepancies were widespread across the company, and that Toshiba had overstated its earnings by $1.2 billion between 2008 and 2014. In particular, the company had understated costs on long-term projects and had misvalued some of its inventory. From the time the issue had surfaced in April, Toshiba's stock had fallen by 25 percent.

The independent experts' report pointed out that as demand for Toshiba's products fell, its CEOs had subjected subordinates to intense pressure in order to meet sales targets, with the pressure usually coming just before the end of a quarter or fiscal year.[14] The report suggested that this pressure induced employees to postpone losses or push forward sales, in an effort to increase operating earnings. Toshiba's then-CEO Hisao Tanaka resigned, deeply apologizing for "inappropriate accounting," which he said was unintentional. He also stated that the issue had created the "largest damage ever" to Toshiba's corporate image.[15]

The committee's report also singled out other senior executives for blame, saying that they found "systematic involvement" by top management among others, whose goal had been the intentional inflation of the firm's earnings, along with "a systematic cover-up." It also noted that Toshiba's corporate culture made it impossible to oppose "one's bosses' wishes."

More resignations followed, and included among others Tanaka's immediate predecessor Norio Sasaki, who served as the firm's vice-chair, and Sasaki's predecessor Atsutoshi Nishida, who held a nonexecutive position as senior adviser. All told, half of Toshiba's 16-member board resigned. The firm's chairman, Masashi Muromachi took over as interim President and CEO. Speaking at a news conference, Muromachi described the issue as the company having been "carried away" by a concern for the "quarter at hand." Notably, the firm assigned one of the independent directors to head the audit committee, which had previously been headed by an inside (interested) director.

Case Analysis Questions

1. What does the information presented in the minicase suggest about goal setting at Toshiba?
2. Discuss the issue of process loss in the events described in the minicase.
3. What are the major lessons to be learned from the minicase about corporate governance?

Chapter Twelve

Application of Real-Option Techniques to Capital Budgeting and Capital Structure

The main objective of this chapter is for students to demonstrate that they can identify the manner in which psychological phenomena impact managers' use of real-option techniques.

After completing this chapter students will be able to:

1. Explain why opaque framing causes managers to refrain from using real-option techniques.
2. Explain how excessive optimism affects the investment policies of managers who use real-option techniques.
3. Explain how overconfidence affects the investment policies of managers who use real-option techniques.
4. Explain why excessive optimism and overconfidence mitigate the impact of agency conflicts associated with debt overhang and asset substitution.
5. Describe how real-option techniques can mitigate managers' tendencies to throw good money after bad.

This chapter is available at www.mhhe.com/shefrin2e

Chapter Thirteen

Behavioral Aspects of Investments

The main objective of this chapter is for students to demonstrate that they can identify key psychological phenomena that impact decisions by investors.

After completing this chapter students will be able to:

1. Explain what investors who seek to exploit market inefficiencies need to understand in order to generate positive alpha.
2. Identify the manner in which psychological phenomena impact investors' judgments about the relationship between risk and return.
3. Describe how psychological phenomena impact investors' judgments and decisions about portfolio selection.
4. Articulate a series of nudges to help investors improve their judgments and choices about portfolio selection.

This chapter is available at www.mhhe.com/shefrin2e

Glossary

acceptance Group discussion tends to induce group members to accept a decision too readily.

accuracy Groups outperform individuals when it comes to intellectual tasks, but do worse than individuals when it comes to judgmental tasks.

affect Emotional feeling.

affect heuristic Basing decisions primarily on intuition, instinct, and gut feeling.

anchoring and adjustment People form an estimate by beginning with an initial number and adjusting to reflect new information or circumstances. However, they tend to make insufficient adjustments relative to that number, thereby leading to anchoring bias.

anomalies Empirical phenomena that appear to be puzzles with respect to the efficient market hypothesis.

availability People overweight information that is readily available and intuitive relative to information that is less salient and more abstract, thereby biasing judgments.

aversion to a sure loss People choose to accept an actuarially unfair risk in an attempt to avoid a sure loss.

base rate information Information pertaining to the general environment.

Bayes rule The relationship linking the probabilities of two events F and D expressed as $P(F|D = P(F) \times P(D|F)/P(D)$ where $P(F)$ is called the prior and $P(F|D)$ is called the posterior.

BPV, behavioral APV The inclusion of behavioral elements in the adjusted present value formula to reflect either mispricing or managerial biases.

behavioral life cycle hypothesis Over the course of their lives, people use mental accounts to cope with potential self-control problems that cause inadequate savings.

bias A predisposition toward error.

big five A psychological framework characterizing people's personalities on five traits.

casino effect Preference for the small probability of a large payoff.

capital gains overhang A variable measure of the magnitude of paper gains (unrealized capital gains), where a negative gain signifies a loss.

catering Choosing a dividend policy with the purpose of responding to investors' psychological needs, be those needs associated with preferences or with investor sentiment.

closed-end fund An investment company whose primary assets are financial assets, which can include stocks or bonds. Unlike an open-end fund which issues new shares in connection with cash inflows, and repurchases shares in response to cash outflows, the number of shares of a closed-end fund are fixed, the same as with an operating company.

confirmation bias People attach too much importance to information that supports positions which they are evaluating or views which they hold relative to information that runs counter to those positions or views.

conjunction fallacy Miscalculating the probability of an event that is defined as the conjunction or simultaneous occurrence of a series of separate events.

cortisol A steroid hormone generated during prolonged periods of stress.

debiasing A process for mitigating bias.

desirability One of the factors contributing to excessive optimism, commonly understood to be wishful thinking.

dilution cost The value that acquirers believe that the target's shareholders receive because the acquiring firm's stock is undervalued in the market.

endowment effect People attach a greater value to an object once they regard it as part of their endowment than before it becomes part of their endowment.

escalation of commitment The tendency to throw good money after bad.

excessive optimism People overestimate how frequently they will experience favorable outcomes and underestimate how frequently they will experience unfavorable outcomes.

extrapolation bias or hot-hand fallacy Unwarranted extrapolation of past trends in forming forecasts.

familiarity Essentially a form of availability bias, where available information is familiar information.

fourfold effect When probabilities of nonzero extreme outcomes are moderate, risk aversion in the domain of gains, and risk seeking in the domain of losses. When probabilities of extreme nonzero outcomes are small, risk seeking in the domain of gains, and risk aversion in the domain of losses.

frame Synonymous for description.

framing effect A person's decision is influenced by the manner in which the setting for the decision is described.

gamblers' fallacy The tendency to overweight the probability of an event because it has not recently occurred at a frequency that reflects its probability.

groupthink The drive for achieving group consensus overrides the realistic appraisal of alternative courses of action.

hedonic editing People prefer to experience gains separately rather than together, but integrate small losses into larger gains.

heuristic A rule of thumb used to make a decision.

hindsight bias The tendency to view events as obvious or almost certain in hindsight when they are neither obvious nor almost certain when viewed in foresight.

home bias The term used to describe the disproportionately high number of investments in securities that are "close to home."

hot issue market Demand for new issues is relatively high.

hubris hypothesis Firms experience the winner's curse in mergers and acquisitions because of hubris.

illusion of control People overestimate the extent to which they can control events.

illusion of effectiveness Unwarranted confidence in the decision.

incentive compatibility constraint The principal chooses the carrot-and-stick differential in terms of pay for performance so as to induce the agent to represent the interests of the principal.

initial underpricing The offer price is too low, resulting in a large first-day price pop.

inside view Taking a perspective on a project by focusing on the details specific to that particular project.

limits of arbitrage Smart investors do not fully exploit mispricing because of the attendant risks that the mispricing will become larger before it becomes smaller.

longholders Excessively optimistic, overconfident CEOs who hold their executive options into the final year.

long-term underperformance New issues earn lower returns than stocks with comparable characteristics against which they have been matched.

loss aversion Psychologically, people experience a loss more acutely than a gain of the same magnitude.

March-Shapira framework A model with two reference (focal) points, one low (survival) and one high (aspiration), with only one point operative at any one time, and risk appetite increasing with the absolute distance between the current situation and the reference point.

mental accounting Mentally separating information into manageable pieces, by maintaining separate accounts.

momentum Recent losers tend subsequently to underperform the market, and recent winners tend subsequently to outperform the market.

narrow framing Treating a risk in isolation.

net asset value (NAV) The intrinsic value of a closed-end fund, equal to the market value of its holdings.

nonoverpayment constraint The principal does not overpay the agent.

nudge A form of weak intervention for helping people avoid psychological pitfalls and make better choices.

1/*n* heuristic A simple rule of thumb that assigns equal weight to all choices under consideration.

opaque framing Describing a decision task in a manner that renders the consequences of the decision difficult to discern.

outside view Taking a perspective on a project by comparing the characteristics of a specific project with a large population of projects which are similar in nature.

overconfidence People know less than they think they know and view themselves as better than they actually are.

overreaction The percentage change in market price in response to an event is too large.

overweighting of small probabilities People tend to overweight low probabilities attached to extreme events.

participation constraint The principal offers attractive enough terms to the agent to induce the agent to participate.

P/E heuristic An approach to valuation based on multiplying a P/E ratio and an earnings forecast.

PEG heuristic An approach to valuation based on multiplying a PEG ratio, an earnings forecast, and a forecast of the growth rate.

polarization Group processes tend to accentuate attitudes toward risk.

poor information sharing Group members fail to share enough information with other group members.

post-earnings-announcement drift The stocks of firms that announce positive earnings surprises experience positive drift after the announcement, while the stocks of firms that announce negative earnings surprises experience negative drift after the announcement.

preference reversal Choosing low-value alternatives over high-value alternatives.

prefrontal cortex The front part of the human brain associated with higher order thinking and executive function.

press coverage overconfidence indicator The press uses the words *optimistic* and *confident* to describe an executive.

price-to-sales heuristic An approach to valuation based on multiplying a price-to-sales ratio and a sales forecast.

proportion of gains realized (PGR) The fraction of all capital gains sold on a particular day.

proportion of losses realized (PLR) The value of all the stock positions that were classified as capital losses sold on that day.

prospect theory A general psychological approach that describes the way people make choices among risky alternatives.

quasi-hedonic editing After a recent prior gain, people are more willing to take risks that will not jeopardize the recent gain, whereas after a recent prior loss, they become less willing to take a subsequent risk that would accentuate the recent loss.

reference class Past similar projects that are small enough in number to compare to the given project, but large enough to enable meaningful statistical analysis.

reference point Benchmark used to measure gains and losses.

regret An emotion that occurs when people imagine having taken a different decision than the one they actually took, one that would have turned out favorably rather than unfavorably.

representativeness People make judgments based on stereotypic thinking, asking how representative an object or idea is for the class to which it belongs.

self-attribution error The tendency for people to take credit for positive outcomes and to blame others or bad luck for negative outcomes.

self-control The act of exercising control over one's impulses, usually to delay gratification.

sensitivity of investment to cash flow Investment depends on how much cash a firm holds.

sentiment Aggregate investor error, usually considered as either excessive optimism or excessive pessimism.

singular information Unique information directly related to a situation or object.

social loafing Group members reduce their contributions, instead relying on others to exert the requisite effort.

status quo bias Inertia, reluctance to make changes from default positions.

sunk cost An expenditure made in the past that is irrevocable.

System 1 The fast, automatic, and intuitive processes associated with thinking.

System 2 The slow, deliberate, conscious processes associated with thinking.

testosterone A steroid hormone associated with risk taking, aggression, and sexuality.

transparent framing Describing a decision task in a manner that renders the consequences of the decision easy to discern.

underreaction The percentage change in market price in response to an event is too small.

visibility How noticeable a project or activity is to others.

willingness to pay How much a person or group is willing to pay to acquire something.

winner's curse The winning bid in an auction results in the winner overpaying.

winner–loser effect Extreme past losers tend subsequently to outperform the market, and extreme past winners tend subsequently to underperform the market, where by past is meant past three years, and by subsequent is meant subsequent five years.

Endnotes

Chapter 1

1. See N. Weinstein, "Unrealistic Optimism about Future Life Events," *Journal of Personality and Social Psychology* 39 (5), 1980, pp. 806–820.
2. People are not uniformly optimistic about all events. For unfavorable events, most people are exceptionally optimistic that they will not be fired from a job. They are less optimistic about gum disease.
3. Undergraduates tend to be more optimistic about unfavorable events than MBA students.
4. For the being fired question, the standard deviations for within-class responses typically lie in the range 2.1 to 3.7, indicating the degree of interpersonal differences. The magnitudes of standard deviation for the other three questions were generally in line with the being fired question.
5. For a discussion about dispositional optimism see M. F., Scheier, C. S., Carver, and M. W. Bridges, "Distinguishing Optimism from Neuroticism (and Trait Anxiety, Self-mastery, and Self-esteem): A Re-evaluation of the Life Orientation Test," *Journal of Personality and Social Psychology*, 67, 1994, pp. 1063–1078. On a scale of 0 to 100, for the general population, the score for dispositional optimism lies in the range 59.7 to 63.1. Additional results, reported below, are based on H. Shefrin, *Behavioral Risk Management*, New York: Palgrave MacMillan, 2016. The mean dispositional optimism score for the 222 undergraduate finance majors mentioned above was 62.7. In respect to excessive optimism, the undergraduate finance majors' mean response for favorable events was 7.7 and for unfavorable events was 6.0. The correlation between their dispositional optimism scores and the favorable unfavorable differential measuring excessive optimism was 0.29. In this regard, mean dispositional optimism for individual students whose responses were above 7 for favorable events and below 7 for unfavorable events, was 65.2. In contrast for students whose responses for unfavorable events were not lower than for favorable events, mean dispositional optimism was 60.3. For the investment professionals mentioned in the body of the text, the mean dispositional optimism score was 70.5, well above the top end of the range for the general population. Professionals' mean response for favorable events was 7.2 and for unfavorable events was 6.2. In this regard, mean dispositional optimism for professionals whose responses were above 7 for favorable events and below 7 for unfavorable events, was 70.5. For these professionals, those whose responses for unfavorable events was not lower than for favorable events, mean dispositional optimism was 68.2. The intergroup difference is similar to the intergroup difference for undergraduates, except for lack of statistical significance: The correlation between dispositional optimism and excessive optimism, in a sample size of 146, was close to zero.
6. See M. Puri and D. Robinson, "Optimism and Economic Choice," *Journal of Financial Economics,* vol. 86, no. 1, 2007, pp. 71–99.
7. See S. Oskamp, "Overconfidence in Case-Study Judgments," *Journal of Consulting Psychology* 29 (3), 1965, pp. 261–265.
8. The trivia test is adapted from J. E. Russo and P. Schoemaker, *Decision Traps.* New York: Simon and Schuster, 1989.
9. Interestingly, people are not equally overconfident across all questions. For example, the hit rate for the Boeing 747 question is almost always considerably lower than the hit rate for the OPEC question or the Mozart question. A typical hit rate for the Boeing question is around 10 percent, while for the Mozart question it is 50 percent or more. There is variation across groups. The Boeing question hit rate might be as high as 25 percent. The Mozart question might be as high as 75 percent.
10. See P. Wason, "Reasoning," in *New Horizons in Psychology,* ed. B. Foss (Harmondsworth: Penguin Books), 1966, pp. 135–151. Confirmation bias pertains to positions that people are evaluating or to views that they hold. Technically, confirmation bias refers to positions people are examining, and "motivated reasoning" applies to views that they hold. See sammcnerney, "Psychology's Treacherous Trio: Confirmation Bias, Cognitive Dissonance, and Motivated Reasoning," September 7, 2011, https://whywereason.com/2011/09/07/psychologys-treacherous-trio-confirmation-bias-cognitive-dissonance-and-motivated-reasoning/.
11. There is an interesting exception to the general conclusion. See L. Cosmides and J. Tooby, "Cognitive Adaptations for Social Exchange." In J. Bankow, L. Cosmides, and J. Tooby (eds.), *The Adequate Mind: Evolutionary Psychology and the Generation of Culture.* New York: Oxford, 1992.

12. See E. Langer, "The Illusion of Control," *Journal of Personality and Social Psychology* 32 (2), 1975, pp. 311–328.

13. See A. Tversky and D. Kahneman, "Judgment Under Uncertainty: Heuristics and Biases," *Science,* New Series, 185 (4157), 1974, pp. 1124–1131. A. Tversky and D. Kahneman, "Availability: A Heuristic for Judging Frequency and Probability," *Cognitive Psychology* 5, 1973, pp. 207–232. The latter article discusses three specific psychological phenomena: representativeness, availability, and anchoring and adjustment.

14. Typically more than 60 percent answer this way. However, there can be wide variation, and it is not rare for 100 percent of a class to think it more likely that Linda is a feminist bank teller than a bank teller.

15. The material for the discussion in this subsection is based on P. Slovic, E. Peters, M. Finucane, and D. MacGregor, "Affect, Risk, and Decision Making," *Health Psychology*, Vol. 24, No. 4(Suppl.), 2005, pp. S35–S40.

16. See D. Kahneman and A. Tversky, "Prospect Theory: An Analysis of Decision Making under Risk," *Econometrica,* 5(2), 1979, 263–291; A. Tversky and D. Kahneman (1992), "Advances in Prospect Theory: Cumulative Representation of Uncertainty," *Journal of Risk and Uncertainty* 5, 1992, pp. 297–323.

17. See L. Lopes, "Between Hope and Fear: The Psychology of Risk," *Advances in Experimental Social Psychology* 20, 1987, pp. 255–295.

18. See J. March and Z. Shapira, "Managerial Perspectives on Risk and Risk Taking," *Psychological Review* 99, 1992, pp. 172–183.

19. See R. Thaler and C. Sunstein, 2008. *Nudge: Improving Decisions About Health, Wealth, and Happiness*, New Haven: Yale University Press. Six specific principles underlie the nudge approach, which can be described using the acronym NUDGES. Listed below are the six principles, with bolded upper case letters used to identify the letters of the acronym. (1) Identify how i**N**centives influence choice; (2) **U**nderstand the conditions which foster or impede effective decision making; (3) take into account the degree to which people become anchored to **D**efault positions; (4) **G**ive people feedback about the consequences of their decisions; (5) **E**xpect people to make mistakes; and (6) **S**tructure complex choices by careful attention to framing.

20. See B. Knutson, E. Wimmer, C. Kuhnen and P. Winkielman, "Nucleus Accumbens Activation Mediates the Influence of Reward Cues on Financial Risk Taking," *NeuroReport* 19(5), 2008, pp. 509–513.

21. See J. Coates, *The Hour Between Dog and Wolf: How Risk Taking Transforms Us, Body, and Mind*, New York: Penguin, 2012.

22. See A. Cuddy, C. Wilmuth, A. Yap, and D. Carney, "Preparatory Power Posing Affects Nonverbal Presence and Job Interview Performance," *Journal of Applied Psychology*, Vol 100(4), 2015, pp. 1286–1295. There is some controversy about the findings in this paper, but not about winners displaying power poses. See T. Harford, "The Dubious Power of Power Poses," *The Financial Times*, June 10, 2016, https://next.ft.com/content/9adf11ca-2dcb-11e6-a18d-a96ab29e3c95.

23. See W. Mischel, *The Marshmallow Test: Mastering Self-Control*, New York: Little, Brown and Company, 2014.

24. See T. Hare, C. Camerer, and A. Rangel, "Self-Control in Decision-Making Involves Modulation of the vmPFC Valuation System," *Science* May 1; 324(5927), 2009, pp. 646–648.

25. The correct answers are: 1. 250,000 pounds; 2. 1513; 3. 191; 4. 10,543. 5. 2.6; 6. 8.3 million; 7. 18 million; 8. 4,000; 9. 1,044; 10. 9.5 million.

26. See W. Bogdanich, J. Williams, and A. Graciela Mendez, "The New Panama Canal: A Risky Bet," *New York Times,* June 22, 2016, http://www.nytimes.com/interactive/2016/06/22/world/ameri-cas/ panama-canal.html?hp&action=click&pgtype=Homepage &clickSource=story-heading&module=first-column-region&region=top-news&WT.nav=top-news.

27. See J. Kasperkevic, "Panama Canal Reopens with Hopes for Trade Boost as 'Center of the Americas,'" *The Guardian,* June 27, 2016, https://www.theguardian.com/world/2016/jun/27/panama-canal-expansion-reopens-trade.

28. Interview with Robert Dunham, June 27–28, 2016, who served as a consultant on the project.

29. See G. Ellison, "Soo Locks Breakdown Would Plunge America into Recession, Cost 11M Jobs," *MLive Media Group,* March 4, 2016, http://www.mlive.com/news/index.ssf/2016/03/soo_locks_breakdown_would_plun.html.

Chapter 2

1. See J. Graham, C. Harvey, and M. Puri, "Managerial Attitudes and Corporate Action," *Journal of Financial Economics* 109, 2013, pp. 103–121.

2. See M. Puri and D. Robinson, "Optimism and Economic Choice,"*Journal of Financial Economics,* vol. 86, no. 1, 2007, pp. 71–99.

3. See J. Siegel, "Big Cap Tech Stocks Are a Sucker Bet," *The Wall Street Journal,* March 14, 2000; "Not-Quite-So-Big-Cap Tech Stocks Are Still a Bad Bet," *The Wall Street Journal,* March 19, 2001.

4. See S. Gervais and T. Odean, "Learning to Be Overconfident," *Review of Financial Studi*es vol. 14, 2001, pp. 1–27.

5. See "Bank of America Roundtable On: The Real Options Approach to Creating Value in the New Economy," *Journal of Applied Corporate Finance,* vol. 13, no. 2, 2000, pp. 45–63.
6. "Why Sun Microsystems Failed," *CNN Money,* 2:04, May 27, 2011, http://money.cnn.com/video/technology/2011/02/28/ctd_mcnealy_sun_oracle.fortune/.
7. See A. Wilde Mathews and B. Martinez, "E-Mails Suggest Early Vioxx Worries—As Evidence of Heart Risk Rose, Merck Officials Played Hardball; One Internal Message: 'Dodge!'" *The Wall Street Journal,* November 2, 2004.
8. "MIT Sloan Alumna Judy Lewent on the Future of Finance," January 9, 2012, http://mitsloanexperts.mit.edu/mitsloan-alumna-judy-lewent-on-the-future-of-finance/.
9. "Merck's Judy Lewent: Once Again, 'Talking About the Future'," November 1, 2006, http://knowledge.wharton.upenn.edu/article/mercks-judy-lewent-once-again-talking-about-the-future/.
10. J. Graham, "How Big Are the Tax Benefits of Debt?" *Journal of Finance* 55, 2000, pp. 1901–1941.
11. R. Brealey, S. Myers, and F. Allen, *Principles of Corporate Finance*, 10th ed. (Burr Ridge: McGraw-Hill Irwin, 2011), 444.
12. Ibid., 459.
13. See B. Fischhoff, "Debiasing." In D. Kahneman, P. Slovic, and A. Tversky (eds.), *Judgment Under Uncertainty: Heuristics and Biases.* Cambridge, MA: Cambridge University Press, 1982.
14. See M. Puri and D. Robinson, "The Economic Psychology of Entrepreneurship and Family Business," *Journal of Economics and Management Strategy* 22, no. 2, 2013, pp. 423–444.
15. B. Oskin, "Japan Earthquake & Tsunami of 2011: Facts and Information," *LiveScience*, May 7, 2015, http://www.livescience.com/39110-japan-2011-earthquake-tsunami-facts.html.
16. See J. Makinen, "4 Years after Fukushima, Japan Considers Restarting Nuclear Facilities," *Los Angeles Times*, March 30, 2015.
17. World Nuclear Association, "Fukushima Accident," last updated October 2015, http://www.worldnuclear.org/info/safety-and-security/safety-of-plants/fukushima-accident/.
18. World Nuclear Association, "Safety of Nuclear Power Reactors," last updated February 2015, http://www.worldnuclear.org/info/Safety-and-Security/Safety-of-Plants/Safety-of-Nuclear-Power-Reactors/.
19. J. Acton and M. Hibbs, "Why Fukushima Was Preventable," *The Carnegie Papers,* March 6, 2012, http://carnegieendowment.org/2012/03/06/why-fukushima-was-preventable.
20. M. Fackler, "Japan's 'Hail Mary' at Fukushima Daiichi: An Underground Ice Wall," *The New York Times,* August 29, 2016, http://www.nytimes.com/2016/08/30/science/fukushima-daiichi-nuclear-plant-cleanup-ice-wall.html?hp&action=click&pgtype=Homepage&clickSource=story-heading&module=second-column-region&region=top-news&WT.nav=top-news
21. In Excel, the binomial distribution function for making this computation is BINOM.DIST. Further information about BINOM.DIST is available by using Excel's help menu, by clicking the circled question mark (?) in the top right corner of the screen.

Chapter 3

1. Brealey-Myers-Allen, Ibid., use present value of growth opportunities (PVGO), and Ross-Westerfield-Jaffe (*Corporate Finance,* 10-th edition, Burr Ridge: McGraw-Hill Education, 2012) use net present value of growth opportunities (NPVGO).
2. See F. C. Evans, "Valuation Essentials for CFOs," *Financial Executive,* March/April 2002.
3. See P. Dechow and H. You, "Understanding and Predicting Target Price Valuation Errors," Working paper: University of California, Berkeley, 2014. This paper also provides evidence about agency issues discussed in section 3.8.
4. See P. Asquith, M. Mikhail, and A. Au, "Information Content of Equity Analyst Reports," Working Paper, Sloan School of Management, Massachussetts Institute of Technology, 2004.
5. See M. A. Ostrom, "Net Stocks Enjoying a Revival," *San Jose Mercury News,* May 3, 2003.
6. This was a joint chapter meeting of the Santa Clara Valley chapter and the San Francisco chapter.
7. Mark Rubash was the vice president, finance and investor relations and the chief accounting officer for eBay Inc. He discussed these issues with an executive MBA class at Santa Clara University on May 9, 2003.
8. The report is available at the McGraw-Hill web site **www.mhhe.com/shefrin2e.**
9. See the note at the bottom of Exhibit 3-3, explaining the rationale for how the Morgan Stanley team developed the discount rate they used in their analysis.
10. The Morgan Stanley team used 330,259,000 shares outstanding, and adjusted the present value of the free cash flows by debt and cash holdings.
11. See http://data.worldbank.org/indicator/NY.GDP.DEFL.KD.ZG?page=2.
12. "eBay Inc at Citi Global Technology Conference," 2014. CQ FD Disclosure, *FNDW*, September 4, 2014.
13. The authors of the report are M. Rowen, A. Landwehr, and A. Wickland.

14. See Pablo Fernandez, "CAPM: An Absurd Model," http://ssrn.com/abstract=2505597.
15. Recall Rajiv Dutta's comparison of eBay and Wal-Mart. For the record, Wal-Mart closed 2004 at $52.79, almost exactly where it had been on April 1, 2003.
16. The authors of the report are W. Hood and M. Laing.
17. Wingfield reports that he also sought to interview Mary Meeker, but she did not respond to his request.
18. The source material for this question comes from: Morgan Stanley report on eBay, April 22, 2010, by Mary Meeker, Scott Devitt, Collis Boyce, and Colter Van Domelen. "CQ1: Turnaround on a Track." Morgan Stanley report on eBay, October 17, 2013, by Scott Devitt, Stephen Shin, and Nishant Verma. "Guidance Disappoints."
19. See Morgan Stanley report on eBay, July 23, 2015, by Brian Nowak, Michael Costantini, and Owen Hyde, entitled "Wanted: More Buyers and Buybacks; Initiate at EW, $29 PT."
20. Material, including quotations are taken from M. Warner, "Aetna 2nd-Quarter Net Up 17% on Membership; Raises Year View," *Dow Jones Global News Select*, July 30, 2013.
21. D. Einhorn, 2013, "UPDATE: Citigroup Raises PT on Aetna Following 2Q13 EPS Analysis," *Benzinga.com,* July 31.

Chapter 4

1. An early seminal article that focused on the application of behavioral finance to capital budgeting, and describes some of the survey data discussed in this section, is M. Statman and D. Caldwell, "Applying Behavioral Finance to Capital Budgeting: Project Termination," *Financial Management,* Winter, 2007, pp. 7–15.
2. See A. Marshall and W. Meckling, "Predictability of the Costs, Time, and Success of Development," that appeared in the National Bureau of Economic Research *The Rate and Direction of Investive Activity: Economic and Social Factors,* Princeton, NJ: Princeton University Press, 1962.
3. See B. Flyvbjerg, M. Skamris Holm, and S. Buhl, "Underestimating Costs in Public Works Projects: Error or Lie?" *Journal of the American Planning Association,* Summer, 2002, pp. 279–295. The transportation infrastructure projects are as prone to cost underestimation as other types of large projects.
4. See D. Axson, "It Doesn't Have to Be Spend and Hope," *Financial Executive,* September/October, 1996, pp. 18–24.
5. For projects requiring small technological advances, the ratio was 1.82.
6. See chapter 5 of E. Mansfield, J. Rapoport, J. Schnee, S. Wagner, and M. Hamburger, *Research and Innovation in the Modern Corporation.* New York: Norton, 1985.
7. See B. W. MacKenzie, "Looking for the Improbable Needle in a Haystack: The Economics of Base Metal Exploration in Canada," *CIM Bulletin,* vol. 74, no. 829, pp. 115–123, 1981. See also W. E. Roscoe, "Probability of an Economic Discovery in Canada," *CIM Bulletin,* vol. 64, 1971, pp. 134–137.
8. See E. Mansfield and R. Brandenburg, "The Allocation, Characteristics, and Outcome of the Firm's Research and Development Portfolio: a Case Study," *Journal of Business,* 1966, pp. 447–464.
9. See D. S. Tull, "The Relationship of Actual and Predicted Sales and Profits in New-Product Introductions," *Journal of Business,* 1967, pp. 233–250. Tull studied 24 firms and found that actual sales fell short of predicted sales in 66 percent of new products.
10. See E. Mansfield, J. Rapoport, J. Schnee, S. Wagner, and M. Hamburger, *Research and Innovation in the Modern Corporation.* New York: Norton, 1985.
11. See P. Hall, *Great Planning Disasters.* Berkeley, California: University of California Press, 1980.
12. J. Wild, "Channel Tunnel's 20th Birthday Holds Lesson on Big Projects," *The Financial Times*, May 5, 2014 http://www.ft.com/intl/cms/s/0/ba54bd0c-d468-11e3-a122-00144feabdc0.html#axzz3xcD9aeuU

    The Economist, "Eurotunnel, The Next 20 Years: A Bad Project Comes Good—With Better Yet in Store," May 10, 2014, http://www.economist.com/news/business/21601882-bad-project-comes-goodwith-better-yet-storenext-20-years?zid=303&ah=27090cf03414b8c5065d64ed0dad813d
13. "Why Do So Many Projects Still Miss Deadlines and Bust Budgets?" *Computing,* October 13, 1988.
14. These data are described in the Standish Research Paper, Chaos Study. See **www.standishgroup.com.** The data are also discussed in a web site article, January 5, 2003, by J. Suzuki entitled "Why Do Software Development Projects Fail So Often?" See **members.cox.net/johnsuzuki/softfail.htm.**
15. Similar findings can also be found in an August 2007study by Dynamic Markets, which surveyed 800 information technology managers from eight countries, and found the following:
    - 62 percent of projects ran over on time.
    - 49 percent of projects ran over on budget.

- 47 percent of projects experienced higher than expected maintenance costs.
- 28 percent of organizations experienced projects that did not fit requirements.
- 25 percent of organizations found that business users were reluctant to adopt new systems.
- 16 percent of organizations reported negative effects of projects on existing systems.
- 13 percent of organizations stated that projects did not deliver expected ROI.

See Dynamic Markets, "IT Projects: Experience Certainty," Independent Market Research Report commissioned by Tata Consultancy services.

16. There are critiques of the findings reported by the Standish Group, suggesting that in view of agency cost issues associated with their consulting activities, the data they present are exaggerated and self-serving. See J. L. Eveleens and C. Verhoef, 2010. "The Rise and Fall of the Chaos Report Figures," *IEEE Software*, January/February, 30-36. http://www.cs.vu.nl/~x/the_rise_and_fall_of_the_chaos_report_figures.pdf. Also see S. Ambler, 2014. "The Non-Existent Software Crisis: Debunking the Chaos Report," February 4. http://www.drdobbs.com/architecture-and-design/the-non-existent-software-crisis-debunki/240165910.
17. See A. Snow and M. Keil, "A Framework for Assessing the Reliability of Software Project Status Reports," *Engineering Management Journal*, vol. 14, no. 2, 2002, pp. 20–26.
18. Exhibit 4-1 updates data taken from the Standish company reports, originally reported in endnote 14. The information updating Exhibit 4-1 and also underlying Exhibit 4-2 is taken from the following web site: http://www.infoq.com/articles/standish-chaos-2015, which is the link to an article entitled "Standish Group 2015 Chaos Report - Q&A with Jennifer Lynch" that was posted by Shane Hastie and Stéphane Wojewoda on October 4, 2015.
19. These failures are documented in R. Glass, *Software Runaway: Lessons Learned from Massive Software Project Failures.* Upper Saddle, NJ: Prentice-Hall, 1998.
20. See K. Cortés, R. Duchin, and D. Sosyura, "Clouded Judgment: The Role of Sentiment in Credit Origination," *Journal of Financial Economics,* forthcoming. The authors report that the approval rate for credit applications increases by 52 basis points (or 0.80 percent) on perfectly sunny days and drops by 113 basis points (or 1.41percent) on overcast days. In addition, a one standard deviation reduction in the deseasoned cloud cover on the day of the loan approval is associated with a 2.7 percent higher loan default rate, controlling for observable loan characteristics.
21. D. Hirshleifer, A. Low, and S. H. Teoh, "Are Overconfident CEOs Better Innovators?" *Journal of Finance,* 67(4), 2012, pp. 1457–98.
22. See H. Wolinsky, "Iridium Failure Brought Motorola Back Down to Earth," *Chicago Sun-Times,* September 25, 2003.
23. See J. Graham, C. Harvey, and M. Puri, "Managerial Attitudes and Corporate *Actions," Journal of Financial Economics* 109, 2013, pp. 103–121.
24. A. Goel and A. Thakor, "Overconfidence, Leadership Selection, and Corporate Governance, *Journal of Finance* 63, 2008, pp. 2737–2784.
25. See I. Ben-David, J. Graham, and C. Harvey, "Managerial Miscalibration," *Quarterly Journal of Economics* 128(4), 2013, pp. 1547–1584.
26. See Ben-David et al., 2013, cited earlier.
27. See J. Flynn, P. Slovic, and C. K. Mertz, "Gender, Race, and the Perception of Environmental Health Risks," *Risk Analysis,* vol. 14, no. 6, 1994, pp. 1101–1198.
28. See "Protecting Value Study: Has the World of Risk Really Changed?" Factory Mutual Insurance Company and Financial Executives Research Foundation, 2003.
29. Much of the evidence presented in this chapter is taken from survey data. The major surveys used are as follows:

Group Surveyed	Survey Conducted by	Issues Surveyed
1. Financial executives	L. Gitman and P. Vandenberg	Use of capital budgeting evaluation techniques
2. Financial executives belonging to FEI	FEI/Duke University	Use of capital budgeting evaluation techniques
3. Financial executives and risk managers	Financial Executives Research Foundation, FM Global, and National Association of Corporate Treasurers	Sources of risk to earnings
4. Software project managers	Standish Group	Budgets, schedules, and features in software projects

30. See J. Graham and C. Harvey, "The Theory and Practice of Corporate Finance: Evidence from the Field," *Journal of Financial Economics,* vol. 60, nos. 2–3, 2001, pp. 187–243. Of 4,400 firms, CFOs from 392 responded. Question responses were on a scale from 0 (not important) to 4 (very important). From the third quarter of 1996 through the second quarter of 2004, the group at Duke University that conducted the surveys, led by John Graham, partnered with FEI. The surveys in the third and fourth quarters of 2004 were conducted solely by Duke University surveys, using mailing lists based on email addresses of previous survey respondents, as well as purchased email lists. From the first quarter of 2005, the Duke group partnered with *CFO Magazine.*
31. See L. Gitman and P. Vandenberg, "Cost of Capital Techniques Used by Major US Firms: 1997 *vs.* 1980," *Financial Practice and Education,* vol. 10, no. 2, 2000, pp. 53–68.
32. See also R. F. Bruner, K. M. Eades, R. S. Harris, and R. C. Higgins, "Best Practices in Estimating the Cost of Capital: Survey and Synthesis," *Financial Practice and Education,* vol. 8, no. 21, 1998, pp. 13–28.
33. Because 75 percent of CFOs report using IRR and 75 percent using NPV, some managers must use both NPV and IRR.
34. There is a modified version of the payback method that uses discounted cash flows. However, Graham and Harvey report that few use it.
35. G. Gigerenzer, *Gut Feelings: The Intelligence of the Unconscious,* 2007, Penguin Group, New York. See also S. Mousavi, G. Gigerenzer and V. Smith, "On Ecological Rationality and Heuristics," in R. Frantz, S. Chen, K. Dopfer, and S. Mousavi (Eds.) *Routledge Handbook of Behavioral Economics.* Taylor & Francis, forthcoming. J. Graham, C. Harvey, and M. Puri, "Capital Allocation and Delegation of Decision-Making Authority with*in Firms," Journal of Financial* Economics 115, 2015, pp. 449–470.
36. See A. Tversky and R. H. Thaler, "Anomalies: Preference Reversals," *Journal of Economic Perspectives,* 4, 1990, pp. 201–11.
37. B. Flyvbjerg, Ph.D. & D. Techn. "From Nobel Prize to Project Management: Getting Risks Right," *Project Management Journal,* vol. 37, no. 3, 2006, pp. 5–15. http://flyvbjerg.plan.aau.dk/Publications2006/Nobel-PMJ2006.pdf
38. Nevertheless, the 73 percent is a significant improvement over the 44 percent figure that prevailed in 1980.
39. These findings are reported in Y. Cai and H. Shefrin, "Acquisition Risk and Psychology," Working paper, Santa Clara University, 2016. The paper discusses a sample of 87,518 firm-year observations from 1990 to 2010.
40. See L. May, "Sunk Costs Are Not So Fully Drowned after All," *Australian Financ*ial *Review,* July 8, 1988; B. Staw, "Knee-Deep in the Big Muddy: A Study of Escalating Commitment toward a Chosen Course of Action," *Organizational Behavior and Human Performance,* vol. 20, 1976, pp. 27–44.
41. See C. Frydman and C. Camerer, "Neural Evidence of Regret and Its Implications for Investor Behavior," Working paper: USC Marshall School of Business and Caltech, 2016. The paper reports that regret signals are stronger for young subjects, but are absent in healthy older subjects.
42. J. Nathan traces the history of Sony Corporation in his book *Sony: The Private Life.* Boston: Houghton Mifflin Company, 1999.
43. Quoted in "Has Syntex Run Out of Steam? Wall Street Is Impatient with Sluggish Sales and Few New Products," *Businessweek,* July 12, 1993, pp. 144–146.
44. See D. Yermack, "Flights of Fancy: Corporate Jets, CEO Perquisites, and Inferior Shareholder Returns," *Journal of Financial Economics* 80(1), 2006, pp. 211–242.
45. See D. Lovallo and D. Kahneman, "Delusions of Success," *Harvard Business Review,* July 2003, pp. 56–60.
46. See G. Reynolds, "Risk Management in a Resource Industry," MBA dissertation, Michael Smurfit Graduate School of Business, University College, Dublin, 2000. The survey used a Delphi technique.
47. See *PRS Newswire,* "MGM Mirage and Dubai World Complete CityCenter Joint Venture Transaction," November 15, 2007.
48. See L. Benston, "A Financial History of the CityCenter Project," *Las Vegas Sun,* March 28, 2009, http://www.lasvegassun.com/news/2009/mar/28/financial-history-citycenter-project/.
49. See *Wall Stre*et *Journal,* "CityCenter Budget Timeline," December 14, 2009, http://www.wsj.com/articles/SB126081974132291021.
50. J. Heywood, interview, January 29, 2016.
51. See A. Gregor, "Building It Big in Las Vegas," *The New York Times,* May 26, 2009, http://www.nytimes.com/2009/05/27/realestate/commercial/27vegas.html?_r=0.
52. See D. Hodge, "Las Vegas Trophy Project Becomes Symbol of Trouble," *Reuters,* April 9, 2009, http://www.reuters.com/assets/print?aid=USTRE53800Q20090409.

Chapter 5

1. See E. Fama, "Random Walks in Stock Market Prices," *Financial Analysts Journal,* vol. 21, no. 5, September/October 1965, pp. 55–59.
2. E. Fama and K. French, "Dissecting Anomalies with a Five-Factor Model," *Review of Financial Studies,* forthcoming.
3. J. Campbell and R. Shiller, "Valuation Ratios and the Long-Run Market Outlook," *Journal of Portfolio Management* 24, no. 2, 1998, pp. 11–26. Campbell and

Shiller's argument focused on the dividend yield D/P and a price-to-earnings ratio P/E, with P being the mean price within a given month and E being annualized average monthly earnings during the prior ten years.

4. The point at the far right of the exhibit corresponds to December 1999, which was three months before the peak of the dot.com bubble, with December 2009 occurring nine months after the bottom of the global financial crisis.
5. M. Baker and J. Wurgler, "Investor Sentiment and the Cross-Section of Stock Returns," *Journal of Finance* 61, 2006, pp. 1645–1680; M. Baker and J. Wurgler, "Investor Sentiment in the Stock Market," *Journal of Economic Perspectives* 21, 2007, pp. 129–151.
6. A. Shleifer and R. Vishny, "The Limits of Arbitrage," *Journal of Finance* 52, 1997, pp. 35–56. Limits to arbitrage apply to many phenomena. For example, there is evidence suggesting that low CAPM-beta stocks outperform high-beta stocks on a risk-adjusted basis. In this regard, Warren Buffett appears to have exploited the low-beta anomaly to earn positive abnormal returns over four decades for his conglomerate firm Berkshire Hathaway, whose stock had the best risk-adjusted return among all U.S. stocks from 1976 on, outperforming many mutual funds. Moreover, Buffett magnified these abnormal returns using leverage. Notably, Buffett's leverage stemmed from borrowing from the insurance division of Berkshire Hathaway. In contrast, pension schemes and mutual funds are limited in their ability to borrow money. Therefore, they take risk by buying high-beta stocks, and as a result shun low-beta stocks, leading the latter to be undervalued. Buffett famously quipped: "It's far better to buy a wonderful company at a fair price than a fair company at a wonderful price." See A. Frazzini and L.H. Pedersen, "Betting Against Beta," *Journal of Financial Economics* 111, 2014, pp. 1–25. Also see 'A. Frazzini, D. Kabiller, and L.H. Pedersen, 2012. "Buffett's Alpha." Unpublished Working paper. AQR Capital Management and New York University, Greenwich, CT and New York, NY.
7. Fama and French initially constructed a three-factor model with factors relating to market returns, size, and B/M. Mark Carhart suggested adding momentum as a fourth factor. See M. Carhart, "On Persistence in Mutual Fund Performance," *Journal of Finance* 52, no. 1, 1997, pp. 57–82.
8. "Ideas That Changed the Theory and Practice of Investing; A Conversation with Eugene Fama, Ph.D.," *Journal of Investment Consulting*, 2008, pp. 6–14.
9. J. Sommer, "Eugene Fama, King of Predictable Markets," *The New York Times*, October 26, 2013, http://www.nytimes.com/2013/10/27/business/eugene-fama-king-of-predictable-markets.html.
10. L. Muelbroek, "An Empirical Analysis of Illegal Insider Trading," *Journal of Finance* 47, 1992, pp. 1661–1699; H. N. Seyhun, "Why Does Aggregate Insider Trading Predict Future Stock Returns?" *Quarterly Journal of Economics* 107, 1992, pp. 1303–1331.
11. F. Degeorge, J. Patel, and R. Zeckhauser, "Earnings Management to Exceed Thresholds," *Journal of Business* 72, no. 1, 1999, pp. 1–33.
12. D. Bergstresser and T. Philippon, "CEO Incentives and Earnings Management, *Journal of Financial Economics* 80, 2006, pp. 511–529.
13. M. Bradshaw, S. Richardson, and R. Sloan, "The Relation between Corporate Financing Activities, Analysts' Forecasts and Stock Returns," *Journal of Accounting and Economics* 42, 2006, pp. 53–85.
14. See J. Fox, "Learn to Play the Earnings Game (and Wall Street Will Love You)," *Fortune Magazine,* March 31, 1997, 76–80.
15. See J. Graham, C. Harvey, and S. Rajgopal, "The Economic Implications of Corporate Financial Reporting," *Journal of Accounting and Economics* 40, 2005, pp. 3–73.
16. See M. Bange and W. De Bondt, "R&D Budgets and Corporate Earnings Targets," *Journal of Corporate Finance,* vol. 4, 1998, pp. 153–184.
17. R. Brealey, S. Myers, and F. Allen, *Principles of Corporate Finance,* 10th ed. (Burr Ridge: McGraw-Hill Irwin, 2011), 330. The text states that the second lesson of market prices is to trust market prices. As behavioral finance has developed over time, successive editions of this textbook have qualified the lesson, so that trusting market prices is now a "starting point," given that sorting out behavioral puzzles will take time.
18. See E. Fama, L. Fisher, M. Jensen, and R. Roll, "The Adjustment of Stock Prices to New Information," *International Economic Review,* 1969. These authors show that for the period 1926–1960, companies that split their stocks saw their market cap rise prior to the split. See D. Ikenberry, G. Rankine, and E. Stice, "What Do Stock Splits Really Signal?" *Journal of Financial and Quantitative Analysis,* vol. 31, no. 3, 1996, pp. 1–21.
19. See D. Ikenberry and S. Ramnath, "Underreaction to Self-Selected News: The Case of Stock Splits," *Review of Financial Studies,* vol. 15, no. 2, 2002, pp. 489–526.
20. See M. Schnurman, "Radio Shack Parent Tandy Corp. to Split Stock 2-for-1," KRTBN Knight-Ridder Tribune Business News: Fort Worth Star-Telegram, May 26, 1999.
21. See T. Loughran and J. Ritter, "The New Issues Puzzle," *Journal of Finance,* vol. 50, 1995, pp. 23–51. The seminal work in this area is E. Miller, "Risk, Uncertainty, and Divergence of Opinion," *Journal of Finance, 32*, 1977, pp. 1151–1168.
22. See T. Loughran and J. Ritter, "The Operating Performance of Firms Conducting Seasoned Equity Offerings," *Journal of Finance,* vol. LII, no. 5, December 1997, pp. 1823–50.

23. Exhibits 5-1 to 5-4 are based on data available at Jay Ritter's web site (**bear.cba.ufl.edu/ritter**).
24. See A. Alti, "How Persistent Is the Impact of Market Timing on Capital Structure?" *Journal of Finance* 61(4), 2006, pp. 1681–1710.
25. See T. Loughran and J. Ritter, "Why Has IPO Underpricing Changed over Time?" *Financial Management,* vol. 33, no. 3, 2004, pp. 5–37.
26. See T. Loughran and J. Ritter, "Why Don't Issuers Get Upset About Leaving Money on the Table in IPOs?" *Review of Financial Studies,* vol. 15, 2002, pp. 413–443. A. Ljungqvist and W. Wilhelm, Jr., 2005. "Does Prospect Theory Explain IPO Behavior?" *Journal of Finance,* 60, 1759–1790.
27. See SEC litigation release 17327, January 22, 2002.
28. See A. Brav and P. Gompers, "Myth or Reality? The Long-Run Underperformance of Initial Public Offerings, Evidence from Venture and Non-Venture-Backed Companies," *Journal of Finance,* vol. 52, no. 5, 1997.
29. In personal correspondence, Jay Ritter reports that he calculated the median book-to-market equity ratio each year, using the post-issue number of shares outstanding and the first closing market price to calculate market value and the post-issue book value of equity. He notes that the yearly medians varied from 0.409 in 1984 to 0.147 in 1999, but that in most years medians were close to the overall median of 0.277. He implemented a simple cutoff, designating any IPO from 1980–2013 (N = 7,854) as a value stock if its post-issue, book-to-market ratio exceeded 0.277. He used annual sales rather than market capitalization to differentiate between big and small firms, using a $100 million (in 2014 dollars) as the cutoff. In respect to a two-by-two analysis, he reports results for three-year mean buy and hold return (BH) for individual stocks, and associated market adjusted returns (VW) using the value weighted CRSP index.

    Small value (N =2,328) BH = 17.9 percent, VW = −28.5 percent

    Small growth (N = 2,635) BH = 8.1 percent, VW = −27.9 percent

    Big value (N = 1,599) BH = 41.0 percent, VW = −1.5 percent

    Big growth (N = 1,292) BH = 36.7 percent, VW = −1.7 percent

    These results suggest that size, measured by sales, is much more important than the book-to-market in respect to IPO pricing.
30. See G. Zuckerman, "CEOs Turn Mum About Projecting Earnings," *The Wall Street Journal,* March 1, 2005.
31. E. Rusli, "Groupon Shares Rise Sharply After I.P.O.," *New York Times*, November 4, 2011, http://dealbook.nytimes.com/2011/11/04/groupon-shares-spike-40-to-open-at-28/?hp.

Chapter 6

1. See R. Brealey, S. Myers, and F. Allen, *Principles of Corporate Finance,* 8th ed., New York, NY: McGraw-Hill/Irwin, 2006, p. 154.
2. See I. Welch, "Views of Financial Economists on the Equity Premium and on Professional Controversies," *Journal of Business,* vol. 73, no. 4, 2000, pp. 501–537. See A. Damodaran, "Equity Risk Premiums (ERP): Determinants, Estimation and Implications—The 2015 Edition," updated March 2015, downloaded from http://pages.stern.nyu.edu/~adamodar/. Damodaran's estimate of the equity premium is in line with the mean estimates provided by academics, and between 2010 and 2016 varied within the range 5 percent to 6 percent.
3. In their 1992 analysis, Fama and French noted that sorting stocks on market beta does not sharply differentiate realized returns across beta-deciles. Based on results from Fama and French's 1992 analysis, the coefficient on beta in a simple regression of realized return on beta, features a coefficient of 0.003 and a t-statistic of 0.46. See E. Fama and K. French, "The Cross-Section of Expected Stock Return," *Journal of Finance,* XLVII(2), 1992, pp. 427–465. See also endnote 6 in chapter 5.
4. For example, SMB stands for "small minus big" and denotes the return to a portfolio of small cap stocks minus the return to a portfolio of large cap stocks. Similarly, HML stands for "high minus low" and refers to book-to-market equity. UMD stands for "up minus down" and refers to recent returns related to momentum. The historical geometric mean for the size factor SMB is 2.1 percent, for the book-to-market factor HML is 4.0 percent, and for the momentum factor UMD is 6.8 percent. As discussed in Chapter 5, Fama and French have added two new factors to their original three. In this regard, they note that their five-factor model is better than their three factor model at capturing the relationship between realized return and sensitivity to the market return.
5. See J. Graham and C. Harvey, "The Theory and Practice of Corporate Finance: Evidence from the Field," *Journal of Financial Economics,* vol. 60, nos. 2–3, 2001, pp. 187–243.
6. For judgments about the risk free rate, the range was 0 to 8 percent and the standard deviation was 1.1 percent.
7. The data for the excess premium are provided as part of the Fama-French factors, and are available from www.wrds.wharton.upenn.edu.
8. Coefficient values are approximately 0.02 with associated t-statistics below 0.26.
9. See P. Andreassen, "On the Social Psychology of the Stock Market: Aggregate Attributional Effects and the Regressiveness of Prediction," *J. Pers. Soc.Psychol.* 53(3), 1987, pp. 490–496.

P. Andreassen, "Explaining the Price-Volume Relationship: the Difference Between Price Changes and Changing Prices," *Organ. Behav. Hum. Decis.Process.* 41(3), 1988, pp. 371–389.

P. Andreassen and S. Kraus, "Judgemental Extrapolation and the Salience of Change," *J. Forecasting* 9(4), 1990, pp. 347–372.

10. See C. Harvey, "Implications for Asset Allocation, Portfolio Management, and Future Research II," *AIMR,* 2002, no. 1, pp. 97–99.
11. The estimate of volatility is based on a statistical formula: estimate of return standard deviation is equal to the difference between the worst case and best case, divided by 2.65.
12. On average, disagreement among CFOs' estimates of the risk premium, as measured by standard deviation, was 4.7 percent. Notably, the relationship between expected return and volatility is statistically insignificant, as is the relationship between the estimate of the risk premium and volatility.
13. The magnitude of the overconfidence is so marked, that it raises the question of whether the survey questions, by priming respondents in respect to the risk free rate, induce anchoring bias.
14. See D. Jenter, "Market Timing and Managerial Portfolio Decisions," *Journal of Finance,* 60(4), 2005, pp. 1903–1949. See also M. S. Rozeff, and M. A. Zaman, "Overreaction and Insider Trading: Evidence from Growth and Value Portfolios," *Journal of Finance,* vol. 53, 1998, pp. 701–716.
15. See J. Graham and C. Harvey, cited earlier.
16. See P. Krüger, A. Landier, and D. Thesmar, "The WACC Fallacy: The Real Effects of Using a Unique Discount Rate," *The Journal of Finance*, vol. 70, 2015, pp. 1253–1285. They measure the value loss due reliance on a single discount rate in the case of acquisitions. They find that in diversifying mergers and acquisitions, when the bidder's beta exceeds that of the target, bidder abnormal returns are higher. They conclude that on average, the present value loss is about 0.8 percent of the bidder's market equity.
17. See J. Graham and C. Harvey, cited earlier.
18. See R. Jagannathan, D. Matsa, I. Meier,and V. Tarhand, "Why Do Firms Use High Discount Rates?," 2015, Working paper: Northwestern University.
19. Notably, during the financial crisis, two thirds of CFOs responded affirmatively to the question about refraining from undertaking positive NPV projects.
20. At the 10% level of significance: I thank Ravi Jagannathan for this insight, communicated in private email correspondence.
21. See A. Landier and D. Thesmar, "Financial Contracting with Optimistic Entrepreneurs," *Review of Financial Studies,* 22(1), 2009, pp. 117–150.
22. Interview, February 9, 2001.
23. S. Poole, "Elon Musk by Ashlee Vance Review – How One Tech Billionaire Plans to Save the World," *The Guardian*, March 17, 2016.
24. J. Davis, "How Elon Musk Turned Tesla into the Car Company of the Future," *Wired*, 2010. http://www.wired.com/2010/09/ff_tesla/
25. B. Cornell and A. Damodaran, "Tesla: Anatomy of a Run-Up," *Journal of Portfolio Management*, Fall 2014, pp. 139–151.
26. P. LeBeau, "Elon Musk: Tired But Optimistic About Tesla's Future," *CNBC*, Wednesday, 21 Aug 2013, http://www.cnbc.com/id/100979018
27. http://aswathdamodaran.blogspot.com/2014/03/return-to-firing-line-revisiting-tesla.html
28. D. Leggett, "US: Tesla Q4 Earnings Boost Pleases Investors," *Just-Auto*, February 22, 2014.
29. http://seekingalpha.com/article/3966011-tesla?auth_param=1b6ob2:1bhabpl:6d93e6db5520a80512757dfc236038a7&dr=1#alt1
30. See R. Rescigno, "Detroit Is Thriving Again," *Barron's*, April 15, 2016.
31. See S. Pulliam, M. Ramsey, and I. J. Dugan, "Elon Musk Sets Ambitious Goals at Tesla—and Often Falls Short," *The Wall Street Journal*, August 15, 2016, http://www.wsj.com/articles/elon-musk-sets-ambitious-goals-at-teslaandoften-falls-short-1471275436.
32. See "Pop Goes The Tesla Bubble," Oct. 22, 2015, http://seekingalpha.com/article/3593586-pop-goes-the-teslabubble.
33. See "If You're Short Tesla Stock, You're Fooling Yourself," April 19, 2016. http://seekingalpha.com/article/3966280-short-tesla-stockfooling?auth_param=1b6ob2:1bhcnhv:3d5d06b74aaef7b51abc8ed9133dd7fa&dr=1

Chapter 7

1. See M. Baker and J. Wurgler, "Behavioral Corporate Finance: An Updated Survey," *Handbook of the Economics of Finance,* vol. 2, eds. G. Constantanides, M. Harris, and R. Stulz (Amsterdam: Elsevier, 2012).
2. See P. Sweeney "Capital Structure: Credibility and Flexibility," *Financial Executive,* 2003, pp. 33–36.
3. See M. Baker and J. Wurgler, "Market Timing and Capital Structure," *Journal of Finance,* vol. 57, no. 1, 2002, pp. 1–32.
4. See D. Jenter, "Market Timing and Managerial Portfolio Decisions," *Journal of Finance,* 60(4), 2005, pp. 1903–1949.
5. See Baker and Wurgler, cited previously.
6. Interview with Eddie Le, Corporate and Investment Banking, Banc of America Securities, November 5, 2004.

7. See S. Pulliam, "Mixed Blessing: How Hedge-Fund Trading Sent a Company's Stock on Wild Ride," *The Wall Street Journal,* December 28, 2004.
8. The top four are (1) earnings dilution, (2) amount of mispricing, (3) if the stock price has recently risen, and (4) providing stock in connection with employee stock ownership.
9. See E. Fama and K. French, "Testing Tradeoff and Pecking Order Predictions about Dividends and Debt," *Review of Financial Studies* 15, 2002, pp. 1–37; R. Huang and J. Ritter, "Testing Theories of Capital Structure and Estimating the Speed of Adjustment," *Journal of Financial and Quantitative Analysis* 44, 2009, pp. 237–271; I. Welch, "Stock Returns and Capital Structure," *Journal of Political Economy* 112, 2004, pp. 106–131.
10. See M. Flannery and K. Rangan, "Partial Adjustment toward Target Capital Structures," Working Paper, University of Florida, 2004; and M. Leary and M. Roberts, "Do Firms Rebalance Their Capital Structures?" Working Paper, Duke University, 2004. See also A. Alti, "How Persistent Is the Impact of Market Timing on Capital Structure?" Working Paper, University of Texas, Austin, 2004.
11. See R. Huang and J. Ritter, "Testing the Market Timing Theory of Capital Structure," Working Paper, University of Florida, 2004.
12. The growth opportunities-based counterargument to Baker and Wurgler's claim that timing new issues has long-term effects on capital structure can be found in A. Hovakimian, "Are Observed Capital Structures Determined by Equity Market Timing?" *Journal of Financial and Quantitative Analysis* 41, 2006, pp. 221–243. However, there are other counterarguments. In arguing that the issue is not settled, Huang and Ritter, 2009, cited in a previous endnote, establish that the tendency for a firm to fund a financing deficit with equity actually decreases when the cost of equity is low.
13. See J. Graham, "How Big Are the Tax Benefits of Debt?" *Journal of Finance,* vol. 55, 2000, pp. 1901–1941.
14. I. Ben-David, J. Graham, and C. Harvey, "Managerial Miscalibration," *Quarterly Journal of Economics* 128, no. 4, 2013, pp. 1547–1584.
15. Y. Cai and H. Shefrin, "Acquisition Risk and Psychology," Working paper, Santa Clara University, 2016.
16. See Goldberg, L. R., 1993. "The Structure of Phenotypic Personality Traits". *American Psychologist,* 48 (1): 26–34.
17. See I. Gow, S. Kaplan, D. Larcker, and A. Zakolyukina, "CEO Personality and Firm Policies," Working paper: University of Chicago, 2016.
18. See C. Mayer and O. Sussman, "A New Test of Capital Structure," Working Paper, Saïd Business School, University of Oxford, 2004. Also see the Huang-Ritter paper.
19. See D. Reilly, "Overheard: Facebook Pulls Ahead of J.P. Morgan," *The Wall Street Journal Online,* October 27, 2014, http://blogs.wsj.com/moneybeat /2014/10/27 /facebook-pulls-ahead-of-j-p-morgan/.
20. J. Hough, "3 Blue-Chips Buying Back Their Undervalued Stocks," *Barron's Online*, March 18, 2016, http://www.barrons.com/articles/3-blue-chips-buying-back-their-undervalued-stocks-1458301063.
21. J. Bennett, "GE: Peltz, Dividend, Stock Buybacks Make it a Buy," *Barron's Online*, April 22, 2016, http://www.barrons.com/articles/ge-peltz-dividend-stock-buybacks-make-it-a-buy-1461347164.
22. T. Loughran and J. Ritter, "The New Issues Puzzle," *Journal of Finance* 50, 1995, pp. 23–51.
23. Some scholars suggest that there is no separate IPO or SEO phenomenon, and that mispricing is completely related to style. See A. Brav and Paul A. Gompers, "Myth or Reality? The Long-Run Underperformance of Initial Public Offerings: Evidence from Venture Capital and Nonventure Capital-Backed Companies," *Journal of Finance* 52, 1997, pp. 1791–1822. P. Gompers and J. Lerner, "The Really Long-Run Performance of Initial Public Offerings: The Pre-Nasdaq Evidence," *Journal of Finance* 58, 2003, pp. 1355–1392.
24. M. Baker and J. Wurgler, "The Equity Share in New Issues and Aggregate Stock Returns," *Journal of Finance* 55, 2000, pp. 2219–2257. Baker and Wurgler find that the underperformance of −6 percent is 15 percent below the average market return.
25. See T. Burch, W. Christie, and V. Nanda, "Do Firms Time Equity Offerings? Evidence from the 1930s and 1940s," *Financial Management* 33, 2004, pp. 5–23.
26. D. Ikenberry, J. Lakonishok, and T. Vermaelen, "Market Underreaction to Open Market Share Repurchases," *Journal of Financial Economics,* vol. 39, 1995, pp. 181–208.
27. I. Dichev, "What are Stock Investors' Actual Historical Returns? Evidence from Dollar Weighted Returns," *American Economic Review* 97, 2007, pp. 386–402.
28. In terms of mean ratings, the findings were 1.89 for borrowing short-term when they feel that short rates are low relative to long rates, 1.78 in respect to expecting long-term rates to decline, 2.19 in respect to low foreign interest rates affecting the decision to issue abroad, 2.33 in respect to small firms, and 2.27 in respect to growth.
29. See P. Marsh, "The Choice between Equity and Debt: An Empirical Study," *Journal of Finance* 37, 1982, pp. 121–144. Marsh studies a sample of U.K. firms and finds that the choice between debt and equity appears to be impacted by the level of interest rates. See also J. Guedes and T. Opler, "The Determinants of the Maturity of Corporate Debt Issues," *Journal of Finance* 51, 1996, pp. 1809–1833.Guedes and Opler study the survey responses regarding the effect of the yield curve. They use a sample of 7,369 U.S. debt issues between 1982 and 1993, and find that maturity is strongly negatively related to the difference between long- and short-term bond yields.

30. See K. Spiess and J. Affleck-Graves, "The Long-Run Performance of Stock Returns Following Debt Offerings," *Journal of Financial Economics* 54, 1999, pp. 45–73. The authors of this study report that the mean underperformance for straight debt is an insignificant 14 percent over five years, although the median underperformance is significant, while the 37 percent underperformance of convertible issuers is significant.
31. See K. Spiess and J. Affleck-Graves, 1999, cited in an earlier endnote. Spiess and Affleck-Graves examine 392 straight debt issues and 400 convertible issues between the years 1975 and 1989. See also S. Richardson and R. Sloan, "External Financing and Future Stock Returns," University of Pennsylvania working paper, 2003. Richardson and Sloan use a much broader panel and also find that net debt issuance is followed by low stock returns. Despite financial executives' responses in the Duke/FEI survey suggesting that they do not time their idiosyncratic credit quality, the shares of unrated issuers have a median five-year underperformance of 54 percent.
32. See M. Baker, J. Stein, and J. Wurgler, "When Does the Market Matter? Stock Prices and the Investment of Equity-Dependent Firms," Quarterly *Journal of Economics* 118, 2003, pp. 969–1006. Baker, Stein, and Wurgler suggest that equity overvaluation relaxes a binding leverage constraint, creating debt capacity that subsequently gets used up. However, because debt is correctly priced in this framework, debt market timing per se is not possible.
33. Over 60 percent would reduce repurchases, but less than 30 percent would reduce dividends.
34. See J. Stein, "Rational Capital Budgeting in an Irrational World," *Journal of Business,* vol. 69, 1996, pp. 429–455.
35. See J. Stein, "Agency, Information, and Corporate Investment." In George Constantinides, Milton Harris, and René Stulz (eds.), *Handbook of the Economics of Finance,* forthcoming.
36. This section is based on a presentation that Adaptec's chief financial officer at the time, David Young, made on November 9, 2001, at Santa Clara University.
37. See O. J. Blanchard, F. Lopez-de-Silanes, and A. Shleifer, "What Do Firms Do with Cash Windfalls?" *Journal of Financial Economics,* vol. 36, 1994, pp. 337–360.
38. See K. Froot, "The Market for Catastrophe Risk: A Clinical Examination," NBER Working Paper no. 8110, February 2001. Revised in *Journal of Financial Economics,* vol. 60, 2001, pp. 529–571.
39. There are several studies documenting this phenomenon. See O. Lamont, "Cash Flow and Investment: Evidence from Internal Capital Markets," *Journal of Finance,* vol. 52, no. 1, 1997, pp. 83–109.
40. See T. Burch, W. Christie, and V. Nanda, "Do Firms Time Equity Offerings? Evidence From the 1930s and 1940s," *Financial Management* 33, 2004, pp. 5–23.
41. See M. Glaser, T. Langer, and M. Weber, "True Overconfidence in Interval Estimates: Evidence Based on a New Measure of Miscalibration," *Journal of Behavioral Decision Making* 26, no. 5, 2013, pp. 405–417. This article compares responses in three types of overconfidence assessments over time using both students and investment professionals. In respect to forecasting returns, the authors also report research indicating that forecasts over short periods such as a week or less tend to feature underconfidence rather than overconfidence.
42. R. Greenwood and S. Hanson, "Waves in Ship Prices and Investment," *The Quarterly Journal of Economics*, 2015, pp. 55–109.
43. See N. Genniaoli, Y. Ma, and A. Shleifer, "Expectations and Investment," Working paper: Universita' Bocconi and Harvard University, 2016.
44. See A. Hovakimian and G. Hovakimian, 2005. "Cash Flow Sensitivity of Investment: Firm-Level Analysis," Working paper Baruch College and Fordham University.
45. U. Malmendier and G. Tate, "Who Makes Acquisitions? CEO Overconfidence and the Market's Reaction," *Journal of Financial Economics*, 89(1), 2008, pp. 20–43.
46. U. Malmendier and G. Tate, "Behavioral CEOs: The Role of Managerial Overconfidence," *Journal of Economic Perspectives*, 29(4), 2015, pp. 37–60.
47. Inclusion in this sample is based on lists compiled by *Forbes* magazine during the period.
48. See U. Malmendier and G. Tate, "CEO Overconfidence and Corporate Investment," *Journal of Finance,* 60(6), 2005, pp. 2661–2700.
49. U. Malmendier and G. Tate, "Does Overconfidence Affect Corporate Investment? CEO Overconfidence Measures Revisited," *European Financial Management,* 11(5), 2005, pp. 649–659.
50. Boards with 12 or fewer members are considered stronger than boards that have more than 12 members. Growth opportunities are typically measured by Tobin's Q, the ratio of the market value of a firm divided by the replacement cost of its assets.
51. See "Buyback Binge of U.S. Companies Is Getting Costly—Firms Reverse Strategy, Buy Shares When Prices Are High," *The Wall Street Journal,* by staff reporters R. McGough, S. McGee and C. Bryan-Low in New York, December 19, 2000.
52. See J. Creswell, "J. Crew Flounders in Fashion's Shifting Tides," *The New York Times*, June 10, 2015, http://www.nytimes.com/2015/06/11/business/j-crew-flounders-in-fashions-shifting-tides.html?ref=dealbook.
53. C. Leonnig and J. Stephens, "Solyndra Went on a Spending Spree After Getting Loan," *The Washington Post*, September 22, 2011, http://www.thefiscaltimes.com

/Articles/2011/09/22/WP-Solyndra-went-on-a-spending-spree-after-getting-loan.

54. Notably, his acquisition of PSINet and other related firms brought valuable "peering" arrangements to Cogent, allowing its network to connect without charge to larger networks such as Verizon, AT&T, France Telecom, and Scandinavia's largest telecom company, TeliaSonera.

55. Cogent's aggressive business strategy led to its being involved in dramatic conflicts with several of its much larger peering partners, such as France Telecom, Level 3 Communications, and TeliaSonera. For example, Cogent's salespeople tried to undercut TeliaSonera by offering to charge 70 percent less than TeliaSonera was charging for the same service. Telia reacted by slowing down Cogent's Swedish customers' Internet speeds, and Schaeffer countered by blocking all of Telia's traffic that went out on Cogent's network. Because the inconvenience to Telia customers, who could not access web sites outside of Sweden, was far greater than the inconvenience to Cogent's Swedish customers, Telia relented, agreeing to terms acceptable to Cogent.

Chapter 8

1. See Merton, Miller, and Franco Modigliani, "Dividend Policy, Growth, and the Valuation of Shares," *Journal of Business,* vol. 34, 1961, pp. 411–433.
2. See J. Ablan, "Bird in the Hand: Suddenly, Dividend Stocks Don't Look So Old-fashioned, After All." *Barron's*, April 23, 2001, p. 22. J. Clements, "The Party Seems to Be Over, Now What?—It's Time to Adjust Your Investment Strategy to a More Lackluster Market." *The Wall Street Journal*: Personal Finance & Spending, September 8, 2000, p. 28. J. Clements, "When Retirement Experts Talk, Why Doesn't Anybody Listen?" *The Wall Street Journal*, Getting Going, June 20, 2007, p. D1. C. De Aenlle, "Is It Time for Dividends to Get Some Respect?" *The New York Times*, Sunday Money: Investing, June 11, 2006, 6. http://www.nytimes.com/2006/06/11/business/yourmoney/11divi.html?_r=0.
3. See J. Moore and Olivia. Mitchell, "Projected Retirement Wealth and Savings Adequacy in the Health and Retirement Study," National Bureau of Economic Research, Working Paper 6240, 1997.
4. See H. Shefrin and M. Statman, "Explaining Investor Preference for Cash Dividends," *Journal of Financial Economics,* 13(2), 1984, pp. 253–282.
5. See Y. Grinstein and R. Michaely, "Institutional Holdings and Payout Policy," *Journal of Finance,* forthcoming.
6. See F. Allen and R. Michaely, "Payout Policy." In G. Constantinides, M. Harris, and R. Stulz (eds.), *North-Holland Handbooks of Economics,* North Holland Amsterdam, 2001.
7. See S. Hartzmark and D. Solomon, "The Dividend Disconnect," Working paper: University of Chicago and University of Southern California, 2016.
8. See J. Lintner, "Distribution of Incomes of Corporations among Dividends, Retained Earnings, and Taxes," *American Economic Review,* vol. 46, no. 2, 1956, pp. 97–113.
9. See A. Brav, J. Graham, C. Harvey, and R. Michaely, "Payout Policy in the 21st Century." Working Paper, Duke University, 2004. Survey responses were obtained from 300 CFOs who filled out a questionnaire, and 23 CFOs or treasurers of prominent corporations who participated in a one-hour field survey. By way of contrast, Lintner's study involved 30 companies.
10. There was over 80 percent agreement with the first three statements, over 70 percent agreement with the fourth, and over 60 percent agreement with the fifth.
11. This quotation is taken from the version of the paper, dated November 14, 2002.
12. Discussed in Chapter 7.
13. J. Ablan, "Bird in the Hand: Suddenly, Dividend Stocks Don't Look So Old-Fashioned, After All." *Barron's,* April 23, 2001, p. 22.
14. See J. Long, "The Market Valuation of Cash Dividends: A Case to Consider," *Journal of Financial Economics,* vol. 6, 1978, pp. 235–264.
15. See M. Baker and J. Wurgler, "A Catering Theory of Dividends," *Journal of Finance,* vol. 59, 2004, pp. 271–288. These authors define catering more narrowly than in the chapter, essentially focusing on initiating dividends to exploit mispriced equity.
16. See S. Benartzi, R. Michaely and R. Thaler, "Do Changes in Dividends Signal the Future or the Past?" *Journal of Finance,* vol. LII, no. 3, 1997, pp. 1007–34.
17. See Chapter 5 on inefficient markets.
18. See also J. Aharony and I. Swary, "Quarterly Dividend and Earnings Announcements and Stockholders' Returns: An Empirical Analysis," *Journal of Finance* 35, 1980, pp. 1–12. They report that in a 21-day window surrounding a dividend decrease, the average cumulative abnormal return was approximately five percentage points. In contrast, the average cumulative abnormal return surrounding a dividend increase was approximately one percentage point.
19. See R. Michaely, R. Thaler, and K. Womack, "Price Reactions to Dividend Initiations and Omissions: Overreaction or Drift?" *Journal of Finance,* vol. L, no. 2, 1995, pp. 573–608.
20. The material in this section is mostly based on M. Baker, Malcolm, B. Mendel, and J. Wurgler, "Dividends as

Reference Points: A Behavioral Signaling Model," *Review of Financial Studies*, forthcoming.

21. The author of the article is Amy Baldwin.
22. See "Unsafe Harbors: Folks Who Like to Buy a Stock and Forget It Face Rude Awakening" that appeared on the front page of the February 7, 2001, issue of the *Wall Street Journal.*
23. See G. Zuckerman and J. Bandler, "Investors Seek to Rewind Kodak," *The Wall Street Journal,* October 21, 2003.
24. See E. S. Browning, "Dividend Stocks Haven't Caught Investors' Fancy," *The Wall Street Journal,* January 31, 2005.
25. See K. Fuller and M. Goldstein, 2004. "Do Dividends Matter More in Declining Markets?" Working paper, University of Georgia.
26. See Barron's Blog, "AAPL: Bulls See Plenty of Room for Bigger Payout; Options Pricing in Status Quo," *Barron's Blog,* February 8, 2013.
27. See C. Mead and S. Gangar, "Apple Raises $17 Billion in Record Corporate Bond Sale," *Bloomberg,* April 30, 2013, http://www.bloomberg.com/news/articles/2013-04-30/apple-plans-six-part-bond-sale-in-first-offering-since-1996-1-/.
28. See "Heard on the Street: Sour on Apple," *The Wall Street Journal,* March 1, 2014.
29. See B. Chen, "A Conversation with Yukari Kane, Author of 'Haunted Empire: Apple after Steve Jobs,'" *The New York Times,* March 18, 2014.
30. See F. Manjoo, "Apple after Jobs: Pretty Much the Same as Ever," *The New York Times,* March 20, 2014.
31. D. Wakabayashi, "Tim Cook's Vision for 'His' Apple Emerges," *The Wall Street Journal,* July 8, 2014.
32. R. Ruiz, "Apple Says Its Chief of Finance Will Retire," *The New York Times,* March 5, 2014.
33. See D. Wakabayashi and E. Chasan, "Apple Appoints New Finance Chief," *The Wall Street Journal,* March 5, 2014.
34. D. Wakabayashi, "Apple Moves to Reward Investors," *The Wall Street Journal,* April 24, 2014.
35. See S. Russolillo, "Facebook Is Gaining on Google," *The Wall Street Journal,* February 1, 2016.
36. See P. La Monica, "IBM: The Dow's Big Blah Stock," *CNN Wire,* December 8, 2014.
37. See M. Cherney, "Investors Take a Large Bite of Apple," *The Wall Street Journal,* April 30, 2014.
38. See B. Chen, "Apple Goes Big with iPhone 6, and Small with a Smartwatch," *The New York Times,* September 10, 2014.
39. See B. Chen, "Apple Goes Big with iPhone 6, and Small with a Smartwatch," *The New York Times,* September 10, 2014.
40. See S. Russolillo, "Facebook Is Gaining on Google," *The Wall Street Journal,* February 1, 2016.

Chapter 9

1. See E. Rasmussen, *Games and Information: An Introduction to Game Theory.* Blackwell, Malden, MA, 2001.
2. See M. C. Jensen and K. Murphy, "CEO Incentives—It's Not How Much You Pay, But How," *Harvard Business Review,* no. 3, May–June 1990, pp. 138–153. See also M.C. Jensen and K. J. Murphy, "Performance Pay and Top Management Incentives," *Journal of Political Economy,* vol. 98, 1990, pp. 225–264. As mentioned in the paragraph, the rate of dismissal is also an issue. For a discussion about dismissal and compensation risk, see F. Peters and A. Wagner, "The Executive Turnover Risk Premium," *Journal of Finance,* 69(4), 2014, pp. 1529–1563.
3. "The Brookings Institution Holds a Discussion on 'Is it Time to Reform Executive Compensation and Stock Option Grants?" September 27, 2012. See A. Lund and G. Polsky, "Can Executive Compensation Reform Cure Short-Termism?" 2013, http://www.brookings.edu/research/papers/2013/03/18-executive-compensation-polsky-lund.
4. See S. Kedia and A. Mozumdar, "Performance Impact of Employee Stock Options," Working Paper, Rutgers University, 2002.
5. See L. Bebchuk and J. Fried, *Pay without Performance: The Unfulfilled Promise of Executive Compensation* (Cambridge: Harvard University Press, 2004); L. Bebchuk, M. Cremers, and U. Peyer, "The CEO Pay Slice," *Journal of Financial Economics* 102, no. 1, 2011, pp. 199–221.
6. R. Fahlenbrach and R. Stulz, "Bank CEO Incentives and the Credit Crisis," *Journal of Financial Economics* 99, 2011, pp. 11–26.
7. See R. Morck, "Behavioral Finance in Corporate Governance—Economics and the Ethics of the Devil's Advocate," *Journal of Management & Governance* 12, 2009, pp. 179–200; R. Morck, "Loyalty, Agency Conflicts and Corporate Governance," in H. K. Baker and J. Nofsinger, eds., *Behavioural Corporate Governance* (John Wiley & Sons, 2010), pp. 453–474.
8. M. Conyon, "Executive Compensation and Board Governance in US Firms," *Economic Journal* 124, 2014, pp. F60–F89. See also A. Wagner and C. Wenk, "Agency versus Hold-up: On the Impact of Binding Say-on-Pay on Shareholder Value," Working paper: University of Zurich, 2015, suggesting that say-on-pay can introduce distortions to ex-ante managerial incentives for extra-contractual firm-specific investments.
9. See P. A. Gompers, J. L. Ishii, and A. Metrick, "Corporate Governance and Equity Prices," *Quarterly Journal of Economics,* vol. 118, no. 1, February 2003, pp. 107–155.

10. See Carol J. Loomis, "Executive Pay: 'This Stuff Is Wrong.' That's the Conclusion of Most of the Insiders Who Talked to *Fortune*—Candidly—about CEO Pay. And You Know What's Even Worse? They Don't See How the Overreaching Can Be Stopped," *Fortune,* June 11, 2001, vol. 143, iss. 14, p. 72. In the interest of taste, some quotations from this article that appear in the text have been edited for colorful language.

11. See J. Stein, "Efficient Capital Markets, Inefficient Firms: A Model of Myopic Corporate Behavior," *Quarterly Journal of Economics,* vol. 104, 1989, pp. 655–669. Stein discusses a model of rational signal jamming, where managers take excessive risk to distinguish themselves relative to others, because they are rewarded in good times but are not penalized in bad times when many firms experience unfavorable outcomes.

12. See N. Bergman and D. Jenter, "Employee Sentiment and Stock Option Compensation," Working Paper, Massachussetts Institute of Technology, 2003.

13. See S. Gervais, J.B. Heaton, and T. Odean, "Overconfidence, Compensation Contracts, and Capital Budgeting," *Journal of Finance* LXVI, no. 5, 2011, pp. 1735–1777.

14. Technically, the four categories correspond to different ranges for what is known as the coefficient of risk aversion. The ranges are: below 1.0, between 1.0 and 1.99, between 2.0 and 3.6, and above 3.6. A variant of this question is discussed in Chapter 1, where people are simply asked what percentage cut they would tolerate for a 50 percent chance to double their income for life. The responses to this version of the question are similar to Concept Preview Question 9.1, but not exactly the same. Although there is variation across groups, the same people often provide precise answers that are inconsistent with the way they answer Concept Preview Question 9.1. The consistency rate typically varies between 60 percent and 80 percent.

15. See J. Graham, C. Harvey, and M. Puri, "Managerial Attitudes and Corporate Actions," *Journal of Financial Economics* 109, 2013, pp. 103–121. For the most part, the results reported here are for U.S. CEOs and CFOs. The original study also included non-U.S. CEOs and CFOs, who tend to be more risk averse than their U.S. counterparts.

16. I thank Song Ma, who was a research assistant at Duke University working on Graham, Harvey, and Puri, 2013, for providing additional analysis of the data. This analysis shows, for example, that for CEOs the proportion of CEO compensation received in the form of stock and stock options rises monotonically across the four groups from approximately 8.5 percent for the most risk-averse to 12 percent for the least risk-averse. However, for CFOs the pattern is U-shaped, at approximately 10.5 percent for the extremes and 8.5 percent in the middle.

17. See R. Frank and C. Sunstein, "Cost-Benefit Analysis and Relative Position," *The University of Chicago Law Review*, Spring 2001, pp. 323–374. Concept Preview Question 9.2 comes from this article. Frank and Sunstein review the literature on relative income, including issues related to pay differentials.

18. See D. Kahneman and A. Deaton, "High Income Improves Evaluation of Life But Not Emotional Well-Being," *Proceedings of the National Academy of Sciences* 107, no. 38, 2010, pp. 16489–16493.

19. See M. Statman, "Fairness Outside the Cocoon," *Financial Analysts Journal* 60, no. 6, 2004, pp. 34–37.

20. F. Degeorge, J. Patel, and R. Zeckhauser, "Earnings Management to Exceed Thresholds," *Journal of Business* 72, 1999, pp. 1–33.

21. C. Carslaw, "Anomalies in Income Numbers: Evidence of Goal Oriented Behavior," *The Accounting Review* 63, 1988, pp. 321–327; V. Bernard, "Post-Earnings Announcement Drift: Delayed Price Response or Risk Premium?" *Journal of Accounting Research* 27, 1989, pp. 1–36.

22. D. Bergstresser and T. Philippon, "CEO Incentives and Earnings Management," *Journal of Financial Economics* 80, 2006, pp. 511–529.

23. R. Sloan, "Do Stock Prices Fully Reflect Information in Accruals and Cash Flows About Future Earnings?" *The Accounting Review* 71, 1996, pp. 289–316.

24. S. H. Teoh, I. Welch, and T. J. Wong, "Earnings Management and the Long-Run Market Performance of Initial Public Offerings," *Journal of Finance* 53, 1998a, pp. 1935–1974; S. H. Teoh, I. Welch, and T. J. Wong, "Earnings Management and the Underperformance of Seasoned Equity Offerings," *Journal of Financial Economics* 50, 1998b, pp. 63–99.

25. See M. Schroeder, "Under Gun from SEC, Bristol, Others Divulge Accounting Issues," *The Wall Street Journal,* August 15, 2002.

26. K. Kelly, "Sealed, Delivered but Not Yet Signed by CEOs," *The Wall Street Journal,* July 25, 2003.

27. See D. Denis, P. Hanouna, and A. Sarin, 2005. "Is there a Dark Side to Incentive Compensation?" Working paper, Purdue University.

28. See "A Diagnosis of Fraud at HealthSouth," *Financial Times,* April 14, 2003.

29. See "Excerpts of Recorded Conversation Between Scrushy and Owens," *The Associated Press,* April 11, 2003.

30. See K. Whitmire, "Ten Years after His Fraud Trial, Richard Scrushy Tells the Truth," *AL.com*, January 25, 2015, http://www.al.com/opinion/index.ssf/2015/01/ten_years_after_his_fraud_tria.html. Also, see Richard Scrushy's personal web site, http://richardscrushy.com/.

31. See "Report Card 2002: The Ethics of American Youth," Survey conducted by the Josephson Institute of Ethics, **www.josephsoninstitute.org.**
32. See "30 Students Accused of Cheating on Ethics Essay," *National Post*, March 27, 2002.
33. See "The Man Behind the Deal Machine: As Creator of iffy Enron Partnerships, Ousted CFO Andrew Fastow is a Prime Target for Investigators," by Wendy Zellner, Mike France, and Joseph Weber, *Businessweek*, February 4, 2002.
34. C. B. Zhong, V. Bohns, and F. Gino, "Good Lamps Are the Best Police: Darkness Increases Dishonesty and Self-Interested Behavior," *Psychological Science* 21, no. 3, 2010, pp. 311–314.
35. S. Pagliaro, N. Ellemers, and M. Barreto, "Sharing Moral Values: Anticipated Ingroup Respect as a Determinant of Adherence to Morality-Based (But Not Competence-Based) Group Norms," Personality and Social *Psychology Bulletin* 37, 2011, pp. 1117–1129.
36. F. Gino, S. Ayal, and D. Ariely, "Contagion and Differentiation in Unethical Behavior," *Psychological Science* 20, no. 3, 2009, pp. 393–398.
37. M. Pitesa and S. Thau, "Masters of the Universe: How Power and Accountability Influence Self-Serving Decisions under Moral Hazard," *Journal of Applied Psychology* 98, no. 3, 2013, pp. 550–558.
38. F. Gino and L. Pierce, "The Abundance Effect: Unethical Behavior in the Presence of Wealth," *Organizational Behavior and Human Decision Processes* 109, no. 2, 2009, pp. 142–155.
39. F. Gino, M. Schweitzer, N. Mead, and D. Ariely "Unable to Resist Temptation: How Self-Control Depletion Promotes Unethical Behavior," *Organizational Behavior and Human Decision Processes* 115, no. 2, 2011, pp. 191–203. See also R. Gibson, C. Tanner, and A. Wagner, "Preferences for Truthfulness: Heterogeneity Among and Within Individuals," *American Economic Review,* 103(1), 2013.
40. See N. Mazar, O. Amir, and D. Ariely, "The Dishonesty of Honest People: A Theory of Self-Concept Maintenance," *Journal of Marketing Research* XLV, 2008, pp. 633–644.
41. M. Bazerman and A. Tenbrunsel, *Blind Spots: Why We Fail to Do What's Right and What to Do about It*, (Princeton, NJ: Princeton University Press, 2012).
42. See http://josephsoninstitute.org/surveys/. The 2009 Josephson study reports the following specific findings: "Teens 17 or under are five times more likely than those over 50 to hold the cynical belief that lying and cheating are necessary to succeed (51% v 10%), nearly four times as likely to deceive their boss (31% v. 8%), more than three times as likely to keep change mistakenly given to them (49% v. 15%), and more than three times as likely to believe it's okay to lie to get a child into a better school (38% v. 11%)." The study also reports the following: "Young adults (18–24) are more than three times more likely to have inflated an insurance claim than those over 40 (7% vs. 2%) and more than twice as likely to lie to their spouse, boyfriend, girlfriend, or partner about something significant (48% v. 18%). Attitude matters—regardless of age, people who believe lying and cheating are a necessary part of success (the report calls them cynics) are more likely to lie and cheat. In fact, this belief is one of the most significant and reliable predictors of dishonest behavior in the adult world."
43. J. Toobin, "A Bad Thing," *The New Yorker,* March 22, 2004, p. 60.
44. See Hertz Global Holdings, "Notice of Annual Meeting of Stockholders and Proxy Statement," May 14, 2014, page 7.
45. See T. Whitehouse, "Compliance Week: How Wheels Came Off of Hertz's Accounting," *News Quotes,* June 2014.
46. See Hertz Global Holdings, Form 10-K, filed July 16, 2015, https://www.documentcloud.org/documents/2185606-htz-hertz-global-holdings-10-k-2015-07-16.html.
47. See T. Whitehouse, "Compliance Week: Robert Rostan 'Hertz Restatement Drives Home Top-Level Control Issues,'" *Training the Street*, July 28, 2015, http://trainingthestreet.com/compliance-week-robert-rostan-hertz-restatement-drives-home-toplevel-control-issues/.
48. See T. Whitehouse, "Compliance Week: Robert Rostan 'Hertz Restatement Drives Home Top-Level Control Issues,'" *Training the Street,* July 28, 2015, http://trainingthestreet.com/compliance-week-robert-rostan-hertz-restatement-drives-home-toplevel-control-issues/.http://www.rgl.com/news/xprNewsDetail.aspx?xpST=NewsDetail&news=512
49. COSO, *Internal Control, Integrated Framework: COSO Executive Summary,* May 2013, http://www.coso.org/documents/990025p_executive_summary_final_may20_e.pdf.

Chapter 10

1. See R. Roll, "The Hubris Hypothesis of Corporate Takeovers." In R. H. Thaler (ed.), *Advances in Behavioral Finance,* New York: Russell Sage Foundation, 1993, pp. 437–458.
2. See E. C. Capen, R. V. Clapp, and W. M. Campbell, "Competitive Bidding in High-Risk Situations," *Journal of Petroleum Technology,* vol. 23, 1971, pp. 641–53.

3. See S. Moeller, F. Schlingemann, and R. Stulz, "Wealth Destruction on a Massive Scale? A Study of Acquiring-Firm Returns in the Recent Merger Wave," *Journal of Finance,* vol. LX, no. 2, 2005, pp. 757–782.
4. C. Christensen, R. Alton, C. Rising, and A. Waldeck, "The Big Idea: The New M&A Playbook," *Harvard Business Review*, March 2011, https://hbr.org/2011/03/the-big-idea-the-new-ma-playbook. The 70-to-90 percent figure was reiterated. See D. McCann, "M&A: The Good, The Bad, The Ugly," *CFO.com*, November 14, 2012.
5. See U. Malmendier and G. Tate, "Who Makes Acquisitions? CEO Overconfidence and the Market's Reaction," *Journal of Financial Economics,* 89(1), 2008, pp. 20–43
6. See T. Lys and L. Vincent, 1995. "An Analysis of Value Destruction in AT&T's Acquisition of NCR," *Journal of Financial Economics,* 39, 353–378, p. 27.
7. See "The McKinsey Quarterly Chart Focus Newsletter," March 2005, **www.mckinseyquarterly.com/newsletters/chartfocus/2005_03.htm,** "Where Mergers Go Wrong," May 5, 2005; The McKinsey Quarterly, **www.mckinseyquarterly.com/article_abstract.aspx?ar=1402&L2=5&L3=4&srid=63&gp=0;** and Kris Frieswick, "Fool's Gold," *CFO Magazine,* February 1, 2005.
8. See D. Durfee, "A Question of Value," *CFO Magazine,* March 1, 2005.
9. See J. Graham, C. Harvey, and M. Puri, "Managerial Attitudes and Corporate Actions," *Journal of Financial Economics* 109, 2013, pp. 103–121. I thank Song Ma, who had been a research assistant at Duke University working on Graham, Harvey, and Puri, 2013, for providing additional analysis of the data in that paper.
10. See J. Graham, C. Harvey, and M. Puri, "Capital Allocation and Delegation of Decision-Making Authority within Firms," *Journal of Financial Economics* 115, 2015, pp. 449–470.
11. See M. Serfling, "CEO Age and the Riskiness of Corporate Policies," *Journal of Corporate Finance* 25, 2014, pp. 251–273. See S. Yim, "The Acquisitiveness of Youth: CEO Age and Acquisition Behavior," *Journal of Financial Economics* 108, no. 1, 2013, pp. 250–273. See M. Cain, and S. McKeon, "CEO Personal Risk-Taking and Corporate Policies," *Journal of Financial and Quantitative Analysis* 51, 2016, pp. 139–164.
12. Operationally, the market's reaction to an acquisition announcement is interpreted to be "sharply negative" when the acquiring firm's value drops by 3 percent or more, measured on a cumulative abnormal return basis, during a three-day window beginning the day before the announcement. Effectively, the market judges deals that go forward under this condition to be "bad acquisitions." In contrast, the market judges deal announcements associated with the acquirer's stock increasing by 3 percent or more during the three-day window as "good acquisitions." Acquisitions which are neither good nor bad by this criterion are deemed to be "neutral."
13. Buy and hold returns are style-matched, similar to the style matching discussed in Chapters 5 and 7.
14. These findings are reported in Y. Cai and H. Shefrin, "Acquisition Risk and Psychology," Working paper, Santa Clara University, 2016. The paper discusses a sample of 87,518 firm-year observations from 1990 to 2010. Notably, 9.7 percent of sample firm-years feature any type of acquisition activity, with the breakdown being 2.5 percent that are bad, 3.8 percent that are good, and 4 percent that are neutral. For an average firm in the sample having $2.2 billion market capitalization, shareholders lose $66 million around the deal announcement when the three-day cumulative abnormal return is −3 percent. However the market capitalization of a firm in the bad acquisition group is higher, at $3.1 billion. As a general matter, acquiring firms are larger than firms that do not engage in acquisitions, whether measured by total assets or by market capitalization. Notably, acquirers engaged in bad acquisitions are larger than acquirers engaged in both good and neutral acquisitions. Acquisitions are more frequent in growth firms, meaning those with high market-to-book ratios, with bad acquisitions having especially high market-to-book ratios. The same statement applies to sales growth. Cash flow volatility post-acquisition is higher for firms engaged in bad acquisitions than for firms in any other category. CEOs associated with bad acquisitions tend to be younger and have less tenure, by between one and two years, than other CEOs. Younger CEOs with less tenure are also more prone to make acquisitions than their counterparts, perhaps because they feel they have something to prove. The mean age for CEOs is approximately 55, and the mean tenure in the sample lies between 10 and 11 years.
15. See B. Fredrickson and D. Kahneman, "Duration Neglect in Retrospective Evaluations of Affective Episodes," *Journal of Personality and Social Psychology.* 65(1), 1993, pp. 45–55.
16. See A. Shleifer and R. Vishny, "Stock Market Driven Acquisitions," *Journal of Financial Economics* 70, 2003, pp. 295–311.
17. See D. Ravenscraft, and F. Scherer, *Mergers, Sell-Offs, and Economic Efficiency* (Washington, D.C.: Brookings Institution, 1987, p. 40.
18. See P. Klein, "Were the Acquisitive Conglomerates Inefficient?" *RAND Journal of Economics* 32, 2001, pp. 745–761.
19. See Ravenscraft and Scherer, 1987, pp. 24, 161, 218.

20. In addition to Klein, 2001 mentioned in an earlier endnote see the following: L. Lang, and R. Stulz, "Tobin's Q, Corporate Diversification and Firm Performance," *Journal of Political Economy 102,* 1994, pp. 1248–1280; P. Berger and E. Ofek, "Diversification's Effect on Firm Value," *Journal of Financial Economics* 37, 1995, pp. 39–65.
21. See D. Golbe and L. White, "A Time Series Analysis of Mergers and Acquisitions in the US economy," in A. Auerbach, ed., *Corporate Takeovers: Causes and Consequences* (NBER: University of Chicago Press, 1988). Also see T. Loughran and A. Vijh, "Do Long-Term Shareholders Benefit from Corporate Acquisitions?" *Journal of Finance* 52, 1997, pp. 1765–1790; R. Rau and T. Vermaelen, "Glamour, Value and the Post-Acquisition Performance of Acquiring Firms," *Journal of Financial Economics* 49, 1998, pp. 223–253.
22. J. Ang and Y. Cheng, "Direct Evidence on the Market-Driven Acquisition Theory," *Journal of Financial Research* 29, 2006, pp. 199–216; M. Dong, D. Hirshleifer, S. Richardson, and S. H. Teoh, "Does Investor Misvaluation Drive the Takeover Market?" *Journal of Finance* 61, 2006, pp. 725–762.
23. See M. Rhodes-Kropf and S. Viswanathan, "Market Valuation and Merger Waves," *Journal of Finance* 59, 2004, pp. 2685–2718. Also see C. Bouwman, K. Fuller, and A. Nain, "The Performance of Stock-Price Driven Acquisitions," 2003, University of Michigan working paper.
24. See C. Chabris and D. Simons, *The Invisible Gorilla* (New York: Crown Publishing Group, 2010).
25. In 2002, the New York State Attorney General published e-mails in which Blodget's assessments about stocks conflicted with what he publicly stated. A year later, the SEC charged Blodget in a civil case with having committed fraud, which resulted in his agreeing to a permanent ban from the securities industry, a $2 million fine, and $2 million disgorgement. Blodget went on to become editor and CEO of the firm *Business Insider*, and host of *Yahoo! Daily Ticker*, a finance show on Yahoo.
26. See S. Miles, "AOL Slides on Doubts about Post-Merger Value: Seagram Shrugs Off Drop: Wall Street Darling May Lose its Allure as Internet stock," *Financial Post*, January 12, 2000. In addition to quoting Blodget, this article quotes several other analysts. It mentions Arthur Newman, an analyst at Schroder & Co., who changed his recommendation on AOL from "significantly outperform" to "outperform," and reduced his 12-month price target from $105 to $85. Newman stated that his valuation reflected a much lower growth rate going forward. The article also mentions analyst Paul Noglows from Hambrecht & Quist. Noglows pointed out that Time Warner's cash flow was growing at approximately 11 percent a year, whereas AOL's growth rate was 75 percent a year.
27. See G. Colvin, "Time Warner, Don't Blame Steve Case," *Fortune,* February 3, 2003.
28. See A. Klein, *Stealing Time: Steve Case, Jerry Levin and the Collapse of Time Warner,* Simon & Schuster, July 2003. Klein is a Washington Post reporter who covered AOL for that paper. His book draws on extensive reporting and sources within AOL, including confidential internal memos. New York, NY.
29. For a general treatment of acquirers exploiting mispricing, see Andrei Shleifer, and Robert Vishny, cited above.
30. See D. Usborne, "A Megamerger That Will Change Our Lives," *The San Diego Union-Tribune,* January 16, 2000. In the interest of taste, this quotation has been edited.
31. See D. Ignatius, "AOL Grows Up," *The Washington Post,* January 11, 2000.
32. See A. Patrick, "Ted's Deal as Sweet as Love," *Australian Financial Review,* January 12, 2000.
33. See K. Harris, "Turner Quits—But Will He Leave Quietly?" *Dominion Post,* February 1, 2003.
34. See M. Peers and K. Brown, "AOL's Winners and Losers," *The Wall Street Journal,* January 14, 2003.
35. See "Time Warner drops AOL name: Board of No. 1 Media Company Votes to Drop AOL from Front of Name; Stock Symbol Changing," **www.cnn.com**, September 18, 2003.
36. See "Levin, Case Incompatible from the Start," *Newsweek,* 12/9/02, vol. 140, iss. 24, p. 53.
37. January 11, 2003.
38. The article was written by Eric Wieffering and appeared on July 13, 2003.
39. See "A Scapegoat Named Steve Case," *Businessweek,* 1/27/03, p. 124.
40. See S. Lohr, "AOL Failed to Perform as a Growth Engine for Time Warner," *The New York Times,* January 16, 2003.
41. S. Case, "It's Time to Take It Apart," *The Washington Post*, December 11, 2005, http://www.washingtonpost.com/wp-dyn/content/article/2005/12/10/AR2005121000099.html.
42. J. Pepitone, "AOL Founder Steve Case: "It's disappointing and frustrating" to look back," *CNN*, December 3, 2010, http://money.cnn.com/2010/12/03/technology/steve_case/.
43. I thank Jeff Clarke and Chris Robell from Hewlett-Packard for their assistance in preparing material for this section, and Brigida Bergkamp for her assistance in coordinating the interviews.
44. G. Anders, *Perfect Enough: Carly Fiorina and the Reinvention of Hewlett-Packard.* Portfolio, 2003.

45. Additional information comes from Bank of America Research. These estimates were dated October 11, 2001.
46. This figure was based on management's estimated pretax synergies of $2.17 billion in calendar year 2003 and earnings before interest and taxes (EBIT) impact from revenue loss of ($493 million) in calendar year 2003. The calculation assumes a 26 percent effective tax rate.
47. This calculation assumes that H-P shareholders would own 64.4 percent of the combined company at 0.6325 times the share-exchange ratio.
48. See J. Eisinger, "H-P's Next Step Is to Unlock Value," *The Wall Street Journal,* February 10, 2004.
49. See https://www.financialexecutives.org/eweb/upload/chapter/SV/SEPT05%20OnlineNews.pdf.
50. T. Lee, "Why is HP Splitting into Two Companies?" *VOX,* October 6, 2014, http://www.vox .com/2014/10/6/6919841/the-hp-split-explained.
51. J. Stewart, "Léo Apotheker May Have Been Worse H.P. Chief than Carly Fiorina," *The New York Times*, October 8, 2015, http://www.nytimes.com/2015/10/09/business/leo-apotheker-may-have-been-worse-hp-chief-than-carly-fiorina.html?rref=collection%2Fcolumn%2FCommon%20Sense. The sentiments expressed are taken from an interview Stewart did with Jeffrey Sonnenfeld, a professor at the Yale School of Management.
52. See "University of Maryland Roundtable on Real Options and Corporate Finance," *Journal of Applied Corporate Finance,* vol. 15, no. 2, 2003, pp. 8–23.
53. See M. Malone, "Microsoft's Yahoo Gambit," *The Wall Street Journal,* February 5, 2008, A17.
54. See K. Delaney, R. Guth, and M. Karnitschnig, "Microsoft Makes Grab for Yahoo—Software Giant's Bid is Aimed at Google; Tapping Ads, Customers." *The Wall Street Journal,* February 2, 2008, http://www.wsj.com/articles/SB120186587368234937.
55. See Y. Kane, Y. Iwatani, and R. Guth, "How Yahoo's Stakes in Asia May Affect Microsoft's Bid," *The Wall Street Journal,* February 27, 2008, B1.
56. See K. Haywood, "Credit Markets: Open Arms for Microsoft Debt? —Possible Bond Offering To Help Fund Yahoo Bid Generates Enthusiasm," *The Wall Street Journal,* February 5, 2008, C6.
57. See S. Miles, "AOL Slides on Doubts about Post-Merger Value: Seagram Shrugs Off Drop: Wall Street Darling May Lose Its Allure as Internet Stock," *Financial Post,* January 12, 2000.
58. See D. Berman, "Microsoft's Bid for Yahoo: Deal Journal / Breaking Insight," *The Wall Street Journal,* February 2, 2008, A4.
59. See R. Guth and P. Dvorak, "Unified Ad System Is Key to Making A Merger Successful," *The Wall Street Journal,* February 4, 2008, B1.
60. See J. Pepitone, "Yahoo's Carol Bartz Out as CEO," CNN, September 6, 2011, http://money.cnn.com/2011/09/06/technology /yahoo_carol_bartz/index.htm?iid=HP_LN.
61. See N. Carlson, "What Happened When Marissa Mayer Tried to Be Steve Jobs," *The New York Times*, December 17, 2014, http://www.nytimes.com/2014/12/21/magazine/what-happened-when-marissa-mayer-tried-to-be-steve-jobs.html?hp&action=click&pgtype=Homepage&module=second-column-region&region=top-news&WT.nav=top-news&_r=0.
62. See *Wall Street Journal,* "Marissa Mayer Wants Three More Years to Turn Around Yahoo," http://blogs.wsj.com.libproxy.scu.edu/digits/2016/03/11/marissa-mayer-wants-three-more-years-to-turn-around-yahoo/.
63. See D. MacMillan and D. Benoit, "Yahoo Reaches Deal with Starboard to Add Board Members," *The Wall Street Journal,* April 27, 2016, http://www.wsj.com/articles/yahoo-reaches-deal-with-starboard-1461762387.
64. See J. Herrman, "Marissa Mayer's Media Problem at Yahoo Is Now Verizon's to Solve," *The New York Times,* July 26, 2016, http://www.nytimes.com/2016/07/27/business/media/marissa-mayers-media-problem-at-yahoo-is-now-verizons-to-solve.html?hp&action=click&pgtype=Homepage&clickSource=story-heading&module=second-column-region&region=top-news&WT.nav=top-news.
65. See N. Carlson, "What Happened When Marissa Mayer Tried to Be Steve Jobs," *The New York Times*, December 17, 2014, http://www.nytimes.com/2014/12/21/magazine/what-happened-when-marissa-mayer-tried-to-be-steve-jobs.html?hp&action=click&pgtype=Homepage&module=second-column-region&region=top-news&WT.nav=top-news&_r=0

Chapter 11

1. A. Edmans, "Does the Stock Market Fully Value Intangibles? Employee Satisfaction and Equity Prices," *Journal of Financial Economics* 101, no. 3, 2011, pp. 621–640.
2. See J. E. Russo and P. Schoemaker, *Decision Traps: The Ten Barriers to Brilliant Decision-Making and How to Overcome Them,* New York: Simon & Schuster, 1989.
3. This material is taken from the lecture notes of John Payne and Gerry DeSanctis, who in 2000 taught "Managerial Effectiveness" at the Fuqua School of Business, Duke University.
4. See I. Janis, *Groupthink,* Houghton-Mifflin, Boston, MA, 1982.

5. See R. Charan, and G. Colvin. "Why CEOs Fail," *Fortune,* June 1999, pp. 68–79.
6. See C. Fracassi and G. Tate, "External Networking and Internal Firm Governance," *Journal of Finance,* 67(1), 2012, pp. 153–194, and Y. Cai, and M. Sevilir, "Board Connections and M&A Transactions," *Journal of Financial Economics* 103(2), 2012, pp. 327–49.
7. See G. Stasser and W. Titus, "Pooling of Unshared Information in Group Decision Making: Biased Information Sampling During Discussion," *Journal of Personality and Social Psychology,* vol. 48, no. 6, 1985, pp. 1467–1478.
8. See the following: M. Nisen, "Alan Mulally Explains How He Turned Around Ford," *Business Insider*, November 6, 2013, http://www.businessinsider.com/alan-mulally-leadership-style-2013-11; T. Leggett, "How Ford's Alan Mulally Turned Around its Fortunes," *BBC News*, July 1, 2014, http://www.bbc.com/news/business-28087325; H. Kraemer, "How Ford CEO Alan Mullaly Turned a Broken Company into the Industry's Comeback Kid: A True Leader," June 18, 2015, http://qz.com/431078/how-ford-ceo-alan-mullaly-turned-a-broken-company-into-the-industrys-come back-kid/.
9. *Financial Crisis Inquiry Report*, Washington, D.C.: U.S. Government Printing Office, 2011, available at http://fcic.law.stanford.edu/.
10. FCIC report, p. 111.
11. See J. Nelson, "Paper Dragon Thieves," *Georgetown Law Journal* 105, 2017, forthcoming.
12. See J. Ewing and H. Tabuchi, "Volkswagen Scandal Reaches All the Way to the Top, Lawsuits Say," *The New York Times*, July 19, 2016, http://www.nytimes.com/2016/07/20/business/international/volkswagen-ny-attorney-general-emissions-scandal.html?hp&action=click&pgtype=Homepage&clickSource=story-heading&module=first-column-region&region=top-news&WT.nav=top-news.
13. See J. Soble, "Scandal Upends Toshiba's Lauded Reputation," *The New York Times,* July 21, 2015, http://www.nytimes.com/2015/07/22/business/international/toshiba-chief-and-7-others-resign-in-accounting-scandal.html?_r=0.
14. See L. Du, "Things To Know about Toshiba's Accounting Scandal," *The Wall Street Journal,* http://blogs.wsj.com/briefly/2015/07/21/5-things-to-know-about-toshibas-accounting-scandal-2/.
15. See B. Dipietro, "Crisis of the Week: Accounting Problems Hobble Toshiba," *The Wall Street Journal,* July 27, 2015, http://blogs.wsj.com/riskandcompliance/2015/07/27/crisis-of-the-week-accounting-problems-hobble-toshiba/.

Index

See Endnotes section for additional references.